PALESTINE AT THE
TIME OF CHRIST

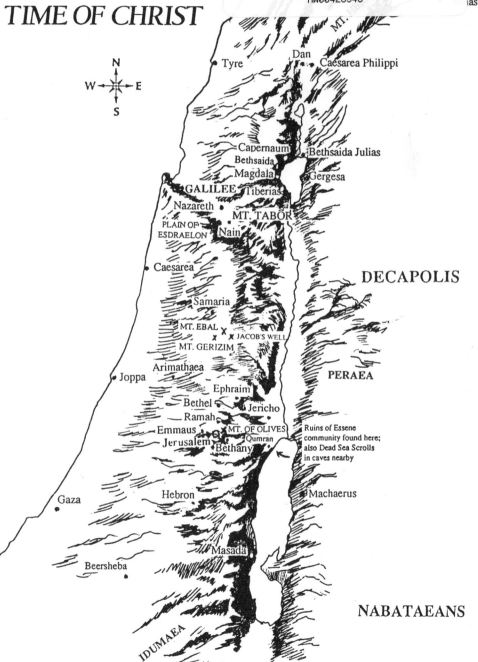

Damascus

N
W←✧→E
S

MT.

Tyre
Dan
Caesarea Philippi

Capernaum
Bethsaida
Bethsaida Julias
Magdala
Gergesa
GALILEE Tiberias
Nazareth
MT. TABOR
PLAIN OF
ESDRAELON Nain

Caesarea

DECAPOLIS

Samaria

MT. EBAL
X X JACOB'S WELL
MT. GERIZIM

Arimathaea
Joppa
PERAEA
Ephraim
Bethel
Jericho
Ramah
Emmaus MT. OF OLIVES
Jerusalem Qumran
Bethany

Ruins of Essene
community found here;
also Dead Sea Scrolls
in caves nearby

Gaza
Hebron
Machaerus

Masada
Beersheba

NABATAEANS

IDUMAEA

J. Kimber

Days of the
LIVING
CHRIST

CHRIST
by Greg K. Olsen

This beautiful new painting of the Savior by Greg Olsen is used by permission. Prints of this painting are available by writing to:

Greg Olsen
735 S. University Ave.
Provo, Utah 84606
(800) 366-2781

Days of the LIVING CHRIST

VOLUME ONE

W. CLEON SKOUSEN

ENSIGN PUBLISHING CO.
SALT LAKE CITY, UTAH

ISBN 0-916095-46-0

The Ensign Publishing Co.
Salt Lake City, Utah

Distributed by:
Sounds of Zion
6973 S. 300 W., Midvale, Utah 84047

Cover design by:
James Fedor

1st Printing, July 1992
2nd Printing, January 1993
3rd Printing, December 1994

This Book Is In Honor of

JEWEL ALMIRA PITCHER SKOUSEN

*Loving wife, mother of eight,
co-editor, and proofreader,
without whose help and encouragement
this book might never have been completed.*

THIS BOOK IS DEDICATED TO:

THE JEWS

Whom Jesus loved because they were his own people, and because they assisted him in going through his assigned ordeal of providing a redemptive sacrifice for all mankind.

THE ARABS

Who are the seed of Abraham, and on whom Jesus has already laid claim. Isaiah names the lands occupied by the great Arab nations in the latter days, and says they will be blessed by the Lord, and be called "my people," and "the work of my hands," at the very same time Israel becomes "mine inheritance."[1]

THE GENTILES

Among whom Jesus has already raised up the descendant of the Patriarch Joseph whom the Jews have been expecting as their "Messiah ben Joseph." Through him the prophetic "Ensign" has been raised up.[2] Israel has been promised that in the latter days the Gentiles will assist them in returning to the land of their former inheritances.[3].

THE LAMANITES—THE AMERICAN ISRAELITES

Isaiah called these American Israelites a people "scattered and pealed," and inhabiting a great land "beyond the rivers of Ethiopia" (Africa).[4] Isaiah knew their land would be among "the islands of the sea," and the ancient American prophets knew Isaiah was looking at the western hemisphere where they dwelt.[5]

The Lamanites represent three royal bloodlines—Ephraim and Manasseh (of the tribe of Joseph), and the people of Mulek (of the tribe of Judah), Mulek being a direct descendant of King David.[6]

---

[1]Isaiah 19:25.
[2]Isaiah 11:12.
[3]Isaiah 49:22.
[4]Isaiah 18:1-2.
[5]2 Nephi 10:19-22, *Book of Mormon*, hereafter cited as B. of M.
[6]Helaman 8:21, B. of M.

Contents – Volume 1

Preface

This study did not start out to be a book. It was simply the earnest desire of the author to gain a deeper understanding of the life and mission of our Savior, Jesus Christ. But, at this somewhat late stage of life, I decided to record my feelings and conclusions after these many years of exciting and inspirational study.

Right here at the beginning, it is worth noting that at least 95% of the Savior's life and teachings are described with clarity and understanding which practically all of us can agree upon as we read the scriptures together. Nevertheless, there are a few obscure areas where the scriptures are sufficiently vague so that a variety of possibilities exist. Most of these relate to dates when certain events occurred, or the exact order of events mentioned in the Gospels. In this shadowy area a question may even arise concerning the exact meaning of a particular passage of scripture.

In these "problematical" dimensions of the scriptures, many different opinions have arisen, both by scholars and laymen. I have learned to respect these various opinions, because a careful scrutiny of each one has demonstrated that some are more credible than others. I have also found that all of these opinions contain assumptions, and the task is to test the assumptions logically, historically and scripturally, while keeping in mind that the certainty of the whole truth will not be finally and conclusively determined until the Lord reveals it.

And we must not forget that this is precisely what he has promised to do. The scripture says:

"Verily, I say unto you, in that day when the Lord shall come, he shall reveal all things—Things which have passed, and hidden things which no man knew...."[1]

Meanwhile, it will be observed that NONE of these problematical opinions are *sine quo non* or absolutely essential to a staunch testimony of Christ's divine mission or the efficacy of his atoning sacrifice which is available to all who will humbly come unto him.

---

[1]Doctrine and Covenants 101:32-33.

It is obvious that whether Jesus was crucified on Thursday or Friday might make an interesting discussion, but nobody's salvation is dependent on the answer, regardless of which day it was. This same thing is true of the various opinions which relate to practically all of the "problematical" areas of the scriptures.

I have seen lifelong friendships shattered by well-meaning individuals trying to win a debate over some trivial detail where the whole truth is not yet known. Too often these heated controversies are not wholesome or friendly "discussions," but contests of polemic contention where the goal is pride in winning, rather than a tolerant, patient consideration of one another's point of view.

I have spent many years of my life as a teacher, and the most a teacher can do for his students is to share his best thinking after a season of careful, prayerful study.

That is what this book is designed to do. It is the author's best thinking concerning each facet of the Savior's life as of the time it was written. However, the author reserves the privilege of extrapolating, clarifying or altering any part of this book which future research or divine revelation might warrant.

Only the truth is sacred, and that is all this writer is anxious to record. In this study, where opinions have been expressed, the basis for the conclusions have been documented, but during a lifetime of study, this author has changed his mind on enough occasions to welcome the opinions of others.

Nevertheless, when all of the opinions have been expressed, the primary reality in life is the supreme joy of knowing that Jesus is the Christ, that God is the Savior's Father, and that we, like the Savior, are his children.

ACKNOWLEDGMENTS

One of the most difficult tasks of an author is adequately acknowledging the hundreds of people to whom he is indebted for the completion of a book, especially after twenty-five years.

In this instance I will mention a few names as space permits, and hope that the remainder will know how precious they are and how deeply I appreciate their friendship and assistance, even though they may not be specifically identified.

First and foremost, I must express my heartfelt gratitude to my loving wife, Jewel, who has been my full-time partner during all the years we have worked together composing over thirty-five books.

Her spirit of enthusiasm and support has been reflected in all of our children and their married companions. They have sacrificed and rendered yeoman service during each of our writing projects.

In preparing this present two-volume publication, my sons Harold, Paul, and Eric have been directly involved during the reviewing and production stage. Meanwhile, our other children—David, Brent, Sharon and their companions—have been strong supporters. Our daughter Julianne Kimber prepared the maps for both volumes.

Several of our children are experts in computer technology and they, along with Jerry Gallacher, have helped immensely in teaching this longtime operator of the manual and electric typewriter how to perform on a computer keyboard.

The backup team also includes Andrew Allison (well-known biographer of both Jefferson and Franklin), and Jim Fedor, whose talent is reflected in the beautiful cover design. Every major publication tends to go through a major crisis as the final deadline approaches. My sons, Harold and Paul, stayed with me through several days and nights to complete the typesetting and make last-minute additions. Yvonne Winn was also with us during the crisis epoch and provided extremely efficient support in completing the project. I would also like to express my appreciation to Lynda Richards, who has served a number of years as my executive secretary.

Jo Ann Skousen contributed her professional writing and editing skills to carefully review the text. She made many excellent suggestions and smoothed out a number of wrinkles in type style and punctuation.

Then there is the front line team of Tom, Lanel, and Doyle Peck who published these two volumes and invested the resources necessary to give them the fine quality we needed. Special appreciation is also extended to Greg Olsen whose beautiful painting of the Savior accompanies this volume. His marvelous painting of "The Healer" appears with volume II. His paintings can best be described as highly spiritual, but at the same time powerfully realistic. The painting for the second volume had already been purchased by Glenda Perryman of Houston, Texas, but she was kind enough to contribute its use for the second volume just as Greg Olsen had generously contributed the first painting for volume I.

Long before the computer had developed a comprehensive concordance, I practically wore the covers off "The Exhaustive Concordance" of the modern scriptures by R. Gary Shapiro. I have often blessed his name for this masterful contribution to the collection of a writer's tools.

The list of friends and loved ones who have given encouragement to the completion of this work are numerous, but I will mention two of them: my sister, Rita Miller, and Senator Orrin Hatch who insisted on having a copy of the manuscript even before it was printed.

To all of these and the many other great friends too numerous to mention, I extend my everlasting gratitude and appreciation.

W. Cleon Skousen

* * * *

A NOTE CONCERNING THE SECOND PRINTING

In the second printing an occasional typographical error has been corrected, and slight editorial changes have been added for clarity.

PREPARING TO ENJOY A STUDY OF THE LIFE OF JESUS CHRIST

There is a special way to study the life of the Savior.

Because this is a spiritual exploration into the chronicles of sacred literature, there soon develops a feeling that we are gently advancing into the cloistered precincts of God's own garden. That is why it is entirely appropriate to accompany this study with frequent, personal prayers.

In our prayers there always should be an earnest petition that our Heavenly Father will share with us his Holy Spirit. As Paul taught us in 1 Corinthians 13:12, "we see through a glass darkly," and it is therefore imperative that we have the companionship of the Holy Spirit if we are to understand these pure doctrines, and feel the inspiration of the great gospel truths that gradually emerge from the teachings of Jesus and his apostles.

MODERN STUDENTS HAVE MANY ADVANTAGES OVER THOSE OF THE PAST SEVERAL CENTURIES

Very early in this spiritual journey, we begin to realize that it is far easier to study the life of Christ in our own day than it was two or three centuries ago.

The scriptural resources that have virtually flooded the world since the modern restoration of the Gospel, have greatly enriched our comprehension of many magnificent and inspiring doctrines that had become completely lost.

In addition, these new resources have brilliantly clarified a great many historical relationships that had become totally obscured during the Dark Ages.

THE PURPOSE OF THIS INTRODUCTION

The primary purpose of this introduction is to briefly trace the torturous twisting and turning of Jewish history during the six hundred years prior to the Savior's birth. As we shall see, the volatile and sometimes tragic dynamics of Jewish suffering during these highly significant centuries had a deeply religious and cultural impact on the Jews by the time Jesus came to minister among them.

A further purpose of this introduction is to get us better acquainted with some of those highly trained scholars who have spent their entire lives searching out the mood and manners of the Jews during New Testament times. One of the most penetrating and gratifying studies in this field is the classical work of Dr. Alfred Edersheim.

THE STORY OF A FAMOUS JEWISH SCHOLAR
WHO BECAME A CHRISTIAN

Alfred Edersheim was born in Vienna in 1825. He matriculated through his early years of educational training in his home community and was finally graduated from the University of Vienna.

He later traveled to England, and while serving as a tutor, came under the influence of a Scottish Presbyterian chaplain named John Duncan.

Before long, Edersheim had made a careful study of the tenets of Christianity, and even though he felt the loving persuasion and social pressure of his own people to resist it, he became a believer in the Jewish Messiah from Nazareth. He was baptized into the Presbyterian faith, and soon afterwards was ordained a minister in the Scottish Presbyterian Church.

Later, Edersheim's talents as a scholar in classical languages led him to undertake graduate studies at the New College in Edinburgh, and later at the University of Berlin.

During these years, this new Jewish convert gradually began to realize that most Christian scholars had a very inadequate understanding of the Savior's Jewish background. He therefore undertook to prepare an extensive study of the Old Testament from a Jewish perspective so that he could share the Savior's religious and cultural background with his fellow Christians.

THE NEED TO STUDY THE OLD TESTAMENT
IN ORDER TO UNDERSTAND THE NEW TESTAMENT

In presenting the saga of the Old Testament, Dr. Edersheim hoped Christians would be able to comprehend to a greater extent the tumultuous anguish which the Jewish people endured for centuries in order to bring the great Messiah-Redeemer to the world.

From a modern source we discover that even the Savior was anxious to have the Gentiles appreciate the history of the Jews and the contribution they have made to the Christian legacy. He said:

"O ye Gentiles, have ye remembered the Jews, mine ancient covenant people? Nay; but ye have cursed them, and have hated them, and have not sought to recover them. But behold, I will return all these things upon your own heads; for I the Lord have not forgotten my people."[1]

The Savior also had something to say about the role of the Jews in giving us the Bible. He said modern man could not pretend to love the Bible and simultaneously despise the people who preserved it. Speaking of the Gentiles, he said:

"They [the Gentiles] shall have a Bible; and it shall proceed forth from the Jews, mine ancient covenant people. And what thank they the Jews for the Bible which they receive from them? Yea, what do the Gentiles mean? Do they remember the travails, and the labors, and the pains of the Jews, and their diligence unto me, in bringing forth salvation unto the Gentiles?"[2]

---

[1] 2 Nephi 29:5, B. of M.
[2] 2 Nephi 29:4, B. of M.

EDERSHEIM'S SEVEN-VOLUME WORK
ON THE OLD TESTAMENT

Therefore, to help Gentile Christians appreciate the Old Testament from the Savior's perspective, Edersheim wrote his comprehensive seven-volume work entitled: *Bible History—Old Testament.*

His goal was to demonstrate that throughout the centuries, the mission of the "people of the covenant" was to prepare the world for the coming of their great Messiah. Of course, in their long history, the Jews often wandered away into strange paths, but, in the final analysis, they did give mankind what God had intended—the Messiah and the Bible.

When this writer became a professor at the Brigham Young University, he also felt the necessity to become immersed in the great treasures of Jewish writings during the first four thousand years of human history. It required more than fifteen years to complete the research and write three volumes on the epoch of the Old Testament. These were then used as college texts in the author's classes.

The most gratifying satisfaction to grow out of these fifteen years of research and writing was the discovery that not only the students became enthusiastically interested in a study of the Old Testament, but so did the general public. This is reflected in the following history of these three books:

The First Two Thousand Years—From Adam to Abraham (published in 1953, now in its 43rd printing.)

The Third Thousand Years—From Abraham to David (published in 1964, now in its 26th printing.)

The Fourth Thousand Years—From David to Christ (published in 1966, now in its 20th printing.)

DR. EDERSHEIM WAS ANXIOUS TO HAVE CHRISTIANS KNOW MORE ABOUT THE JEWISH TEMPLE AND THE JEWISH PEOPLE

The next thing Dr. Edersheim wanted Christians to appreciate were the sacred ceremonies and sacrifices connected with the Holy Temple. He wanted them to picture in their minds the rich tapestry of Jewish religious fervor that centered around the Holy of Holies and the altar of sacrifice during the period in which Jesus lived.

For this reason he called his second Jewish missionary book to the Christians *The Temple—Its Ministry and Services as They Were in the Time of Christ.*

Dr. Edersheim's third literary contribution was entitled *Sketches of Jewish Social Life in the Days of Christ.*

In his later life (1875), Alfred Edersheim became a clergyman in the Church of England, and was then recruited to be a lecturer at Oxford University in 1884.

Finally, he dedicated the last seven years of his life to writing his most famous work *The Life and Times of Jesus the Messiah.*

In this writer's opinion it required a scholarly Jewish Christian to perform this great labor. Dr. Edersheim gives modern students the authentic touch that he was so eminently qualified to provide. He died shortly after this book was completed in 1889.

When this two-volume work was published, it soon became a bestseller. Today, it is described as the most widely used reference work in the English language on the New Testament.

JOSEPHUS, THE JEWISH GENERAL WHO BECAME THE JEWS' MOST FAMOUS HISTORIAN

Another famous Jewish writer who contributed a profusion of valuable knowledge concerning the culture and history of the Jews was Flavius Josephus.

Josephus was born in 37 A.D., about four years after the crucifixion of the Savior. His father was a leader in one of the most distinguished families of priests, and his mother belonged to the Hasmonean (Maccabee) family which made Josephus of royal lineage.[3]

By the age of 14 his penetrating study of the law had attracted the attention of the learned men of Jerusalem. His next project was to carefully study the Sadducees, the Pharisees and the Essenes. Josephus wanted to make sure which one was the most correct exponent of God's law. In the process, he even spent three years (from age sixteen to nineteen) with a hermit in the desert, where he existed on roots, fruits, nuts and herbs. In the end he became a devoted Pharisee.

When Josephus was twenty-seven years of age (66 A.D.) he went to Rome to plead for the release of certain priests who had been arrested by the Romans for some minor offenses. He made friends quickly among the Roman elite and was introduced to the empress. Through her influence he succeeded in gaining the release of the Jewish priests.

While in Rome, Josephus was tremendously impressed with the military might and the highly trained skill of the Roman legions encamped near the capital. This was uppermost in his mind when he returned to Jerusalem and found the Jews conspiring to launch a violent insurrection against the Roman rulers.

The whole idea left him with ambivalent feelings. At first he strongly argued against the revolt because he felt it might lead to a disaster for the Jews. Nevertheless, he loved his people, and the traditional vision of freedom and independence such as they had enjoyed under the Maccabees led him to accept an assignment to go up to Galilee and recruit an army.

---

[3]The autobiography of Josephus is contained in the complete works of Josephus which were published in 1960 by the Kregel Publishers, Grand Rapids, Michigan.

He actually succeeded in mobilizing a creditable force and put the new, raw troops through intensive training. However, when the Romans appeared on the scene it struck a paralyzing fear in every heart. As a spirit of panic seized them, the Galileans broke rank and many fled. Josephus was forced to take refuge at Jotapata but after a siege of six weeks his weakened army was slaughtered and he was taken captive.

Josephus travelled south as a Roman prisoner and quickly realized it was suicidal for his people to continue their struggle any further. The Romans had conquered the entire country except Jerusalem, and that great city was under a deadly siege. Within a short time the defenders were starving, and eating their own dead. Josephus did everything possible to dissuade his people from continuing their stubborn resistance, but all he got for his effort was the humiliation of being called a traitor.

Josephus then became a translator for General Vespasian, and a warm relationship developed between the two. By the time Vespasian had became the new emperor, Josephus was treated almost as though he were a member of the emperor's family. Perhaps this is why he adopted the family name of the emperor and thereafter became known as "Flavius" Josephus.

JOSEPHUS SAW THE FALL OF JERUSALEM AND
THE TOTAL DISINTEGRATION OF THE JEWISH NATION

The fall of Jerusalem cost over a million Jewish lives, and the pillaging of the land cost several million more. Just before the great last surge of destruction, Josephus was asked if he wanted to rescue anything from the city before it was totally demolished. Josephus requested permission to gather up all of the "holy books," which we assume to have been the temple library. This treasure of historical and scriptural records proved of inestimable value when Josephus began writing his history of the Jewish people.

Many of the captive Jews were crucified. Among them, Josephus found three of his old friends. He succeeded in getting permission to have all three of them taken down from their crosses, but for two of them it was too late. Even with the care of the best physicians, they died.

Josephus returned to Rome with the victorious legions, and, in process of time, he was made a Roman citizen and given an estate with a pension for life. This allowed him to use the rest of his years (which ended around 100 A.D.) in research and writing.

Josephus became famous for two major works. His first important book was called *Wars of the Jews*, written soon after the destruction of Jerusalem in 70 A.D. while all of the facts were fresh in his mind. Several years later he wrote *Antiquities of the Jews*, which is a comprehensive history of the Jews and their patriarchal ancestors back to Adam. At one point he virtually abandoned the effort until some of his Greek friends, including Epaphroditus, induced him to continue. These Greek friends said it was not only to satisfy their curiosity concerning the history of the Jews, but also to learn about the laws which their prophets said were received directly from God.[4]

The best English translation of Josephus thus far is that of William Whiston.

BY THE TIME OF CHRIST, THE JEWS HAD BEEN SCATTERED ALL ACROSS THE EARTH

From Josephus and other sources, we learn that, contrary to popular belief, the Jews were not concentrated in Palestine when Jesus came to minister among them. They had been sifted across the face of the earth like chaff before the wind.

The great crisis date for the *first* scattering of the Jews began around 600 B.C.[5]

---

[4]Josephus, *Antiquities of the Jews*, Grand Rapids, Michigan, Kregel Publications, Preface, para. 2.
[5]This is the precise date designated by the prophet Nephi as the first year of the reign of Zedekiah who was put on the throne by the Babylonians after Nebuchadnezzar's first attack on Jerusalem. This date for Zedekiah was ridiculed when the Book of Mormon was first published in 1830 because secular chronologists had decided that the first year of the reign of King Zedekiah was 553 B.C. [B. H. Roberts, *Studies of the Book of Mormon*, Chicago: University of Illinois Press, 1985, pp. 2-3]. TODAY, however, the chronologists have gradually changed their date until now they are designating 598 B.C. as the correct one. This honest attempt to persist in their research so as to accurately target the proper date for the beginning of Zedekiah's reign, has now brought these scholars 45 years closer to the date divinely revealed in the American scripture. They have only two more years to go.

That was the year King Nebuchadnezzar from Babylon moved in against Jerusalem with his massive war machine. However, at that time he did not destroy Jerusalem. Instead, he came to teach them a lesson. His first act was to put a new king (Zedekiah) over the Jews, and collect the delinquent tribute. He raided the temple— confiscating many of its treasures—and then decided to take back to Babylon ten thousand of the most talented Jewish artisans. One of them was the prophet Ezekiel.

Unfortunately, during the following thirteen years, the Jewish leaders not only failed to pay their annual tribute, but—worst of all—they entered into a military alliance with Egypt, which was Babylon's foremost enemy.

It was just a question of time until Nebuchadnezzar came charging down on Jerusalem with the intention of obliterating the whole Jewish nation from the face of the earth. That fatal date turned out to be 587 B.C.

THE DESTRUCTION OF JERUSALEM
AND SCATTERING OF THE JEWS

When the Babylonian tornado of destruction descended on Jerusalem in 587 B.C., it was accompanied by all of the horrors of rapine, burning, looting and killing that characterized the techniques of conquest in those blood-thirsty days.

For weeks the fires of Jerusalem and other settlements in Palestine filled the air with the pungent stench of burning flesh and the odor of smoldering ruins. Within a few days starvation set in, crushing out the lives of old and young alike. Other tens of thousands—without any mercy from their captors—died from the scourges of various contagious diseases. Still other thousands fled in all directions to seek safety in neighboring nations.

When it was all over there was a mere fragment of the population huddled together like terrified sheep near the ruins of Jerusalem. These were roughly herded together and marched off across the mountains and deserts to Babylon. There they were placed in a concentration camp called Tel Abib.

The scripture says that in the miserable and depressed condition the Jews mourned out their days of wretched existence for seventy years. In fact, the only thing that saved them was a mighty political convulsion among the world powers.[6]

THE BABYLONIANS ARE CONQUERED BY THE PERSIANS

In 539 B.C. a horde of Medes and Persians descended on Babylon while the king and all his courtiers were celebrating a great feast.[7] The attack was in the darkness and came as a complete surprise. In a single night the glory of Babylon was crushed into the dust after Cyrus breached the walls and poured in upon the city like a legion of avenging angels.

By morning the Jews found themselves under the dominion of a completely different kingdom.

A TINY FRAGMENT OF THE JEWS RETURNED TO JERUSALEM

Nearly 150 years earlier, the Lord revealed to Isaiah that it would be a man named Cyrus who would befriend the Jews and send them back to Jerusalem to rebuild the temple.[8] The Lord even called Cyrus "my shepherd."[9]

Significantly, it was the very next year after the triumphant Cyrus conquered Babylon that he authorized 50,000 Jews to return to the site of Jerusalem and rebuild the Lord's holy house. From this fragile beginning, the Jews began the restoration of their nation and their sacred city.

Later, Ezra journeyed to Jerusalem to institute certain reforms and teach the people the Mosaic law from scriptures which he took with him.[10] A few years after that, the brilliant Nehemiah—who was not only a Jew but the highly trusted cupbearer to King Cyrus—gained

---

[6]Jeremiah 25:11-12.
[7]W. Cleon Skousen, *The Fourth Thousand Years*, Salt Lake City, Utah: Bookcraft, 1966. pp. 758-9.
[8]Isaiah 44:28.
[9]Ibid.
[10]Skousen, *The Fourth Thousand Years*, pp. 787-790.

permission to go to Jerusalem and supervise the reconstruction of the city's protective walls.[11]

THE BUILDING OF THE SECOND TEMPLE

As the second temple neared completion, it did not in any way compare with the world-famous grandeur of Solomon's original temple. Nevertheless, it generated a sense of identity and national unity for the Jews. At least they had their own holy house, structured on sacred ground, where their daily sacrifices could send up a sweet smell to heaven, and where the people would be provided with a center for daily worship as well as sabbath services.

The second temple was dedicated with elaborate ceremonies in 516 B.C.

BY THE TIME OF CHRIST, MANY OF THE SCATTERED JEWS HAD BECOME WEALTHY AND HIGHLY INFLUENTIAL AMONG THE GENTILE NATIONS

Meanwhile, just as the Lord had told the prophet Ezekiel, tens of thousands of the Jews had been scattered in every direction—east, west, north, and south.[12]

To confirm the reality of the widespread dispersion of the Jews, we turn to Philo, a Jewish philosopher of Alexandria, Egypt, who was a contemporary of Jesus. He states that as of his day the Jews were in "all the cities of Europe, in provinces of Asia, and in the islands."[13]

Although the Lord told Ezekiel that the dispersion of the Jews was a well-deserved punishment, it turned out that in God's wisdom it became a great blessing for many of the Jews as well as the Gentiles.

---

[11]Ibid. pp. 790-792.

[12]Ezekiel 5:12.

[13]Quoted by Alfred Edersheim in *The Life and Times of Jesus the Messiah*, Grand Rapids, Mich., Wm. B. Eerdmans Publishing Co., vol. I:6.

Edersheim tells us that by the time Jesus was born, many of these Jews in gentile nations had become some of the richest and most powerful "behind-the-scenes" leaders in trade, ship-building, banking, and politics.[14]

This is confirmed by Strabo (63 B.C.–28 A.D.), the noted Greek historian, who is quoted by Josephus as saying:

"It is not easy to find a place in the world that has not admitted this [Jewish] race, *and is not mastered by it.*"[15]

There is an interesting reason why some of the Jews became masters "behind the scenes" in many of the nations where they settled.

THE TALENTS OF THE JEWS

It seems that the very nature of the Jewish character creates a remarkable cultural phenomenon wherever these scattered Israelites become established.

First of all, many Jews have natural capabilities required for leadership. They are aggressive, resourceful, intelligent, and willing to take risks for their convictions. These attributes are qualities which rulers quickly recognize and often employ to their own advantage. Consequently it was not long before many of the *diaspora* (dispersed or scattered) Jews were trained and used by rulers to fill difficult and highly responsible positions.

This is precisely what King Nebuchadnezzar did in Babylon before he felt provoked to attack Jerusalem. He had Daniel as his chief adviser at the gate of judgment, and Daniel's three friends, Shadrach, Meshach, and Abed-nego, were appointed by the king to be the three chief administrators over the entire province of Babylon.[16]

---

[14]Ibid., pp. 73-74.
[15]Josephus, *Antiquities of the Jews*, Book 14, 7:2.
[16]Daniel 2:48-49.

Later, we find the beautiful Queen Esther—who turned out to be of the house of Judah—married to the king of Persia.[17] And her uncle, named Mordecai, was made the king's chief minister.[18]

These examples merely illustrate how the scattered Jews gradually became so influential in nearly every country where they settled, and why Strabo of Alexandria would say they had become "masters," as it were, behind the scenes in those countries.

WHY THE JEWS WERE PERSECUTED

However, in spite of the wealth and influence which many of the Jews achieved individually, there were a number of reasons why the Jews were disliked and resented as a people.

The first problem was their resistance to assimilation. They would serve the Greeks, the Romans, the Asiatics, or the Europeans, but nevertheless remained first and foremost, "Jews."

This was not only true of the orthodox Jews, but even of those who did their best to shatter the Ten Commandments on a regular basis between sabbaths.

The second factor was the Jewish resistance to pagan idol worship. To most Greeks and Romans, the myths of the gods was a routine way of life. Disbelief was no sin, but failure to join in the feasts, ceremonies and celebrations which honored the gods was considered a threat to the fundamental keystone of their civilizations.

From a gentile perspective, "to get along, you go along," but when it came to pagan idols, the Jews did not go along.

The third element that kept the Jews apart was their sense of divine destiny. Eventually, they felt it was the intention of God to set up a worldwide kingdom under their Jewish King-Messiah.[19] They

---

[17]Esther 2:16-17.
[18]Esther 8:2.
[19]Edersheim, *Life and Times of Jesus*, vol. I, pp. 78-79.

believed that, as Daniel had predicted, God's kingdom would someday replace all other kingdoms and last forever.[20]

THE RESTRUCTURING OF THE WORLD BY THE GREEKS

Eventually, there was another convulsion in world politics.

It will be recalled that the Medes and Persians conquered Babylon in 539 B.C., but between 334 and 328 B.C., the Persian empire was conquered by Alexander the Great, and the Greeks became the new rulers of the whole civilized world.

The Jews fared rather well under Alexander, but in 323 B.C., while Alexander was in Babylon, he suddenly died of a malignant fever. Instead of leaving his empire to a single heir, Alexander left various segments of his empire as a legacy to each of his leading generals.

For over a century, these ambitious generals and their descendants fought each other trying to take over the whole empire. When the dust had finally settled, the heirs of general Seleucus Nicator had established authority over Alexander's eastern conquests and these became known as the Seleucid empire.

Egypt and the Greek provinces in Africa became the holdings of the heirs of General Ptolemy.

The descendants of the one-eyed General Antigonus Cyclops managed to acquire Macedonia, and part of Asia Minor.

To the Jews, the most significant outcome of all this restructuring of Europe and Asia was the fact that the Seleucid empire included Syria and Palestine. The Seleucids established the capital of their empire at Antioch on the Arontes river, 300 miles north of Jerusalem.

---

[20]Daniel 2:44.

As it turned out, the Seleucid kingdom soon became the center for the worst persecution the Jews had suffered in more than 300 years.

THE GREEK RULER, ANTIOCHUS EPIPHANES, TRIES
TO FORCE THE JEWS TO BECOME PAGANS

The Seleucid ruler who left the most bitter memory in the minds of the Jews, was Antiochus Epiphanes (Antiochus IV), whose worst abuses reached their height around 170 B.C. The well-known historian, Will Durant, describes the character of the man who ruled the Jews during this particular period:

"Antiochus IV....loved wine, women and art; he drank to excess, and left his royal seat, at banquets, to dance naked with the entertainers, or to carouse with wastrels; he was a Bohemian whose dream of power had come true."[21]

The ambition of this new ruler was to subjugate the Jews economically, and then compel them to adopt the pagan religion of the Greeks. Concerning his economic exploitation of the Jews, Durant says:

"He ordered the Jews to pay in taxes one third of their grain crops and one half of the fruit of their trees."[22]

However, the heavy taxes were nothing compared to the shattering impact of a desolating religious persecution which Antiochus IV imposed on the Jews. Durant continues:

"Antiochus...marched up to Jerusalem, slaughtered Jews of either sex by the thousands, desecrated and looted the temple, appropriated for the royal coffers its golden altar, its vessels, and its treasuries....

---

[21]Durant, Will, *The Life of Greece*, New York: Simon and Schuster, 1939, pp. 573-4.
[22]Ibid. p. 581.

"He commanded that the temple be rededicated as a shrine to Zeus, that a Greek altar be built over the old one, and that the usual sacrifices be replaced with a sacrifice of swine.

"He forbade the keeping of the Sabbath of the Jewish festivals, and made circumcision a capital crime....Greek [pagan] ritual was made compulsory on pain of death. Every Jew who refused to eat pork, or who was found possessing the Book of the Law, was to be jailed or killed, and the Book, wherever found, was to be burned."[23]

JERUSALEM DESTROYED THE SECOND TIME

The determination of Antiochus Epiphanes [IV] to compel the Jews to practice pagan rites bordered on insanity. When the Jews resisted, Durant writes:

"Jerusalem itself was put to the flames, its walls were destroyed, and [many of] its Jewish population [were] sold into slavery."[24]

But during all of these outrages against the economy and the religious culture of the Jews, there was one family for whom all this abuse and persecution became completely unbearable. This family was known as the Hasmoneans.

The head of the Hasmonean family was an aged priest named Mattathias. He lived with his family at Modin, about 17 miles northwest of Jerusalem.

THE HASMONEAN REVOLT AND
THE RISE OF THE MACCABEES

The incident which ignited the old man's emotional explosion occurred when the old priest came upon a Greek who had built an altar in Modin and had compelled a Jew to sacrifice a pig in honor of Zeus. When Mattathias saw with his own eyes this blasphemous pagan sacrifice, he rushed forward, sword in hand. Josephus describes it as follows:

---

[23]Ibid. p. 582.
[24]Ibid.

"Mattathias had great indignation...and slew the man himself that sacrificed, and Apelles the king's general, who compelled them to sacrifice....He also overthrew the idol altar, and cried out, 'If' said he, 'any one be zealous for the laws of his country, and for the worship of God, let him follow me;' and when he had said this, he made haste into the desert with his sons, and left all his substance in the village."[25]

Word spread throughout Judea that old Mattathias and his sons were rising up in revolt. Almost before Epiphanes realized what was happening, the Seleucids had a violent civil war on their hands.

Mattathias died the following year, which was 166 B.C., but the Hasmonean brothers decided to carry on the war. They rallied all their strength around their third brother, whose name was Judas. This young Jew called himself by the name of Maccabee, which is said to have meant "the hammer." He and his brothers determined to be the Jewish hammer to beat down their oppressors and restore their freedom.[26]

Thus began the great rebellion of the Jews which is known in history as the revolt of the Maccabees.

No doubt Epiphanes and his Greek armies would have ended this revolt in a bloody genocidal destruction of the Jews if the Greeks had not suddenly faced a new threat which arose out of the west. The legions of Rome appeared on the scene in one of their early eastward thrusts to lay the foundation for their own world empire. When Epiphanes saw the strength of the Romans, he dared not become involved with a war against the powerful legions and risk the possibility of losing part of his kingdom. He therefore negotiated for peace and agreed to pay a heavy tribute to the Romans each year.

---

[25]Josephus, *Antiquities of the Jews*, Book 12, 6:2.
[26]Durant, op. cit, p. 584.

HANUKKAH—THE CLEANSING AND
REDEDICATION OF THE TEMPLE

This outside distraction was the break the Jews needed. While Epiphanes was abroad trying to raise money for the tribute to the Romans, the Maccabees led the Jews in a valiant attack on the Greek-Syrian troops guarding Jerusalem, and they succeeded in taking possession of the city.

The priests immediately cleansed the temple, and held an eight-day rededication service. This event became one of the most celebrated occasions in Jewish history.

Today, usually during December, the Jews memorialize this great victory with the celebration of *Hanukkah*, which means "dedication." It is also called the "Feast of Lights" because traditionally, it is said that the priests could only find a single cruse of oil that was still pure and uncontaminated. To the amazement of the people, that single cruse of oil kept the lights burning in the temple throughout the entire celebration of eight days. It is said that the people considered this a benediction from heaven, a veritable miracle.

Of course, this was not the end of the fighting, but eventually the Jews gained their freedom and acquired full control of their affairs. But they paid a heavy price. During all those dark days of trouble and strife, each of the five Hasmonean brothers died a violent death. They have been honored ever since as five of the nation's greatest heroes.

THE JEWS DIVIDE ALONG RELIGIOUS LINES

For several generations it had been increasingly apparent that there were a number of diametrical differences among three segments of the Jewish population. They had developed divergent religious views concerning the beliefs and practices of their forefathers. The three groups were:

1. THE SADDUCEES. Jewish history tells us that the Sadducees were the wealthy, priestly class who had charge of the temple, but were considered rank apostates by the Pharisees.

The Sadducees were much taken up with the things of the world. They liked the sophistry as well as the philosophy of the Greeks. They were very careless about keeping the sabbath and made no secret of the fact that they did not believe in a resurrection, the existence of angels or spirits, and they positively denied that God was responsive to prayers or involved in the affairs of man. They also ignored prophecy, thinking it had no validity whatever.

The Sadducees promoted the idea of a warm accommodation with the religion and culture of the Greek-Syrian rulers and later with the Romans. The Pharisees called them the "worldly" Jews.

Nevertheless, the Sadducees were zealots when it came to enforcing "an eye for eye, tooth for tooth, stripe for stripe, and burn for burn." They refused to accept the policy of Moses who said the purpose of the law was "reparation," and a person could redeem an eye or an injury with money damages. The Sadducees said God wanted a literal application of the law—a poked out eye, an extracted tooth, a chopped off hand, or a searing burn.[27]

2. THE PHARISEES. The Pharisees, of course, were at the other end of the spectrum. They were much taken up with obeying God's law according to every jot and tittle, but they followed the example of Moses in allowing an offender to compensate for any injury to a neighbor or damage of his property with payments of money. Beyond that, however, they enforced the laws of the Torah with vigor. They prescribed exactly how far you could walk on the sabbath, how much you could carry on the sabbath, and were even critical of Jesus when he healed cripples on the sabbath.[28]

However, the Pharisees differed sharply from the Sadducees in that they believed in immortality, the existence of angels and spirits, the validity of prophecy, and the intervention of God in the personal affairs of mankind. The Pharisees emphasized that they considered

---

[27]James E. Talmage, *Jesus the Christ*, Salt Lake City, Deseret Book, 1970, p. 66.
[28]Durant, *Caesar and Christ*, pp. 536-37.

themselves to be the orthodox Jews, and looked upon the Sadducees as atheists.[29]

3. THE ESSENES. The "Puritans" among the Jews were called the Essenes. They lived in communities separate from populated centers so as to avoid their corruption and apostasy. Josephus has the following to say about the Essenes:

"They teach the immortality of souls, and esteem that the rewards of righteousness are to be earnestly striven for....They do not offer sacrifices...on which account they are excluded from the common court of the temple, but offer their sacrifices themselves."[30]

He goes on to say that they obeyed God's law with the utmost strictness and had all things in common, "so that a rich man enjoys no more of his own wealth than he who hath nothing at all."[31]

However, the Essenes were few in number, and Josephus felt their total membership did not exceed 4,000 men.[32]

Foremost among the great treasures left by the Essenes were the so-called "Dead Sea Scrolls" which began to be discovered in 1947. They were found located in caves near Qumram, not far from the shores of the Dead Sea and about 10 miles south of Jericho. These were family scriptures copied on strips of leather or parchment. The famous Isaiah scroll was inscribed on copper. Several thousand of the family scriptures of the Essenes have been recovered, and they date from around 300 B.C. to 70 A.D. Of course, they were originally copied from ancient records which have been long since lost, so the writings of the Essenes now constitute some of the oldest scriptural records in existence.

---

[29]Josephus, *Antiquities of the Jews*, Book 18:3.
[30]Ibid., paragraph 5.
[31]Ibid.
[32]Ibid.

EVENTS LEADING UP TO THE CONQUEST
OF THE JEWS BY THE ROMANS

The Romans had been occasionally swinging around the Eastern Mediterranean ever since they made vassals of the Syrian-Greeks. But by 63 B.C. the famous general Pompey was moving down the Levant after a whole series of triumphant victories in Greece and Asia Minor.

The conquest of the Jews came about as a result of two politically ambitious brothers of the Hasmonean dynasty quarreling over who would get the throne and the office of High Priest. For awhile, Hyrcanus was made king by their mother, Queen Salome. Then the younger brother demanded the throne. His name was Aristobulus II.

It was in the midst of this quarrel that the Roman legions arrived on the scene under General Pompey. Each of the quarreling Hasmonean princes went secretly to Pompey seeking his support, but both of them failed. In the end, Pompey ran roughshod over both of the Jewish princes and laid siege in the name of Rome.

It was 63 B.C. when the iron-tired wheels of Pompey's Roman chariots rumbled through the streets of Jerusalem, and after 12,000 Jews had been slain, the Roman eagles were implanted on top of Mount Zion.[33]

Now a Roman governor would preside over the affairs of the Jews.

THE ROLE OF THE ROMANS DURING CHRIST'S MINISTRY

It turned out the dominant role of the Romans was very important during the three-year ministry of Jesus Christ. And it was equally important during the subsequent ministry of the apostles.

Unlike the Greeks, the Romans had no desire to impose their pagan religion on conquered countries. Their passion was for peace, order, Roman justice, and the prompt payment of tribute.

---

[33]W. O. E. Oesterley, and T. H. Robinson, *A History of Israel.* Oxford, Clarendon Press, 1939, vol. II, p. 302.

In retrospect, it is rather fascinating that wherever the Romans went, they took the greatest delight in building thousands of miles of paved roads, turning deserts into oases, building mile after mile of brilliantly engineered viaducts, and then embellishing every major city with amphitheaters, coliseums, palaces, temples, and race tracks. There had never been anything like it in the history of the world. Their goal was to spread their kind of civilization under *Pax Romana* from England to India.

But there was always a vehement political-military power struggle at the top. By 53 B.C., the two top contenders were Julius Caesar and General Gnaeus Pompey, who had conquered the Jews. Eventually, Caesar won out, and the most significant development for the Jews was the fact that Caesar selected one of his allies, an Idumean Arab, to be the procurator over Palestine.

THE IDUMEAN ARABS

The Idumean Arabs were descendants of Esau, the twin brother of Jacob. The Jews even believed that in heaven or the pre-existence, Jacob's spirit was born before Esau's spirit.[34] In any event, here on earth both Arabs and Jews knew they were closely related, and both were descendants of Abraham. However, the Jews had tried to maintain the original teachings of the patriarchs, whereas the Arabs had built up a religion of their own.

Down through the ages, the Arabs and the Israelites have been helpful to each other at critical moments in history. For example, it is interesting that it was the Arabic tribes, called the Hyksos, who conquered Egypt around 1,750 B.C. Therefore, it was not the Egyptians, but the Arab Hyksos, who were the rulers of the Egyptians and who made Joseph (the son of Jacob) their prime minister. Consequently, it was Joseph under the Hyksos who saved both the Egyptians and the Israelites from starvation when the great famine came.[35]

---

[34]Edersheim, *Life and Times of Jesus*, vol I, p. 42 note.
[35]Werner Keller, *The Bible in History*, New York: William Morrow and Co., 1956, p. 93.

Some 200 years later, when Moses led the Israelites out of Egypt, the Lord commanded Moses not to molest the Arabs—who were called the Edomites and were located just south of the Dead Sea. The area of Edom was later called Idumea (Greek for Edom) and it was there that Antipater, the new friend of Julius Caesar, was raised.

Antipater was no ordinary Arab. Both he and his father (named Antipas) had been governors of Idumea, and were very influential among the desert tribes. Antipater had four sons and one daughter. Phasael was his oldest son, but he committed suicide. Thereafter Herod became Antipater's heir.

Herod emerges on the stage of history after his father, Antipater, was murdered by an administration of poison. It almost seems as though the tragic events of Phasael's suicide and Antipater's murder became symptomatic of the dark shadow of the poison cup, the dagger and the sword that would hang over Herod's head the rest of his life.

THE *HOMICIDE MANIA* OF THOSE WHO BECAME RULERS

The modern student is seldom prepared to comprehend the savage destruction of human life among practically all of the men and women who rose to positions of power during these centuries. We might call it a psychoneurosis of "*homicide mania*".

Rulers like Herod who suffered from this terrible affliction were perpetually terrified by the haunting possibility that someone was out to kill them and seize their thrones. They became so paranoid that they would kill some of their former best friends, their own relatives, even their own children. In some cases there were certain seditious individuals who actually did conspire to seize their thrones, but, more often than not, the suspicions fell on innocent victims who were helpless and unable to save themselves from rulers who had absolute power over life and death.

It will be recalled that even the great King David suffered an attack of *homicide mania* and had one of his most loyal generals killed in an effort to cover up his adulterous act with the general's wife, Bath-sheba.[36]

Cleopatra is another example of a ruler who fell victim to *homicide mania*. At a time when Cleopatra imagined that her lover, Mark Antony, had the prospect of becoming the new emperor of Rome—with herself as his queen of the empire—she decided to eliminate all possible competitors. Josephus says:

"Cleopatra...put to death all her kindred, till no one near her in blood remained alive, and after that she fell [to] slaying those [in] no way related to her."[37]

Of course, Mark Anthony and Cleopatra lost their great naval battle at Actium in 31 B.C., and both committed suicide in 30 B.C. Cleopatra's death brought to an end the famous Greek family of the Ptolemys, who had ruled Egypt for nearly 300 years.

THE TRAGIC EXAMPLE OF HEROD THE GREAT

Now that we have examined the pattern of this psycho-neurotic affliction of *homicide mania*, we turn to the amazing career of Herod the Great who suffered from this horrible malady.

Historians are generally complimentary of Herod during the early part of his life. He was tall, strong, handsome, and skilled in the arts of war. After his father's death, Herod cultivated the friendship of the Romans so that by the time he was 26 the handsome Herod was made the tetrarch of Galilee.

But ambitious Hasmonians (remnants of the Maccabees) resisted Herod because he was an Idumean Arab rather than one of their own. After barely escaping assassination, he fled to Rome. However, the Roman Senate was highly indignant that the Jews had violently evicted one of their appointed officials. They therefore sent Herod back to Palestine with enough legions to crush every faction of resistance. Herod triumphantly entered Jerusalem in 36 B.C. and was

---

[36]Skousen, *The Fourth Thousand Years*, pp. 134-142.

[37]Josephus, *Wars of the Jews*, Grand Rapids, Mich., Kregel Publications, Book I, 18:4.

not only given authority over Galilee, but became the undisputed ruler of all Judea. He was then 37 years of age.

HEROD'S FIRST SYMPTOMS OF *HOMICIDE MANIA*

We are told that Herod fell deeply in love with a Jewish princess named Mariamne, whom he married, and by her he had two sons. But trouble began when his new mother-in-law, Alexandra, began stirring up all kinds of strife and jealousy among members of the family. Before long, Herod began to feel the terrors of a ruler who could not retire to his bed without fearing that before morning he might have a stiletto thrust between his ribs, or at his next meal he might get the deadly draft of poison that would end his life.

Herod's pathological suspicions first fell upon Aristobulus, Mariamne's brother, whom she and her mother had demanded that Herod appoint to the office of high priest even though he was only 16 years of age. Herod reluctantly consented, but after a little more than a year, Aristobulus was murdered—Josephus says by drowning.[38]

Later, Herod returned from a trip to Rome and immediately heard rumors that while he was gone his own uncle Joseph had taken advantage of his wife. Mariamne took an oath that the charge was false, but Herod reached his own conclusion and had his uncle executed.[39]

Herod then targeted Mariamne's grandfather, Hyrcanus II, who was made to appear guilty of treasonous plots against Herod, and before another month had passed he was sentenced to be executed.[40]

Herod's next shadow of suspicion fell upon Mariamne, herself. It seems that Herod found it necessary to take another extended trip, but before leaving he decided to place Mariamne and Alexandra—his troublesome mother-in-law—under the immediate guardianship of

---

[38]Oesterley, *History of Israel*, vol. 2:357, note 3.
[39]Ibid. vol. 2:360.
[40]Ibid. vol. 2:360.

a trusted friend, named Sohemus. However, upon Herod's return, certain palace gossips claimed that, in spite of all the precautions Herod had taken, there had been an affair between the trusted Sohemus and Mariamne. The gossips even extended their story to allege that Sohemus had laid an elaborate plan to poison Herod.

The enraged king ordered Sohemus executed without even holding a trial.[41]

Mariamne was next, but she did have a trial—a public trial. The evidence against her seemed somewhat tenuous, but the verdict was pronounced and she was found guilty of adultery and plotting to poison the king. After she was executed the sorrow of Herod was so great that he fell ill and refused to be comforted. In fact, he mourned the loss of Mariamne all the rest of his life.[42]

Nevertheless, the purging of the palace continued, and the death of Mariamne was followed by the extermination of Alexandra, the meddling mother-in-law.[43]

Then Herod ordered the execution of Mariamne's two sons, Alexander and Aristobulus, because palace spies reported that they were plotting to avenge their mother's death. Following their arrest, both died by strangulation.[44]

A CONTRASTING ELEMENT IN HEROD'S PERSONALITY

In spite of the revolting trail of blood and tears during the opening years of Herod's reign, historians find some surprising contrasts during the years that followed.

For example, he was a far better administrator of the affairs of the Jewish people than they had received in the past. He maintained order and put down insurrections with a firm hand. Nevertheless, he never indulged in religious persecution. Although he was totally

---

[41]Ibid. vol. 2:363.
[42]Ibid.
[43]Ibid.
[44]Josephus, *Antiquities of the Jews*, Book 16, 11:7.

irreligious himself, Herod treated the leading dignitaries of the Pharisees, Polio and Sameas, with the most profound respect.[45]

When famine struck the country, Herod stripped the rich furniture in his palace of gold and silver, and melted down the most expensive and beautiful vessels to buy grain from Egypt so the people could have bread. He even arranged to have provisions cooked and sent to those who were old or sick or without ovens and cookware. In this same spirit he spent a fortune on clothes and emergency shelter for those who were destitute.[46]

When he succeeded in getting Augustus Caesar to protect the unique life style of the Jews in Palestine, he induced the emperor to extend those same privileges to Jews throughout the whole empire.[47] Out of respect for the second commandment, which forbade graven images, Herod did not allow any images or statues within the buildings he erected in Jewish territory. Similarly, he did not allow the engraving of an effigy of himself to be placed on the face of Jewish coins.[48]

HEROD SPENDS FORTUNES BUILDING ROMAN-TYPE CITIES

To increase the respect of the Romans for himself and his administration, Herod began expending fabulous amounts of money building Roman-type cities throughout Palestine. It was primarily for this that he became known as Herod the Great.

He completely restructured Jerusalem so that it had paved streets, marble palaces, aqueducts, stadia, theaters, a hippodrome for horse racing, sumptuous baths, and all the embellishments which the Romans considered essential for a higher quality of life.

Herod built the finest harbor between Joppa and Dora at Caesarea on the Mediterranean. He beautified the hot baths at

---

[45]Hastings, *Dictionary of the Bible*, New York: Chas. Schribner's Sons, 1936, vol. 2, p. 356.
[46]Josephus, *Antiquities of the Jews*, Book 15, 9:2.
[47]Hastings, op. cit, p. 356.
[48]Ibid.

Tiberias on the sea of Galilee. He built a model city with marble streets and palaces at Samaria, the former capital of the Ten Tribes, and then renamed it "Sebaste" which is the Greek for Augustus. He rebuilt and expanded the seaport at Joppa; and even extended himself by enriching a number of foreign Roman cities such as Damascus, Antioch and Rhodes.[49]

HEROD SEEKS THE GOOD WILL OF THE JEWS
BY REBUILDING THEIR ANCIENT TEMPLE

It is not difficult to imagine the intense hatred of the Jews toward Herod after he had practically wiped out the royal line of the Maccabees, executed his Jewish wife Mariamne—and her two sons—and even strategized the death of her mother and grandfather.

But all of that had happened during the earlier years when Herod first became king in 37 B.C.

By 22 B.C. Herod somehow wanted to achieve a reconciliation with the Jews. He therefore offered to tear down their dilapidated, 400-year-old temple and build them a beautiful new one.

The Jews reared back in fear and distrust. They suspected Herod of a plot to tear down their old temple and then refuse to build a new one. To reassure them, Herod promised to purchase and gather together all of the materials for the new structure before the old temple was demolished. To show his good faith, he employed 10,000 workers and spent two years gathering and preparing the needed materials. Only then did the Jewish leaders finally consent to let him go ahead and tear down the old temple so as to begin work on the new structure in 20 B.C.

The new temple was an architectural jewel, but not large. Its dimensions were exactly the same as those of Solomon's temple. If we use 18 inches for each cubit, it was thirty feet wide, ninety feet long, and forty-five feet high. It was completed in the unbelievably short period of only eighteen months.[50]

---

[49]Josephus, *Antiquities of the Jews*, Book 15, chapters 8 and 9.
[50]Skousen, *The Fourth Thousand Years*, p. 215, note 17.

However, the temple esplanade of nearly 35 acres, with its huge courtyards and vast complex of buildings, was not completed for another 46 years—long after Herod was dead.

A DESCRIPTION OF THE TEMPLE ESPLANADE
AT THE TIME OF JESUS

Herod wanted to build a temple that would require twice as much space on the top of Mount Moriah as the temple of Solomon.[51]

To do this it was necessary to bring up huge monolithic stones from the bowels of the mountain and structure them together with lead and iron. The highest pinnacle of this wall is the southeast corner, which can be seen today. It rises 170 feet above the Kidron valley. The interior was designed to accommodate a series of arches with 88 pillars supporting a huge platform at the top which became part of the expanded temple area.

Altogether, Herod's "Temple Square" was a massive engineering feat which eventually provided the crowning attraction of a magnificent acropolis—600 feet square on each side. This allowed God's holy temple to be seen from every part of the city.

The lowest courtyard was the largest in size and was called the Court of the Gentiles. This court was open to anyone. The next tier was up a few steps and closer to the temple. It was called the Women's Court, where Jews—both men and women—met to worship each day. The elaborate entrance to this area of worship was called the "Gate Beautiful."

It is said that during special convocations these two courtyards could accommodate tens of thousands.

Moving westward toward the temple, there were 15 steps leading up to the Court of the Priests. In this court was the huge altar of sacrifice with its gigantic laver of water and multitude of drains to carry away the blood and water from numerous sacrifices (such as

---

[51]There is a good description of Herod's Temple in the *LDS Bible Dictionary*, pp. 781-783.

those at the Feast of the Passover) so they could flow down to fertilize the Royal Gardens far below.

From the Court of the Priests there were 12 steps leading up to the porch of the temple itself.

THE TEMPLE OF HEROD

The temple had been built by the priests with thousands of workmen carefully prefabricating the stone so that the sound of their mallets would not disturb the peace of the sacred mount.

The interior of the temple was divided into the "Holy Place," and the "Holy of Holies." The Holy Place had its large menorah for light, a golden altar of incense for the daily prayer service, and a golden table of shew bread. Beyond this, two heavy veils divided the Holy place from the Holy of Holies. The Holy of Holies had once been the place reserved for direct communications with God. It was also the sanctuary for the Ark of the Covenant, but this had been lost or hidden when Jerusalem was destroyed in 587 B.C.

We should mention that in the northwestern corner of the temple square was a military fortress overlooking their acropolis. It was called the Antonia in honor of Herod's friend, Mark Anthony.[52] Roman soldiers manned the Antonia and were on the alert to rush down to restore the peace in case of any disturbances.

A GLORIOUS SURPRISE FOR THE JEWS

So the temple itself was completed, and this holy house was ready for any communication the Lord God Jehovah might wish to share with his chosen people.

However, so far as the Jewish record shows, this people had not received a revelation from God for over 400 years. The heavens had been sealed and silent as though they were made of brass. There had been no prophets, no heavenly revelations, no angelic beings, no word from the Lord.

---

[52]Josephus, *Antiquities of the Jews*, p. 335.

But the people were ready. Each morning the savor of the sweet smell of the daily sacrifices ascended into the heavens. The priests were in their places, the incense was burning, and the people assembled in the Court of the Women for their daily prayers. How could they have guessed that for the Lord God Jehovah, this was enough.

Without their ever suspecting it, they were about to be visited by an angel of God.

*   *   *   *

CHAPTER 1

THE REAL STORY OF CHRISTMAS

The most important events in history often burst in upon us unannounced.

It was during the year of the Romans 752[1] that the heavens began to unfold the opening scenes of a monumental event which God's prophets had been predicting since the days of Adam.[2] The setting was in Jerusalem, and the place was Herod's Temple.

As the first wisps of dawning light filtered up through the eastern sky, a silver trumpet sent three clarion calls from the heights of the temple to awaken the city.[3]

There were already about fifty priests on duty at the temple, and they were intently going about their various tasks. The first duty was to use torches in order to inspect the various courtyards to make certain that each one was clean and secure. After that they came together and each of the priests received his allotted assignment. When they were all in their respective places, the great gates of the temple were slowly opened to welcome the early worshippers.[4]

At the moment, the major center of activity was the Court of the Priests, where preparations were being made for the daily sacrifice. The fire on the altar had to be rekindled and stirred into a lively flame. Live coals had to be carried into the temple to provide the hot bed for the golden Altar of Incense. The wicks of the Menorah had to be trimmed,[5] and the lamb for the sacrifice had to be brought up.

---

[1]Appendix C in vol. 2 points out that the Lord's dating system seems to be four years later than the current secular chronology.

[2]Moses 6:57, P.G.P..

[3]Edersheim, *Life and Times of Jesus*, 1:133.

[4]Ibid.

[5]In the Temple of Solomon there were seven lights on a stand called the Menorah, whereas in the

PREPARING THE DAILY SACRIFICE

As the early worshipers filtered into the vicinity of the Court of the Priests, they saw the lamb being prepared for the morning sacrifice. It had to be carefully inspected so the priests could certify to its fitness, and then it was given water from a golden bowl. When all was in order, the lamb was laid out on the north side of the altar with its face toward the west.[6]

All of this was to memorialize the traumatic moment when Isaac was brought to this same Mount Moriah—perhaps near this very spot—and bound by his father so he could be presented to the Lord as a sacrificial offering.[7]

Of course, as the Bible tells us, Isaac was never sacrificed, but the scripture says the Father wanted Abraham to know, in a finite way, what it would be like when the Father would have to sacrifice his Beloved Son in the meridian of time.[8]

Meanwhile, on the altar at Herod's Temple, the sacrifice of a lamb was consummated. As the blood spilled forth, it was caught in a golden bowl and sprinkled on two sides of the altar. Then the carcass of the lamb was prepared in the manner required for a burnt offering.[9]

THE PRAYER SERVICE AND THE BURNING OF THE INCENSE

By this time the crowd of worshipers would have probably multiplied sufficiently to require that they be assembled together in the Court of the Women which was just a few steps below the altar of sacrifice. This courtyard was the place of general assembly with the men occupying the main floor and the women being seated in the two galleries above.[10]

---

second temple there was only one candlestick. When the Romans raided Herod's Temple in 70 A.D. they found a seven-lamp Menorah which is shown in statuary portraying the "triumph" of Titus when he returned to Rome.

[6]Edersheim, *Life and Times of Jesus*, 1:134.

[7]Genesis 22:2; 2 Chronicles 3:1.

[8]Jacob 4:5, B. of M.

[9]W. Cleon Skousen, *The Third Thousand Years*, Salt Lake City: Bookcraft, 1964, p. 339.

[10]Edersheim, *Life and Times of Jesus*, vol. 1, p. 245.

It will be appreciated that there were no blood sacrifices offered inside the temple. The only altar within the walls of this sacred building was the altar of incense where the priest would shortly send the perfumed vapors heavenward to represent the prayers of the people ascending to God.

We should also mention that there were no worship services inside the temple. The congregation remained outside in the court where both men and women worshipped together while the priest represented them in the House of God.

ZACHARIAS, AN ELDERLY PRIEST, PRESIDES AT THE PRAYER SERVICE AND OFFERS THE INCENSE

The Bible tells us that on this particular day, an ancient Levite priest—named Zacharias—came to the temple to burn the incense and wish Godspeed to those who came to pray.

As the old priest entered the main room of the temple he stood in what was called the Holy Place.

He saw straight before him the sacred veils behind which lay the Holy of Holies. To the right of the veils was the golden altar of incense with its glowing coals brought in from the altar of sacrifice a short time before. Along the right wall of the Holy Place was the table of shew bread and against the opposite wall stood the golden candlesticks or Menorah which provided the only light.

THE SPECIAL PRAYER OF ZACHARIAS

Zacharias, like the other worshipers, had come to the temple this day with a special prayer in his heart. However, his petition was not a new prayer. It had been the burden of his soul for many years. He longed for a son.

Of course, he was now an old man and the time had long since passed when he might expect a son, but almost out of habit as it were, he continued to make his supplication to the Lord. It was the uppermost thought in his mind as he approached the altar of incense.

THE FIRST APPEARANCE OF THE CHRISTMAS MESSENGER

Suddenly, Zacharias stopped. He was almost blinded as the dim half-light of the Holy Place was shattered by the brilliant appearance of a glorious being. An angel stood to the right of the altar surrounded by an intense heavenly light.[11] For the first time in more than 400 years of Hebrew history, a revelation had been granted to a priest of the Jewish people.

In terror Zacharias began to retreat toward the door, but the messenger stopped him and said,

"Fear not Zacharias, for thy prayer is heard and thy wife Elisabeth shall bear thee a son, and thou shalt call his name John."[12]

The humble Levite priest could scarcely believe his ears, but the angel continued:

"He shall be great in the sight of the Lord...and shall make ready a people prepared for the Lord."[13]

This was too much for Zacharias. How could Elisabeth have a son? It was impossible! She was too old. In this doubting spirit, he challenged the angel:

"Whereby shall I know this? I am an old man and my wife is well stricken in years."[14]

Now the angel was offended. The eyes that looked down on Zacharias must have been deep as eternity. Did Zacharias doubt the power of God? Had he forgotten the mother of Samson, the mother of Samuel, and the mother of Isaac—all of whom received their children through a special blessing from heaven? Or did he doubt the authority of the angel?

---

[11]Luke 1:11.
[12]Luke 1:13.
[13]Luke 1:15-17.
[14]Luke 1:18.

In tones of solemn rebuke the angel declared:

"I am Gabriel, that stands in the presence of God; and am sent to speak unto thee, and to shew thee these glad tidings.

"Behold, thou shalt be dumb, and not able to speak...because thou believest not my words."[15]

Instantly, the angel was gone.

Almost as though he were stunned, Zacharias proceeded with the rite of the incense burning and the perfumed vapors filled the Holy Place. Then the aged priest walked out before the people.

CONSEQUENCES OF AN ENCOUNTER WITH AN ANGEL

The people had become worried about the old man. Why had he taken so long? No one was allowed to go into the temple to investigate so they were greatly relieved when he finally came out and stood before them. But to their amazement he acted as though he couldn't speak. Nevertheless, he tried to make gestures with his hands to let them know he had seen a heavenly vision.[16]

It would be exciting to know what happened when Zacharias returned home. No doubt Elisabeth was astounded when she discovered that her husband could not speak, but undoubtedly her greatest shock came when Zacharias communicated with her in writing that he had seen an angel of God who said Elisabeth was going to have a baby. The angel said this special baby was to be given the name of John, and that when he grew up he was to go before the face of the coming Messiah to prepare his way.

For a woman old enough to be a grandmother, this was not only startling but frightening news. The Bible says Elisabeth was "well stricken in years,"[17] and the prospect of her antiquated body giving birth to a baby imposed on Elisabeth an enormous test of faith.

---

[15]Luke 1:19-20.
[16]Luke 1:22.
[17]Luke 1:18.

Nevertheless, it all came to pass. Although relatives and neighbors would have pronounced it impossible, the powers of procreation actually returned to this aged couple, and before long Elisabeth was able to confirm to Zacharias that she was with child.

NAZARETH—THE RESIDENCE OF FORGOTTEN ROYALTY

Now the scene was set for the next episode in this real-life drama from Biblical history. It was time for Gabriel to make another visit to the earth.

This event occurred about eighty miles north of Jerusalem in a certain sheltered valley surrounded by the hills of Galilee. In this valley there was a modest peasant village called Nazareth. Here lived a daughter of Israel who was to become the most famous woman in the world. Her name was Miriam. Today we call her "Mary," which is derived from the Greek translation of her name.[18]

Miriam (or Mary) was a very popular name among the Jews. Perhaps this was because the prophets had predicted that this would be the name of the Messiah's mother.[19]

By right of birth, Mary was a Jewish princess. She was a direct descendant of King David. We know this because the Savior's only mortal lineage was through his mother, and the scripture specifically says that the Messiah would be of the "fruit of the body" of David.[20] To fulfill this prophecy Mary would have to be the one to give Jesus his royal Davidic inheritance. The Jews were well acquainted with this lineal descent. When they were asked, "What think ye of Christ? Whose son is he? They say unto him, The Son of David."[21]

It was only a short time earlier that this beautiful girl had become betrothed to a young man who was also a descendant of David. His name was Joseph.[22]

---

[18]Hastings *Dictionary of the Bible*, vol. III, p. 278 under "Mary."
[19]Mosiah 3:8, B. of M.
[20]Psalms 132:11.
[21]Matthew 22:42.
[22]Luke 1:26-27.

Because the world would not know the divine identity of the Savior's real Father, both Matthew[23] and Luke[24] went out of their way to protect Jesus by showing that Joseph, his foster father, was of the Davidic line. However, these two genealogical tables are not the same, and Dr. James E. Talmage offers the following explanation:

"These records present several apparent discrepancies, but....the consensus of judgment on the part of investigators is that Matthew's account is that of the royal lineage, establishing the order of sequence among the legal successors to the throne of David, while the account given by Luke is a personal pedigree, demonstrating descent from David without adherence to the line of legal succession."[25]

But the fact that two young heirs to the throne of King David were living in the obscure village of Nazareth was of no particular consequence to the Jews just then. Nor to the Romans. The main concern of the Romans was to keep a tight rein on a non-Jewish king who ruled the Jews. His name was Herod—Herod the Great.

SECOND APPEARANCE OF THE CHRISTMAS ANGEL

It was just six months after Elisabeth knew she was with child that Gabriel made his second visit to the Holy Land. This time it was to Mary, a descendant of King David, who was living in Nazareth.

She was alone when the celestial vision opened before her. As with Zacharias, she was deeply frightened. The sudden brilliance of the heavenly messenger momentarily overwhelmed her and even before she could speak, the salutation of the glorious Gabriel fell upon her ears.

"Hail thou that are highly favoured. The Lord is with thee! Blessed art thou among women!"[26]

---

[23]Matthew, chapter 1.
[24]Luke, chapter 3.
[25]Talmage, *Jesus the Christ*, pp. 85-86.
[26]Luke 1:28.

Instinctively Mary drew back, but in a tone of comforting assurance the angel quickly added,

"Fear not, Mary, for thou hast found favour with God."[27]

Then in solemn words designed to inspire confidence and understanding, he delivered his precious message:

"Behold, thou shalt conceive in thy womb, and bring forth a son, and shalt call his name JESUS.

"He shall be great, and shall be called the Son of the Highest: and the Lord God shall give unto him the throne of his father David:

"And he shall reign over the house of Jacob for ever; and of his kingdom there shall be no end."[28]

Mary could not comprehend all of this, but as she reflected on the words of the angel and gained some semblance of composure, she asked:

"How shall this be, seeing I know not a man?

"The angel answered and said unto her, The Holy Ghost shall come upon thee, and *the power of the Highest shall overshadow thee*: therefore...that holy thing which shall be born of thee shall be called the Son of God."[29]

Mary responded to this thrilling message with words which reflect the depth of her spirituality and the beauty of her character. She said, very simply:

"Behold the handmaid of the Lord; be it unto me according to thy word."[30]

---

[27]Luke 1:30.
[28]Luke 1:31-33.
[29]Luke 1:34-35.
[30]Luke 1:38.

WHO WAS GABRIEL?

It is doubtful that either Mary or Zacharias knew the true identity of the angel who called himself Gabriel.

Nevertheless, this heavenly harbinger must have thrilled as he stood before this beautiful girl. He knew she was a person of true nobility. He knew that her identity and mission had been revealed to the prophets centuries before she was born.[31] Gabriel also knew that Mary was one of his own descendants.

This messenger from heaven who called himself Gabriel was none other than the prophet Noah.[32] As Mary looked up into his brilliant countenance she was beholding the unresurrected spirit of her own great patriarchal ancestor who survived the great flood.

When Gabriel had finished delivering his message, he confided to Mary that her aged cousin, Elisabeth, had conceived by divine intervention and was already in her sixth month. No doubt the shocked look on Mary's face led the angel to say:

"With God nothing shall be impossible!"[33]

Left to herself, Mary treasured up the words of the angel in secret. However, a secret is a burden—a terribly heavy burden—especially a secret as monumental as this one. But whom could she tell? Apparently she did not tell her parents, and we know she did not tell Joseph. But there was one person she could tell—Elisabeth! She therefore made haste to go straightway and visit her.

However, sometime prior to Mary's departure—perhaps it was only a few days before she left—the glory of God encompassed her and, for Mary, the miracle of new life began.[34]

---

[31]1 Nephi 11:18; Mosiah 3:8; Alma 7:10, B. of M.
[32]*Documentary History of the Church*, Salt Lake City: Deseret News, 1904, vol. III, p. 386
[33]Luke 1:37.
[34]Talmage, *Jesus the Christ*, pp. 83-84.

THE MOTHER OF JESUS VISITS
THE MOTHER OF JOHN THE BAPTIST

Zacharias and Elisabeth lived in the hill country of Judea, not far from Jerusalem.[35] However, from Nazareth, it was a difficult journey of nearly a hundred miles over treacherous roads.

As Mary drew near her cousin's home, a marvelous thing happened to Elisabeth.

Through the months Elisabeth had known that she was preparing the earthly tabernacle for John, and his mission was to go before the Messiah to prepare his way. Therefore she knew that somewhere in this land of Israel there must be a Jewish mother who was preparing a temporal body for the very son of God. Who could that be? Then she heard a voice calling from her front door.[36]

Suddenly the Holy Ghost came upon Elisabeth and the babe seemed to leap within her womb.[37] We also know from what she said a few moments later that the Spirit had whispered to her, "You are about to see the mother of the Lord!"[38]

When Elisabeth came to the entryway of her house, she saw the radiant face of her young cousin, Mary. In an outburst of joyous excitement, Elisabeth exclaimed:

"Blessed art thou among women, and blessed is the fruit of thy womb!

"And whence is this to me, that *the mother of my Lord* should come to me?"[39]

No doubt Mary was amazed to hear these words. Obviously Elisabeth already knew her secret! Mary therefore replied:

---

[35]Luke 1:39.
[36]Luke 1:40.
[37]Luke 1:41.
[38]Luke 1:43.
[39]Luke 1:42-43.

"My soul doth magnify the Lord."[40]

Then Mary poured forth a cadence of poetic expression which is called the "Magnificat" or Mary's Song of Thanksgiving. What a tremendous blessing to be allowed to be the chosen daughter in Israel who would be the mother of the Savior.[41]

During the following three months, Mary stayed with Elisabeth to await the time when this elderly woman would be delivered of her special child.[42]

When the time came, the baby was a male child just as Gabriel had predicted.[43]

For Zacharias and Elisabeth this baby was a triumphant blessing. It was almost unbelievable that a woman who was "stricken in years," and had long since passed her child-bearing years, would be renewed in her procreative strength and give birth to her first child. Relatives, neighbors and friends joined in the rejoicing, and all of them gathered to witness the naming of this wonderful infant born out of season.[44]

JOHN THE BAPTIST IS NAMED AND ORDAINED

However, not until the ceremony was actually in progress, did the officiating priest attempt to determine the name which should be pronounced on this baby.

Then he found himself in the midst of a family dispute. Elisabeth said the name of the child should be John. Indignant male relatives ordered the priest to name the child after his father. Certainly he was not likely to have another son to carry his name.[45]

---

[40]Luke 1:46.
[41]Luke 1:47-55.
[42]Luke 1:56.
[43]Luke 1:57.
[44]Luke 1:58-59.
[45]Luke 1:59-61.

Finally, when Elisabeth continued to object, an appeal was made to Zacharias. This was done by signs, for he was deaf as well as dumb.[46]

Zacharias motioned for a tablet, and when they obtained one, he wrote with the stencil, "His name is John."[47]

This caused the relatives to marvel. They thought surely the devout Levite would want his only child to bear the name of his father.[48]

But in a moment, they had greater cause for astonishment. Zacharias suddenly began to speak. For the first time in nearly a year, his tongue was loosed. "Blessed be the Lord God of Israel!" he exclaimed. Then, gazing proudly on his new infant son and being filled with the spirit of prophecy, Zacharias declared:

"Thou, child, shalt be called the prophet of the Highest: for thou shalt go before the face of the Lord to prepare his ways."[49]

Later that same day, probably in the privacy of their own home, an angel came and ordained the infant John to the priesthood.[50]

Never before in history had such a procedure been followed, but here was a choice child, filled with the Holy Ghost from the time of his birth,[51] ordained to his high calling at the age of eight days. Of him Jesus would later say:

"Among those that are born of women there is not a greater prophet than John the Baptist."[52]

---

[46]Luke 1:62.
[47]Luke 1:63.
[48]Luke 1:61.
[49]Luke 1:76.
[50]Doctrine and Covenants 84:28.
[51]Doctrine and Covenants 84:27.
[52]Luke 7:28.

MARY RETURNS TO NAZARETH

Now Mary returned to her home in Nazareth, and there Joseph anxiously awaited her.

No doubt Mary approached this homecoming with the deepest apprehension. It is believed that already she had been with child around three months. What would Joseph think? What would her parents think? What could she tell them without revealing her sacred mission? No doubt Mary probably assumed that her betrothal to Joseph would have to be forfeited because of her great mission. Yet there is every reason to believe that she loved him deeply.

How long it was before Joseph learned Mary was with child we do not know, but when he did become aware of it, he was overwhelmed with grief. Under Jewish law a betrothal was almost as sacred and binding as marriage itself, and faithlessness could be punished by death.[53] The only alternative was to "put her away" by a bill of public divorcement which would have made Mary an object of public disgrace.

Joseph was not bitter against Mary, merely sorrowful. To this righteous young Hebrew it must have seemed impossible that his beautiful Mary would be gone for such a short time and somehow betray their love. Apparently, they never discussed it, but Joseph determined not to embarrass her with a public denunciation of their betrothal, but just simply "put her away privily."[54]

It is interesting that during this moment of anguish and deep emotional strain, not a word of explanation escaped Mary's lips. In fact, she herself was probably unaware of just what the will of the Lord might be concerning her.

Meanwhile, Joseph was beyond all consolation. His Mary was the most beautiful girl in the province. One of the prophets who had

---

[53]Deuteronomy 22:23-24.
[54]Matthew 1:19.

seen her in vision, exclaimed that she was "most beautiful and fair above all other virgins."[55]

But one dark night while Joseph feverishly pondered the sudden shipwreck of his prospective marriage, the angel of the Lord appeared to him in a dream, and said:

"Joseph, thou son of David, fear not to take unto thee Mary thy wife: for that which is conceived in her is of the Holy Ghost.

"And she shall bring forth a son, and thou shalt call his name JESUS: for he shall save his people from their sins."[56]

Who could describe the transitional joy which flooded the mind of Joseph as this revelation inspired in his mind a beautiful and sympathetic understanding of Mary's sacred calling? And who could record the tender scene when Joseph took Mary to a quiet place and lifted her face toward his to tell her about the angel? Although it is not in the scripture, we surmise it went something like this:

"Mary, I know your great secret!"

"You do?"

"Yes, the angel appeared to me."

"He did? What did he say?"

"He told me about the baby. And he said we are to be married."

"Oh, Joseph!"

Joseph's marriage to Mary must have taken place immediately, for the angel commanded it,[57] and by the time of the taxing or

---

[55]1 Nephi 11:15, B. of M.
[56]Matthew 1:20-21.
[57]Matthew 1:20.

census ordered by Caesar, Joseph and Mary are specifically referred to as husband and wife.[58]

WHEN WAS JESUS BORN?

It is now known that it was early in April that Joseph and Mary made their way to Bethlehem.

The exact date of these events was not verified with certainty until 1830 when the Lord affirmed that April 6th of that year marked one thousand, eight hundred, and thirty years since the Savior came in the flesh.[59]

Prior to that time, no one knew the precise date. Authorities conceded, however, that December 25th was not celebrated as Christmas until the fourth century A.D. In fact, it was established on that date simply for convenience.

When Christianity was adopted as the official religion of Rome, the emperor asked the date of the Savior's birth. No one knew. It was therefore decided that since Rome celebrated the birthday of the Roman god, Sol, on December 25th, they would adopt it by decree as the birth date of Christ. And that was that.[60]

Of course, historically, this didn't fit the account in the scriptures since there would be no grazing of the sheep by night in December. The new grass does not come out until sometime in March. Furthermore, as we shall see shortly, the Savior was born at the time of the Passover, and that wouldn't happen until early in April. In fact, Dr. Edersheim tells us that Jewish tradition speculated that the Messiah would come at Passover time.[61]

IN HER NINTH MONTH, MARY JOURNEYS TO BETHLEHEM

Since Bethlehem was originally the "City of David," it was therefore the ancestral home of both Mary and Joseph. The decree of

---

[58]Luke 2:5.
[59]Doctrine and Covenants 20:1.
[60]*Collier's Encyclopedia*, New York: Crowell Pub. Co., 1962, vol. 6, p. 403 under "Christmas."
[61]Edersheim, *Life and Times of Jesus*, vol 1, p. 171.

the emperor required that everyone should return to their ancestral homes to register for the new taxation. For this reason Mary and Joseph made their way to the ancient city of David.

This was a critical time for Mary. She was in her ninth month and very close to delivery.[62] To have walked that distance would have been virtually impossible, and to ride a donkey would seem distressful. However, anyone acquainted with riding a donkey knows that if one is seated far back on the hips of this little animal, the feet go clipping along under him while the hips scarcely move. Such a ride on a donkey has been compared with sitting in a comfortable rocker at home.

As we have mentioned, the great Feast of the Passover took place in the early part of April.[63] For this feast tens of thousands flooded into Jerusalem. The crowds always swelled to such proportions that they not only filled up Jerusalem, but spilled over into every town and hamlet for several miles around. This would include Bethany, Bethphage, and most assuredly, Bethlehem.

THE FIRST CHRISTMAS EVE

Bethlehem is six to seven miles south of Jerusalem. As Mary and Joseph came toward the end of this long journey, they passed flocks of sheep grazing on the hills. Here their great ancestor, David, had tended his flocks as a youth. In the valley below, Ruth, their maternal ancestor, had gleaned in the fields of grain. To Mary and Joseph this was home and every foot of it seemed saturated with sacred history.

But Bethlehem did not welcome them. As they threaded their way among the teeming crowds, Joseph must have felt increasing apprehension. Where would they stay? Everywhere they were met with the same rebuff: "No room!"[64]

---

[62]Luke 2:5-6.
[63]Peloubet's *Bible Dictionary*, Philadelphia: Universal Book and Bible House, 1913, under "Passover."
[64]Luke 2:7.

As time passed the situation became desperate. Knowing Mary's great mission and the identity of the child about to be born, it must have seemed incomprehensible to Joseph that all doors should be closed against them.

Overwhelmed with anxiety, Joseph finally accepted the offer at one of the inns to make their bed in what he normally would have rejected with disgust. A stable![65]

But this was no time to quibble. Already Mary was beginning to feel the pangs of imminent childbirth. Joseph's soul must have been harrowed to the quick as he led his trembling young wife into this humble abode made for cattle. In haste he no doubt prepared for her the most meager semblance of comfort as the hour drew near for her baby's birth.

Of course, having a baby is not a simple affair, but anyone who has been around Jewish women knows that they would never have permitted Joseph to handle this situation alone. This writer believes that when the women at the inn heard that a baby was about to be born, their maternal instincts undoubtedly took over and relieved Joseph of the whole project.

And when Jewish women take over a delivery, there is an unimaginable amount of happy hustle, bustle and excited chatter. One would think each one was a professional midwife. So we think that when this little baby was born, no one could have been greeted with more warmth and joy than that which came from this excited cluster of Jewish women who had happily provided the services.

But they would have been shocked into speechless amazement if they had known who this baby was.

But Mary knew. So did Joseph. Who could describe their joy and relief as this little baby was tightly wrapped in swaddling clothes—as was the custom with the Jewish newborn—and tenderly placed in the soft hay of the manger.

---

[65]Luke 2:7.

LET THE HEAVENS RESOUND!

In what is believed to have been the 753rd year of the Romans,[66] the Jewish nation would never have dreamed that this was to be the year of their great Messiah.

But in the celestial courts of heaven, the seraphic hosts of angels had no doubt stood at attention waiting for the supreme moment when the great Jehovah would take the plunge into the forgetfulness of the Second Estate.

At one moment he was in heaven managing the Father's universal kingdom. An instant later he was no longer in heaven. In fact, he did not know where he was, who he was, or why he was suddenly feeling very tired and very hungry.

But the hosts of heaven knew. This was the moment that would divide history. No doubt the ancient saints from Adam to Malachi had waited tensely as this great drama began to unfold. And finally, it was actually happening.

AND THERE WERE SHEPHERDS ABIDING IN THE FIELDS

Only about a mile distant, hovering over the outskirts of Bethlehem, were certain angels preparing to make their presence known. Below them was a group of humble shepherds, abiding in the fields and watching their flocks by night. These had been chosen to see a marvelous vision that they would be talking about the rest of their lives.

It all commenced the moment Mary's precious infant was born. Immediately, the shepherds saw the veil of mortality sheered back, and an angel stood before them with a glory that bathed the surrounding terrain in a radiant light.

The shepherds thought they would be consumed and shrank back in fright, but the angel said:

---

[66]Talmage, *Jesus the Christ*, pp. 102-3.

"Fear not: for, behold, I bring you good tidings of great joy, which shall be to all people.

"For unto you is born this day in the city of David a Saviour, which is Christ the Lord.

"And this shall be a sign unto you; Ye shall find the babe wrapped in swaddling clothes, lying in a manger."[67]

At that moment the hosts of heaven could no longer be restrained. The majestic choir of thousands of heavenly voices burst into song. It appears that these vast angelic choirs must have repeated one line of the song several times because the shepherds never forgot it. They remembered how the angels sang:

"Glory to God in the highest, and on earth peace, good will toward men."[68]

THE UNKNOWN KING

When the vision closed, the shepherds left immediately to go into Bethlehem and seek out the location of the child "lying in a manger." Perhaps the flickering flame of an olive oil lamp sent its rays into the night to guide them to the stable's portals.

As the shepherds stood watching Joseph, Mary, and the baby, they saw that the little one was indeed wrapped in swaddling clothes and lying in a manger. There is no record of any conversation. Perhaps they just looked.

What they saw was a humble Galilean peasant and his wife with a newborn child. There were no halos of light about their heads, no visible cherubim. Nevertheless, with the glory of the angels still fresh in their minds, the shepherds looked upon the sleeping child with devotion and awe. Jehovah had entered mortality![69]

---

[67]Luke 2:10-12.
[68]Luke 2:14.
[69]The exact location of the nativity scene in Bethlehem is not known. A little over 300 years after the Savior's birth, Helena, the mother of Constantine, made a pilgrimage to Bethlehem to locate the

When the shepherds finally left the stable they ran swiftly to awaken their friends and neighbors. To all who would listen they related the wonderful night vision and the things they had been told concerning the newborn child. Amazingly, these relatives and friends were not impressed. They didn't even get up to go look for themselves. The scripture says they just "wondered."[70]

But this did not dampen the spiritual zeal of the shepherds. Luke says they returned to their flocks "glorifying and praising God for all the things they had heard and seen."[71]

And so the early morning hours of the first Christmas passed without further incident. While the baby slept, Mary treasured in her heart the thrilling triumph of this hour.

But where were the Wise Men? Although Christmas pageants have it otherwise, there were no Wise Men present on the night of the nativity. In fact, they were in their homeland hundreds of miles to "the East." During the early hours of the first Christmas morning they saw a great new star in the heavens.[72]

The Nephites probably could not see the star this first night because the western hemisphere was bathed in light so that there was no night. But they would see this brilliant new stellar orb the next night when darkness once more came at the close of the day.[73]

---

place of the nativity. Justin Martyr who lived less than a century after Christ, said the scene of the nativity was a cave which was often part of the "khan" or stable that innkeepers maintained for their guests. The mother of Constantine selected one of several grottos or caves as the most likely site, and Constantine built a church over it. (F. W. Farrar, *The Life of Christ*, New York: Thomas P. Cromwell & Co., p. 24) The present church was built by Justinian, but was greatly altered by the Crusaders. The grotto which was believed by Helena to be the scene of the nativity, is beneath the church. Fixed to the floor is a huge silver star inscribed with the Latin words: "Here, of the Virgin Mary, Christ was born." A few feet away is a very ornate "Chapel of the Manger," where Mary's child is said to have been cradled in the hay.

[70]Luke 2:18.
[71]Luke 2:20.
[72]Matthew 2:2.
[73]3 Nephi 1:12-15, 19-21, B. of M.

Meanwhile, the Wise Men were mounting their camel caravan and traveling toward the west to find the new king. They knew the beautiful new Christmas star was the prophetic sign that the Christ child had been born.[74]

* * * *

TOPICS FOR REFLECTION AND DISCUSSION

1. How did the Jews begin each day at the temple? How early did they start? How did the people of Jerusalem know when to awaken? What were some of the tasks of the priests as they prepared for the morning sacrifice? Where did the sacrifice take place? Immediately afterwards, where did the people meet for their prayer services?

2. What was the special assignment which Zacharias, the priest, had to perform within the temple? Did the people get to go into the temple with him? What had been the special prayerful petition of Zacharias for many years? When the angel appeared to the right of the altar what did he tell Zacharias?

3. In what way was Zacharias punished for doubting the message of the angel? Why was Elisabeth shocked and surprised when she learned what the angel had said? Why would this require a miraculous blessing and a lot of faith on her part?

4. About how long after the angel's appearance in the temple did he appear to Mary up in Nazareth? To whom was Mary betrothed? They were both descendants of what famous king? What was Mary's Hebrew name? Had the prophets known about her in advance? Had they known her name?

5. Whose power did the angel say would overshadow Mary to bring about her conception? Therefore, what would her son be called? Had Gabriel previously lived upon the earth? Who was he? What did Gabriel tell Mary concerning her cousin Elisabeth?

---

[74]Matthew 2:2.

6. Why is a secret a burden? Whom did Mary decide to tell? When Mary visited Elisabeth, what happened as she reached the front door? How long did Mary stay with Elisabeth? When she returned to Nazareth, why was she so worried? Did she give Joseph any explanation of why she was with child? How did he find out who the baby was? What was he commanded to do?

7. Approximately how close was Mary to the birth of her baby when she made the journey to Bethlehem? Would she be terribly uncomfortable riding a little donkey? What was going on in Jerusalem that made it impossible to find lodgings in the surrounding towns?

8. Who probably volunteered to take over the task of helping with the Savior's birth? What does it mean to "plunge into the forgetfulness of the Second Estate?" In the beginning would Jesus know who he was, where he was, or what his mission in life would be? Is this also true of each of us?

9. What leads us to suppose there was a gigantic congregation of the righteous in heaven just before Jesus was born? When the angel appeared to the shepherds, what were the three main things he announced to them? Where did he say they could find the Christ Child?

10. When the shepherds found the stable and entered, what did they see? Is there any indication they talked with Joseph or Mary? But whom did they awaken to tell about the exciting things that had been happening to them? Were these people impressed? Did they rush to the stable to see the Baby? Where were the Wise Men on Christmas eve? How did they know the Christ Child had been born? Who else had received a heavenly sign of the Savior's birth?

*   *   *   *

CHAPTER 2

MARY'S CHILD IS NAMED

And Barely Escapes Assassination

When Mary's baby was eight days old, he was taken to the priest to be circumcised and given a name.[1]

The rabbi was instructed by Mary and Joseph to give the baby the Hebrew name of "Joshua," which means "Jehovah is our salvation."[2] What better name could have been given this particular child? After all, he *was* Jehovah, and it would be through his life and death that salvation would become a reality for all the world.

Of course, we are not accustomed to thinking of the Savior by the name of Joshua. Rather, we think of him by the name of Jesus which is based on the Greek translation of that name. So, just as we know his mother, Miriam, as Mary, so we speak of her son, Joshua, as Jesus.[3]

It is important to remember that this name of Joshua or Jesus was not given to the Savior by accident. When the angel appeared to Joseph, he specifically commanded that this should be the name by which Mary's child should be known.[4] Adam knew that the Father's only begotten son would be called by this name.[5] So did Enoch[6] and Noah.[7] One scripture says that "none of the prophets" wrote

---

[1] Luke 2:21.
[2] Peloubet's *Bible Dictionary*, under Joshua.
[3] In the New Testament the prophet Joshua is sometimes referred to as Jesus: Acts 7:45; Hebrew 4:8.
[4] Matt. 1:20-21.
[5] Moses 6:52, 57, *Pearl of Great Price*, hereafter cited as P. of G. P.
[6] Moses 7:50, P. of G. P.
[7] Moses 8:24, P. of G. P.

without referring to Jesus the Christ who would come.[8] Among the Nephite prophets in America, the name of Jesus was mentioned 45 times during the Old Testament epoch.[9]

JESUS IS PRESENTED IN THE TEMPLE

The Jews celebrated the birth of a child in a very special way. As we have already seen, the pattern for a male child was to have him presented to the priest on his eighth day for the circumcision and conferring of his name. Thirty-two days later the baby was taken to the temple.[10]

Because Jesus was Mary's firstborn son, there was a special ceremonial procedure. It was required that Jesus be dedicated to the Lord to commemorate the time when God spared the children of the Israelites on the night that the firstborn of the Egyptians were slain.[11] The Lord declared that henceforth the firstborn male in every Israelite family must be dedicated to the Lord.[12]

If possible, this dedicatory service was to take place at the temple; therefore, Mary and Joseph took their infant son to Jerusalem which was a journey of six or seven miles from Bethlehem.

If the people could afford it, the parents were required to bring a lamb for a sacrifice. However, if the parents were poor, they could sacrifice two doves.[13] It seems significant that the economic circumstances of Joseph and Mary were such that they brought "a pair of turtledoves or two young pigeons."[14]

---

[8]Jacob 7:11, B. of M.
[9]See R. G. Shapiro, *An Exhaustive Concordance of the Book of Mormon*, Salt Lake City: Hawkes Publishing Co., 1977, under "Jesus."
[10]Leviticus 12:2-4.
[11]Exodus 12:23, 29.
[12]Exodus 13:1-2, 15.
[13]Leviticus 12:8.
[14]Luke 2:24.

THE HOLY GHOST BRINGS SIMEON
TO SEE THE CHRIST CHILD

There was an elderly man living in Jerusalem at this time who had been a righteous servant of God. His name was Simeon. Earlier in his life, Simeon had received a revelation that contained a very special promise. He was told he would not die until he had seen the Messiah.[15]

Consequently, when Mary and Joseph brought their baby to the temple, it became the greatest day in Simeon's life. Apparently he was going about his regular business in the city when the Spirit suddenly constrained him to get to the temple where his long-awaited expectation would be fulfilled.[16]

It is a steep climb up Mount Moriah to the temple courts, and no doubt the elderly Simeon was breathless when he finally entered the temple gate. Nevertheless, it seems that the Spirit led him directly to the particular priest who was in the process of dedicating Mary's son to his Heavenly Father. This was such a thrilling moment for Simeon that he didn't even wait for the ceremony to be completed. He strode forward and tenderly took the baby into his arms.[17] The priest as well as Mary and Joseph must have been astonished as the radiant old man reverently lifted his face toward heaven and said:

"Lord, now lettest thou thy servant depart in peace, according to thy word:

"For mine eyes have seen thy salvation, which thou hast prepared before the face of all people;

"A light to lighten the Gentiles, and the glory of thy people Israel."[18]

---

[15]Luke 2:25-26.
[16]Luke 2:27.
[17]Luke 2:28.
[18]Luke 2:29-32.

In these few words the old man bore testimony that this child was indeed the divine personality Simeon had been promised he would see "according to thy word." Furthermore, he knew Jesus had been "prepared" for a great mission. It is understandable why the scripture says Mary and Joseph "marvelled" at the things Simeon said as he lifted his voice to heaven in prayerful adoration while holding this precious baby in his arms.[19]

The inspired old man blessed both Mary and Joseph, and then turned directly to Mary, and said:

"Behold, this child is set for the fall and rising again of many in Israel; and for a sign which shall be spoken against."[20]

As the Spirit whispered these profound diadems of prophetic wisdom to the mind of Simeon, we wonder if the benevolent old patriarch understood the full implication of the words he spoke. Sometimes inspired men say things that come as a surprise to them as well as to those who are listening. We especially wonder if Simeon knew the full meaning of his next prophecy as he said to Mary:

"Yea, a sword shall pierce through thy own soul also, that the thoughts of many hearts may be revealed."[21]

Thirty-three years later, as Mary stood sobbing at the foot of her son's cruel Roman cross, she would learn the tragic and literal meaning of Simeon's ominous and mysterious words which he uttered in the temple that day.

THE PROPHETESS ANNA

Simeon was not the only righteous person in Jerusalem who felt the magnetic power of the Holy Ghost drawing him to the temple and the Christ Child. The scripture says there was also a very famous woman who felt this same Spirit. Her name was Anna. Luke says:

---

[19]Luke 2:33.
[20]Luke 2:34.
[21]Luke 2:35.

"And there was one Anna, a prophetess, the daughter of Phanuel, of the tribe of Aser [Asher]: she was of a great age, and had lived with an husband seven years from her virginity;

"And she was a widow of about fourscore and four years, which departed not from the temple, but served God with fastings and prayers night and day."[22]

This tells us seven remarkable things about Anna.

To begin with, she had enjoyed the ministration of the Holy Ghost sufficiently to give her the reputation of being a "prophetess." However, she was not a Jew, but belonged to the tribe of Asher, the eighth son of Jacob by Zilpah, Leah's handmaid.[23]

Furthermore, she was a descendant of Phanuel, who apparently was one of those who had escaped the captivity of the Assyrians in 721 B.C. when the ten tribes were conquered and carried away. This is all the more remarkable because the inheritance of the tribe of Asher lay directly in the path of the conquering invaders from Assyria.

Equally remarkable was the fact that this woman had lived with her husband only seven years when he died, and—since then—she had been a widow for 84 years. We can understand why Luke would say that she was "of a great age," because, by the most conservative estimates, she would have been at least a hundred years old. To illustrate, let us assume she was 17 when she married, and then became a widow at the age of 24. Add 84 years of widowhood to this figure and we realize that she would have been 108 years old by this time.

Luke tells us that this aged woman lived right on the temple esplanade and "served God with fastings and prayers night and day." No wonder this venerable "prophetess" was rewarded with a

---

[22]Luke 2:36-37.
[23]Genesis 30:13.

personal revelation indicating that the Christ Child had not only arrived on earth, but he was at the temple that very day.

We imagine there may have been a small group of people attracted by the excitement that old Simeon created as he interrupted the dedicatory ceremonies to bear his testimony. The gathering of a crowd is suggested by the manner in which Anna bore her testimony. Luke says she "spake of him to all them that looked for redemption in Jerusalem."[24]

Anna's reference to the "redemption in Jerusalem" would not be interpreted by the Jews to mean salvation of the human soul. As our story unfolds, we will discover that the Jews interpreted the "redemption in Jerusalem" to be a monumental event of the future when God would devastate the Romans with fire and brimstone and restore Jerusalem as the capital of a mighty Israelite nation.

The salvation or redemption of the human soul was a concept that had been completely obscured by the rabbinical emphasis on the "works" of the Mosaic law. When we come to the story of Nicodemus we will discover how painfully difficult it was for the rabbinically trained mind to grasp the glorious message of individual salvation and the redemption of the human soul.

JOSEPH AND MARY BEGIN THEIR LIFE AS HUSBAND AND WIFE

After going to the temple, Mary and Joseph returned to Bethlehem with the baby. Now they began living together as husband and wife for the first time. The scripture says:

"And he knew her not till she had brought forth her firstborn son,"[25] [and the forty days of "purification" had been fulfilled.][26]

Because Mary and Joseph are such notable personalities in sacred history, it is difficult to think of them in their role as young

---

[24]Luke 2:38.
[25]Matthew 1:25.
[26]Leviticus 12:2-4.

lovers who were betrothed to each other and were making exciting plans for their marriage just before Gabriel suddenly appeared on the scene.

But, of course, Gabriel changed everything.

For Mary there had followed an inspiring interlude of events too sacred to be recorded in detail. However, we know she was told of her calling as the mother of the Savior, and that she was quickened by the Holy Ghost when the power of the Highest overshadowed her. We know she was told about her aged cousin, Elisabeth, conceiving for the first time, and that Elisabeth's baby would grow up to become the great prophet who would prepare the way for the ministry of Mary's son.

We recall how Mary hastened to see Elisabeth so she could share her great secret, but the Holy Ghost had already told Elisabeth. Then there were those three wonderful months which Mary spent with Elisabeth waiting for John the Baptist to be born. After that she returned home, wondering what Joseph would think when he realized she was with child. But Mary was relieved and overjoyed when she learned that the angel had told Joseph about her baby and commanded them to be married immediately.

For Joseph, the past year had been entirely different. At first there was the feeling of elation at the time of their betrothal, but that was followed by several months of loneliness while Mary was visiting Elisabeth. Then came the horrible discovery that Mary was with child, and the agonizing weeks of torment and anguish until the heavenly messenger appeared to Joseph and told him what was happening.

Of course, from then on he played his assigned role knowing that Mary was one of the most choice and divinely blessed women in history. The best part was the good news from the angel that Joseph would be allowed to become her husband after all!

When Joseph and Mary took Jesus to Bethlehem, they faced all the harsh realities of life. They had this precious baby, but they also had the pressing responsibility of securing a home and earning a living.

From Matthew we learn that they did succeed in securing a house,[27] and while they did not yet know it, Mary and Joseph were about to receive a bounty of rich treasures from the East that would relieve them of some of their immediate financial worries.

THE COMING OF THE WISE MEN

We do not know how many months were required before the wise men were able to reach Palestine from the East, but it was undoubtedly a long and tedious journey. The wise men appear to have belonged to one of the priesthood colonies that seem to have survived in various places from ancient times.[28] Like the priesthood colony in America, these men knew about the coming of the Savior, and were immediately aware that he had been born in the land of Jerusalem for they had seen the great new star.[29]

Enroute, they probably discussed the excitement they expected to encounter among the Jews since the Messiah had been born among them. Upon their arrival, however, they were no doubt amazed to discover there was no excitement at all. The Jews didn't seem to know anything about the birth of their Messiah. When these distinguished visitors made contact with Herod, they found the king of the Jews totally ignorant of the great event which the wise men were certain had occurred. In fact, the scripture says the belief of the wise men that a new king of the Jews had been born troubled Herod greatly.[30]

For years, there was nothing that could ignite the mind of Herod into a flaming furnace of murderous hatred more quickly than a rumor that there was some "pretender" rising up to claim his throne. As we have already seen, such rumors had cost the lives of several people in Herod's own family, including his wife Mariamne and two of his sons.

---

[27]Matthew 2:11.
[28]W. Cleon Skousen, *The First 2,000 Years*, Salt Lake City, Bookcraft, 1953, chapter 25.
[29]Matthew 2:1-2.
[30]Matthew 2:3.

Herod had a network of spies in every part of the land, and it is not unreasonable to assume that he might have already heard rumors that certain shepherds claimed they had seen angels, heard heavenly choirs, and even seen the Christ Child in a manger.[31]

But regardless of the rumors that might be floating about, what shocked Herod was the tangible reality of three venerable men standing before him who had travelled hundreds of miles to see the newborn king of the Jews. They even claimed there was a new star on the night of his nativity which they had been told to expect as the divine sign of his birth.[32]

Hurriedly, Herod conferred with the priests and scribes. Where did tradition and prophecy say their Messiah would be born? "In Bethlehem, the City of David," they said.[33]

Frantically, Herod conjured up a scheme. Surely he must not stand by after all he had done, even killing his own wife and children, and allow his throne to be snatched away by some nefarious infant whom the superstitious populace might rally around and claim as their divine king! In this spirit of desperate hatred, Herod plotted murder for the child.

The problem was to find him.

Calling the wise men to him "privily," he extracted from them the precise date when the great new star was first seen in their own country.[34] This is significant, because it meant that once Herod learned when the star appeared, he knew exactly how old Jesus was.

Herod then proceeded to shrewdly extract from the wise men a solemn promise that if they found the child, they would promptly inform the king so he could visit the child and honor him also.[35]

---

[31]Luke 2:15-16.
[32]Matthew 2:2.
[33]Matthew 2:5-6.
[34]Matthew 2:7.
[35]Matthew 2:8.

The wise men assured the king they would return and report to him once the child was found. Then they prepared to depart.

THE WISE MEN JOURNEY TO BETHLEHEM

It is thought that King Herod was staying at his winter palace at this time which was not far from the city of Jericho. If this was the case, the wise men had about sixteen miles of uphill travel to reach Jerusalem, and then another six or seven miles southward to reach Bethlehem.

The scripture says they left King Herod at night and, as they began their journey in the darkness, they suddenly saw the Christmas star again. Matthew says:

"When they saw the star, they rejoiced with exceeding great joy."[36]

They had good reason to rejoice. The wise men were strangers and had no idea where they were. Furthermore, there were many side roads and detours on the road leading up toward Jerusalem, and just as many along the winding road leading to Bethlehem.

But there was something very special about this star. It did not remain high in the heavens to be admired by star gazers. It was more like a satellite that moved directly ahead of the wise men as it guided them along the way. As Matthew says:

"And lo, the star, which they saw in the east, went before them."[37]

To gain some appreciation of the miraculous importance of this star, one only needs to visit a Judean town on a dark night and imagine the predicament of the wise men when they arrived in Bethlehem. They were seeking for a house at an unknown location, inhabited by people whose names they had never heard, and whose faces they had never seen.

---

[36]Matthew 2:10.
[37]Matthew 2:9.

This beautiful Christmas star is one of the neglected miracles of the Bible. Here is what Matthew says it did:

"And lo, the star, which they saw in the east, went before them, till it came and stood over where the young child was."[38]

At this point we learn that Mary, Joseph, and Jesus, were no longer in a humble stable. As soon as the Passover crowds had gone, they apparently had no difficulty finding better quarters. Matthew assures us that this had happened. When the beautiful satellite star stopped over the place where Mary, Joseph, and Jesus were staying, the wise men dismounted, and the Gospel writer says:

"When they were come into the *house*, they saw the young child with Mary his mother, and fell down, and worshipped him: and when they had opened their treasures, they presented unto him gifts; gold, and frankincense, and myrrh."[39]

One can only imagine the amazement of Mary and Joseph as they saw these princely strangers from a distant land come into their house and spread before them a display of wealth beyond anything they had seen in their whole lives—gold, frankincense, and myrrh.

At this time, Mary and Joseph did not know it, but the gift of gold would serve them well on the long journey they would have to make before they reached their final destination at Nazareth.

In addition to the gold, there was the frankincense. This was the expensive crystalline resin extracted from trees in Arabia, and used in synagogues and the temple for incense burning. Everywhere it could be exchanged for a handsome price.

The myrrh was also from an Arabian tree and when collected in any appreciable quantity, it was worth a small fortune. The myrrh was a highly fragrant resin used as a perfume as well as a cosmetic.

---

[38]Matthew 2:9.
[39]Matthew 2:11 (emphasis added).

It must have been a most inspiring visitation for Mary and Joseph as they listened to the story of these strangers. And it must have been equally inspiring to these gifted patriarchs as they gazed on the gentle countenance of Mary's baby. As we have already mentioned, they were undoubtedly members of a body of righteous priesthood holders in their own country. The very fact that they knew about the Christmas star, and were aware that it signified the birth of the Savior, suggests that they were far closer to the source of heavenly knowledge than the main body of the Jews.

A further evidence of their spiritual affinity and divine approbation was a revelation which they received while staying overnight with Mary and Joseph. Matthew says:

"And being warned of God in a dream that they should not return to Herod, they departed into their own country another way."[40]

So this is all we know about the wonderful story of the wise men. Out of the unknown they came, and into the unknown they departed. We do not know their nationality, their names, or their exact number. Their entire history is contained in just twelve verses of Matthew. Nevertheless, we are promised that someday we will have their whole story.[41]

JESUS BECOMES A CAPITAL FUGITIVE

Barely had the wise men departed from Bethlehem before Joseph received what is believed to have been his second revelation. Matthew says:

"And when they were departed, behold, the angel of the Lord appeareth to Joseph in a dream, saying, Arise, and take the young child and his mother, and flee into Egypt, and be thou there until I bring thee word: for Herod will seek the young child to destroy him."[42]

---

[40]Matthew 2:12.
[41]2 Nephi 27:10,22, B. of M.
[42]Matthew 2:13.

Only a few nights earlier, Herod had felt the wise men were his personal allies since they had promised to return and tell Herod where they found the Christ Child. However, when they did not return, the desperate Herod resolved to take matters into his own hands with a wrathful vengeance.[43]

All historians agree that Herod was a pathological murderer when it came to protecting his throne. His entire history as a king is drenched with blood of both relatives and friends whom he suspected of possible duplicity.[44]

But now he was dealing with something intangible—a rumor about an unidentified stranger, and a child at that. Spies and paid informers were no doubt spread out among the people to get some kind of lead. There were rumors and suspicions, but nothing tangible. One of the best leads turned out to be an aged priest named Zacharias. He had a son born to him only a short time before the time when the wise men said the Star first appeared. Furthermore, the wife of Zacharias was said to be a relative of a young woman who was the mother of the "child pretender."

The failure of Herod's officers to locate Jesus drove the frustrated king into a resurgence of his *homicide mania*. As his psychoneurosis of senseless rage inflamed his mind, he ordered his soldiers to sweep down on Bethlehem and slaughter every child under the age of two. Since Herod knew the exact age of Jesus, this decree was designed to include every child around his age. It is estimated that Jesus was probably twelve to fourteen months old when the decree was issued.

Matthew tells us that the decree not only included all of the children of Bethlehem, but the soldiers were ordered to then go into all the "coasts" of Bethlehem and slay the children in those villages and towns as well.[45]

---

[43]Matthew 2:16.
[44]See *Josephus, Complete Works*, Grand Rapids, Mich., 1960, Kregel Publications, where these crimes are itemized under "Herod" in the index.
[45]Matthew 2:16.

Who can imagine the horror of all those parents who found their precious little ones being stripped from their arms and thrust through with a sword before their very eyes. This tragedy became known as the "slaughter of the innocents."

Matthew believed the prophet Jeremiah was referring to this terrible massacre when he wrote:

"In Rama was there a voice heard, lamentation, and weeping, and great mourning, Rachel weeping for her children, and would not be comforted, because they are not."[46]

We notice that Jeremiah says this tragic killing of the children would occur in "Rama." There were a number of places in Israel and Judea called Rama or Ramah, and it is assumed that this also may have been one of the names associated with Bethlehem.

THE INFANT JOHN THE BAPTIST BARELY ESCAPES

We now know that just before this terrible slaughter of the children took place, the aged priest, Zacharias, learned of it. At this point we gain a new insight from a modern revelation concerning the life-threatening crisis which now descended on the old man and his young son, John. We know that Zacharias and Elisabeth had their home in the "hill country" of Judea,[47] and this was apparently in the "coasts" of Bethlehem.

While working on the inspired translation of the Bible, Joseph Smith learned the following about Zacharias and his little family in this hour of peril. He wrote:

"When Herod's edict went forth to destroy the young children, John was about six months older than Jesus, and came under the hellish edict, and Zacharias caused his mother [the aged Elisabeth] to take him into the mountains where he was raised on locusts and wild honey."[48]

---

[46]Matthew 2:17-18; Jeremiah 31:15.
[47]Luke 1:39.
[48]*Teachings of the Prophet Joseph Smith*, Salt Lake City: Deseret Book Co., 1973, p. 261.

Apparently Herod learned that the son of Zacharias had escaped the massacre of the children, and perhaps thought that both Jesus and John were hiding in the same place. Herod told his soldiers to extract this information from the old priest, even on pain of death. Zacharias therefore became the immediate target of Herod's wrath, and Joseph Smith describes the outcome:

"When the father [Zacharias] refused to disclose his [John's] whereabouts, and being the officiating high priest at the temple that year, he was slain by Herod's order, between the porch and the altar, as Jesus said."[49]

So the murder of Zacharias can be added to Herod's other crimes.

What happened to Elisabeth and John after they went into hiding is an interesting story by itself, but we will learn more about that in a later chapter.

THE DEATH OF KING HEROD

It was an ironic twist of fate, or more likely, a providential decree, that just after Herod had ordered the massacre of the children of Bethlehem the grim reaper descended on Herod himself. History has left no doubt as to the agony of his last days. He was taken down with a "loathsome disease," and Frederic W. Farrar describes his condition as follows:

"On his bed of intolerable anguish, in that splendid and luxurious palace which he had built for himself under the palms of Jericho, swollen with disease and scorched by thirst, ulcerated externally and glowing inwardly with a 'soft slow fire,' surrounded by plotting sons and plundering slaves, ...longing for death as a release from his tortures yet dreading it as the beginning of worse terrors, ...devoured by the premature corruption of an anticipated grave, eaten of worms as though visibly smitten by the finger of God's wrath after seventy years of successful villainy, the wretched old man, whom men had called the Great, lay in savage frenzy awaiting his last hour."[50]

---

[49]Ibid.
[50]Frederic W. Farrar, *The Life of Christ*, New York: Thomas Crowell and Co., 1874, pp. 54-55.

When death came, it was a relief to both Herod and his people.

FROM EGYPT TO NAZARETH

The news of Herod's death reached Mary and Joseph in Egypt even sooner than the fastest courier. It came by a heavenly messenger. Matthew says:

"But when Herod was dead, behold, an angel of the Lord appeareth in a dream to Joseph in Egypt,

"Saying, Arise, and take the young child and his mother, and go into the land of Israel: for they are dead which sought the young child's life."[51]

It is interesting that the angelic messenger was very non-specific about the place where Mary and Joseph should take up their residence in "the land of Israel."

As we pointed out earlier, all the circumstances suggest that Joseph and Mary had settled in Bethlehem with the intention of making it their permanent home. This is further demonstrated by their decision to go back to Bethlehem when they came up out of Egypt. Matthew continues:

"And he arose, and took the young child and his mother, and came into the land of Israel.

"But when he heard that Archelaus did reign in Judaea in the room of his father Herod, he was afraid to go thither: notwithstanding, being warned of God in a dream, he turned aside into the parts of Galilee.

"And he came and dwelt in a city called Nazareth."[52]

---

[51]Matthew 2: 19-20.
[52]Matthew 2:21-23.

So Joseph and Mary had gone the full cycle. How could they have guessed when they set out to register for the taxation in Bethlehem that all this would happen to them?

It is rather amazing that while on this adventurous journey, the child of Mary had fulfilled three separate prophecies, each of which seemed to contradict the others.

The first prophecy said the Messiah would be born in Bethlehem.[53]

The second prophecy said he would come up out of Egypt.[54]

The third prophecy said he would be a Nazarene.[55]

The literal fulfillment of these three prophecies illustrates what we will find in every facet of the Savior's earthly career. No prediction by any prophet concerning the life and mission of the Son of God was allowed to remain neglected or unfulfilled.

* * * *

TOPICS FOR REFLECTION AND DISCUSSION

1. What is the meaning of the name, "Joshua"? Why was it particularly appropriate for Mary's son? Who chose the name? How long after his birth was Jesus taken to the temple? Why did this happen only to Jesus, and not to his subsequent half-brothers?

2. How do we know Simeon was loved of the Lord? How did he find Jesus at the temple? Did he interrupt the service? What did he say to the Lord as he held Jesus in his arms? Name two things Simeon knew about Mary's baby.

3. Name four of the seven things Luke revealed about Anna. Where did she live? What did she tell the people about Jesus? After Joseph

---

[53]Micah 5:2.
[54]Hosea 11:1, Matthew 2:15.
[55]Matthew 2:23. Matthew cites this prophecy without indicating the source.

and Mary returned to Bethlehem, what were some of their most pressing problems? Did they stay in the stable?

4. Why were the wise men not present the night Jesus was born? Do we know their number? Their names? Their nationality? What would suggest that perhaps they were a group of priesthood holders similar to the Christian Nephites?

5. Why do we think they went to inquire about the newborn king from Herod? Why did Herod react so violently to such a simple question? How did Herod learn from the wise men how old Jesus was by this time? What shrewd promise did he extract from the wise men?

6. When the wise men left Herod's palace, what made them rejoice as they moved out into the darkness? What was so miraculous about the Christmas star? Why did the wise men have to depend upon it so completely? Why do some say this is one of the most neglected miracles in the Bible?

7. Where did the wise men find Joseph, Mary, and Jesus? In what way was the gift of gold so important later on? Describe the nature of frankincense. Describe the nature of myrrh. What led the wise men to take a detour route back home? What was Joseph's second revelation?

8. When Herod issued a decree to have the children under age two massacred, what famous person besides Jesus was put in jeopardy? What did his father do about it? Then what happened to the father? Who revealed this new information to us?

9. About how soon after the massacre of the children did Herod discover he was on his death bed? What kind of a disease did he have? Why did he suffer mentally as well as physically?

10. How did Joseph get the news of Herod's death down in Egypt? What was he told to do? Why didn't Joseph and Mary raise Jesus in Bethlehem, the city of David? Where did they go? Name the three prophecies which seemed to contradict each other. Which ones did Jesus literally fulfill?

* * * *

CHAPTER 3

THE EARLY YEARS OF JESUS

Many years ago, Bruce Barton wrote a national bestseller entitled, *The Man Nobody Knows.*[1] This book was about the life of Jesus Christ. It is true that nobody knows the Savior completely except the Father. In fact, when Jesus was born to Mary, he, himself, did not know who he was.

The Lord has promised that someday we will be told "all things,"[2] and it will be fascinating to learn how Jesus first found out about himself and was able to learn the true identity of his real father. It will be equally interesting to know who told him.

FRAGMENTS OF THE "HIDDEN YEARS"

As far as the record shows, most of the early portions of the life of Christ were "hidden years." This leaves a huge section of empty pages in our story. But when "all things" are revealed, we will no doubt discover that those were exciting times. They were his growing-up years, his learning years, his years of preparation.

It is interesting that the Savior's "hidden years" extended clear up until he was nearly thirty. It was only as he prepared to launch into his public ministry that Jesus emerged from the obscurity of his early life. But this was not unique. The law of Moses did not allow a young Jew to assume the responsibilities of his ministry until he was thirty. The Lord told Moses:

"From thirty years old and upward even unto fifty years old, [was] every one that came to do the service of the ministry, and the service of the burden in the tabernacle of the congregation."[3]

---

[1]Bruce Barton, *The Man Nobody Knows*, New York, Grosset & Dunlap, 1924.
[2]2 Nephi 27:22, B. of M.
[3]Numbers 4:47.

So all during these years, Jesus was gradually finding out who he really was, and preparing himself for what he was to become.

WHY DO WE ENTER MORTALITY
WITH NO MEMORY OF OUR PAST?

It is significant that during his earth life, the Great Jehovah had to be told who he was. He was the victim of what science calls "amnesia." This occurs when a person completely forgets his past and has no recollection of his true identity.

And just as it was with Jesus, so it is with us. We have no memory of our experiences before this earth life. Obviously, there must be an important reason for this, but it leads us to ask, "Why must we enter earth life as an unknown entity?" One scripture says it is because this is our probationary estate. The Lord said:

"We will prove them...to see if they will do all things whatsoever the Lord their God shall command them."[4]

Since the testing in this life will determine our entire eternal existence for the future, the Father had to set it up so we would all begin our mortal estate on an equal basis. That meant we must have no recollection of our pre-earth life. It meant we would enter this life without knowing whether we were leaders or followers before we came here. We must not even know whether we had been foreordained to accomplish some monumental mission, as was Jeremiah, who had to be told he was foreordained to be a prophet.[5]

It would be impossible for us to imagine what a traumatic experience it must have been for the great Jehovah—the Master Intelligence who had been the Father's general manager for this portion of the Father's kingdom[6]—to suddenly take the breathless plunge into the Second Estate. In a split second, this transition into mortality swept away his memory of who he was, where he was, or why he was here. It was a gigantic leap into a dark labyrinth of

---

[4]Abraham 3:25, P. of G.P.
[5]Jeremiah 1:5.
[6]Moses 1:33, P. of G.P.

unknown dimensions. As with all of us, he entered his life on earth without any comprehension of its height, breadth, or depth.

However, Jesus had known this would happen, and many centuries before his birth he selected Mary to be his mother. As we have mentioned earlier, the mother of Jesus was not only predetermined and foreordained, but she was given her earthly name hundreds of years before she was born.[7]

When Jesus chose her as his mother, he knew this would be the woman who would have him in her care during those perilous years when he would not know who he was. No greater compliment could have been paid to Mary than to have had the great Jehovah select her, not only to be his mother, but also his teacher, protector, and guardian during his critical years of earthly preparation.

WHAT IT MUST HAVE BEEN LIKE
TO BE THE MOTHER OF JESUS

Among the hundreds of millions of mothers who have blessed this earth, which one would venture to imagine what it must have been like to be the mother of Jesus?

Many times during those early years, Mary must have looked at her son, and said to herself: "My little one, you don't even know who you are." But his mother knew. So did Joseph. Nevertheless, they did not know he had come to be crucified.[8] We will have more to say about that in a later chapter.

When Mary first received her divine calling, she had a ministering angel to tell her what to do and what to expect. But after her baby was born, there is no indication that she had Gabriel or any other heavenly messengers to guide her as she anxiously endeavored to nurture and raise up her son. Apparently, like other mothers, she was left to the whisperings of the Spirit and the guidance of her own maternal instincts as she prayerfully and carefully proceeded one day at a time to perform her great task.

---

[7]Mosiah 3:8, B. of M.
[8]Doctrine and Covenants 133:66.

The Psalmist said that when the Messiah came, there would be guardian angels to watch over him,[9] but to what extent, Mary and Joseph probably never knew.

We can assume that Mary and Joseph did everything possible to train Jesus in all of the traditional ways that would prepare him for his life of service. They not only had to teach him what to do, but what *not* to do.

THE YOUNG PHARISEE

During this period of Jewish history, nearly all of the common people belonged to the religious sect of Judaism called the Pharisees. In a religious sense, they were fundamentalist Jews. They believed in a life of strict obedience to the entire code of divine law given to Moses. Therefore, it is reasonable to assume that Jesus was carefully trained in all the disciplines of the Mosaic law as taught by the rabbinical scholars.

Among other things, this meant he had to learn at least two languages—the classical Hebrew, so he could study the scriptures, and the Aramaic, which was the dialect or language of the common people.[10] There were also many in Palestine and Syria who spoke Greek, the classical language of the Mediterranean.[11] Among the Jews, this was particularly true of those who were patrons of the Greek culture. They called themselves "Hellenists."

Furthermore, since the Romans were the rulers of the western world, the people would be inclined to learn some elements of Latin. Dr. Edersheim suggests that by the time Jesus launched into his ministry, he seems to have had some understanding of both Greek and Latin, since he conversed with people of both cultures.[12]

---

[9]Psalms 91:11.

[10]Farrar, *Life of Christ*, op. cit, p. 83.

[11]Ibid. pp. 83-84.

[12]Edersheim, *Life and Times of Jesus*, vol. 1, p. 253.

Education was of primary importance to the Jews, and, in the days of Jesus, every Jewish child was required to attend school beginning at the age of five or six.[13]

The Jews also emphasized the need to begin training for a profession early in life. From his youth, the Savior was taught carpentry by Joseph, his foster father.[14] In a land where timber was scarce, this profession was arduous. This implies that Jesus had to rise early, work hard, and perfect the skills of his trade.

There was also the need to develop the social graces of kindness, patience, a controlled temper, and thoughtfulness in dealing with others. Each day there were special times for prayer and scripture study. On the sabbath, the older members of the family attended the local synagogue. Jesus would never have guessed that it would be from this very synagogue that these townspeople would one day carry him bodily to the precipice of a high hill and try to cast him down to his death on the rocks below.[15]

As Jesus responded to the gentle persuasion of his mother, and the firm guidance of Joseph, these anxious parents must have felt a sense of genuine satisfaction as Jesus exhibited all of the qualities of a righteous and superior child. The scripture leaves no doubt that their efforts were successful. Luke says:

"And Jesus increased in wisdom and stature, and in favour with God and man."[16]

THE HALF-BROTHERS AND HALF-SISTERS OF JESUS

Of course, we have to keep in mind that Joseph and Mary were also involved in raising other children besides Jesus.

---

[13]Ibid. p. 230.
[14]Mark 6:3.
[15]Luke 4:28-30.
[16]Luke 2:52.

The scriptures indicate that after Jesus was born, Joseph and Mary had four sons.[17] Their names were James, Joses (Joseph), Simon, and Judas. The scripture also says there were "sisters,"[18] but we are not told their names or the number. If we assume that in addition to Jesus, there were at least two sisters and four brothers, it would mean that Mary and Joseph were raising a family of seven children while Jesus was growing up.

It is reasonable to assume that the Savior's four brothers (and perhaps the sisters) would have noticed the constant anxiety of their mother for the welfare of Jesus. There is nothing in the records to indicate that any feelings of jealousy arose between these younger siblings and their older half-brother, but it would be understandable if there might have been just a little twinge of resentment. We can also imagine the occasional reaction of growing up with an older brother who didn't do *anything* wrong![19]

The possibility that there might have been some degree of estrangement is perhaps implied by the fact that later on, when Jesus began his great ministry, not one of his brothers believed in him—not even when he began performing hundreds of miracles.[20]

Nevertheless, the story has a happy ending. It was no accident that these four men were chosen to be his brothers, and shortly after the Savior's resurrection, he took special care to appear to his half-brother, James.[21] And what is even more significant, this beloved half-brother not only became a devout disciple of Jesus, but was later ordained to be an apostle![22]

It is equally gratifying to learn that in due time, the other brothers and sisters apparently were converted. This is suggested in the first chapter of Acts where it says that after the Savior's resurrection, all his other brothers appear to have been numbered

---

[17]Matt. 13:55.
[18]Matt. 13:56.
[19]Hebrews 4:15.
[20]John 7:5; Mark 6:4.
[21]1 Corinthians 15:7.
[22]Galatians. 1:19.

among the members of the church.[23] Surely their sisters would not have been left behind.

GROWING UP IN NAZARETH

The Savior's growing up years seem to have been simple, carefully structured, and productive. There was school, carpentry work, Hebrew studies, scripture studies, occasional discussions with the rabbi, and the normal social activities of a rural community.

There is also evidence that Jesus joined his family several times a year to make the long trek to Jerusalem to attend the religious celebrations on the great feast days.

As was the case with many families, they probably took along one of their own sheep for a peace offering. It was the prescribed procedure to give a portion to the priests,[24] and then the family had the rest of the meat to provide them with an important part of their food during the three or four days they were in the holy city. A modern Jew would refer to this process of sanctifying their meat as making it "kosher," or proper to eat.

All Jewish fathers were "bound to teach their sons."[25] They had the responsibility of teaching their sons the Ten Commandments, the eighty or so statutes of the law (expanded into 613 by the rabbis), and the "judgments." The judgments consisted of a long list of blessings the Lord promised to the people if they were faithful,[26] followed by a long list of cursings which would befall them if they became wicked.[27]

THE HIGHLIGHTS OF BIBLE HISTORY

Joseph also had to teach his sons concerning the major events in the religious history of God's people. This would include sacred

---

[23]Acts 1:14.

[24]Leviticus 7:32.

[25]Edersheim, *Life and Times of Jesus*, vol. 1, p. 230.

[26]Deuteronomy 28:1-14.

[27]Ibid. 28:16-68.

events as well as incidents in the lives of God's prophets. All of these were closely associated with the Biblical timetable.

During the years the present author was teaching at the Brigham Young University, each of his one thousand students per semester was required to memorize the same timetable the Savior was probably required to know. To this day, many of those students express appreciation for this requirement.

Memorizing this timetable is the most efficient and effective way to study the Old Testament as well as ancient history. This timetable consists of a comparatively short list of "hook" dates. Once these have been memorized, they constitute a frame of reference or "hook" for all of the other important events which are related to that same period.

To illustrate the value of a hook date as a memory device, we might mention that scarcely anyone can remember the date for the great Battle of Granada when all of the Jews and Moors were driven out of Spain. However, once it is pointed out that this battle occurred in 1492, a student never forgets it. The year Fourteen Ninety-Two is riveted into the mind of every school child. It is a wonderful hook date.

The highlights of the Biblical timetable go something like this:

4,000 B.C.—the beginning of human history after the Fall.

2,344 B.C.—the year of the great universal flood.

2,000 B.C.—the century that belonged to Abraham (who lived between 2022 and 1847 B.C., but these dates need not be memorized.)

1,900 B.C.—the century that belonged to Isaac (who lived between 1922 and 1742 B.C.)

1,800 B.C.—the century that belonged to Jacob (who lived between 1862 and 1715 B.C.)

1,700 B.C.—the century that belonged to Joseph (who lived between 1771 and 1661 B.C.)

1,500 B.C.—the century that belonged to Moses (who lived between 1597 and 1477 B.C.)

1,400 B.C.—the beginning of Israel's great dark ages (when apostasy engulfed the people for several centuries.)

1,100 B.C.—the century that belonged to Samuel and King Saul.

1,000 B.C.—the century that belonged to King David (who lived between 1032 and 962 B.C.) and King Solomon (who lived between 987 and 922 B.C.)

922 B.C.—the year the ten northern tribes separated from the two tribes of Judah and Levi.

900 B.C.—the century that belonged to Elijah.

800 B.C.—the century that belonged to Elisha.

721 B.C.—the year the northern ten tribes were conquered and carried off to Assyria.

700 B.C.—the century that ended with the great prophet Isaiah at the height of his ministry.

600 B.C.—the century that belonged to four great prophets: Jeremiah, Lehi, Daniel, and Ezekiel.

587 B.C.—the conquest of the Jews by Babylon, the destruction of Jerusalem, with the remnant of the Jews being carried off to Babylon.

538 B.C.—The year Cyrus conquered Babylon (539 B.C.) and allowed the Jews to return to Jerusalem and rebuild their temple.

516 B.C.—The Second Temple was dedicated. It became known as the temple of Zerubbabel, being named after the governor of Jerusalem.

458 B.C.—Ezra leaves Persia to launch a religious reform in Jerusalem, taking with him the books which became the Old Testament.

445 B.C.—Nehemiah comes to Jerusalem from Persia to rebuild the walls of the city.

400 B.C.—The prophet Malachi closes the Old Testament epoch with the promise that someday Elijah would come to turn the hearts of the fathers to the children and of the children to the fathers.

Of these 22 dates, 13 are even numbers and rather easily memorized when associated with the name of a particular prophet. The remainder can be committed to memory with a little effort, and together they become an invaluable historical treasure for ready reference.

THE GRADUAL AWAKENING OF JESUS

Who would dare tell Jesus who he was?

The task of gradually sharing with Jesus the shocking and virtually unbelievable story that he was literally the Son of God was no doubt too frightening for either Joseph or Mary to undertake. During those tender years of the Savior's life, we imagine that both of them kept silent, hoping that someday, somehow, the Father would share with Jesus a complete knowledge of both his identity and his mission.

As we shall see in a moment, it came as a complete surprise to both Joseph and Mary when the twelve-year-old Jesus revealed that he knew who he was. No doubt they wondered, as we do today, just *who* it was that had the thrilling assignment of sharing with Jesus the astonishing disclosure that he was actually Jehovah, the very Son of God.

We shall also see in a moment that by the age of twelve, Jesus had received extensive instructions concerning the meaning of the scriptures and the words of the prophets.

It will be recalled that the birthday of the Savior was associated with the Feast of the Passover, which occurred during the early part of April each year.[28] We have a particular interest in this Feast of the Passover which marked the date when Jesus reached the age of twelve.[29]

The age of twelve was—and still is—a very special year for Jewish boys. That was the year when each twelve-year-old was expected to demonstrate that he was ready to be considered a "son of the law."[30] It seems that at the Passover it was the custom for a boy of this age to make himself available to the rabbis and priests so that he could be questioned concerning his knowledge of the law and the teachings of the prophets. Today, every religious Jewish boy at this age is tested in a similar way to see if he is prepared for his "bar Mitzvah" or becoming a "son of the Law" by the time he reaches thirteen.

When Jesus was taken to the temple to follow the custom of making contact with the learned rabbis, two interesting things occurred.

First of all, Jesus found that he was in possession of many insights and treasures of scriptural knowledge that exceeded the wisdom and learning of these rabbis and priests who interrogated him. This would have been exciting for a mature scholar, let alone a twelve-year-old boy from a ne'er-do-well town like Nazareth.

---

[28]Doctrine and Covenants 20:1.
[29]Luke 2:42.
[30]Edersheim, *Life and Times of Jesus*, vol. 1, p.235.

In the second place, it would have been rather astonishing to the rabbinical scholars at the temple to discover this youngster from a small northern village of Galilee who seemed to be so intellectually brilliant.

One might well imagine these rabbis calling to one another and inviting their learned friends to come and listen to this amazing twelve-year-old initiate.

The scripture tells the story as follows:

"Now his parents went to Jerusalem every year at the feast of the passover.

"And when he was twelve years old, they went up to Jerusalem after the custom of the feast.

"And when they had fulfilled the days, as they returned, the child Jesus tarried behind in Jerusalem; and Joseph and his mother knew not of it.

"But they, supposing him to have been in the company, went a day's journey; and they sought him among their kinsfolk and acquaintance.

"And when they found him not, they turned back again to Jerusalem, seeking him.

"And it came to pass, that after three days they found him in the temple, sitting in the midst of the doctors, both hearing them, and asking them questions.

"And all that heard him were astonished at his understanding and answers."[31]

---

[31]Luke 2:41-47.

WHAT HAD REALLY HAPPENED?

The last two verses contain several significant details. First of all, Joseph and Mary saw him "sitting in the midst of the doctors." Dr. Edersheim explains:

"We read in the Talmud that the members of the Temple-Sanhedrin...from the close of the Morning to the time of the Evening Sacrifice, were wont on Sabbaths and *feast days* to come out upon the Terrace of the Temple, and there to teach. In such popular instruction the utmost latitude of questioning would be given. It is in this audience, which sat on the ground, surrounding and mingling with the Doctors—and hence *during, not after* the Feast—that we must seek the Child Jesus."[32]

Luke says it was there that Mary and Joseph found him "hearing [the doctors] and asking questions."[33] But he was not only asking questions. He was adding his own comments to the responses of the learned rabbis. It says:

"And all that heard him were astonished at his *understanding and answers.*"[34]

So it is not difficult to imagine what had been happening to this twelve-year-old boy. Once Jesus felt the youthful exuberance of being accepted—even praised—by the temple elite, all else seems to have evaporated from his mind. He had become so pre-occupied with the thrill of this new experience that he either temporarily forgot about his parents or felt assured they would understand when they learned what a tremendous thing had happened to him.

This would also lead us to assume that each day Jesus would talk himself into exhaustion and then fall asleep at night right there among the pillars of Solomon's porch where the learned men often assembled. As for food, everyone brought extra food to these feast

---

[32]Edersheim, *Life and Times of Jesus*, vol. 1, p. 247.
[33]Luke 2:46.
[34]Luke 2:47.

day celebrations, and no doubt there were plenty of rations to share with this bright young boy who had attracted so much attention.

But this went on for three days![35]

JESUS LOST, JESUS FOUND

Only parents who have lost a child for several days will have any conception of the emotional trauma which Joseph and Mary must have felt when they suddenly realized Jesus was not in their "company" returning to Nazareth.[36]

Their mental anguish was no doubt multiplied at least a hundred times by the realization that this precious boy entrusted to them was the very Son of God. Through their carelessness, it appeared they had lost him. He could have been hurt, kidnapped, or wandered away and become disoriented.

Apparently Mary and Joseph stayed together as they looked frantically for this precious boy. Finally they found him—in the temple courtyard, of all places, and "sitting in the midst of the doctors."[37]

As they rushed forward in excited relief, Mary made no attempt to hide her feelings of agonizing worry. The scripture says:

"And when they saw him, they were amazed: and his mother said unto him, Son, why hast thou thus dealt with us? behold, thy father and I have sought thee sorrowing."[38]

The feelings of Jesus at this time must have been completely ambivalent. On the one hand, he had been a great trial to his parents; in fact, he had been unforgivably remiss in his familial duties by not making an effort to let them know where he was. But, on the other hand, if he had gone seeking his parents, he could have missed these

---

[35]Luke 2:46.
[36]Luke 2:44.
[37]Luke 2:46.
[38]Luke 2:48.

three glorious days of profound gospel conversations with the most learned men in the country.

As Jesus quickly tried to sort out the dichotomy between his sense of guilt and the euphoria of a complete childhood triumph, he finally came up on the side of the triumph. He said:

"How is it that ye sought me? wist ye not that I must be about my Father's business?"[39]

JESUS SHARES HIS GREAT SECRET

It is from this electrifying statement that we learn that by this time Jesus knew who he was. And, as we have mentioned earlier, this leads us to assume that either the Father or a heavenly messenger had revealed to Jesus the same great secret which Gabriel had shared with Mary. Gabriel had told her she would be quickened by the Holy Ghost, and the power of the Highest would overshadow her; consequently, the child that she conceived would be the very Son of God.

Now Jesus knew he was that child.

The Savior's statement to his mother also indicates that while Jesus knew he may have committed a serious offense against his mother and Joseph, nevertheless he had made the Father's teachings available to these men who were some of the greatest scholars in Jerusalem. And he could see that they loved it!

There is also one further element to be considered. In examining the question, "How is it ye sought me?" we need to consider the possibility that Jesus had a different view of the situation than his parents. For example, the Feast lasted two days, but many people lingered and visited with friends and relatives the rest of the week. This was especially true of people who had come a long distance, such as the worshipers from Nazareth.

---

[39]Luke 2:49.

It is possible that Jesus thought his parents were still in Jerusalem and having a pleasant time. This would account for his statement, "How is it that ye sought me?" If they were having a good time, why would they want to seek him out and interrupt the wonderful experience he was having?

In any event, Jesus closed the discussion with that profound and wonderful statement, "Wist ye not that I must be about my Father's business?"

MARY AND JOSEPH FAIL TO COMPREHEND

Amazingly, Joseph and Mary were so relieved and thankful to find this precious son that they completely missed the meaning of what he said. Luke confirms this by saying:

"And they understood not the saying which he spake unto them."[40]

This clearly implies that neither Mary nor Joseph were even aware that Jesus had been having a whole series of training sessions with ministering angels, or perhaps even with his Father. Nor did they realize he already knew the identity of his real Father.

One might challenge the idea that this choice son of Mary would receive heavenly visitations without telling her about it, but that has happened before.

By way of example, there is no indication that Mary ever told her parents about Gabriel. She travelled close to 80 miles to visit Elisabeth so she would have someone with whom she could share her secret.

Young Joseph Smith, at the age of seventeen, was visited by the angel Moroni three times in one night. On the last visit, Moroni told Joseph to relate to his father everything that had happened. He didn't do it. When the angel came again, he asked Joseph why he had not

___

[40]Luke 2:50.

told his father. Joseph simply replied, "I was afraid he would not believe me."[41]

In the case of Jesus, we do not know why the twelve-year-old had not told his mother about the thrilling angelic visits he had been receiving. But obviously he had not. If they had known of his heavenly visitations, they would have comprehended what Jesus was talking about. Luke assures us that "they understood not the saying" when he mentioned his "Father's business."[42]

Nevertheless, Mary did not forget what he said. The scripture says "his mother kept all these sayings in her heart."[43]

The scripture also assures us that all of this exciting attention Jesus received from the learned men at the temple did not go to his head. Luke says that Jesus obediently returned to Nazareth with his parents and "was subject unto them."[44]

MARY AND JOSEPH FIND THEMSELVES RAISING A PRECOCIOUS SON

Nevertheless, it was not long before Mary and Joseph—and probably the rabbi at the local synagogue—began to realize that the carpenter and his wife were nurturing and raising up a remarkably brilliant son. Whenever someone undertook to teach him anything, it seemed as though he already knew it. The scripture says:

"And it came to pass that Jesus grew up with his brethren, and waxed strong, and waited upon the Lord for the time of his ministry to come.

"And he served under his father, and he spake not as other men, neither could he be taught, for he needed not that any man should teach him."[45]

---

[41]Lucy Mack Smith, *History of Joseph Smith*, Salt Lake City: Stevens and Wallis, Inc., 1945, p. 79.
[42]Luke 2:50.
[43]Luke 2:51.
[44]Ibid.
[45]JST Matthew 3:24-25.

Except for this one passage, the Bible now skips nearly eighteen years in the Savior's life. We assume that during this time he would be going to Jerusalem for the feasts, especially the feast of the Passover. No doubt he made a few friends in Jerusalem and developed a broader understanding of the Romans, the Jewish "Hellenists" or Greeks, and also the Pharisees and the Sadducees who were the two principal sects of the Jews.

It is also very likely that it was during some of these visits that he first became acquainted with three wonderful young people—Mary, Martha, and their brother Lazarus—who lived in Bethany on the eastern slopes of the Mount of Olives. During his ministry, Jesus displayed a love for these three young people which sometimes seemed to exceed that which he exhibited for his half-brothers and half-sisters, perhaps even for the Twelve.

WHAT HAPPENED TO JOSEPH?

Something else important happened during those eighteen years. Mary's husband disappeared from the story. Apparently, during that lapse of time, he died. There is no reference to his death in the scripture, but this is assumed from the fact that Joseph is never mentioned again. In fact, after Jesus entered his ministry there are several references to Mary and her children, but they are always mentioned without Joseph. For some reason, Joseph is gone, and that is the basis for our presumption that he had died.

It is sometimes suggested that perhaps Joseph was an older man when he was betrothed to Mary, and that since thirty years had passed away by the time Jesus began his ministry, Joseph may have died of natural causes incident to old age. However, this does not seem to be a logical explanation.

To begin with, it was very uncommon among the Jews for a young girl to enter into a betrothal with an older man. This writer was told at the Hebrew University that ordinarily it was traditional for the parents of a young woman to "arrange" a betrothal when she was in her late teens, and the young man who had been chosen and "arranged" to be her husband was in his early twenties.

The suggestion that Joseph was an older man when he became engaged to Mary does not fit the Jewish tradition in the Savior's era. Nevertheless, as we have pointed out, the absence of Joseph from the Gospel accounts would indicate that Joseph had died sometime before the ministry of Jesus began.

JESUS HAD TO ACCOMPLISH TWO THINGS BEFORE HIS MINISTRY COMMENCED

As Jesus entered his twenty-ninth year, he had to accomplish two things. First, he had to "fulfill all righteousness," by finding John the Baptist and receiving the sacred ordinance of baptism from him. John was six months older than Jesus, and was already at the River Jordan, baptizing vast numbers of people.[46] Elsewhere, we learn that John had also been administered to by an angel and was expecting Jesus.[47]

Secondly, Jesus knew he must begin searching out the twelve men scattered among the Jews who were ordained before they were born to be his apostles.[48]

This was going to be an eventful year.

* * * *

TOPICS FOR REFLECTION AND DISCUSSION

1. Why do you think Bruce Barton called his book on the life of Christ, *The Man Nobody Knows?* How much better do you think we know the Savior since the restoration of the gospel? Give some examples.

2. What do you think would have concerned Mary the most as she undertook to rear Jesus? Jesus had a strong personality which usually spells problems for parents. Was this a problem for Mary and Joseph as they raised Jesus?

---

[46]Matthew 3:5-6; John 1:28.
[47]John 1:26-27, 33.
[48]Romans 8:29-30; Jeremiah 1:5; Alma 13:3, B. of M.

3. How do you account for the fact that the four brothers of Jesus did not become the Savior's disciples until after he was resurrected? Were you surprised that one of his brothers became an apostle?

4. Have you made an attempt to memorize the 22 "hook" dates in Old Testament history? Name three advantages to be gained by memorizing these dates. When did the great battle of Granada occur that drove the Jews and the Arabs out of Spain? Why will you be able to remember the date of that battle in the future?

5. Describe the principal highlights in the story of the Savior's visit to Jerusalem when he was twelve years old. Why is age twelve so important to a Jewish boy today?

6. How would you describe the feelings of Jesus when he discovered that he knew more about the scriptures than the learned men at the temple? Why do you think he continued his dialogue with these men for three days without going out to find his parents?

7. Why was it customary for the rabbis to question boys at this age? What was Jesus doing at the temple which Jesus said he considered to be his "Father's business?" Did Mary and Joseph understand what he meant?

8. As the years passed by, why does the scripture say it was difficult to teach Jesus anything? Did this seem to make him proud or arrogant?

9. By the time Jesus was ready to begin his ministry, it appears that Joseph may have died. What circumstances suggest that this was the case? Why do the scholars at the Hebrew University think it was unlikely that Joseph was an older man when he was betrothed to Mary?

10. Jesus had to do two things before he entered into his ministry at the age of thirty. What were they? How do we know John the Baptist was expecting him?

* * * *

CHAPTER 4

THE SUDDEN APPEARANCE OF JOHN THE BAPTIST

Not since the famous Hasmonean family of Judah had launched the Maccabee revolution against the Greek occupation 195 years earlier had there been such a stir among the Jewish people. Crowds swarmed down the Jericho road to hear the trumpeting voice of John the Baptist on the shores of the Jordan river.

This rough rustic had suddenly appeared on the scene dressed in a leather girdle tied about his waist—not unlike a Scottish kilt—and wearing a hair-shirt mantle made of camel wool.[1] It gave this bearded man from the wilderness the very appearance attributed to Elijah the prophet.[2]

BUT THE THING WHICH STIRRED
THE PEOPLE WAS HIS MESSAGE

Every student of the Hebrew scrolls knew that some day there would come among the Jews a "voice of him that crieth in the wilderness, Prepare ye the way of the Lord, make straight in the desert a highway for our God."[3]

Suddenly here was John, emerging out of the wilderness, and proclaiming the exciting news that the long awaited Messiah—the Anointed One of Israel—was about to come forth among the people. In no uncertain terms he declared that the Jews must immediately "prepare the way of the Lord." To do this, they must repent of their sins and be baptized.

---

[1]Mark 1:6.
[2]2 Kings 1:8.
[3]Isaiah 40:3; Malachi 3:1; 1 Nephi 10:7-10, 2 Nephi 31:4-8, B. of M.

The scripture leaves no doubt that John's message had its impact on the hearts and minds of the populace. Mark tells us:

"And there went out unto him all the land of Judaea, and they of Jerusalem, and were all baptized of him in the river of Jordan, confessing their sins."[4]

WHERE HAD JOHN BEEN ALL THESE YEARS?

By this time, Elisabeth's son, John, had reached thirty years of age. This was the maturity required before a priest was allowed to serve in the ministry or in the temple.[5]

It will be recalled that he had been born in the vicinity of Bethlehem where his parents lived in "the hill country" of Judeah.[6] In connection with the massacre of the children at Bethlehem, Herod tried to kill the baby John, and his father, Zacharias, lost his life rather than reveal his whereabouts. As we indicated earlier, Joseph Smith described these circumstances as follows:

"When Herod's edict went forth to destroy the young children, John was about six months older than Jesus, and came under the hellish edict, and Zacharias caused his mother to take him into the mountains, where he was raised on locust and wild honey."[7]

In due time, Herod apparently learned that the son of Zacharias had escaped the massacre of the children at Bethlehem. It is very likely that he also thought both Jesus and John were hiding in the same place. For this reason, Zacharias became the target of Herod's wrath, hoping he could force the aged priest to tell where the children were.

Joseph Smith describes the outcome:

---

[4] Mark 1:5.
[5] Numbers 4:3; 1 Chronicles 23:3.
[6] Luke 1:39-40.
[7] *Teachings of the Prophet Joseph Smith*, p. 261.

"When the father [Zacharias] refused to disclose his [John's] whereabouts, and being the officiating high priest at the temple that year, he was slain by Herod's order, between the porch and the altar, as Jesus said."[8]

During his ministry, Jesus referred to this tragic event and equated it with the murders of many other prophets down through the years. He said:

"Therefore also said the wisdom of God, I will send them prophets and apostles, and some of them they shall slay and persecute:

"That the blood of all the prophets, which was shed from the foundation of the world, may be required of this generation;

"From the blood of Abel unto the blood of Zacharias, which perished between the altar and the temple."[9]

Notice that according to Luke, Jesus made no attempt to identify which Zacharias he was talking about, because no doubt this heinous murder of the priest at the temple just three decades earlier was fresh in the minds of all the people.

However, since there were numerous prophets by this or similar names in the Bible, some ancient scribe who was working on the Gospel of Matthew decided to identify this Zacharias mentioned by Jesus as the "son of Barachias."[10] This created all kinds of problems because the ancient prophet Zechariah (note the slight difference in spelling)—who is described as "the son of Berechiah,"[11]—was not slain in the temple. He was one of the prophets involved in the building of the second temple (Temple of Zerubbabel dedicated in 516 B.C.), but there is no indication he was slain there.[12]

---

[8]Ibid.
[9]Luke 11:49-51.
[10]Matthew 23:35.
[11]Zechariah 1:1.
[12]See LDS Dictionary under 51 "Zachariah."

Nevertheless, there was another ancient prophet named Zechariah who was slain in the temple, but he was the "son of Jehoiada."[13]

All of this confusion was eliminated when Joseph Smith learned that Jesus was not talking about either of those ancient prophets. He was talking about Zacharias, the father of John the Baptist.

Many years after Joseph Smith's death, Bible scholars found certain early Christian writings that sustained Joseph Smith's statement concerning Zacharias.

Dr. Robert Matthews, in his splendid definitive work on the life of John the Baptist, quotes this material. He said there is:

"...a very old tradition, as old at least as the second century, that Herod also sought to destroy at the same time the son of Zacharias and Elisabeth—the young St. John, whose greatness had been foretold to him; that Elisabeth escaped with her son from amid the slaughter, and was afterwards miraculously preserved, and that Herod, in his rage at being thus baffled, sent and slew Zacharias between the altar and the Temple."[14]

JOHN'S LIFE IN THE DESERT

The scripture could not be more striking in its description of the frugal existence of John during the first 30 years of his life than to say that he survived primarily on "locusts and wild honey."[15]

Locusts, or grasshoppers, were a legitimate form of food under the law of Moses.[16] Locusts are still the principal diet of the poor in many parts of the east. They are gathered in nets, plunged into salted

---

[13]2 Chronicles 24:20-21.

[14]Robert Matthews, *A Burning Light*, Provo, Utah: BYU Press, 1972, p. 25; a similar account has also been found in the *Apocryphal New Testament*, published in 1953, and quoted by Dr. Matthews in his book on p. 26.

[15]Matt. 3:4.

[16]Leviticus 11:21-22.

boiling water, dried in the sun, and eaten with butter made from goat's milk.[17]

Early Christian tradition states that the elderly Elisabeth died while John was still a boy and he was thereafter adopted by one of the desert communities.[18] The "Essenes" were the best known of these groups, but there were many others. As mentioned in the Introduction, these are the people to whom we are indebted for the "Dead Sea Scrolls."

These desert societies were largely dissident protesters who were disgusted with the corruption of the religious leaders at Jerusalem. They were therefore seeking to practice a very conservative and fundamentalist version of the Mosaic code.[19] As one might suspect, these people generally trained their children under a disciplined regimen of reading the scriptures, memorizing the law, reciting the judgments (the cursings and the blessings), and following a pattern of hard labor and regulated living according to the strictest interpretation of the law.

All of this was an ideal setting for the growing up years of a Levite youth who was a direct descendant of Aaron and had been born to become "the voice of one crying in the wilderness, Prepare ye the way of the Lord."[20]

WHAT JOHN KNEW ABOUT HIMSELF

Before her death, Elisabeth undoubtedly shared with her son the details of the appearance of the angel Gabriel in the temple, and how, through the blessing of God, she was able to give birth to John in her old age.

She would also want him to know about the angel who came to their home—when John was only eight days old—and ordained him "to overthrow the kingdom of the Jews, and to make straight the way

---

[17]Cunningham Geike, *Life and Words of Christ*, vol. 1, pp. 354-5.
[18]Matthews, *A Burning Light*, p. 27.
[19]Ibid.
[20]Isaiah 40:3.

of the Lord...to prepare them for the coming of the Lord."[21] He would also need to know that he had been given the "keys" to the Aaronic Priesthood, as indicated by the prophet Joseph Smith.[22]

There was also the amazing miracle that occurred on the day John was circumcised and named. His father, after being unable to speak for over nine months, was miraculously healed. Being endowed by the Holy Ghost, the old priest proved eloquent as he blessed the infant John and said he would not only "go before the face of the Lord to prepare his way," but he would "give... salvation unto his people," and be a "light to them that sit in darkness."[23]

In other words, John would proclaim the FULLNESS of the gospel.

Of course, John could not teach these precious principles—which had been lost to the Jews—unless he first learned them himself. This would lead us to conclude that John received the ministering of angels just as Jesus did. In fact, John refers to one of these ministering angels who told him how to recognize the Christ himself.[24]

JOHN LAUNCHES HIS MINISTRY AT BETHABARA

Around 600 B.C., the prophet Lehi saw a vision of the opening of the ministry of John the Baptist, and he recognized the place. He said he saw John preaching and baptizing at Bethabara.[25] The apostle John also mentions Bethabara and describes where it was located. He says:

"These things were done in Bethabara beyond Jordan, where John was baptizing."[26]

---

[21]Doctrine and Covenants, 84:28.
[22]*Teachings of the Prophet Joseph Smith*, p. 272.
[23]Luke 1:76-79.
[24]John 1:33.
[25]I Nephi 10:9, B. of M.
[26]John 1:28.

In other words, John launched his ministry on the eastern side of the Jordan river at a community called Bethabara. Occasionally it was called "Bethany," but not the same Bethany as the one where Mary, Martha, and Lazarus lived.[27]

However, since the prophet Lehi had lived in Palestine and called it "Bethabara," we conclude that this was the correct name. Bethabara means *House of the Ford*, or the lower crossing of the Jordan River.

All of the gospel writers emphasize that John's opening proclamation was "repent and be baptized." However, when it became a popular fad to follow the crowds going down to Bethabara, many of them arrived at the River Jordan to discover there was much more to it than merely a baptismal ceremony. John challenged each group to repent of those sins which characterized their profession or lifestyle.

Imagine trekking happily all the way down from Jerusalem, crossing the River Jordan, and then having John the Baptist suddenly stand up and say:

"O generation of vipers, who hath warned you to flee from the wrath to come?

"Bring forth therefore fruits worthy of repentance....

"And the people asked him, saying, What shall we do then?

"He answereth and saith unto them, He that hath two coats, let him impart to him that hath none; and he that hath meat, let him do likewise.

"Then came also publicans [tax collectors] to be baptized, and said unto him, Master, what shall we do?

---

[27]Matthews, *A Burning Light*, p. 34, note.

"And he said unto them, Exact no more than that which is appointed you.

"And the soldiers likewise demanded of him, saying, And what shall we do? And he said unto them, Do violence to no man, neither accuse any falsely; and be content with your wages."[28]

I once heard a prominent philosopher say, "I love to hear a good sermon on repentance—just don't be too specific." John the Baptist was specific.

THE FULLNESS OF THE GOSPEL RESTORED

Once John had gathered about himself a creditable congregation of repentant disciples, he began to teach them the fullness of the gospel.

Joseph Smith stated that when John commenced his ministry, he was actually inaugurating and setting up the kingdom of God.[29]

Some have thought the kingdom of God was not set up until the day of Pentecost, but Joseph Smith said it began with John. Nevertheless, it was a simple beginning. No miracles. No structured organization. No officers. Just faith, repentance, and baptism.

Joseph Smith learned many new things about the ministry of John when he was preparing the inspired version of the Bible. Most of the following citations are from the King James Translation, but where we have cited from the inspired translation of Joseph Smith, we will indicate it in the footnotes with the letters "JST," meaning the Joseph Smith Translation, or "Inspired Version."

After reviewing all that John taught concerning the gospel, we find 33 different doctrinal principles that John shared with those who were willing to stay with him and listen. He taught the following:

---

[28]Luke 3:7-14.
[29]*Teachings of the Prophet Joseph Smith,* p. 273.

1. To be a true disciple requires a frank and sincere confession of sin.[30]

2. Confession must be accompanied by a determination to repent of those sins, and forsake them. These are what he called the "fruits" of repentance.[31]

3. Repentance and reform should be followed by entering into a covenant with God to obey his commandments and "endure to the end." This covenant was made through baptism by immersion at the hands of one having the priesthood authority to perform the ordinance. Part of John's message was that he had the authority to perform "legal" baptisms; in other words, baptisms that would be acceptable to God.[32]

4. John said he came in the spirit of Elias as a forerunner for the Messiah.[33]

5. He said that there would be another Elias come after him who would restore all things. He identified this second Elias as the one who would baptize them with the Holy Ghost. This Elias turned out to be the Savior—*the* Elias who would restore all things.[34]

6. John testified that an angel told him the Messiah would be identified for him by the sign of the dove descending upon the Messiah.[35]

7. When John saw this happen he went forth boldly to testify that Jesus was indeed the long-awaited Messiah.[36]

---

[30]Matt. 3:6.
[31]Matt. 3:8.
[32]*Teachings of the Prophet Joseph Smith*, p. 336.
[33]JST John 1:20-24.
[34]JST John 1:26-28; compare with KJT.
[35]JST John 1:32; compare with KJT.
[36]JST John 1:31, 33; compare with KJT.

8. John knew Jesus by the name which the angel attributed to him—namely "the Lamb of God."[37] He also said the Messiah would "take away the sins of the world."[38]

9. John taught that Jesus was with the Father in the pre-mortal existence.[39] Although this scripture is usually attributed to the apostle John, a modern revelation indicates that this is actually the testimony of John the Baptist.[40] The apostle John simply quoted the baptist's testimony, and the modern revelation clarifies who originally said it.

10. John the Baptist knew that in the pre-earth life Jesus or Jehovah was often referred to as "the Word," since he communicated to the intelligences of the universe the will of the Father and the "good news" of the gospel.[41]

11. John the Baptist taught that all things were created by Jehovah or "the Word" under the direction of the Father.[42]

12. John knew that Jesus, as the ante-mortal Jehovah, increased from grace to grace until the governing of all things was placed in his hands by the Father. Some have thought Jesus did not receive the fullness of power until after Christ's resurrection and his ascension into heaven. However, John says Jesus increased from grace to grace in the pre-earth life and that the Father gave all power into his hands before he ever came to this earth.[43]

That is why Jesus prayed: "And now, O Father, glorify thou me with thine own self with the glory which I had with thee before the world was."[44]

---

[37]John 1:36.
[38]JST Luke 3:5; compare with KJT.
[39]John 1:1,14.
[40]Doctrine and Covenants 93:7-15. Verse 15 specifically identifies which John is bearing this testimony.
[41]John 1:1 plus Doctrine and Covenants 93:8 where the "Word" is identified as the "messenger of salvation" or Christ.
[42]John 1:3 plus Doctrine and Covenants 93:9-10.
[43]Doctrine and Covenants 93:13-17.
[44]John 17:5.

13. John taught that the people must obey God's commandments and bring forth good fruit or they would be "hewn down and cast into the fire."[45]

14. They must cultivate brotherly kindness, honesty, and justice.[46]

15. They must pray often.[47]

16. They must fast.[48]

17. They must be morally clean.[49]

18. They must testify of the divinity of Christ.[50]

19. John the Baptist said Christ's atonement would bring salvation to the heathen nations, and not just the Jews.[51]

20. Although Jesus restricted his preaching almost exclusively to the Jews, John said he would eventually launch a program to preach the gospel to the gentiles.[52]

21. John taught that Christ would ultimately gather Israel again.[53]

22. He said Jesus would bring to pass the resurrection of ALL the dead, whether they were good or evil.[54] However, he did not say they would all get the same glory!

---

[45]Luke 3:9.
[46]JST Luke 3:15-21; compare with KJT.
[47]Luke 11:1.
[48]Matt. 9:14.
[49]Matt. 14:3-4.
[50]John 1:36.
[51]JST. Luke 3:5; compare with KJT.
[52]JST Luke 3:6; compare with KJT.
[53]JST Luke 3:5; compare with KJT.
[54]JST Luke 3:7; compare with KJT.

23. John the Baptist also taught that Christ would ascend into heaven and take his place at the right hand of the Father until the fullness of time.[55]

24. John said it would be during the fullness of time that the law and the testimony would be sealed up ready for the final judgment of God.[56]

25. That would be the time when the keys of the kingdom would be delivered to the Father.[57]

26. John the Baptist said it would be the long-awaited time when Jesus Christ would come in glory.[58]

27. And when Jesus came it would be the great day of God's judgment.[59]

28. At last the world would see the administration of true, Godly justice.[60]

29. He said God's judgment would be based on the works or deeds of each person.[61]

30. Incidental to the Second Coming of Christ, John said there would be a tremendous manifestation of God's great power.[62]

31. He said the whole surface of the earth would be restructured with the mountains and rough places becoming smooth, and the valleys either filled up or raised.[63]

---

[55]JST Luke 3:7-8; compare with KJT.
[56]JST Luke 3:8; compare with KJT.
[57]JST Luke 3:8; compare with KJT.
[58]JST Luke 3:9; compare KJT.
[59]JST Luke 3:9; compare KJT.
[60]JST Luke 3:9; compare KJT.
[61]Ibid.
[62]JST Luke 3:10; compare KJT.
[63]Ibid.

32. John made it clear that this amazing display of God's power would not be just for the members of God's kingdom, but that all flesh would see the salvation of God together.[64]

33. John promised that Jesus would be the second Elias who would "restore all things."[65] This turned out to include the ministering of the gifts of the Holy Ghost, restoring the Melchizedek Priesthood, setting up the structure of the church organization, and establishing all of the higher ordinances, including eternal marriage and the temple endowment. He also initiated vicarious work for the dead. As we shall see later, these are the "things" Jesus taught his apostles during the forty days between the resurrection and the ascension.

Nevertheless, it is impressive that John the Baptist taught every aspect of the entire gospel except the crucifixion and the work reserved for his Master who would "restore all things."

JOHN'S MOST DIFFICULT PROBLEM

From the very beginning it appears that John seemed to sense that his greatest challenge would be to convince his converts to leave him and join Jesus.

Even before he had met the Savior, he was promoting the idea that a far greater leader was about to arrive on the scene. John had the keys to the kingdom, but only the preparatory kingdom.[66]

Notice how carefully John tried to prepare his followers for a transition from himself to the Savior:

"I indeed baptize you with water unto repentance: but he that cometh after me is mightier than I, whose shoes I am not worthy to bear: he shall baptize you with the Holy Ghost, and with fire."[67]

---

[64]JST Luke 3:10.
[65]JST John 1:26-28; compare KJT.
[66]Doctrine and Covenants 94:26.
[67]Matthew 3:11.

Another scripture is even more explicit. John the Baptist is quoted as saying:

"There standeth one among you, whom ye know not;

"He it is, who coming after me is preferred before me, whose shoe's latchet I am not worthy to unloose."[68]

The most ironic thing about all of this is the fact that many of the multitude who hurried to the River Jordan hailed John as a prophet but rejected his testimony concerning the divinity of Jesus. The scripture says:

"...many received John as a prophet, but they believed not on Jesus."[69]

THE IMPACT OF JOHN'S TEACHINGS

The scripture leaves no doubt as to the effectiveness of John's powerful proclamation of the fullness of the gospel. As we shall see in a moment, his teachings inspired repentance in some of the lowest and most wicked elements among the people.

The only level of society which rigidly rejected his message was the sophisticated rabbinical clergy who had their own private vested interests to protect. This is why Jesus denounced them, saying:

"Verily I say unto you...the *publicans [tax collectors] and harlots* go into the kingdom of God before you.

"For John came unto you in the way of righteousness, and ye believed him not: but the publicans and the harlots believed him."[70]

Jesus told the Pharisees that John was "a burning and a shining light, and ye were willing for a season to rejoice in his light."[71]

---

[68]John 1:26-27.
[69]JST John 4:2; compare KJT.
[70]Matthew 21:31-32 (emphasis added).
[71]John 5:35.

He was simply saying that in the beginning it was popular to join up with John as he went forth preaching repentance and baptism. However, when he bore testimony that Jesus of Nazareth was the long-awaited Messiah, these fair-weather converts virtually fled in terror, lest their ears become tainted by the words of John which they equated with blasphemy.[72]

By doing this, these former zealots of John not only rejected the Savior, but they also turned their backs on one of the greatest prophets who ever lived. Joseph Smith describes why Jesus would later give him such high praise:

"How is it that John was considered one of the greatest prophets? His miracles could not have constituted his greatness.

"First. He was entrusted with a divine mission of preparing the way before the face of the Lord. Whoever had such a trust committed to him before or since? No man.

"Secondly. He was entrusted with the important mission...to baptize the Son of Man. Whoever had the honor of doing that?...Whoever led the Son of God into the waters of baptism, and had the privilege of beholding the Holy Ghost descend in the form of a dove, or rather in the *sign* of the dove?....

"Thirdly. John, at that time, was the only legal administrator in the affairs of the kingdom there was then on earth....The son of Zacharias wrested the keys, the kingdom, the power, the glory...by the holy anointing and decree of heaven, and these three reasons constitute him the greatest prophet born of a woman."[73]

JESUS COMES TO BE BAPTIZED OF JOHN

An angel prepared John for his first meeting with Jesus. John later told the people:

"And I knew him not: but he that sent me to baptize with water, the same said unto me, Upon whom thou shalt see the Spirit

---

[72] JST John 4:2; compare KJT.
[73] *Teachings of the Prophet Joseph Smith*, pp. 275-6.

descending, and remaining on him, the same is he which baptizeth with the Holy Ghost.

"And I saw, and bare record that this is the Son of God."[74]

According to the Inspired Version, we have the following expanded and more complete account of Jesus coming to be baptized of John:

"Then cometh Jesus from Galilee to Jordan unto John, to be baptized of him.

"But John *refused* him, saying, I have need to be baptized of thee, and *why* comest thou to me?

"And Jesus answering said unto him, Suffer *me* to be *baptized of thee*: for thus it becometh us to fulfil all righteousness. Then he suffered him.

"And John went down into the water and baptized him.

"And Jesus, when he was baptized, went up straightway out of the water: and *John saw, and lo,* the heavens were opened unto him, and he saw the Spirit of God descending like a dove, and lighting upon him:

"And lo, *he heard* a voice from heaven, saying, This is my beloved Son, in whom I am well pleased, *Hear ye him.*"[75]

This statement was apparently addressed to John.

JOHN SEES THE HOLY GHOST DESCENDING LIKE A DOVE

As we mentioned earlier, John had been told by the same heavenly messenger who sent him forth to preach and baptize, that

---

[74]John 1:31-34. The Inspired Version gives verse 31 a little differently, but does not change the point of this discussion.
[75]JST Matthew 3:41-46; compare KJT (emphasis added).

the one on whom he saw the Spirit "descending like a dove" would be the Messiah who would baptize with fire.[76]

There has been considerable debate as to what John saw. Did he see the Spirit descending "like" a dove, or did he see a dove symbolizing the Holy Ghost?

It turns out that the Spirit of the Holy Ghost personally descended upon Jesus "like" a dove, but there was also a dove present as a symbol or "sign" of the Holy Ghost. Joseph Smith clarified this scriptural problem in the following words:

"The sign of the dove was instituted before the creation of the world, a witness for the Holy Ghost, and the devil cannot come in the sign of a dove. *The Holy Ghost is a personage, and is in the form of a personage.* It does not confine itself to the *form* of a dove, but in the *sign* of the dove. The Holy Ghost cannot be transformed into a dove; but the sign of a dove was given to John to signify the truth of the deed, as the dove is an *emblem* or token of truth and innocence."[77]

This would therefore lead us to conclude that John witnessed two things:

1. He saw the heavens opened and the Holy Ghost descending as a personage of spirit,[78] which "abode" upon him.[79]

2. Then John saw the "sign" or "emblem" of the Holy Ghost in the "bodily shape like a dove."[80] The presence of a dove alighting upon the Savior just as the personage of the Holy Ghost descended upon him, confirmed to John that this was indeed the Christ, the very Son of God, the Messiah.

---

[76]John 1:33.
[77]*Teachings of the Prophet Joseph Smith*, pp. 275-276.
[78]Doctrine and Covenants 130:22.
[79]John 1:32.
[80]Luke 3:22.

To confirm the identity of Jesus as the Messiah, the Father spoke from the heavens and said:

"This is my beloved Son, in whom I am well pleased. HEAR YE HIM."[81]

For those who have been taught that the Trinity is "three in one and one in three," these verses are highly instructive. Here was Jesus—as a mortal being—coming up out of the water, while the Holy Ghost came down out of heaven; and the voice of the Father was heard coming out of heaven, assuring John that this was his Beloved Son.

As the Lord has explained in a modern revelation, the members of the Godhead are three separate persons even though they are ONE in PURPOSE.[82]

THE NEXT IMPORTANT STEP IN THE SAVIOR'S PREPARATION

Mark says that "immediately" after the baptism of Jesus, the Spirit directed the Savior into the wilderness for a period of intensive instruction and testing.

The beginning of the ministry of Jesus was barely a couple of months away, and there was much that he had to be told about his mission and about himself.

* * * *

TOPICS FOR REFLECTION AND DISCUSSION

1. What do you consider to be the two most important reasons why John's ministry created so much excitement among the Jews? Why do you think religious revivals, such as the one John initiated, tend to lose public support after a short period of time?

2. We listed many important things Elisabeth would have wanted her son to know as he was growing up. Can you list four of them?

---

[81]JST Matthew 3:46; compare KJT.
[82]Doctrine and Covenants 130:22; John 17:20-22.

According to tradition, what happened to John's mother after she and John had lived in the wilderness for awhile? And what does this tradition say about John's upbringing after he was left an orphan?

3. Describe the circumstances under which John's father was killed. Can you think of two major advantages John would have had in a desert community that he might not have had if he were raised in Jerusalem?

4. Can you find Bethabara on a Bible map? On which side of the river was it located? What is this region called today? What does the name of Bethabara tell you about this location? Around 600 B.C., who saw a vision of John baptizing at this place?

5. When the multitude came down to be baptized, John called them a generation of vipers. What kind of repentance did he demand of the tax collectors? What did he tell the soldiers they must do?

6. In preaching the fullness of the gospel, John taught at least 33 things that we can identify in the scriptures. Did he know about the Second Coming? Did he know about the final judgment? Can you name five other doctrines he taught?

7. Can you name three things John the Baptist did not teach? Why do you think he refrained from doing this?

8. Who did Joseph Smith say launched "the kingdom of God" in the meridian of time? What kind of priesthood keys did John hold? Who held the higher keys?

9. How did Joseph Smith justify the statement of the Savior that there was never a greater prophet than John the Baptist? What was John's greatest challenge during his ministry?

10. How do you account for the fact that many people were willing to accept John as a prophet, but would not accept Jesus as the Messiah even though John testified of his divinity?

*   *   *   *

CHAPTER 5

WHY DIDN'T THE JEWS RECOGNIZE CHRIST?

Before we proceed further with the life of the Savior, we must try to find the answer to one of the major riddles in the New Testament. A Christian cannot read the story in the Gospels without wondering why the Jews did not recognize the true identity of Jesus Christ. The reason is simple: They were NOT expecting a Redeemer Christ.

WHAT KIND OF MESSIAH WERE THE JEWS EXPECTING?

The Jews were expecting a Messiah, but it was to be a King-Messiah, a divinely endowed replica of the mighty King David, one who could call down fire from heaven, demolish the Romans, and set up the kingdom of Israel the way Daniel described it. Daniel's prophecy read as follows:

"And in the days of these kings shall the God of heaven set up a kingdom, which shall never be destroyed: and the kingdom shall not be left to other people, but it shall break in pieces and consume all these kingdoms, and it shall stand for ever."[1]

As Dr. Alfred Edersheim, the distinguished Jewish convert to Christianity, says:

"...all that Israel hoped for, was national restoration and glory. Everything else was but [the] means to these ends; the Messiah Himself [being] only the grand instrument in attaining them. Thus viewed, the picture presented would be of Israel's exaltation, rather than the salvation of the world....In such a picture there would be neither room nor occasion for a Messiah-Saviour....The sum total of Rabbinic expectations, scarcely entered into the teaching of Jesus about the Kingdom of God....He was not the Messiah of Jewish conception."[2]

---

[1] Daniel 2:44.
[2] Edersheim, *Life and Times of Jesus*, vol. 1, p. 164.

Another Jewish scholar from the modern Hebrew University in Jerusalem, points out that according to the prevailing teachings of the rabbis, Jesus did not provide the necessary "proof" of his Messiahship. All he provided were miracles.

Dr. Gershom Scholem says the Jews had been forewarned by their leading scholars that they should not be misled by the mere demonstration of the power to perform miracles. The scribes and priests had said that unless the man claiming to be the Messiah actually destroyed the enemies of the Jews and restored Israel to its former Davidic glory, he was to be rejected. Here is the way Dr. Scholem describes the rabbinical teachings of the Savior's day:

"The Messiah will arise and restore the kingdom of David to its former might. He will rebuild the sanctuary and gather the dispersed of Israel....Do not think that the Messiah needs to perform signs and miracles, bring about a new state of things in the world, revive the dead, and the like. It is not so."[3]

Then he summarizes the teachings of the great Jewish scholar Moses Maimonides (1135-1204), and says:

"The intervention of heaven on earth constitutes no criterion for the legitimacy of the Messiah and his mission. He [Maimonides] will allow only one criterion: whether the Messiah succeeds in his endeavors [to restore the glorious Davidic kingdom]. The Messiah must prove his identity to justify skeptics, NOT by cosmic signs and miracles, but by historical success."[4]

WHY HAD THE RABBIS MISSED THE OLD TESTAMENT
PROPHECIES CONCERNING THE COMING OF A MESSIAH?

This mistaken expectation of the Jews was no accident. It was the result of a thousand years of rabbinical book burning. For reasons that we shall consider in a moment, this mighty tribe of Israel had undertaken to erase from their scriptures the entire story of the First Coming, or misinterpret those that remained.

---

[3]Gershom Scholem, *The Messianic Idea in Judaism*, New York: Schocken Books, 1971, p. 27.
[4]Ibid. p. 30.

This is why the arrival of Jesus as the Lamb of God who would be slain for the sins of the world, caught the Jews completely by surprise. As Jesus said of the Jews in one scripture:

"In that day when I came unto mine own, NO MAN among you received me, and you were driven out."[5]

Or as John said:

"He was in the world...and the world knew him not. He came unto his own, and his own received him not."[6]

In a literal sense, these scriptures mean that not a single Jew recognized Jesus in his Redeemer role when he came among them. And the more amazing fact is that the scriptures verify that all during his mortal ministry, neither his apostles nor his followers recognized him in his true role as one who had come to be sacrificed for the sins of the world.

From the very beginning, they looked upon him as the long awaited King-Messiah, and it was not until after his resurrection that they realized his death and resurrection were both part of God's plan.

BUT DIDN'T JESUS TELL THEM HE WOULD
BE CRUCIFIED AND RESURRECTED?

All of this is rather puzzling since we find in the New Testament several passages where Jesus expressly told his disciples he would be lifted up or crucified, and that he would rise on the third day. For example:

"For he taught his disciples, and said unto them, The Son of man is delivered into the hands of men, and they shall kill him; and after that he is killed, he shall rise the third day."[7]

But notice what Mark says immediately after this verse:

---

[5]Doctrine and Covenants 133:66.
[6]John 1:10-11.
[7]Mark 9:31.

"But they understood not that saying, and were afraid to ask him."[8]

We have the same testimony from Luke:

"Then he took unto him the twelve, and said unto them, Behold, we go up to Jerusalem, and all things that are written by the prophets concerning the Son of man shall be accomplished....They shall scourge him, and put him to death: and the third day he shall rise again."[9]

Then Luke confirms what Mark had previously said, namely:

"And they understood none of these things; and this saying was hid from them, neither knew they the things which were spoken."[10]

No wonder Peter and John thought the Savior's body had been stolen rather than resurrected when they went with Mary and found the body gone and the tomb empty. It says they drew this conclusion because:

"As yet they knew not the scripture, that he must rise again from the dead."[11]

BUT IF THE APOSTLES DID NOT COMPREHEND
WHAT JESUS SAID, HOW COULD THEY LATER
QUOTE HIM IN THEIR GOSPELS?

Jesus anticipated this problem and therefore said to his disciples:

"But the Comforter, which is the Holy Ghost, whom the Father will send in my name, he shall teach you all things, and bring all things to your remembrance, whatsoever I have said unto you."[12]

---

[8]Mark 9:32 (emphasis added).
[9]Luke 18:31,33.
[10]Luke 18:34 (emphasis added).
[11]John 20:9.
[12]John 14:26.

This means that a great many verses of the scripture which quote the Savior in the New Testament, are actually revelations to the Gospel writers by the Holy Ghost. No doubt this is why Mark, Luke, and John all try to explain why some of these verses—which clearly describe the crucifixion and the resurrection of the Savior—were totally incomprehensible to the Twelve when they first heard them.

WHY DID THE SAVIOR LEAVE HIS FOLLOWERS IN THE DARK?

We now know that a very delicate set of circumstances had to be put in place or the crucifixion would never have occurred. And we know that unless the crucifixion did occur the main lynch pin of the whole plan of salvation would have been lost. Now that we know that a redemptive sacrifice was absolutely essential for the success of the plan of salvation, we begin to realize why the setup had to be divinely "arranged" so it would take place.

Paul later realized the delicacy of this arrangement because he said that if the Jews had known Jesus was the real Messiah, they never would have crucified him.[13] And, of course, that would have been disastrous.

This, then, gives us a better understanding of the complexity and delicacy of this whole divine scenario.

Because of what eventually happened, we are led to assume that sometime during the pre-existence there might very well have been a conversation between the Father and the Son that went something like this:

The Father: As you know, with each new round of creation, we have to have a redemptive sacrifice. I am grateful that you volunteered to provide the needed sacrifice for this particular round. Now, who would you want to help you go through that ordeal?

The Son: I would like to have some of those who valiantly supported me during the War in Heaven, and who love me. Since I

---

[13]1 Corinthians 2:8.

will be coming into mortality through the loins of David, I would like to have his people bring about the crucifixion.

The Father: But they would never crucify you if they knew who you were. [As Paul said: "Had they known it, they would not have crucified the Lord of Glory."][14]

The Son: Then I must arrange it so they will not realize who I am until after the crucifixion is over.

The Father: Do you have a plan?

The Son: I will have their prophets reveal that the Messiah will be a Jew but that the Jews will slay me. Of course, their leaders will say that they would never kill their Messiah. They will denounce this prophecy and call it a myth. They will also forbid anyone to teach it. Anything in writing will be removed from their scriptures. This will destroy their knowledge concerning my First Coming as a Redeemer-Messiah.

As a result, when I come to the earth the first time, they will expect me to come in power as the King-Messiah to establish my kingdom. When this fails to materialize, they will think I am an imposter and kill me.

The Father: Then what will happen to those who crucified you as an imposter?

The Son: Those who assented to my crucifixion in ignorance will not have committed any culpable offense for which they cannot be forgiven. After my resurrection, I will invite them to repent and be baptized for the remission of their sins. This will include their assenting to my crucifixion. Their offenses can then be blotted out through my redemptive sacrifice which they helped me achieve. If they accept this invitation I can welcome them into my kingdom.

---

[14]1 Corinthians 2:8.

The Father. And what about those who do not accept your invitation or who knew they were slaying an innocent man?

The Son: They will be like anyone else who knowingly sins against the truth. They will have to suffer the consequences.

The Father. I approve of the plan. It is similar to the one we have followed on other worlds.

THIS IS NOT THE FIRST TIME THE FATHER HAS HAD TO "ARRANGE" CERTAIN CIRCUMSTANCES TO ACHIEVE HIS RIGHTEOUS PURPOSES

The management of the Second Estate (or mortal probation of the human family) has involved many critical situations where the Father had to carefully "arrange" the sequence of events so as to achieve his righteous purposes.

One of these extremely difficult scenarios was arranging for the Fall. The Father could have launched Adam and Eve into this mortal testing ground through a simple metamorphosis of their bodies and their environment. However, the Second Estate is a high-risk experience, and the Father did not want his children railing against the gates of heaven and saying, "Father, look what you did to us!"

It was important to have our first parents enter the Second Estate on their own initiative, and have the Fall come about as a result of their voluntarily disobeying a divine commandment. Thus, the trials and tribulations of the Fall would be perceived as a penalty and the stage would be set for repentance and a strong resolve to obey the Father's commandments in the future.

But the Father had to arrange this. The question was, how do you get two of the most obedient children of the Father to voluntarily disobey a commandment? It wasn't easy. But it worked. And how gloriously relieved the mother of men became when she discovered that they had done just what the Father needed to have done.

No doubt Eve had carried the larger burden of guilt after they were driven out of the Garden of Eden, but when it was explained to them what the Father was trying to achieve, she sang out her triumphant song of vindication, and said:

"Were it not for our transgression we never should have had seed, and never should have know good and evil, and the joy of our redemption, and the eternal life which God giveth unto all the obedient."[15]

Then it says, "Adam and Eve blessed the name of God."[16]

THE LESSONS OF SCRIPTURAL HISTORY

Thus we are introduced to the Father's divine policy of arranging things so his righteous purposes are fulfilled.

Another arranged scenario was raising up Enoch to head off Satan's highly successful campaign to take over the entire human family with his wicked practices.[17]

Later on the Lord had to raise up Noah to build the ark and save his family and the more advanced species of animal life so they would not be destroyed in the great flood.[18]

Around 2,000 B.C., the Lord began arranging a sequence of events that established Abraham as the father of the faithful for all time.[19]

Then came the panorama of miracles associated with the raising up of Moses and the liberating of Israel from the cruel bondage of the Pharaohs in Egypt.[20]

Thereafter, in almost every generation, the intervening hand of the Lord could be discerned. He was with Joshua, Samuel, David,

---

[15]Moses 5:11, P. of G. P.
[16]Moses 5:12, P. of G. P.
[17]Moses 6:26-68; 7:1-69, P. of G. P.
[18]Genesis 6:7-22 plus chapter 8 and 9.
[19]Genesis, chapters 12-25.
[20]Exodus, chapters 7 to 12.

Solomon, Elijah, Elisha, Isaiah, Jeremiah, Ezekiel, Daniel, and all the rest.

We mention these events to illustrate the pattern of the Lord in arranging various scenarios or circumstances so that his purposes can be fulfilled without violating the free agency of mankind.

The Father obviously approved of a similar plan to arrange for the crucifixion.

THE SCRIPTURES VERIFY THAT THIS IS
THE PLAN THE SAVIOR FOLLOWED

It is rather amazing how successfully the proposed plan fell into place as history unfolded.

For example, the Jews were outraged when their prophets began to preach that their Messiah would be a Jew but that *he would be killed by his own people.*

No respectable Jew was going to take that. They were persuaded that this story was not scripture at all, but a myth—a fable some enemy of the Jews had concocted. Perhaps the tribe of Joseph did it!

As we shall see in a moment, it soon became an established policy among the Jews to purge their scriptures of all references to the First Coming. And any person caught teaching this proscribed doctrine—that the Messiah would be slain by his own people—was stoned to death.

TWO SETS OF SCRIPTURES

We wouldn't know about this unless there had been two separate sets of scriptures. It so happened that in addition to the purged scripture of the Jews, there was a separate scripture written on brass plates which was maintained from generation to generation by a remnant of the tribe of Joseph.

We now have portions of the writings from the so-called "Brass Plates," which are quoted in the Book of Mormon. It is primarily from this source that we are able to put together the story of how the

Jewish scholars tried to destroy all of the scriptures describing the First Coming.

Here are some of the Old Testament prophets whose writings refer to the First Coming of Christ—and were preserved in the brass plates—even though they were purged from the Jewish scripture.

ESAIAS

One of these prophets was Esaias, not the prophet Isaiah who lived around 700 B.C., but a prophet who lived around 2,000 B.C.

He was ordained to the priesthood "under the hand of God,"[21] which means his mission under the priesthood was to teach the gospel and proclaim the "good tidings" of the coming of the Prince of Peace.[22]

ABRAHAM

We now know that even Abraham testified of the coming of Christ, but his testimony concerning Jesus is not in the Old Testament. But a prophet who had access to the brass plates says:

"Behold, Abraham saw of his coming, and was filled with gladness and did rejoice....There were many before the days of Abraham who were called by the order of God; yea, even after the order of his Son; and...a great many thousand years before his coming, that even redemption should come unto them."[23]

MOSES

The brass plates also contained the testimony of Moses concerning the coming of Christ. One of the ancient prophets referred to the words of Moses, and said:

---

[21]Doctrine and Covenants 84:12.
[22]Isaiah 52:7; Luke 2:18.
[23]Helaman 8:17-18, B. of M.

"Yea, did he [Moses] not bear record that the Son of God should come? And as he lifted up the brazen serpent in the wilderness, even so shall he be lifted up who should come.

"And as many as should look upon that serpent should live, even so as many as should look upon the Son of God with faith, having a contrite spirit, might live, even unto that life which is eternal."[24]

Moses explained that this represented the Savior who would come in due time and that all who looked upon him and accepted him would be saved from their sins.[25]

Moses also knew that as far back as the days of Enoch it was known that Jesus would die on a cross.[26]

ZENOS, ZENOCK AND NEUM

The dates when these three prophets lived are not indicated, but we know they lived sometime before 600 B.C. when the Brass Plates were taken from Jerusalem because they had the prophecies of Zenos, Zenock and Neum in them at that time. These men plainly taught that when Jesus came to live upon the earth he would be turned over to wicked men, and by them he would be:

"...lifted up...and crucified, and...buried in a sepulchre."[27]

The testimony of Zenos and Zenoch cost them their lives. The scripture says that when Zenos began preaching to the Jews about the First Coming of the Savior, he "was slain."[28] As for Zenock, the records says:

"...because the people would not understand his words they stoned him to death."[29]

---

[24]Helaman 8:14-15, B. of M.
[25]Helaman 8:14-15, B. of M.
[26]Moses 7:55, P. of G. P.
[27]1 Nephi 19:10, B. of M.
[28]Helaman 8:19, B. of M.
[29]Alma 33:17, B. of M.

None of the writings or prophecies of Zenos, Zenock or Neum appear in the Jewish Bible, but exist only in quotations from the brass plates that were preserved by the family of Lehi. In the original scripture we are told that not only did these prophets testify of the coming Christ, but "also Isaiah and Jeremiah."[30]

LEHI, A CONTEMPORARY OF JEREMIAH

The Bible indicates that around 600 B.C., there was a host of prophets, contemporary with Jeremiah, who all proclaimed the word of the Lord to the Jews. But their messages were rejected. The Bible says:

"The Lord God of their fathers sent to them by his messengers...because he had compassion on his people...But they mocked the messengers of God, and despised his words, and misused his prophets,until the wrath of the Lord arose against his people."[31]

One of these prophets was named Lehi, and here is what happened to him:

"For he truly testified of their wickedness...and he testified...OF THE COMING OF THE MESSIAH, and also the redemption of the world. And when the Jews heard these things they were angry with him; yea, even as with the prophets of old, whom they had cast out, and stoned, and slain, and they also sought his life."[32]

THE JEWISH CENSORS FAILED TO PURGE ONE CHAPTER THAT TOLD ABOUT THE FIRST COMING

As the Jewish rabbis and scribes carefully went through the Old Testament trying to eliminate any passages which related to the First Coming, they missed one whole chapter in Isaiah. This is chapter 53.

---

[30]Helaman 8:20, B. of M.
[31]Helaman 8:18-20, B. of M.
[32]1 Nephi 1:19-20 (emphasis added), B. of M.

Fortunately, they misinterpreted this chapter. Just prior to this chapter, Isaiah was writing about the glorious Second Coming.[33] Then Isaiah proceeded to say that this glorified being of the Second Coming would be the same Messiah who would come earlier and be rejected because they found "no beauty that we should desire him."[34] Isaiah then commences to describe what the First Coming would be like.

Let us quote three verses from Chapter 53 to demonstrate how amazing it is that the Jewish scholars failed to recognize this scripture as the First Coming. Isaiah said:

"He is despised and rejected of men; a man of sorrows, and acquainted with grief: and we hid as it were our faces from him; he was despised, and we esteemed him not.

"Surely he hath borne our griefs, and carried our sorrows: yet we did esteem him stricken, smitten of God, and afflicted.

"But he was wounded for our transgressions, he was bruised for our iniquities: the chastisement of our peace was upon him; and with his stripes we are healed."[35]

Then Isaiah tells how he will be "cut off out of the land of the living," and his grave will be with the wicked although his tomb will be with the rich.[36]

Isaiah goes on to say that his death will be an "offering for sin," and this "righteous servant shall justify many for he shall bear their iniquities."[37]

It is amazing how the Jewish scholars interpreted this chapter from Isaiah. They completely missed the clear message that Isaiah was writing about the life, death, and resurrection of the Redeemer-

---

[33]Chapter 52.
[34]Isaiah 53:2.
[35]Isaiah 53:3-5.
[36]Isaiah 53:8-9.
[37]Isaiah 53:11.

Messiah. Instead, Professor Gershom Scholem of the Hebrew University says the rabbis thought Isaiah was talking about the decline and fall "of the entire Jewish people" followed by their ultimate rise to glory and power.[38]

And after Isaiah made this prediction around the eighth century, B.C., the nation of Israel did indeed "decline and fall." Consequently, by the time Jesus arrived on the scene the Jews felt their return to "glory and power" was about to occur. In fact, Dr. Scholem says they were expecting the great Messianic era "to break in abruptly [upon them] at any moment."[39]

This leads us to ask: "What were the historical circumstances in the days of Jesus that made the Jews feel that their King-Messiah would break in abruptly, at any moment?"

CHRIST CAME WHEN THE JEWS BELIEVED THE VISION
OF DANIEL WAS ABOUT TO BE FULFILLED

The Jews believed that when their Messiah came he would restore the Davidic kingdom as described by Daniel. Let us consider the prophecy of Daniel in more detail so we can understand why the Jews thought conditions were prophetically ripe to have their Messiah appear at any moment.

It will be recalled that Daniel was shown a vision so he could interpret a dream for King Nebuchadnezzar of Babylon.[40] In this dream Nebuchadnezzar had seen the grotesque image of a man. The head was of gold (which Daniel said represented Babylon). The chest was of silver (which turned out to represent Persia that would conquer Babylon). The belly and thighs were of brass (representing Greece that would conquer Persia), and the hips and legs were of iron (representing Rome that would conquer Greece).

---

[38]Scholem, op. cit., p. 33.
[39]Ibid., pp. 4-5.
[40]Daniel, chapter 2.

At the time of Christ, the first three kingdoms had come and gone and the iron kingdom of Rome ruled the civilized world. Let us repeat once again what Daniel said would happen next:

"And in the days of these kings shall the God of heaven set up a kingdom, which shall *never be destroyed*: and the kingdom shall not be left to other people, but it shall break in pieces and *consume all these kingdoms*, and it shall stand for ever."[41]

As Professor Scholem indicates above, the mind-set of the learned Jewish scholars had been to conclude that after the "iron kingdom" of Rome took over, the people would know that "the end" was near, and the coming of the Messiah was "about to break in abruptly at any moment." They had forgotten all about the ten toes!

Therefore, as of the moment, it fired the soul of every Jew to contemplate the imminent overthrow of Rome and the setting up of a Davidic king to govern the whole earth.

SO HOW DID THE FOLLOWERS OF JESUS PERCEIVE HIM?

Keeping all of this in mind, consider how Jesus was perceived by his apostles and his followers as he commenced his great ministry.

They saw that he had marvelous powers—power to heal hundreds, walk on the sea, and, by some heavenly endowment, power to feed thousands. It was proof enough that they were seeing the first glimpse of the emerging majesty of their long-awaited King-Messiah. It was easy for them to imagine that at any moment he would commence wiping out the Romans and all other opposition with fire and brimstone.

Hadn't Jesus even told the apostles that "I appoint unto you a kingdom...that ye may eat and drink at my table...and sit on thrones judging the twelve tribes of Israel?"

When we think of it, this was exciting!

---

[41]Daniel 2:44 (emphasis added).

The mind-set of the apostles is dramatically demonstrated on one occasion when Jesus began to be persecuted by the Samaritans. We read:

"And when his disciples James and John saw this, they said, Lord, wilt thou that we command fire to come down from heaven, and consume them...?"[42]

What they didn't know was the fact that this Majestic Being standing before them was not yet the King-Messiah. He had not come to destroy anyone with fire from heaven. Jesus was just what John the Baptist had called him: "the Lamb of God." And he was being prepared for the sacrifice.

WHAT THE APOSTLES DID NOT UNDERSTAND DURING THEIR MINISTRY

We get a whole new perspective of the apostles when we realize how much they did NOT understand:

1. They did not understand his role as the Lamb of God who would be sacrificed for the sins of the world. As one of the Savior's followers said on the way to Emmaus:

"We trusted that it had been he who should have redeemed Israel [as the King-Messiah]."[43]

2. They never expected to see him arrested and abused.

3. They never expected to see him crucified.

4. They never thought he would EVER die, since the prophets said his kingdom would last forever.[44]

5. As we shall see in a modern scripture, when the apostles saw the Savior's mental distress and deep depression at the Last Supper,

---

[42]Luke 9:54.
[43]Luke 24:21.
[44]Daniel 2:44.

they began to lose faith in him. On the way to the Garden of Gethsemane, the scripture says: "The disciples began to be sore amazed, and to be very heavy and to complain in their hearts *wondering if this be the Messiah.*"[45] He was definitely not behaving like the King-Messiah!

So the plan of the Father and the Son had worked. When Jesus came among the Jews, not even his own apostles really knew who he was. Nor did they understand the terrifying dimension of the mission he was foreordained to fulfill during this "First Coming."

That understanding would have to wait until after the resurrection.

*   *   *   *

TOPICS FOR REFLECTION AND DISCUSSION

1. Were you surprised to learn that Jesus said "NO MAN" knew his true mission and identity when he was born among the Jews? Whom did the apostles think Jesus was? Whom did the rulers of the Jews think he was?

2. What did the rabbinical scholars say would be "proof" of the Messiah's true identity? Did they say this would include miracles and manifestations of the power of God?

3. How did the Jews lose nearly all their scriptures describing the First Coming of Christ? Who were some of the prophets who had told about the First Coming? Where could their writings be found even though they had been stripped from the Jewish Old Testament?

4. What was the one chapter in the Old Testament that discussed the First Coming in considerable detail but was missed by the rabbinical censors? What does Professor Scholem of the Hebrew University say the censors thought it meant? What is there in the three verses we quoted from this chapter of Isaiah which makes their distorted interpretation rather amazing?

---

[45]JST Mark 14:36 (emphasis added).

5. Why did the Jews think the prophecy of Daniel was about to be fulfilled in their day? What three kingdoms had already come and gone? Which kingdom was then in power? What did Daniel say God would set up to destroy all other kingdoms and last forever?

6. What happened during and after the Last Supper that shook the faith of the apostles? Did they ever discuss the possibility that he might not be the King-Messiah after all?

7. Since Jesus had told the apostles several times that he would be crucified and then rise the third day, how do you account for the fact that none of them comprehended what he had said? How were they able to recall these statements later on, and include them in the four Gospels?

8. What was the most difficult task confronting the Father and the Son as they set about to arrange for the crucifixion of Jesus Christ?

9. Why do you think Jesus chose the Jews to help him get through the ordeal of the crucifixion? On what basis could the Jews be forgiven for "consenting" to his death? But what did they have to do to be forgiven? What would happen to those who refused to do it?

10. List four things the early apostles never expected to see in connection with the life of the Savior.

*   *   *   *

CHAPTER 6

FORTY DAYS WITH HEAVENLY BEINGS

And a Rendezvous With Satan

At the close of the fourth chapter, we reviewed the inspiring experience of John the Baptist as he immersed the Savior in the River Jordan and then saw the Holy Ghost descending upon him "like a dove." John then heard the voice of the Father say:

"This is my Beloved Son, in whom I am well pleased. HEAR YE HIM."[1]

We sometimes think that Jesus began selecting his disciples immediately after his baptism, but, as we shall see in a moment, most authorities believe this did not take place until later. The Savior's immediate task was to receive extensive instruction from his Father concerning his ministry which would commence in a few months. So the scripture says:

"And immediately the Spirit took him into the wilderness. And he was there in the wilderness forty days."[2]

Except for the final week of his earthly existence, these forty days were probably the most sacred and important sequence of events in the Savior's life. Several miraculous things happened to Jesus during this period of time.

---

[1]JST Matthew 3:46, compare KJT, Matthew 3:27.
[2]JST Mark 1:12-13, compare KJT.

FORTY DAYS WITHOUT FOOD OR WATER

First of all, he was able to exist without food or water for nearly six weeks. Under ordinary circumstances this is physically impossible. The absence of water alone will generally destroy human life in ten days.

A friend of this author, John Noble, spent over nine years in a Soviet slave labor camp, and on one occasion his guards tried to starve him to death. In his well-known book, *I Found God in Soviet Russia,* John Noble describes the rapid deterioration of his brain and body as he was forced to go without food for twelve days:

"Each day my strength diminished. After an entire week without a morsel of food to eat, I found myself too weak to walk....By this time my weakness was so great that I could no longer sleep at night. I did not feel any pain, but felt dizzy and giddy, as if I were intoxicated. It was difficult to keep my thoughts collected. At times I became delirious....

"On the ninth day of the fast, both my bodily strength and my mental processes had sunk to such a level that, in one of the few lucid moments I had in my delirium, I realized death could not be far away....

"The period of systematic starvation did finally come to an end after twelve hideous days. On Tuesday morning, August 14, without explanation, the 'liquid diet' order (consisting of a daily cup of warm water which the guards called 'coffee') was suddenly lifted and we received bread with our 'coffee.'

RAPTUROUS GRATITUDE FOR A FEW CRUMBS OF BREAD

"It was not a full slice, but some stale crumbs on a piece of paper, amounting in all to perhaps two ounces. However, it was our first nourishment of any kind and when I received these crumbs in my hand, I must have sat transfixed for at least a quarter of an hour, trying to comprehend that it was real and that the Lord had seen fit to save my life.

"Tears ran down my eyes and I offered a prayer of gratitude to God. Then I ate each crumb slowly, as though I were partaking of the communion wafer."[3]

But at least John Noble had a cup of water each day. The Savior did not even have that. We learn from the scripture that the Savior's type of "fasting" was done under circumstances similar to that of Moses who did not "eat bread nor drink water" during the entire period of forty days.[4]

To survive under these circumstances would require a miraculous endowment of power so that the physical body could remain in a state of "suspended animation" without the debilitating effects which would otherwise occur. We think of this as some kind of divine "quickening."

A MIRACLE THAT HAS OCCURRED
ONLY FOUR TIMES IN HISTORY

There have been only four known occasions when human beings have lived for forty days and nights without food or water.

The first time was when Moses went up to the top of Mount Sinai to get the pattern for the Tabernacle and receive the stone tablets "written by the finger of God." He was forty days and nights without food or water.[5] However, when he came down from the mount and found the people worshipping the golden calf, he smashed the tablets in anger because he felt the Israelites were entirely unworthy of this divine law.[6]

The second time this miracle occurred was two or three days later when Moses was told to return to the top of the mountain, and this time bring his *own* set of tablets![7]

---

[3]John Noble, *I Found God in Soviet Russia*, New York: St. Martins Publishers, 1969, pp. 41-47.
[4]Deuteronomy 9:9.
[5]Ibid.
[6]Exodus 32:19.
[7]Exodus 34:1-2.

Once again Moses was with the Lord for forty days and nights "and did neither eat bread nor drink water."[8]

This means that except for the nourishment Moses received during the interval of two or three days in the camp, he went without bread or water for a total of 80 days.

The third time a prophet went forty days and nights without food or water was when Elijah fled from the murderous Queen Jezebel and came to the summit of Mount Sinai (sometimes called Mount Horeb). This is the identical mountain where Moses had fasted and communed with the Lord. Now Elijah did the same thing and in the same place. After the Lord told Elijah how to proceed with his ministry, the aged prophet departed.[9]

The fourth time this miracle occurred was when Jesus went up from Jordan and was taken by the Spirit into the wilderness where there were "wild beasts," indicating that it was totally uninhabited by humans.[10]

Luke says, "And in those days, he did eat nothing."[11]

THE SAVIOR'S FORTY DAYS WITH HIS FATHER AND A NUMBER OF MINISTERING ANGELS

As far as we can tell, there were only about three more months before the Feast of the Passover in April when Jesus would be thirty years old. That is when he would go to Jerusalem, boldly cleanse the temple, and launch into his official ministry with a display of miraculous power that would shock the nation. The Inspired Version says that during these forty days he "communed with God," which would be the Father, himself.[12] It also says, "angels ministered unto him."[13]

---

[8]Exodus 34:28.
[9]1 Kings 19:8.
[10]Mark 1:13.
[11]Luke 4:2.
[12]JST Matthew 4:2, compare KJT.
[13]Mark 1:13.

No doubt these ministering angels included a number of the great prophets of the Old Testament who had predicted the Savior's coming. Some of them, like Zenos and Zenock, had been slain for testifying of him.[14] In fact, the scripture says, "Many have testified of these things at the coming of Christ, and were slain because they testified."[15].

What a thrilling experience it must have been for these choice martyrs of past centuries who may have been allowed to visit Jesus in the wilderness, and minister to him.

THE ATONING SACRIFICE

Probably the most important single subject to be discussed with the Savior during these forty days would be the great atoning sacrifice which would come at the end of his ministry.

Because Jesus was the very Son of God, there is a tendency to assume that this was just part of his mission and it automatically followed that he would perform it. But there was nothing automatic about it. It was horrible. It involved the most excruciating suffering. Furthermore, Jesus did not have to do it. He had his free agency. He could have elected at the last moment to turn back and reject this assignment.

And he almost did.

Who would have suspected that this courageous Crown Prince of heaven, this glorified, all-powerful First Counsellor to the Father, would falter as he finally faced the agonizing prospect of the crucifixion?[16]

Later, we will read the Savior's description of the terror and the torturous mental anguish which completely encompassed him as he

---

[14]Helaman 8:19; Alma 33:15-17, B. of M.
[15]3 Nephi 10:15, B. of M.
[16]Mark 14:36.

knelt beneath the olive trees and asked the Father to find some other way.[17]

But in the wilderness, the Father and ministering angels no doubt filled the Savior with the firm resolution to perform his great mission and endure its suffering right through to the bitter end. As we proceed with our study, we will find that Jesus attempted to share this information with his disciples on several occasions, but not one of them believed it nor understood what he was talking about.[18] For at least three years, Jesus carried in his heart the agonizing burden of this great secret alone.

THE COMING FLOOD OF MIRACLES

Another important topic which was undoubtedly discussed during the forty days in the wilderness would be the miraculous powers which Jesus would exercise over the elements during his ministry. So far as the record shows, he had never performed a miracle up to this time.

Soon the Savior's visible power to control the elements would be the most sensational news in the land. Everywhere the word would go forth, "He can heal!"

Not since the days of Moses would there be such an avalanche of miracles among the Jewish people as those which would begin to occur when Jesus launched his ministry on his thirtieth birthday.

The fact that the Savior's control over the elements was a major topic of discussion during the forty days in the wilderness is suggested by the fact that the very *first* thing Satan tried to tempt Jesus to do, was to show that he had power over the elements, and could change stones into bread.

This brings us to the role of Satan during those forty sacred days in the wilderness.

---

[17]Ibid.
[18]Luke 18:31-34.

THE SAVIOR'S RENDEZVOUS WITH SATAN

Now that we have Joseph Smith's Inspired Version of the Bible, we are better informed concerning the events which occurred while Jesus was in the wilderness.

The first thing we learn is that during all those forty days when Jesus was conferring with the Father and enjoying the ministering of angels, Satan was anxiously waiting for his chance to tempt Jesus. The scripture says:

"And he was there in the wilderness forty days, Satan seeking to tempt him."[19]

But the fallen prince of darkness was not allowed to invade these sacred precincts in the wilderness during the forty days of divine instruction. The scripture says it was not until "*after*" the forty days that "the devil came unto him."[20]

Satan apparently thought he could tempt the Savior in three different ways. His intention was to test Jesus in the areas of human weakness where all mankind seem to be the most vulnerable. The first area would be the craving of the physical appetites when the body is famishing for food. The second area would be the instinctive passion of human beings for the acquisition of wealth and power. The third area would be the human instinct to gamble and "take a chance" just to prove a point.

However, before we go into the details of Satan's effort to tempt Jesus, there is one aspect of this encounter that might be overlooked. This is the fact that the "free agency" factor in the Second Estate, gave Satan the *right* to tempt Jesus, just as he has a right to tempt all the rest of the Father's children.

---

[19]JST Mark 1:11, compare KJT Mark 1:13.
[20]JST Luke 4:2.

The divine plan of eternal progression requires that mankind be tested during the Second Estate to demonstrate whether they will exercise their free agency to choose good rather than evil.[21]

In this process, Satan has a part. As the scripture says:

"And it must needs be that the devil should tempt the children of men, or they could not be agents unto themselves."[22]

This is why Satan is able to continually demand equal time to test the Father's children. We might even go further and say that under the principles of eternal law, Satan has a legal *right* to "prove" how each of us will use our free agency in this Second Estate.

From this it is easy to appreciate that whenever the heavens have been opened and marvelous revelations have been bestowed upon an individual, the devil has had a right to demand an equal opportunity to display his own powers.

Brigham Young explained the "equal time" doctrine as follows:

"When individuals are blessed with visions, revelations, and great manifestations, look out, then the devil is nigh you, and you will be tempted IN PROPORTION to the vision, revelation, or manifestation you have received."[23]

In the scriptures there are a number of examples of Satan exercising his right to "equal time."

He did this to Moses.[24] He did it to Joseph Smith.[25] And we shall soon see that he did it to the Savior.

In fact, as we have indicated above, all the time Jesus was being tutored by his Father and receiving the comfort of ministering angels,

---

[21]Abraham 3:25, P. of G. P.; 2 Nephi 2:27-29, B. of M.

[22]Doctrine and Covenants 29:39.

[23]*Journal of Discourses*, vol. 3, p. 206.

[24]Moses 1:12-22, P. of G. P.

[25]Doctrine and Covenants 128:20.

the scripture says Satan was there "seeking to tempt him."[26] This would indicate the devil could hardly wait to test the Savior's mettle.

And another interesting element to be considered in a moment is the fact that since Satan was entitled to equal time, the *Holy Ghost* seems to have helped set up the staging for each of the temptations so Jesus could get it over with as quickly as possible.

THE FIRST TEMPTATION

We should mention that Matthew gives the temptations in a different order than Luke, but Luke seems to follow the more logical sequence, and that is the order we will follow here.

The first temptation was Satan's effort to take advantage of the Savior's hunger. Jesus had been without food or drink for forty days, so the moment the "quickening" power of God was removed from Jesus, his normal appetites returned, and it says:

"In those days, he did eat nothing; and when they were ended, he afterwards hungered."[27]

These were ideal circumstances for Satan's first opportunity to ensnare the Savior. Notice how Satan challenged Jesus as he said:

"*IF* thou be the Son of God, command this stone that it be made bread."[28]

Notice that Satan's first temptation was not merely to satisfy the Savior's hunger, but to *prove* he was indeed the Son of God, with power over the elements.

Satan was also tempting Jesus to display his power before he was scheduled to start performing miracles. If Jesus had responded, the devil would have had the additional satisfaction of seeing his will dominating that of the Savior.

---

[26]JST Mark 1:11, compare KJT Mark 1:13.
[27]Luke 4:2 (emphasis added).
[28]Luke 4:3.

Jesus replied: "It is written, That man shall not live by bread alone, but by every word of God."[29]

THE SECOND TEMPTATION

Jesus was then confronted by his second temptation. Notice, however, that the King James Version of the New Testament states that it was the *devil* who took Jesus up to the high mountain for his second test.[30]   The Inspired Version corrects this error. It was the Holy Ghost who carried him up into the high mountain, and showed him the kingdoms of the world.

The Inspired Version says:

"The *SPIRIT* taketh him up into a high mountain, and he beheld all the kingdoms of the world, in a moment of time."[31]

It seems truly remarkable that the Holy Ghost would participate in setting up the Savior's temptations. As we indicated earlier, it was no doubt to expedite this necessary but irksome procedure so as to get Satan's "equal opportunity" over with as soon as possible.

The Inspired Version continues:

"And the devil came unto him, and said unto him, All this power will I give unto thee, and the glory of them; for they are delivered unto me, and to whomsoever I will, I give them.

"If thou therefore wilt worship me, all shall be thine.

"And Jesus answered and said unto him, Get thee behind me, Satan: for it is written, Thou shalt worship the Lord thy God, and him only shalt thou serve."[32]

It is interesting that Satan claimed that all of the kingdoms which Jesus was shown were under the devil's control. Unfortunately, this

---

[29]Luke 4:4.
[30]Luke 4:5.
[31]JST Luke 4:5, compare KJT.
[32]JST Luke 4:6-8, compare KJT.

was probably true. As far as is known, there was not a single nation on the face of the earth in those days that was righteous.

Even in America, the Nephites had just murdered their chief judge and there had been a complete breakdown of orderly government among the Nephites.[33]

Notice also that Satan not only boasted that all of these nations were under his dominion, but he declared that their wicked rulers were those to whom *HE* had given these kingdoms.

In our own day we see dictators and ruthless demagogues seizing power over various nations and we wonder where they came from. In this scripture we see a strong indication that among all the wicked nations that have rejected the Lord, Satan glories in elevating to power those who are the devil's most depraved and loyal followers.

THE THIRD TEMPTATION

Satan had now used up two-thirds of his equal time or equal opportunity to tempt Jesus. The Holy Ghost therefore prepared to give him his last chance. The scripture says:

"And the *SPIRIT* brought him to Jerusalem, and set him on a pinnacle of the temple, and the devil came unto him and said unto him, *If* thou be the Son of God, cast thyself down from hence:

"For it is written, He shall give his angels charge over thee, to keep thee: And in their hands they shall bear thee up, lest at any time thou dash thy foot against a stone."[34]

In this taunting temptation, Lucifer was asking Jesus to gamble his life just to prove a point. Jesus knew exactly what Satan was trying to do, and so he said, "Thou shalt not tempt the Lord thy God."[35]

---

[33]3 Nephi, chapter 7, B. of M.
[34]JST Luke 4:9-10 (emphasis added). Compare KJT Luke 4:9-11; Psalms 91:11-12.
[35]Luke 4:12.

At this juncture, Lucifer's time was up. The devil had been given three opportunities to tempt Jesus and had failed. In the dark regions of hell, there must have arisen a great lamentation of "weeping and wailing and gnashing of teeth."[36]

Luke concludes this dramatic encounter between Jesus and Satan by saying:

"And when the devil had ended all the temptation, he departed from him for a season."[37]

THE REAL TEMPTATIONS OF JESUS CAME FROM WITHIN HIMSELF

It would seem that for all practical purposes, the three temptations concocted by Satan were not temptations in the real sense of the word. Jesus dispatched each of them almost casually and indifferently.

Nevertheless, Jesus did have the normal roster of genuine temptations as he went through life. These were the same temptations that confront all human beings. As we shall see in a moment, they came primarily from within himself.

The physical body has certain built-in proclivities that are necessary for survival. We call them instincts. However, these instincts are so powerful that a person can be virtually mesmerized into being obnoxiously selfish, vindictive, vengeful, greedy, covetous, avaricious, lustful, hateful, venal, sadistic, mercenary, gluttonous, drunken, a robber, a vandal, a thief, or even a murderer.

Every normal human being struggles throughout his or her life trying to keep these appetites of the flesh under control. Our God-given instincts are necessary for survival, but they are "an enemy to God" if they go beyond the parameters clearly defined by God's law. As one prophet wrote:

---

[36]Moses 1:22, P. of G. P.
[37]JST Luke 4:13.

"For the natural man is an enemy to God, and has been from the fall of Adam, and will be, forever and ever, unless he yields to the enticing of the Holy Spirit, and putteth off the natural man and becometh a saint through the atonement of Christ the Lord, and becometh as a child, submissive, meek, humble, patient, full of love, willing to submit to all things which the Lord seeth fit to inflict upon him, even as a child doth submit to his father."[38]

These instinctive forces, by their very nature, provide the major temptations in life. We know this is painfully true for ourselves, and the scripture says it was equally true for the Savior.

The prophet Alma wanted his people to know that even though the Savior was the Son of God, he would be required to endure all of the normal frailties of the flesh. He said:

"And he shall go forth, suffering pains and afflictions and temptations of every kind; and this that the word might be fulfilled which saith he will take upon him the pains and the sicknesses of his people."[39]

The apostle Paul verified that in order for Jesus to pass through mortal life "without sin," he had to demonstrate that he could do it in spite of all the worst temptations that confront ordinary human beings. He said:

"Jesus the Son of God....was IN ALL POINTS tempted like as we are, yet without sin."[40]

THE APOSTLES WERE CHRIST'S WITNESSES THAT HE RESISTED ALL EVIL

Toward the end of his ministry, Jesus sat with his disciples at the Last Supper, contemplating the blessing of having friends like the faithful eleven who sat at the table with him. He knew they had been

---

[38]Mosiah 3:19, B. of M.
[39]Alma 7:11, B. of M.
[40]Hebrews 4:14-15 (emphasis added).

ordained to be apostles before they were born.[41] They had been diligent, long suffering, and loyal. What was equally important, they had watched him struggle against hunger, thirst, heat, cold, blisters, and fatigue. They had seen him grit his teeth, so to speak, and fight back the surge of a righteous anger when he felt like screaming at the wretched wickedness of the scribes, Pharisees and Sadducees who preyed upon the righteous.

Throughout his ministry, these faithful eleven apostles had watched him overcome the many temptations which had crossed his path, and had observed his struggle with the temptations of the flesh which were all terribly real. Being the Son of God did not alter the fact that his body was "of the earth, earthy." Jesus appreciated their bearing with him through all of his struggles and said:

"Ye are they which have continued with me IN MY TEMPTATIONS."[42]

JESUS DRAWS OUT THREE OF HIS FUTURE APOSTLES

But now we must go back to the time when Jesus came out of the wilderness. His immediate task was to find these eleven men who would become his closest friends, and eventually be ordained apostles. He even had to search out Judas Iscariot, who, like Cain, was foreknown to harbor a nest of serpents in his breast and would sell his soul to perdition for thirty pieces of silver.[43]

John's Gospel tells about the Savior selecting several of his prospective apostles, but the time when this took place is not entirely clear. Most authorities agree that the selection of the apostles did not occur until after the forty days in the wilderness.[44]

Assuming the latter to be the case, here is probably what happened. Jesus came out of the wilderness and immediately

---

[41]Romans 8:29; Alma 13:3, B. of M.
[42]Luke 22:28.
[43]John 17:12.
[44]See Talmage, *Jesus the Christ*, pp. 127-128.

returned to the place where John was preaching and baptizing. The scripture says:

"Again the next day after, John stood, and two of his disciples;

"And looking upon Jesus as he walked, he saith, Behold the Lamb of God!

"And the two disciples heard him speak, and they followed Jesus.

"Then Jesus turned, and saw them following, and saith unto them, What seek ye? They said unto him, Rabbi, (which is to say, being interpreted, Master,) where dwellest thou?

"He saith unto them, Come and see. They came and saw where he dwelt, and abode with him that day: for it was about the tenth hour [around 4 p.m.].

"One of the two which heard John speak, and followed him, was Andrew, Simon Peter's brother."[45]

Notice that John, the Gospel writer, never identifies the second disciple because, out of modesty, he was referring to himself. Throughout his writings, the apostle John always tried to avoid any direct reference to his own person. He would usually say "the one Jesus loved," or, as in this instance, the "other disciple." The scripture continues:

"The first [Andrew] findeth his own brother Simon [Peter], and saith unto him, We have found the Messias, which is, being interpreted, the Christ.

"And he brought him to Jesus. And when Jesus beheld him, he said, Thou art Simon the son of Jona: thou shalt be called Cephas, which is by interpretation, A stone."[46]

---

[45]John 1:35-40.
[46]John 1:41-42.

So Jesus had now sorted out from among John's disciples three of his own future apostles—John, Andrew and (Simon) Peter. Now we are introduced to another future apostle.

THE CALLING OF PHILIP

"The day following Jesus would go forth into Galilee."[47]

Toward the close of the day as Jesus and his tiny band of followers moved up into the region of Galilee, the scripture states:

"Jesus...findeth Philip, and saith unto him, Follow me.

"Now Philip was of Bethsaida, the city of Andrew and Peter."[48]

THE CALLING OF NATHANAEL

It is interesting how the calling of one disciple would set up a chain reaction that always seemed to lead Jesus to another choice disciple. So as soon as Jesus chose Philip, the scripture says:

"Philip findeth Nathanael, and saith unto him, We have found him, of whom Moses in the law, and the prophets, did write, Jesus of Nazareth, the son of Joseph.

"And Nathanael said unto him, Can there any good thing come out of Nazareth?"[49]

Nothing could have expressed more vividly the general contempt of the Galileans for the humble village of Nazareth than this statement by Nathanael. How appropriate that the Son of God who was born in a stable, should be raised in an obscure village with neither distinction nor esteem. But Philip did not argue with Nathanael. He simply said:

"Come and see."[50]

---

[47]John 1:43.
[48]John 1:43-44.
[49]John 1:45-46.
[50]John 1:46.

A few moments later, Nathanael was surprised when he and Philip approached the Savior. The scripture says:

"Jesus saw Nathanael coming to him, and saith of him, Behold an Israelite indeed, in whom is no guile!

"Nathanael saith unto him, Whence knowest thou me? Jesus answered and said unto him, Before that Philip called thee, when thou wast under the fig tree, I saw thee.

"Nathanael answered and saith unto him, Rabbi, thou art the Son of God; thou art the King of Israel.

"Jesus answered and said unto him, Because I said unto thee, I saw thee under the fig tree, believest thou? thou shalt see greater things than these.

"And he saith unto him, Verily, verily, I say unto you, Hereafter ye shall see heaven open, and the angels of God ascending and descending upon the Son of man."[51]

Authorities tend to believe that in the later lists of the Twelve, Nathanael is identical with the Bartholomew who is mentioned several times.[52] Assuming this to be the case, Jesus now had with him five of the foreordained men who would soon become his apostles.

* * * *

TOPICS FOR REFLECTION AND DISCUSSION

1. What are the four occasions when servants of God have gone without food or water for forty days? When John Noble was given no food for a week, what was his condition?

---

[51]John 1:47-51.
[52]Peloubet's *Bible Dictionary*, under "Nathanael."

2. What are we led to assume concerning the physical status of the bodies of the Savior and the prophets who fasted forty days and nights?

3. What leads us to assume that Jesus probably did not fully realize the horrors of the crucifixion until he had reached maturity? Do you think this new understanding was a relief or a terrible burden?

4. Did Jesus have the free agency to turn back from his mission as the appointed Redeemer of the world? Did this possibility become one of his most severe temptations?

5. Why do you think it would be important to discuss with Jesus the power to perform miracles prior to the commencement of his ministry? As far as we know, had Jesus performed any miracles up to this time?

6. Explain why it is necessary for Satan to have "equal time" in tempting mankind. What does it accomplish?

7. Who helped to set the stage for the temptations of Jesus? Was he trying to help Jesus or Satan? In what way?

8. What is the principal source for the greatest temptations of all mankind? At what point do the survival instincts in the flesh become "the enemy of God?"

9. According to the scriptures, how real were the temptations of Jesus? Did he occasionally succumb and commit sin?

10. Who were the first three disciples selected by Jesus who would later become apostles? Who were the next two? In the various lists of the Twelve, which apostle appears to be identical with Nathanael?

*   *   *   *

CHAPTER 7

HOW JESUS CELEBRATED HIS THIRTIETH BIRTHDAY

It appears that after Jesus had selected several new disciples from among the followers of John the Baptist, these new friends and future apostles followed Jesus to his home in Nazareth. The disciples then became the guests of Mary and her family. So far as we can tell, these would be the five we have already met—John, Andrew, Peter, Philip, and Nathanael or Bartholomew.

Now the time for the Feast of the Passover was drawing near. It will be recalled that the birth date of Jesus has been fixed by revelation as the sixth day of April,[1] and we have seen that this coincided with the week of the Passover.

To the Lord, the date of April 6 seems highly significant. We know it was the date of his birth, and we cannot help wondering if it might also have been the date for either his crucifixion or his resurrection. In any event, we know from the scriptures that all three of these events occurred during the same week on the Jewish calendar.

We have reason to believe that Jesus was anxiously looking forward to his upcoming journey to Jerusalem—not only for the sake of the Feast of the Passover, but more especially because he would be thirty years of age and officially entitled to commence his ministry.

THE WEDDING FEAST IN CANA

However, there was an important social event which was scheduled to take place before they left for Jerusalem. It was a wedding feast at Cana, where Mary seems to have been assigned to

---

attend as one of the hostesses. The scriptures indicate that the wedding took place on Tuesday, the third day of the week.[2]

Jesus, of course, was invited to attend, and the disciples of Jesus were invited as well.[3] However, we notice that Joseph, Mary's husband, is not mentioned at this time. From this point on, Joseph is always missing from any reference to Mary and her family. As we have pointed out earlier, this leads us to believe that Joseph had passed away some time earlier.

By this time Mary would be well aware that her son was nearing the moment when it would be legal for him to come out in the open and begin his great mission. But this was not all. The scripture says that all these years she had been hiding in her heart many of the wonderful things she knew about her son.[4]

Mary may have already known that Jesus had some remarkable powers over the elements, and on this special occasion, she may have tantalized her imagination with the thought that if Jesus would just demonstrate some of his remarkable powers for the wedding guests, it would be most gratifying to his mother.

Mothers are like that sometimes.

A STRANGE CONVERSATION BETWEEN MARY AND JESUS

Keeping all of these possibilities in mind, we may discover the explanation for some of the strange circumstances that led up to the performance of the Savior's first miracle. In the Inspired Version we read:

"And when they wanted wine, his mother said unto him, They have no wine.

---

[2]John 2:1.
[3]John 2:2.
[4]For example, Luke 2:51.

"Jesus saith unto her, Woman, what wilt thou have me do for thee? *that will I do*; for mine hour is not yet come."[5]

Notice what a completely different interpretation we derive from the Inspired Version compared to the traditional story based on the King James translation.

In the first place, we see that Mary somehow felt responsible for the lack of wine at the closing hours of the feast. And when she shared her concern with Jesus, he asked her how he could help her. In fact, he said he would do whatever SHE asked him to do.

There is an implication here that he does not want to do anything publicly—in front of all the people—because his "hour had not yet come." His hour would be when he reached thirty years of age, then he could come out before the people in his true role. Meanwhile, he wanted to make his mother happy, but in a private way. Therefore he asks what SHE would like him to do.

Then the scripture says:

"His mother saith unto the servants, Whatsoever he saith unto you, do it."[6]

This sounds as though Mary expected Jesus to do something special to solve her dilemma. And having disclosed her anxiety to Jesus, she left it up to him.

John continues:

"And there were set there six waterpots of stone, after the manner of the purifying of the Jews, containing two or three firkins apiece."[7]

---

[5]JST John 2:3-4, compare KJT John 2:3-4.
[6]JST John 2:5.
[7]John 2:6.

Authorities tell us a "firkin" was approximately nine gallons, therefore, based on "two or three firkins apiece," these water jarsheld from 18 to 27 gallons each.[8] This would mean that the servants filled the six water jars with an excess of more than 100 gallons of fluid. This certainly suggests that the wedding feast was no small affair.

Jesus then undertook to respond to his mother's need. It says:

"Jesus saith unto them, Fill the waterpots with water. And they filled them up to the brim.

"And he saith unto them, Draw out now, and bear unto the governor of the feast. And they bare unto him."[9]

Notice that the servants had barely finished pouring the water into the six jars before Jesus told them to begin drawing the liquid out again. As the servants did so they were no doubt amazed to discover that they were ladling out either purple or white wine.

It was customary in those days to have the master of ceremonies or "ruler of the feast" sample any new batch of wine. In this instance, the ruler of the feast was astonished to discover that this latest beverage was not the customary watered down wine which was usually served at the end of a feast. It was even better than the wine that was served at the beginning.

He therefore called the bridegroom and exclaimed:

"Every man at the beginning doth set forth good wine; and when men have well drunk, then that which is worse: but thou hast kept the good wine until now."[10]

John was probably present with the other four disciples when this amazing episode took place. He closes the incident with this brief comment:

---

[8]Peloubet's *Bible Dictionary*, under "Weights and Measures."
[9]John 2:7-8.
[10]John 2:10.

"This beginning of miracles did Jesus in Cana of Galilee, and manifested forth his glory; and his disciples believed on him."[11]

It is interesting that John would say, "his disciples believed on him." Of course, these humble men had already heard the powerful testimony of their original master, John the Baptist. He had said that Jesus was the Lamb of God, and they had accepted it. Nevertheless, to be present when Jesus changed ordinary drinking water into delicious wine, was certainly something to elevate their testimonies. Surely, this *had* to be power direct from heaven, so now John could say, in a very special way, they "believed on him."

THE SCIENCE OF MIRACLES

How did he do it? The way Jesus changed the water into wine was actually quite simple.

Every molecule of water in those jars comprised a miniature universe consisting of numerous intelligences combined with tiny bits of matter. As a modern prophet said:

"There is an eternity of matter, and it is all acted upon and filled with a portion of divinity....Matter is capacitated to receive intelligence."[12]

These tiny, finite particles of primal matter are united with individual intelligences, and they have been organized into everything we see about us. The Father and the Son can communicate with these intelligences and structure them into whatever kingdoms, orders, or patterns they desire.[13]

In this manner, our Heavenly Father and his Son have organized the entire universe. We read:

"There is not a particle of element which is not filled with life [or intelligence]....It is in the rock, the sand, the dust, in water, air, the

---

[11]John 2:11, compare JST John 2:11.
[12]Brigham Young, *Journal of Discourses*, Liverpool, England: F. D. and S. W. Richards, 1860, 7:2.
[13]Doctrine and Covenants 88:37-38.

gases, and, in short, in every description and organization of matter, whether it be solid, liquid, or gaseous, particle operating with particle."[14]

Then Abraham tells us how he saw the intelligences organized with these particles of element or matter before the world was. The Lord said to Abraham:

"I rule in the heavens above, and in the earth beneath, in all wisdom and prudence, over all the intelligences thine eyes have seen....I came down in the beginning in the midst of all the intelligences.

"Now the Lord had shown unto me, Abraham, the intelligences that were organized before the world was."[15]

WHEN GOD SPEAKS, THESE INTELLIGENCES OBEY

These intelligences love the Father and the Son. They honor them, and therefore they obey them. The scriptures tell us that the Father and the Son govern them by simply speaking to them. When the intelligences obey, the matter which is attached to them automatically follows. They are merely responding to the voice of their Creators or Master Organizers. This is why we read in the scriptures:

"For behold, the dust of the earth moveth hither and thither...at the *COMMAND* of our great and everlasting God.

"Yea, behold at his *VOICE* do the hills and the mountains tremble and quake.

"And by the power of his *VOICE* they are broken up, and become smooth, yea, even like unto a valley.

"Yea, by the power of his *VOICE* do the foundations rock, even to the very center.

---

[14]Brigham Young, *Journal of Discourses*, vol. 3:277.
[15]Abraham 3:21-22, P. of G.P.

"Yea and if he *SAY* unto the earth—Move—it is moved.

"Yea, if he *SAY* unto the earth—Thou shalt go back, that it lengthen out the day for many hours—it is done.

"And thus, *ACCORDING TO HIS WORD* the earth goeth back, and it appeareth unto man that the sun standeth still; yea, and behold, this is so; for surely it is the earth that moveth and not the sun.

"And behold, also, if he *SAY* unto the waters of the great deep—Be thou dried up—it is done.

"Behold, if he *SAY* unto this mountain—Be thou raised up, and come over and fall upon that city, that it be buried up behold it is done."[16]

NO WONDER THE DISCIPLES BELIEVED

We have already seen that Christ's little band of disciples had been amazed when they saw the Savior turn six huge jars of water into wine. Just a few days after this they would be far more amazed when they accompanied Jesus up to the temple and saw him talking to millions upon millions of these tiny intelligences. Suddenly, at his command, the blind would see, the deaf would hear, crippled arms and legs would straighten, and deformed bodies would stand erect.

Just as the prophet explained it in the above scripture, when the Master speaks, the intelligences obey. This is the secret to miracles.

A VISIT TO CAPERNAUM, THEN ON TO JERUSALEM

The scripture says that after the wedding feast at Cana:

"He went down to Capernaum, he, and his mother, and his brethren, and his disciples: and they continued there NOT many days."[17]

---

[16]Helaman 12:8-17 (emphasis added), B. of M.
[17]John 2:12 (emphasis added).

We think there may have been a special reason for this brief stop at Capernaum. When feast days drew near, it was customary for large companies to travel together as thousands of faithful Jews converged on Jerusalem. Mary and Jesus may have gone to Capernaum to join with relatives and friends to make the trek southward.

It is estimated that when the Feast of the Passover occurred, the population of Jerusalem increased to well over a million people.[18]

And the increase was not only in terms of people.

A Roman study revealed that 256,500 lambs were butchered and eaten at one of these feasts.[19] These lambs had to be at least eight days old, but not more than a year.[20] Since the lambing season had just occurred, this meant that a great many ewes would have undoubtedly accompanied their lambs. All of these vast flocks of sheep and lambs would have to be herded in from their early spring pastures and locked up in improvised corrals near the outskirts of the city. Only after the lambs were inspected and approved could they be offered for sale at the courtyard of the temple.[21]

Then there were the dove merchants, and the sellers of special spices, herbs, and vegetables for the Passover feast. In addition to these, there crowded toward the temple heights the peddlers with everything from trinkets to pottery, and headdresses to shoes. This was called the "temple market" located in the Court of the Gentiles.[22] In all probability, the merchants made more at these great feasts than all the rest of the year put together.

In the main courtyard of the temple, there was a large concourse of money changers. Donations had to be made in temple coins and therefore those who had come with Greek and Roman money had to exchange it for sacred temple coins. There was also the annual head tax requiring each Jew to exchange enough foreign coin to pay

[18]James E. Talmage, *Jesus the Christ*, p. 167.
[19]Ibid.
[20]Hastings, *Dictionary of the Bible*, vol. 3, p. 691, under "Passover."
[21]Edersheim, *Life and Times of Jesus*, 1:370, note 1.
[22]Ibid., 1:370-371.

the "atonement tax." This amounted to approximately thirty-four cents in modern money and every faithful Jew paid it for the upkeep of the temple.[23]

Of course, the money changers charged exorbitant rates of exchange, and it is said that the dishonesty and corruption in many of these Passover transactions was enormous.[24]

JESUS, WITH HIS FAMILY AND DISCIPLES, APPROACHES THE TEMPLE

It is only possible to roughly imagine the crowding, pushing, and noisy maneuvering that occurred along the narrow highways as the streams of people, sheep, donkeys, merchants' carts and frightened, crying children, all made their gradual ascent toward Mount Moriah and the temple.

In previous years, when Jesus had come along this same crushing, uncomfortable route, he could only endure it. But on this occasion, as he and his little band approached the temple, his righteous indignation began to swell within him until it inflamed his very soul. Here was his Father's holy house, newly built by Herod, designed to have its courtyards set aside for worship, prayer, and quiet conversations. Instead, it was packed with noisy, clamoring crowds, milling about among the shouting hucksters and merchants, some selling sheep or oxen, others selling trinkets or doves, and in the background could be heard the haggling of the noisy, quarrelsome money changers.

This rabble of irreverent money mongers had turned God's sacred temple courtyards into a pandemonium of commercialized bedlam.

Somewhere along the way, Jesus picked up a whip. Or he may have unravelled a heavy piece of rope and fashioned it into a whip.

---

[23]Ibid., 1:168.
[24]Ibid., 1:370-1.

The Bible says Jesus "made a scourge of small cords,"[25] which is what ropes were made of.

It is clear that Jesus did not use one of the whips which was often employed to drive donkeys, camels or oxen. These were made of tough leather thongs tipped with pieces of metal or bone. Such a whip could cut soft, human flesh to shreds. Jesus had no need of such a whip. He needed a token whip, a scourge, one that might leave a welt, but not a gash. By unwinding a piece of heavy rope Jesus would have his "scourge."

THE CLEANSING OF THE TEMPLE

It must have shocked those who were with Jesus when he suddenly left them, pushed into the crowd, and began turning over tables, driving lambs from their pens, spilling money boxes on the ground, and flaying to the right and the left with his scourge. He cried out:

"Make NOT my Father's house an house of merchandise!"[26]

The apostle John says:

"He drove them all out of the temple, and the sheep, and the oxen; and poured out the changers' money, and overthrew the tables."[27]

From that point where Jesus first began the cleansing, a surge of mass hysteria must have engulfed the thousands of temple patrons, peddlers, and priests. It was as though a spirit of mob terror seized the hearts of people as they fled from the Court of the Gentiles and poured out through the nine huge gates in all directions.

WHAT TERRIFIED THE PEOPLE?

When we think about it, the dimensions of what Jesus did are almost unbelievable. Ordinarily, such action by a single individual

---

[25]John 2:16.
[26]John 2:16 (emphasis added).
[27]John 2:15.

would have brought down on him the fury of perhaps two or three hundred merchants and vendors whose money had been spilled out on the ground. At the very least, it would have resulted in the immediate arrest of Jesus by the temple guards. But none of this happened.

The situation was even more amazing when we recall that there was a whole platoon of Roman soldiers assigned to the Antonia fortress located at the northeast corner of the temple esplanade. However, based on a long-standing arrangement with the Jewish leaders, the Romans did not ordinarily interfere with the crowds on the sacred temple grounds unless they were summoned. Apparently the actions of the Savior were so sudden, and the reaction of the crowd so precipitous, that no one thought to summon them.

It is sometimes suggested that the hysteria which seized the hearts of the people merely demonstrated the growing sense of conscience-stricken guilt which was associated with the desecration of the temple on feast days. Assuming this to be the case, it is thought that perhaps this volatile sense of guilt may have required only a spark from one strong, courageous, and angry man to send them terror-stricken into flight—as though God himself were wielding a scourge behind them, as indeed he was.

Nevertheless, even though the initial hysteria caused the people to flee from the temple in a panic, we realize it would have only been a few minutes before they gathered their wits together and realized they must hurry back to rescue their money bags, merchandise, lambs and birds.

The scripture says that is exactly what happened.

THE MIRACLE WORKER

Crowds of people—accompanied by the merchants and priests—rapidly filtered back into the huge temple courtyard. No doubt most of them were angry, especially the priests and merchants. We assume they returned to the Court of the Gentiles with vengeance in their eyes, but what they saw was enough to stop them in their tracks.

All the crippled beggars who had been too helpless to flee, were being healed by Jesus. No doubt some of them were running, jumping, and praising God for being able to walk, or see, or stand straight. It was enough to make many of the returning Jews outright believers.[28]

But the rabbis had warned the Jews against miracle workers.[29] They said an impostor could deceive them with miracles. Therefore, some of the those who probably were Sadducees and had authority over the temple courts, moved up to Jesus and said:

"What sign showest thou unto us, seeing that thou doest these things?[30]

Since the miracles were not considered a sufficient "sign" to prove the Savior's heavenly credentials, he decided to share with them a heavenly mystery. He said:

"Destroy this temple, and in three days I will raise it up."[31]

As Jesus looked at these self-appointed protagonists, he must have seen confusion written all over their faces. They immediately rose to the bait and said:

"Forty and six years was this temple in building, and wilt thou rear it up in three days?"

Apparently Jesus made no reply, but John adds: "He spake of the temple of his body."[32]

It is clear that these challengers took no action against the Savior, but they probably wandered away mumbling to themselves in perplexed frustration. But they did not forget what Jesus had said. Three years later, they served as witnesses against him, and the

[28]John 2:23.
[29]Gershom Scholem, *The Messianic Idea in Judaism*, op. cit., p. 27.
[30]John 2:18.
[31]John 2:19.
[32]John 2:21.

Sanhedrin—the highest court in the Jewish hierarchy—condemned Jesus to death for saying these words. They called it blasphemy.

Meanwhile, as Jesus turned back to his compassionate ministry of healing the crippled beggars, it must have been a glorious moment for the Father's Beloved Son. No one who saw the humble carpenter from Nazareth on this memorable occasion would ever forget it. The miracles he was performing were so spectacular that a member of the Sanhedrin searched for Jesus to talk with him the very next day.[33]

THE MIRACLES CREATE A CRISIS FOR JESUS

No doubt this series of healings required a very substantial period of time. There were always numerous beggars on the temple concourse and we gain the impression that Jesus healed everyone in sight just as he would do on another occasion.[34]

Nothing like this could have occurred without attracting a huge throng back to the temple. No doubt these Passover crowds watched intently as they saw what Jesus was doing. It must have been a stirring spectacle to see the beggars rising from their suffering and afflictions to sing out their praises to God as they were healed.

In spite of the rabbis' warning against miracle workers, this continuous outpouring of heavenly power could not help but have a lofty and exalting impact on the minds of the people. Consequently, it was not long before the previous anger and resentment of the crowd had turned into a swelling emotion of zeal and adoration. Who could doubt that this miraculous healer was a great prophet, perhaps even the Messiah.

Jesus knew what was happening in the minds of these people. The crowd was ready to surge in upon Jesus to raise him up in wild acclaim. But that must not happen. To prevent it, Jesus decided to perform a miracle on his own behalf.

---

[33]John 3:2.
[34]3 Nephi 17:9, B. of M.

An eye-witness to these events was John the Beloved, and here is what he says happened:

"Many believed in his name, when they saw the miracles which he did. BUT JESUS DID NOT COMMIT HIMSELF UNTO THEM, because he knew all men."[35]

This brief verse tells us three things. First, Jesus would have been accepted by many as the Messiah and king of the Jews if he had allowed them to do so. Second, he did something to prevent them from seizing him, and raising him up as their Messiah. Third, Jesus knew this great throng of people better than they knew themselves.

SEEING THE SITUATION THROUGH THE EYES OF JESUS

If Jesus had committed or surrendered himself to this multitude of admiring Jews, nothing could have been more unfortunate. Not only would this have thwarted the Father's plan for the redemptive sacrifice, but all of the marvelous developments scheduled for the next three years of the Savior's ministry would never have happened.

So how did he escape?

John simply says he did not "commit himself" unto them, but subsequent scriptures describe what Jesus did on a number of occasions when he did not want to "commit himself." During a later visit to the temple, John says:

"Then took they up stones to cast at him: but Jesus hid himself, and went out of the temple, going through the midst of them, and so passed by."[36]

On another occasion the people of Nazareth became so angry with Jesus that they carried him to a high hill so they could throw him over a cliff, but the scripture says:

[35]John 2:23-24.
[36]John 8:59.

"But he passing through the midst of them, went his way."[37]

On another occasion when Jesus wished to disengage from a crowd, John says:

"These things Jesus spake and departed, and did hide himself from them."[38]

After Jesus fed the 5,000 the scripture says:

"When Jesus therefore perceived that they would come and take him by force, to make him a king, he departed again into a mountain himself alone."[39]

The crowd subsequently searched everywhere trying to find Jesus, but he had hidden himself.[40]

This miracle is sometimes called "the veiling of the eyes." In old Testament times, the prophet Elisha used this miracle to disorient the whole Syrian army![41]

HOW WELL DID JESUS KNOW THESE PEOPLE?

It will be recalled that one of the reasons Jesus would not commit himself to the crowds at the temple was "because he knew all men."[42]

Jesus knew that many of these very people who wanted to acclaim him as their Messiah and king on this first day of his ministry, were merely converted by his miracles. He knew that three years later many of these same people would consent to his crucifixion *in spite* of his miracles.[43]

---

[37]Luke 4:30.
[38]John 12:36.
[39]John 6:15.
[40]John 6:24.
[41]2 Kings 6:17-20.
[42]John 2:24.
[43]2 Nephi 10:3-4, B. of M.

After leaving the temple, Jesus and his companions hastened away to their private lodgings where no one would be likely to find them.

As we contemplate the amazing things that had happened during these past few hours, we can only exclaim: "What a way to celebrate a birthday!"

The next time the throngs of Jerusalem heard of Jesus, he would be in Judaea, baptizing those who were humble enough to seek him out.

*   *   *   *

TOPICS FOR REFLECTION AND DISCUSSION

1. Describe the two most interesting things you learned from the story of the wedding feast at Cana. How would we surmise that Mary already knew about the Savior's power over the elements before she came to Cana? Why did Jesus say he would help his mother when he did not want to display his power in public?

2. What must be combined with the primal particles of matter so they can be organized and controlled? What ancient prophet saw how the intelligences were organized before the world was? By what simple means does the Lord get the intelligences to do special things for him?

3. To what extent was the population of Jerusalem increased at the time of the Feast of the Passover? How would you describe living conditions in Jerusalem during one of these Feast days?

4. Name some of the activities during the Feast of the Passover that desecrated God's holy house and its immediate environment.

5. When Jesus cleansed the temple, what kind of a whip did he use? What leads us to think he would not have used an ordinary herdsman's whip?

6. Did he just drive out a few, to set an example, or did he drive the people *en masse* from the temple esplanade? In what particular way did Jesus say the temple was being desecrated?

7. After Jesus cleansed the temple, why would there still be a lot of beggars remaining in the temple courtyard? What did Jesus do for them?

8. One group of authority-minded Jews wanted to challenge the authority of Jesus to do these things. What did they ask him to produce as evidence that he had authority to cleanse the temple and perform these miracles? What did Jesus reply? Did they know what he meant?

9. Does it appear that Jesus healed people in groups or individually? Do you think he just picked out a few people to heal or did he heal everyone in sight?

10. What did the people try to do to Jesus when they witnessed the massive healing of the beggars at the temple? Why would this have been a tragic mistake at the beginning of his ministry? What did Jesus do about it? Where was he the next time the people heard of him?

*   *   *   *

CHAPTER 8

CHRIST'S CONVERSATION WITH NICODEMUS

After Jesus disappeared from among the crowd at the temple, he probably took up residence with his disciples where curiosity seekers were not likely to find him.

But one man did find him. His name was Nicodemus. He was a member of the powerful Jewish Sanhedrin which was the principal governing body of the Jewish religion. Up to this time, the disciples of Jesus were primarily those who had come to him through the ministry of John the Baptist, but Nicodemus had come on his own. In this sense, he might be described as the Savior's first prospective convert.

NICODEMUS WAS NO ORDINARY INVESTIGATOR

John opens the story of Nicodemus by saying:

"There was a man of the Pharisees, named Nicodemus, a ruler of the Jews:

"The same came to Jesus by night...."[1]

The fact that Nicodemus came to Jesus alone and by night would suggest that he was sensitive about his reputation. After all, he was not only a member of the Sanhedrin, but Nicodemus was a leading member of the most popular sect of the Jews, the Pharisees. He apparently wanted to converse with Jesus, but did not want to run the risk of attracting criticism or arousing suspicion that he might be one of the Nazarene's followers.

---

[1]John 3:1.

Nicodemus opened the conversation in a most interesting way. It was almost as though he were trying to justify himself in coming to see Jesus. He began by saying:

"Rabbi, we know that thou art a teacher come from God: for no man can do these miracles that thou doest, except God be with him."[2]

Obviously, Jesus had an admiring friend in this Nicodemus, but not a convert. Jesus read his mind and knew he had come out of intellectual curiosity.

The first task confronting Jesus was to get this investigator to think. The Savior knew his own people. He knew that the mind of this noble man was locked up "with much learning" and encased in a carefully structured intellectual cocoon.

In the famous rabbinical school of Hillel[3]—where Nicodemus was probably trained—the advanced students were infatuated with mysteries in the scriptures. The commentaries on the Torah were elaborately woven into over-arching shadows of mystical speculation that sometimes transformed the simplest truth into a phantom of obscure perplexity.[4]

One prophet, who lived six hundred years before Nicodemus, pronounced a very harsh judgment upon the rabbinical schools. He said:

"Behold...they despised the words of plainness...and sought for things that they could not understand. Wherefore, because of their blindness, which blindness came by looking beyond the mark...God hath taken away his plainness from them, and delivered unto them many things which they cannot understand...."[5]

---

[2]John 3:2.
[3]Edersheim, *Life and Times of Jesus*, 1:240.
[4]Ibid. 1:31-45.
[5]Jacob 4:14, B. of M.

Because of the training of Nicodemus, Jesus decided to confront him with a simple gospel truth that he knew this highly trained Pharisee would probably extrapolate into a tantalizing, mysterious riddle. And that is exactly what happened. Jesus said:

"Verily, verily, I say unto thee, Except a man be born again, he cannot see the kingdom of God."[6]

Nicodemus immediately responded with an exploratory question:

"How can a man be born when he is old? can he enter the second time into his mother's womb, and be born?"[7]

As nearly as we can tell, Jesus was trying to get Nicodemus to humble himself, to acknowledge that he had no idea what Jesus was talking about, and thereby open his heart and mind to the simple truths of the gospel so Jesus could teach him.

Notice how Jesus then gave his investigator a hint that what he had said was merely symbolic. He said:

"Verily, verily, I say unto thee, Except a man be born of water and of the Spirit, he cannot enter into the kingdom of God.

"That which is born of the flesh is flesh; and that which is born of the Spirit is spirit."[8]

From earliest times, the gospel culture of the prophets had taught that the "new birth" of baptism and the gift of the Holy Ghost are symbolic of the natural birth. That is the way it was originally taught to Adam.[9] But Nicodemus, the typically trained Pharisee, did not recognize the code phrase from the gospel culture which Jesus had just pronounced.

---

[6]John 3:3.
[7]John 3:4.
[8]JST John 3:5-6.
[9]Moses 6:59.

Jesus then made one of those decisive statements which appears to have been designed to either make Nicodemus an investigator or break off the dialogue. He said:

"Marvel not that I said unto thee, Ye must be born again.

"The wind bloweth where it listeth, and thou hearest the sound thereof, but canst not tell whence it cometh, and whither it goeth: so is every one that is born of the Spirit."[10]

Obviously, Jesus was probing the mind of Nicodemus for any evidence of a little spiritual curiosity. But he was doing it with more code phrases, and it was going completely over the head of his investigator.

At this point, any experienced missionary would be inclined to ask, "Why is Jesus being so obscure? Why doesn't he just come straight out and tell Nicodemus to repent and be baptized the way John the Baptist proclaimed it?"

In a moment we learn that Nicodemus had already heard the simple invitation of John the Baptist, and Jesus knew he had rejected it.

The Savior loved Nicodemus. He loved him enough to hope he would humble himself and open his mind so the Savior could teach him the most simple truths of the gospel. But this did not happen. What Jesus said to Nicodemus did not arouse his curiosity nor stimulate his desire to have Jesus explain how one might be born of the water and the Spirit.

Instead, Nicodemus simply challenged Jesus by saying:

"How can these things be?"[11]

---

[10]John 3:6-8.
[11]John 3:9.

This was not a humble inquiry, but an intellectual thrust designed to place Jesus on the defensive. Therefore Jesus challenged him right back:

"Art thou a master of Israel, and knowest not these things? "Verily, verily, I say unto thee, We speak that we do know, and testify that we have seen; and YE RECEIVE NOT OUR WITNESS."[12]

Now we begin to understand what has been happening here. The "we" in this statement only fits two people—John the Baptist and Jesus. They have both tried to tell Nicodemus their great message—things they had seen, things that they knew—but he "received not" their witness. This tells us that Nicodemus had been one of those referred to by Luke when he said:

"The publicans justified God, being baptized with the baptism of John. But the Pharisees and lawyers rejected the counsel of God against themselves, being not baptized of him."[13]

Now we begin to see Nicodemus through the eyes of the Savior. This proud Pharisee had confessed that Jesus must be a man of God to perform all those miracles at the temple, but when he came to the Nazarene at night he was not seeking instruction, repentance or baptism. He was simply fascinated by Jesus in an intellectual way, just as the Athenians would later be fascinated with Paul.[14]

We almost detect a note of sadness as Jesus said to Nicodemus:

"If I have told you earthly things, and ye believe not, how shall ye believe, if I tell you of heavenly things?"[15]

---

[12]John 3:10-11 (emphasis added).
[13]Luke 7:29-30.
[14]Acts 17:32.
[15]John 3:3-12.

JESUS BEARS HIS TESTIMONY TO EARS THAT CANNOT HEAR

Every missionary has had the experience of seeking to open the eyes of one who cannot see, and unstop the ears of someone who cannot hear. When all else fails, there is only one thing left to do—bear a fervent testimony.

On that quiet April night in Jerusalem, this is what Jesus did. No human being ever heard a more powerful testimony of the Father and the Son than Jesus gave to Nicodemus. From his own lips, Jesus bore witness that he was indeed the Messiah, the very Son of God.

Jesus began by paying a tender tribute to the greatness of his Heavenly Father. He said:

"For God so loved the world, that he gave his only begotten Son, that whosoever believeth *on* him should not perish, but have everlasting life."[16]

Then Jesus spoke of himself, and said:

"For God sent not his Son into the world to condemn the world; but that the world through him might be saved.

"He who believeth on him is not condemned: but he who believeth not is condemned already, because he hath not believed in the name of the only begotten Son of God *which before was preached by the mouth of all the holy prophets.*"[17]

This last statement was intended to prick the conscience of Nicodemus. If this learned Pharisee had been carefully studying the simple message of the scriptures instead of vaporizing them into mysteries, he would have recognized Jesus, especially after all the miraculous healings at the temple. Every prophet had proclaimed that the Jews would one day see their great Messiah.

---

[16]JST John 3:16, compare KJT.
[17]JST John 3:16-18 (emphasis added), compare KJT.

Then Jesus let the hammer fall. He said:

"THEY TESTIFIED OF ME!"[18]

For some reason the King James Translation does not include this important statement. Jesus then went on to explain why the learned Jews of that generation were not able to recognize their Messiah. He said:

"And this is the condemnation, that light is come into the world, and men loved darkness rather than light, because their deeds were evil.

"For every one that doeth evil hateth the light, neither cometh to the light, lest his deeds should be reproved.

"But he that doeth truth cometh to the light, that his deeds may be made manifest, that they are wrought in God."[19]

Jesus knew that if Nicodemus could have felt even the smallest morsel of humility in his heart, the Holy Spirit could have shot a shaft of light into his soul and converted him. What a marvelous strength Nicodemus could have been to the early church!

But it was not to be.

So far as the record shows, this proud "ruler of the Jews" never quite made it. Nevertheless, he remained a friend. Later, he would defend the rights of Jesus when the Pharisees were going to condemn the Savior without a trial.[20]

Then, after Jesus was crucified and Joseph of Arimathaea had claimed the body, it would be Nicodemus who would bring a hundred pounds of myrrh and aloes for the Savior's burial.[21]

---

[18]JST John 3:18.
[19]John 3:19-21.
[20]John 7:50.
[21]John 19:39.

One cannot help but hope that sometime, somewhere, Nicodemus took hold of the plough and became a full disciple. However, the apostle John seems to have followed Nicodemus closely, and if he had joined the church it is believed that John would have joyfully written about it.

THE HONORABLE MEN OF THE EARTH

During the average lifetime, one meets a considerable number of "good and honorable men" who fit the profile of Nicodemus. We work and pray to bring them into the kingdom, but while they compliment the church and admire its people, they cannot quite muster the strength to make a commitment and become a member.

The Lord needs these people. They could be a great strength to the work of the kingdom. But when they fail to answer the call, they lose their potential blessing of a mansion in the celestial kingdom. The Lord says the following of those who come forth in the terrestrial kingdom:

"These are they who are honorable men of the earth, who were blinded by the craftiness of men. These are they who receive of his glory, but not of his fullness."[22]

Before we leave the discussion between the Savior and Nicodemus, let us briefly consider the full implication of what Jesus meant when he told Nicodemus that he must be born of the water and the Spirit.

WHAT DOES IT MEAN TO BE BORN OF THE WATER?

It is interesting that even today, many modern churches do not know what Jesus really meant when he said that a person must be "born of the water." John had certainly tried to make it clear when he said, "Repent and be baptized."

The original connotation of "baptism" simply meant "to be buried." The ancient baptismal fonts were all large enough to permit

---

[22]Doctrine and Covenants 76:73-76.

baptism by immersion, and the Bible says John baptized at "Aenon...because there was much water there."[23]

The Lord's ordinance of baptism was both beautiful and simple. It had only four basic requirements:

1. The candidates had to be at least eight years old and mentally competent to believe in Jesus Christ and promise the Lord that he or she would obey his commandments.[24]

2. The candidates were required to confess that they had repented of their sins or demonstrated in their lives adequate "fruits meet for repentance."[25]

3. The candidate had to be completely immersed in water.[26]

4. The person performing the ordinance had to be called and ordained to the priesthood of God "as was Aaron."[27]

This holy ordinance was first administered to Adam,[28] and it was thereafter performed for all those who wanted to be identified with God's kingdom on earth.

By the time of Abraham, parents were often neglecting to have their children baptized when they reached the age of eight. They chose to follow the pagan practice of putting the child through an ablution bath administered by the parents, or sprinkling the child with blood, or cutting "a mark in the flesh." The Lord thereupon took advantage of the prevailing vogue and ordered that:

"Every man child among you shall be circumcised. And ye shall circumcise the flesh of your foreskin; and it shall be a token of the

---

[23]John 3:23.
[24]Doctrine and Covenants 68:25.
[25]Matthew 3:8; Moroni 8:25.
[26]Doctrine and Covenants 20:73-74.
[27]Hebrews 5:4; Doctrine and Covenants 20:73.
[28]Moses 6:64-65, P. of G.P.

covenant betwixt me and you. And he that is eight days old shall be circumcised among you, every man child in your generations."[29]

This was not so much for the benefit of the child, but for the parent. The Lord said:

"My people have gone astray from my precepts, and have not kept mine ordinances....They have not observed...the burial or BAPTISM wherewith I commanded them....And I will establish a covenant of circumcision...that thou may knowest for ever that children are not accountable before me until they are EIGHT YEARS OLD."[30]

So male children were to be circumcised at eight DAYS to remind parents that ALL children are to be baptized when they are eight YEARS old.

By the time of Christ, circumcision had become the prevailing ordinance but not baptism. Baptism was used only to initiate gentiles or infidels into Judaism.[31]

Nevertheless, the memory of the former days when everybody was baptized, remained sufficiently strong among the people so that they flocked to Bethabara to be baptized by John when he announced that this was necessary to gain a remission of their sins.

Thus, through the ministry of John the Baptist, the original ordinance was restored.

HOW THE CHRISTIANS LOST THE
TRUE ORDINANCE OF BAPTISM

During the long series of persecutions of the Christians by the Roman emperors, many changes occurred in the ordinances of the early Christian church. Among the casualties was the ordinance of baptism. Over the centuries, this is what happened:

---

[29]JST Genesis 17:15-17.
[30]JST Genesis 17:5-11.
[31]Hastings *Dictionary of the Bible*, vol. 1, p. 239.

1. Instead of baptism by immersion, the practice of sprinkling and pouring was introduced.[32]

2. Bishop Augustine invented the doctrine of "original sin" and required the baptism of all infants for the remission of the sins of Adam and Eve.[33]

3. The ordinance of baptism by immersion, sprinkling, or pouring became acceptable no matter who performed it. All that was required was saying the right words: "In the name of the Father, the Son, and the Holy Ghost." No priesthood was required.[34]

It is interesting that when the gospel was restored in the latter days, and the correct ordinance of baptism was reinstated, some individuals wanted to be members of the church but insisted they had already been baptized in their former churches. To them, the Lord said:

"Behold, I say unto you that all old covenants have I caused to be done away in this thing; and this is a new and an everlasting covenant, even that which was from the beginning.

"Wherefore, although a man should be baptized an hundred times it availeth him nothing, for you cannot enter in at the strait gate by the law of Moses, neither by your dead works.

"For it is because of your dead works that I have caused this last covenant and this church to be built up unto me, even as in days of old.

"Wherefore, enter ye in at the gate, as I have commanded, and seek not to counsel your God."[35]

---

[32]James L. Barker, *Apostasy from the Divine Church*, pp. 189-190.
[33]Ibid., p. 439, 454.
[34]Ibid. p. 216.
[35]Doctrine and Covenants 22:1-4.

So, with the restoration of the gospel, the Lord returned to the original simplicity of the ordinance administered to Adam and practiced in every dispensation thereafter.

By direct revelation the Lord gave careful instructions concerning the ordinance of baptism.

First, the Lord described who could qualify for baptism:

"All those who humble themselves before God, and desire to be baptized, and come forth with broken hearts and contrite spirits, and witness before the church that they have truly repented of all their sins, and are willing to take upon them the name of Jesus Christ, having a determination to serve him to the end, and truly manifest by their works that they have received of the Spirit of Christ unto the remission of their sins, shall be received by baptism into his church."[36]

Then the Lord described how baptisms had always been performed:

"The person who is called of God and has authority from Jesus Christ to baptize, shall go down into the water with the person who has presented himself or herself for baptism, and shall say, calling him or her by name: Having been commissioned of Jesus Christ, I baptize you in the name of the Father, and of the Son, and of the Holy Ghost. Amen.

"Then shall he immerse him or her in the water, and come forth again out of the water."[37]

---

[36]Doctrine and Covenants 20:37.
[37]Doctrine and Covenants 20:73-74.

BAPTISM BY ITSELF DOES NOT
ACHIEVE REMISSION Of SINS

There are three steps to securing the remission of sins. This was described by the Lord in a revelation to Enoch. He said:

1. "By the water ye keep the commandment."

2. "By the Spirit ye are justified."

3. "By the blood ye are sanctified."[38]

Notice that the remission of sins does not come until the sincerity of the candidate has been "justified" by the Spirit of the Lord or the Holy Ghost.

Once the individual has been certified or justified to the Savior, then Jesus exercises the cleansing force of his atoning sacrifice to suspend their sins from the great recording devices of heaven.

This, then, brings us to the subject of being "born of the Spirit."

WHAT DOES IT MEAN TO BE BORN OF THE SPIRIT?

This ordinance is the conferring of a very special gift on those who have repented and been baptized. It is called *THE* gift of the Holy Ghost. This gift comes to the recipient by way of a command. As one of the members of the Melchizedek priesthood lays his hands on the newly baptized member, he says:

"*RECEIVE* the Holy Ghost."

At that moment, the new convert not only becomes a confirmed member of the church, but wonderful blessings immediately begin taking place in heaven which he or she knows nothing about.

First of all, assuming the convert has sincerely repented, then the Holy Ghost will personally, or through his emissaries, certify to the

---

[38]Moses 6:60, P. of G.P.

Savior that this individual is honest and sincere in his desire to enter a covenant with God. This covenant includes a promise to obey God's commandments and serve him faithfully all the days of his or her life. This individual is then "justified" and the ordinance of baptism is "sealed" or certified before the Savior so that the Atonement can begin operating in his or her behalf.[39]

This ordinance will not only completely blot out the guilt for all past sins, but once a person has been baptized, the Atonement will provide a complete forgiveness for any *future* sins when they are accompanied by repentance and a resolution to overcome them.

This is what is meant by being born of the Spirit.[40]

If Nicodemus had humbled himself sufficiently to open his mind and heart and allow Jesus to teach him the first principles of the gospel, this is what he would have heard.

* * * *

TOPICS FOR REFLECTION AND DISCUSSION

1. Describe the position which Nicodemus occupied in Jerusalem and explain why you think he went to see Jesus at night. Did Nicodemus believe Jesus was a man of God? What was the basis for this conclusion?

2. What was there about the education of Nicodemus that made it difficult for him to communicate with Jesus? Did he appear to have come for a spiritual education or an intellectual discussion?

3. What kinds of phrases was Jesus using in his discussion with Nicodemus? Did these seem somewhat obscure to you? Were they obscure to Nicodemus? Why didn't Jesus simply ask Nicodemus to repent and be baptized the way John the Baptist was teaching it?

---

[39]Moses 6:65, P. of G.P.
[40]See also Appendix D, "What Does It Mean to be Baptized with the Holy Ghost and with Fire?"

4. Did Jesus ever tell Nicodemus his own identity and who was talking to him? Did Nicodemus become an enemy of Jesus? What did Nicodemus do when Jesus was about to be condemned without a trial?

5. What did Nicodemus do immediately after the Crucifixion? Is there any evidence that he ever joined the church? When an "honorable man of the earth" admires God's kingdom, but fails to embrace it, what does he lose?

6. What are the four requirements for a proper baptism under the Lord's plan? What did the word "baptism" originally mean?

7. When was circumcision begun? How early in life was it to occur? What was it intended to remind parents to do?

8. What was the main ordinance among the Jews in the days of Jesus? What had happened to baptism? Then how do we account for the response which John the Baptist received when he invited the people to come down to the Jordan and be baptized?

9. What happened to the ordinance of baptism after the days of the apostles? Describe the requirements for baptism under the restored gospel. What else is required after baptism to gain a forgiveness of sins?

10. When a person is confirmed a member of the church, he or she is given a commandment. What is it? Who certifies to the Savior that the ordinance of baptism has been worthily performed? Does the Atonement cleanse us of past sins? Does it cleanse us of any subsequent sins providing we sincerely repent of them?

*   *   *   *

CHAPTER 9

NUMEROUS CONVERSIONS IN JUDEA

But the Savior Travels North After Receiving a Death Threat

After the Savior's conversation with Nicodemus, he appears to have left Jerusalem almost immediately and launched his ministry to the south, which was Judea.

No towns or cities are mentioned in connection with this new field of labor. This leads us to conclude that Jesus moved about in the rural areas. Although we cannot pinpoint the place where he began to preach and baptize, we can eliminate the territory where he probably did not go.

Some have supposed that he would move toward the eastern part of Judaea, but this is extremely unlikely. Between Bethlehem and the Dead Sea is the wilderness of Judea. This is a desolate plateau approximately 15 miles wide.

"Nothing green refreshes the eye over the wide landscape. No stream waters it, except when the rains, for a time, fill the wadis with rushing torrents. Only the black tents of some poor Arabs who manage to find pasture for their goats in the cliffs and hollows of its almost bare rocks, give any human interest to the forbidding landscape."[1]

Along the eastern border of Judea is the formidable Dead Sea. This vast body of water is 1,300 feet below sea level and the wilderness of Judea extends to the edge of its rugged cliffs which look down 2,000 feet to the glistening sheet of salt water below.

---

[1]Cunningham Geikie, *Hours With the Bible*, New York: James Pott and Co., 1903, vol. 3, pp. 192-3.

SITE OF THE JUDEAN MINISTRY

In the light of these circumstances, we conclude that Jesus probably began his first missionary work in the "hill country" of Judea, not far from the area where John's parents—Zacharias and Elisabeth—originally lived.[2]

This was a beautiful rolling countryside where the sheep and cattle grazed along the hills, and the valleys flourished with grapes, figs, vegetable gardens and wheat fields. Furthermore, it was not a great distance from Jerusalem which would make it convenient for truth-seekers to find Jesus.

In this quiet countryside setting the people would be able to hear the Savior's teachings without the confusion and traffic of the towns or the hecklers from the local synagogues. And there were also a number of places in this region where crystal-clear pools of water are fed by springs from subterranean channels. In these pools baptisms could be performed.

A very attractive spot in this area would have been the famous Solomon's Pools which furnished water through the Roman aqueducts to Jerusalem. These were surrounded by trees, gardens, and the dwelling places of those who tended the vineyards.

JESUS AND HIS DISCIPLES BEGIN BAPTIZING

As soon as the word reached Jerusalem that Jesus had been located, there must have been many who were eager to see him. News of the startling miracles which he had performed after the cleansing of the temple undoubtedly spread throughout the city and the surrounding region.

It will be recalled that many of those who saw the miracles at the temple wanted to proclaim Jesus the Messiah immediately, but he withdrew himself. Since these would already have a budding testimony of the divinity of Jesus, they would undoubtedly be among the first to hasten to the hill country to hear him. Others would go

---

[2]Luke 1:39.

out of curiosity. The record is clear that there were many who journeyed into the countryside to hear Jesus and many of those who heard him were baptized.[3]

With large crowds to be taught and many of them to be baptized, it was inevitable that Jesus would turn to his closest disciples to help him. Up to this point the scriptures have only identified five of them.

Most likely, these five would be among those he ordained to help him. There may have been others, but the five the scriptures have already mentioned are Peter, John, Andrew, Philip and Nathanael or Bartholomew.

There is no reference to the time when Jesus ordained these disciples to the priesthood, but we know this occurred because they were soon baptizing more than the Savior himself.

The Inspired Version specifically says that even though Jesus baptized, "he himself baptized not so many as his disciples."[4]

MEANWHILE, WHAT HAD HAPPENED TO JOHN THE BAPTIST?

While the Savior was busily engaged in his ministry in Judea, all kinds of things had been happening to John the Baptist.

We find that John was no longer baptizing at Bethabara on the east side of the Jordan, but had taken his disciples to the community of Aenon, which means a place of *springs* where there was "much water."[5] Aenon is described as being near Salim but the exact location of these two towns has never been determined.

Although there have been a few traditions to the contrary, it appears that John conducted his entire ministry "beyond" the River Jordan. That is where he was preaching at Bethabara on the east side

---

[3]John 3:26.
[4]JST John 4:3, compare with KJT John 4:2.
[5]John 3:23.

of the river at the beginning of his ministry,[6] and he was still there at the end of his ministry when he was arrested by Herod Antipas.[7]

This district was known as Perea, and was governed by Herod Antipas who also governed Galilee.

THE DISCIPLES OF JOHN BECOME ALARMED

The notoriety and success of the Savior's campaign in Judaea came to the attention of the disciples of John the Baptist. They therefore appear to have journeyed into Judea to see what was going on. What they saw alarmed them and so they hastened back to report to John the Baptist. They anxiously told him:

"Rabbi, he that was with thee beyond Jordan, to whom thou barest witness, behold, the same baptizeth, and he receiveth of all people who come unto him."[8]

Most authorities agree that the words of John's disciples reflect a certain spirit of jealousy and resentment. They were saying, in effect, that Jesus was accepting all who came to him as *his* followers, including some of John's disciples.

In this complaint there is no suggestion that Jesus had been rebaptizing John's disciples, but simply that he was accepting them as part of his own entourage of followers.

JOHN'S NOBILITY IS EXHIBITED
IN HIS TRIBUTE TO JESUS

It appears that this incident convinced John that it was now time for him to prepare all of his disciples for the future when Jesus would be their new leader.

However, John's disciples were so loyal that they did not see Jesus in his Messianic role. They instinctively sensed that Jesus was some kind of competitor. Therefore John attempted to straighten out

---

[6]John 1:28.
[7]Mark 6:17.
[8]JST John 3:27.

their thinking once and for all. In John's mind it was extremely important that they understand how he felt about Jesus.

The tribute which John paid to the Savior is quoted by the Gospel of John as a series of one-liners that seem inadequately expressed in our present translation.[9]

Fortunately, a modern apostle, Elder James E. Talmage, has assembled John's testimony in a beautiful, coherent statement that captures the fervent love and respect which John held for the Savior. The modern apostle's summary of John's tribute is as follows:

"A man receives only as God gives unto him. It is not given to me to do the work of Christ. You, yourselves, are witnesses that I disclaimed being the Christ....I said I was one sent before him. He is as the bridegroom; I am only as the friend of the bridegroom, his servant; and I rejoice greatly in being thus near him.

"His voice gives me happiness; and thus my joy is fulfilled. He of whom you speak stands at the beginning of his ministry. I, near the end of mine.

"He must increase, but I must decrease.

"He came from heaven and therefore is superior to all things of earth; nevertheless, men refuse to receive his testimony.

"To such a one, the Spirit of God is not apportioned; it is his in full measure. The Father loveth him, the Son, and hath given all things into his hand.

"He that believeth on the Son hath everlasting life; and he that believeth not the Son, shall not see life; but the wrath of God abideth on him."[10]

---

[9]John 3:27-36.
[10]Talmage, *Jesus the Christ*, p. 164.

In our language, there is no more humble, yet brilliant tribute to Jesus than this epitome of the heartfelt feelings of John the Baptist for the Savior.

JOHN THE BAPTIST IS THROWN INTO PRISON

It was about this same time that Jesus learned that his faithful cousin had been thrown into prison. The scripture tells us that John was arrested because he had dared to criticize the immorality of those who ruled over Perea where John was performing his mission.

As we have already mentioned, Parea was governed by Herod Antipas, son of Herod the Great. To appreciate why John was arrested, we have to know a little more about this tetrarch (governor of a fourth of the country) who ruled both Perea and Galilee under the authority of Rome.

According to Josephus, the famous Jewish historian, Herod Antipas, while visiting Rome, fell madly in love with his brother's wife, whose name was Herodias. He promised her that if she would abandon her husband and return with him, he would divorce his wife and marry her.[11]

Herodias thought she saw an opportunity to advance her personal station in life, and so she agreed. As a result, Herodias, without the benefit of a divorce, married Herod Antipas and thereby created a national scandal in Israel.[12]

Herod's first wife left him as soon as she realized what was happening, and fled back to her father. Her father was King Aretas, who ruled the Arab kingdom just south of the Dead Sea, including Petra. The Arab people who inhabited this area were called the Nabataeans.[13]

This whole affair was further complicated by the fact that Herodias was a niece of both her first husband and his brother, Herod Antipas, with whom she was now living. This meant that

---

[11]Josephus, *Antiquities of the Jews*, Book XVIII, 5:2.
[12]Matthews, *A Burning Light*, p. 87.
[13]Josephus, op. cit., Book XVIII, 5:1.

under the Mosaic law, both of her marriages were incestuous, and her marriage to Herod Antipas was adulterous.[14]

It was under these circumstances that John addressed himself to Herod Antipas and said:

"It is not lawful for thee to have thy brother's wife."[15]

When Herodias heard of John's rebuke she was furious. Mark says:

"[She] would have killed him; but she could not."[16]

AT FIRST, HEROD ANTIPAS PROTECTED JOHN

According to the Gospel of Mark, it was Herod Antipas who prevented Herodias from having John killed. Mark says:

"Herod feared John, knowing that he was a just man and an holy man, and one who feared God, and observed to worship him; and when he heard him, he did many things for him, and heard him gladly."[17]

But under the persistent pressure of teasing and nagging from Herodias, Herod Antipas finally felt compelled to have John arrested and thrown into prison.

According to Josephus, the Jewish historian, Herod Antipas was embarrassed by this arrest, but excused himself to the inhabitants of that region by saying that John had created a division among the people and that he had arrested John to prevent an insurrection.[18]

Matthew had a somewhat different feeling about Herod Antipas. Matthew believed that the only thing which saved John's life was

---

[14]Ibid.
[15]Mark 6:18.
[16]Mark 6:19.
[17]JST Mark 6:21.
[18]Josephus, *Antiquities of the Jews*, Book XVIII, chapter 5:2.

Herod's fear of "the multitude, because they counted him a prophet."[19]

JESUS SENDS ANGELS TO COMFORT JOHN

The scripture states that when Jesus learned of John's imprisonment, he sensed that this was not only the end of John's ministry, but that John would soon seal his testimony with his blood. Therefore the Inspired Version says:

"Jesus knew that John was cast into prison, and he sent angels, and, behold, they came and ministered unto him."[20]

Someday we will know who these angels were, and the details of the conversation they had with John as they comforted him.

It is believed that John was held in prison for approximately a year and a half. The fact that Herodias eventually had to use deceit and intrigue to get John killed suggests that Herod Antipas intervened to protect John during that period.

But during all this time, the hatred in the heart of Herodias continued to fester as she contrived her murderous plot by which she eventually intended to have John executed. As we shall see in a later chapter, her diabolical scheme finally succeeded.

JESUS ENCOUNTERS HIS FIRST DEATH THREAT

After Jesus had enjoyed the thrill of preaching the gospel to multitudes of converts, and helping to baptize many of them, he suddenly found it necessary to make a quick departure for the north. Either by revelation or the warning of friends, he learned that there was a plot to kill him. Apparently this scheme had been brewing for some time. The scripture says:

"They sought the more diligently some means that they might put him to death."[21]

---

[19]Matt. 14:5.
[20]JST Matthew 4:11, compare KJT Matthew 4:12.
[21]JST John 4:2.

The Gospel writer then goes on to say that many of the people who were conspiring to have Jesus killed were those who had accepted John as a prophet, but who would not accept Jesus as the Messiah even though John testified that he was the very Son of God, and the hope of Israel. John writes:

"Many received John [the Baptist] as a prophet, but they believed not on Jesus."[22]

Here was an amazing anomaly. This tells us that when John came without miracles, they believed him, but when Jesus came performing marvelous miracles, they wanted to kill him!

This leads us to conclude that Jesus was already dealing with some of the dark spirits described by a prophet nearly 600 years earlier. As we mentioned earlier, Jacob, the son of Lehi, was told by an angel that when Jesus began his ministry, he would be among people, some of whom were:

"...the more wicked part of the world; and they shall crucify him—for thus it behooveth our God, and there is none other nation on earth that would crucify their God.

"For should the mighty miracles be wrought among other nations they would repent, and know that he be their God.

"But because of priestcrafts and iniquities, they at Jerusalem will stiffen their necks against him, that he be crucified.

"Wherefore, because of their iniquities, destructions, famines, pestilences, and bloodshed shall come upon them; and they who shall not be destroyed shall be scattered among all nations."[23]

As we shall see later, the general populace of the Jews would have liked to have made Jesus their king, but the apostate Jewish rulers who were the servants of the Roman emperor contrived to

---

[22]JST John 4:2.
[23]2 Nephi 10:3-6, B. of M.

deceive the common people and persuade them that Jesus was an impostor.

We have already pointed out that the leaders had the support of the rabbinical scholars who had warned the people that miracles were not sufficient proof that Jesus was the Messiah. They quoted Daniel who had promised that the true Messiah would destroy their enemies and set up a kingdom that would last forever. Unless Jesus did that, he was a deceiver.

Little did they realize that these scholars had misread the final fulfillment of Daniel's prophecies by twenty centuries!

JESUS AND HIS DISCIPLES JOURNEY NORTH

This author has conducted a couple of dozen tours to the Holy Land, but each time when we take the trip from Jerusalem northward, I wish we could abandon the bus and walk along the roadway. This is sacred ground, and every step of the way is saturated with Bible history.

Ordinarily the Savior would not have come this way. He would have taken the "safe" road which went down to Jericho and then up along the River Jordan to Galilee. The river route was generally travelled almost exclusively by Jews so as to avoid going through the territory of the despised Samaritans. However, in spite of this, Jesus suddenly announced to his disciples that "he must needs go through Samaria."[24]

As one walks along this road, the finest guide I know of is an excellent book called *Discovering the World of the Bible,* by Dr. LaMar C. Berrett of the Brigham Young University. With easy-to-read maps and carefully researched commentary, he takes the modern pilgrim mile by mile, town by town, until you feel almost as though it were part of your own heritage—which, in a way, it is.

Barely two miles north of Jerusalem and a little to the east of the main road, Jesus and his disciples would have seen the ancient city

---

[24]John 4:4.

of Nob. At one time the famous Tabernacle was located here, and this is where David went to get the sword of Goliath to use in defending himself against Saul.[25]

About the same distance north of Jerusalem, and somewhat to the west, the Savior and his little band of fellow travelers would have seen Gibeah. This was Saul's hometown. It was anciently called "Gibeah of Saul," and after he was made king this is where Saul had his capital.[26]

As they travelled another two miles northwest from Gibeah, they would have come to the famous site of Mizpah or Mizpeh. This is where the leaders of the Israelites were gathered to proclaim Saul their first king.[27] It was also from this point that Samuel launched his highly successful campaign against the Philistines.[28]

Although they may not have passed through it, no doubt Jesus would have noted Anathoth, just three miles northeast of Jerusalem, which was the birthplace of Jeremiah.[29]

One mile beyond Anathoth was the hometown of Samuel, the famous judge of Israel for so many years. This community still exists and is called Ramah. Samuel died here and his traditional burial place has been honored through the centuries.[30]

Five miles north of Jerusalem, Jesus and his disciples would have passed through Gibeon. This is where the five kings of the Canaanite nations were killed by Joshua. This is also the place where Joshua commanded the sun and the moon to stand still while the Israelites completed their destruction of the Canaanite armies that had attacked them.[31]

---

[25]1 Samuel 21:1-6; 22:17-19.
[26]1 Samuel 10:26.
[27]1 Samuel 10:17.
[28]1 Samuel 7:5.
[29]Jeremiah 1:1.
[30]1 Samuel 25:1.
[31]Joshua 10:12.

Eight miles north of Jerusalem is a more modern city, and it may not have existed at the time of the Savior. Today it is called Ramallah. This is an Arab city. Over 95 percent of its population are Christian Arabs with representatives in the Israeli Knesset or congress.[32]

Eleven miles north of Jerusalem Jesus probably passed through Bethel, one of the most famous cities in the Bible. It was originally called "Luz," meaning light. This is where Jacob had his great vision. He saw the Lord and was promised he would be blessed in obtaining a wife among the relatives of Abraham in Padanaram located on the upper Euphrates.[33]

Twelve miles north of Jerusalem is the city of Ephraim. This was a place not frequented by Jews because of the Samaritan population. Later we will find that after Jesus raised Lazarus from the dead, this is where he retired for a season because the high priest had ordered the murder of both Jesus and Lazarus.[34]

Twenty-one miles north of Jerusalem is Shiloh and it may have been here that Jesus and his disciples stopped for the night. This was the capital of Israel 300 years before the conquest of Jerusalem. The Tabernacle and the Ark of the Covenant were located here for many years during the time of the judges.[35]

If they stopped overnight at Shiloh, Jesus and his disciples would have come to Ophrah early the next morning. This was the hometown of Israel's famous military hero named Gideon. A little further on lies the ancient site of Timnath where Joshua was buried.[36]

Finally, after traveling nearly thirty-five miles north from Jerusalem, Jesus and his disciples came to one of the most famous spots in Bible history. It was the homestead of Jacob, the patriarchal father of the twelve tribes.

---

[32]La Mar C. Berrett, *Discovering the World of the Bible*, Provo, Utah: Young House, 1973, p. 318.
[33]Genesis 28:11-19; 31:13.
[34]John 11:54.
[35]1 Samuel 4:3.
[36]Joshua 24:30.

In Jacob's day the major pagan community in this area was called Shechem (SHEE-kem). Here Jacob bought a "parcel" of land from the local ruler where he could settle his family and his flocks. Then he dug a well. In a very real sense this became Jacob's northern homestead.[37]

Today, when one visits the traditional site of this well, it is easy to imagine how Jesus must have felt as he looked about and thought of the great events that had occurred in this place.

Looking north, Jesus would see the foreboding heights of Mount Ebal, the Mountain of Cursing.[38]

Directly across the valley from Mount Ebal is Mount Gerizim, the Mountain of Blessing.[39]

Between Mount Ebal and Mount Gerizim lies the ancient city of Shechem. It was selected as the first capital by the northern ten tribes after they broke away from Judah around 921 B.C.[40]

However, after the ten tribes were captured and carried away by the Assyrians around 721 B.C., they left behind a small remnant of Israelites. These later intermarried with the Assyrian settlers who were sent back to repopulate the land, and their descendants became known as the Samaritans.[41]

THE JEWS AND THE SAMARITANS

The Samaritans called themselves Israelites, but the Jews looked upon them as half-breeds and a cursed people. The Samaritans did accept the five books of Moses, but none of the prophetic writings. They also offered sacrifices and followed many aspects of the Mosaic law; nevertheless, their beliefs were sufficiently different to make the Samaritans totally abhorrent to the Jews.[42]

---

[37]Genesis 33:18-19.
[38]Berrett, *Discovering the World of the Bible*, p. 325.
[39]Ibid.
[40]Ibid. p. 323, 326.
[41]Peloubet's *Bible Dictionary*, under "Samaritans."
[42]Talmage, op. cit., p. 172.

The Jews considered Samaritans more unclean than the Gentiles, and eating food prepared by a Samaritan was considered worse than eating swine.[43]

JESUS MEETS A WOMAN AT JACOB'S WELL

As soon as Jesus and his disciples reached Jacob's well about noon, the Savior sent the disciples into town to buy food while he remained behind.[44]

While Jesus was waiting for his disciples, a most fascinating encounter took place between Jesus and a woman who came to fetch water. The scripture says:

"There cometh a woman of Samaria to draw water: Jesus saith unto her, Give me to drink....

"Then saith the woman of Samaria unto him, How is it that thou, being a Jew, askest drink of me, which am a woman of Samaria? for the Jews have no dealings with the Samaritans.

"Jesus answered and said unto her, If thou knewest the gift of God, and who it is that saith to thee, Give me to drink; thou wouldest have asked of him, and he would have given thee living water."[45]

The woman was puzzled by this man who had no water, or any way of getting it, but nevertheless suggested she should ask him for a drink of his "living water."

"The woman saith unto him, Sir, thou hast nothing to draw with, and the well is deep: from whence then hast thou that living water?

"Art thou greater than our father Jacob, which gave us the well, and drank thereof himself, and his children, and his cattle?

"Jesus answered and said unto her, Whosoever drinketh of this water shall thirst again:

---

[43]Ibid., pp. 172-3.
[44]John 4:8.
[45]John 4:7-10.

"But whosoever drinketh of the water that I shall give him shall never thirst; but the water that I shall give him shall be in him a well of water springing up into everlasting life."[46]

Now Jesus really had her attention.

It was one thing for him to talk about water when she could see he had none, but for him to tell her that he had a special kind of living water that would quench a person's thirst forever, that indeed was fascinating. Her curiosity literally leaped out at Jesus as she said:

"Sir, give me this water, that I thirst not, neither come hither to draw."[47]

What Jesus did next is rather amazing. He obviously knew she was an extremely worldly woman, and yet he knew that in the depth of her soul she had more potential faith than perhaps any other woman in the city. He planned to bring the true worth of this woman to the surface, so he said:

"Go, call thy husband, and come hither.

"The woman answered and said, I have no husband. Jesus said unto her, Thou hast well said, I have no husband:

"For thou hast had *five* husbands; and he whom thou now hast is *not* thy husband: in that saidst thou truly.

"The woman saith unto him, Sir, I perceive that thou art a prophet!"[48]

It would be difficult to measure this woman's astonishment and surprise as Jesus exposed her marital history in a single sentence. He must indeed be a prophet, and if this were the case, perhaps he might be willing to answer a certain question that had been bothering her for a long time. In a spirit of honest inquiry, she said:

---

[46]John 4:7-14.
[47]John 4:15.
[48]John 4:16-19 (emphasis added).

"Our fathers worshipped in this mountain; and ye say, that in Jerusalem is the place where men ought to worship.

"Jesus saith unto her, Woman, believe me, the hour cometh, when ye shall neither in this mountain, nor yet at Jerusalem, worship the Father."[49]

One might have expected Jesus to pursue this theme concerning the coming destruction of Jerusalem in about thirty-five years, but he did not. Instead, he turned to the subject of God and the worship of God. He said:

"Ye worship ye know not what: we know what we worship: for salvation is of the Jews."[50]

IS GOD A SPIRIT?

Now Jesus was getting down to basics. The Samaritans needed to know more about the deity they worshipped. So he began to tell her. Unfortunately, the next verse in the King James version is poorly translated and leads to some faulty conclusions. Here is what Jesus actually said, according to the Inspired Version:

"But the hour cometh, and now is, when the true worshippers shall worship the Father in spirit and in truth: for the Father seeketh such to worship him.

"For unto such hath God promised his Spirit. And they who worship him, must worship in spirit and truth."[51]

When the King James translators were working on the second verse, it came out as follows:

"God is a Spirit: and they that worship him must worship him in spirit and in truth."[52]

---

[49]John 4:20-21.
[50]John 4:22.
[51]JST John 4:25-26.
[52]John 4:24.

The idea that God is only a spirit and not a tangible being grew out of this verse. The Inspired Version gives us the correct translation and the following passage from a modern revelation gives us the correct doctrine:

"The Father has a body of flesh and bones as tangible as man's; the Son also; but the Holy Ghost has not a body of flesh and bones, but is a personage of Spirit."[53]

JESUS BEARS WITNESS OF HIMSELF

This woman had been extremely honest and forthright in answering the Savior's questions. Now she went further and expressed a profound faith in the coming of a Messiah. She said:

"I know that Messias cometh, which is called Christ: when he is come, he will tell us all things."[54]

Jesus knew he was talking to a woman with eyes that could see and ears that could hear. Therefore, he shared with this humble and honest Samaritan the most exciting news she would ever hear, either in this life or the next. He said:

"I THAT SPEAK UNTO THEE AM HE!"[55]

We wish the scripture gave us some indication of her reaction, but this sacred moment was suddenly interrupted by the return of the disciples. They were astonished to find Jesus conversing with an untouchable Samaritan, but they said nothing. They only marvelled "that he talked with the woman."[56]

But for the Samaritan woman this was time for action. The Bible says:

"The woman then left her waterpot, and went her way into the city, and saith to the men,

---

[53]Doctrine and Covenants 130:22.
[54]John 4:25.
[55]John 4:26.
[56]John 4:27.

"Come, see a man, which told me all things that ever I did: is not this the Christ?

"Then they went out of the city, and came unto him."[57]

THE REAPING OF A SAMARITAN HARVEST

As the crowd came running down the road toward Jacob's well, Jesus said to his disciples,

"Behold, I say unto you, Lift up your eyes, and look on the fields; for they are white already to harvest.

"And he that reapeth receiveth wages, and gathereth fruit unto life eternal: that both he that soweth and he that reapeth may rejoice together.

"And herein is that saying true, One soweth, and another reapeth."[58]

This crowd of approaching Samaritans had been reading the Mosaic scriptures faithfully. Their teachers had sowed the seeds that a Messiah was coming. As a result of sowing these seeds through many generations, the fruit was ripe and ready. Now these disciples had the privilege of reaping the joyous harvest.

But Jesus wanted them to know they were reaping the fruit of other men's labors. He said:

"I sent you to reap that whereon ye bestowed no labour: other men laboured, and ye are entered into their labours."[59]

So the disciples had the supreme satisfaction of reaping a bounteous harvest even though they had not been the original sowers.

---

[57]John 4:28-30.
[58]John 4:35-37.
[59]John 4:38.

This joy of the harvest, whether as a sower or a reaper, constitutes the "wages" or reward of the faithful missionary. The scripture says:

"And many of the Samaritans of that city believed on him for the saying of the woman, which testified, He told me all that ever I did....

"And said unto the woman, Now we believe, not because of thy saying: for we have heard him ourselves, and know that this is indeed the Christ, the Saviour of the world."[60]

What a sensational finale to a simple luncheon stop at Jacob's well. No wonder Jesus said "he must go through Samaria." There would be few occasions when these disciples would experience anything as gratifying as this.

"So when the Samaritans were come unto him, they besought him that he would tarry with them: and he abode there two days.

"And many more believed because of his own word....

"Now after two days he departed thence."[61]

* * * *

TOPICS FOR REFLECTION AND DISCUSSION

1. Approximately how soon after Jesus cleansed the temple did he commence his ministry in Judea? Why do we think many of the people from Jerusalem would seek him out there?

2. Did Jesus baptize? Did his disciples baptize? Is there any record that he ordained them to the priesthood at this time? Are we certain they were ordained?

3. Where was John the Baptist at this time? Why did John's disciples who visited Jesus become alarmed? List three of the highlights of John's tribute to Jesus.

---

[60]John 4:39,42.
[61]John 4:40-41, 43.

4. Why was John arrested? Can you narrate the circumstances that led John to make his charge against Herod Antipas? Who wanted to kill John the Baptist? Who apparently protected John from being killed for quite some time?

5. What made Jesus suddenly decide to leave Judaea and go to Galilee? Why did Jacob, the son of Lehi, say the plot against Jesus was by the apostate leaders who were some of the most wicked people on earth? Why did he say no other people on earth would have killed the Savior?

6. List three things that created a spirit of hostility between the Jews and the Samaritans.

7. What does the Bible tell us about the life of the woman who met Jesus at the well? What did Jesus perceive in her regardless of this background? Did she apparently come up to his expectations?

8. Did Jesus ever tell the Samaritan woman who he was? What convinced the men of the city that they should go out to the well and see Jesus for themselves?

9. Did Jesus and his disciples reap a harvest at Shechem? Who sowed the seeds? What are the richest rewards or "wages" of a missionary?

10. How long did Jesus and his disciples stay in Shechem?

*   *   *   *

CHAPTER 10

JESUS RETURNS TO GALILEE

*No Longer a Mere Carpenter But
Now a National Celebrity*

Only a few weeks earlier, Jesus had left Galilee as a virtual nobody. He was merely the son of a carpenter from Nazareth who took care of his widowed mother. He was a nice enough person, but of no particular significance or renown.

Amazingly, he was now about to return to Galilee as a national celebrity. Some even said he was the long awaited Messiah. Others said he was merely a diviner, a sort of miracle worker, a gifted healer. But there were some who said he was clearly a fraudulent impostor, a knave, a charlatan, a law breaker, perhaps even guilty of the heinous crime of blasphemy.

But whether people loved or ridiculed Jesus, they wanted to see him. Very few people in the region recalled having seen him before. He certainly did not appear to have done anything notable in the past, at least not in Galilee. And it was unbelievable that he would have had the audacity to use a rope whip and drive a whole crowd of Passover patrons from the main courtyard of the temple. Then there were those stories about his healing the beggars, making crippled beggars walk, blind beggars see, deaf beggars hear, and hunchbacks stand up straight.

It did seem most incredible.

But in Galilee the big question among the fishing villages spread along the waterfront was simply "Where is he? When do we see him?"

Some travelers back from Jerusalem said it was rumored that he was in Judea preaching and baptizing. But why didn't he return home? After all, his mother, his brothers, his sisters, friends—they were all waiting for him at Nazareth in Galilee.

JESUS BEGINS THE LAST LEG OF HIS JOURNEY

There must have been a joyous mood among Jesus and his disciples as they departed from Shechem with the enthusiastic acclamation and warm good wishes of a throng of Samaritans who had just become the Savior's newest disciples.

But after leaving Shechem and traveling nine miles up the road, it would have been sobering to the mind and spirit of Jesus to enter the reconstructed precincts of what had once been the notorious and wicked city of Samaria.

Samaria had been the last capital of the northern ten tribes before they were besieged and conquered by the Assyrians. And all historians agree that in its heyday, Samaria had been a cesspool of debauchery and degradation. Today, its rebuilt ruins are called *Sebastia.*[1]

This is where the wicked Jezebel and her weak-minded husband, Ahab, had set up religious brothels dedicated to Baal and Ashtoreth.[2]

This is where Jezebel had sent forth the edict that every prophet of Jehovah in Israel had to be killed. Nevertheless, it was here, in the presence of the king and queen, that Elijah dared to appear and proclaim a deadly famine on this whole region. Then he sped off to the east where he could hide by the brook Cherith to avoid assassination.[3]

It was this city of Samaria where Naaman came to be cured of his leprosy but hesitated to take Elisha's instruction to bathe in the Jordan seven times. Only after his servant induced him to try it, was he cured.[4]

---

[1]Skousen, *The Fourth Thousand Years*, Salt Lake City, Bookcraft, 1966, p. 312.
[2]1 Kings 16:31-32; Geikie, *Hours with the Bible*, Vol. 3, pp. 390-392.
[3]1 Kings 17:2-3.
[4]2 Kings 5: 9-14.

And finally, this was where the apostate Israelites were attacked by the Syrians and endured a siege so terrible that they were compelled to survive by eating their own dead.[5]

Even today, an ugly pall of foreboding seems to hang over Samaria, and it was probably a relief to Jesus and his disciples as they prepared to leave these evil haunts and proceed up the road another fourteen miles to Dothan.

Dothan marks the end of the high country and guards the pass leading down into the rich plains of the Jezreel Valley. It will be recalled that it was near Dothan that Joseph found his brethren and their flocks, but instead of being welcomed by these older brothers, he was stripped of his multi-colored coat and thrown down a dry well.

A short time later, while the brothers were having lunch and trying to decide what to do with Joseph, some distant relatives, the Midianites, discovered Joseph and sold him to a passing caravan of Ishmaelites, who were also distant relatives. It was they who carried Joseph down into Egypt and sold him to Potiphar. Although Joseph began his career in Egypt as a slave, he ended up becoming prime minister of the whole land. Indeed, we can say that truth is often stranger than fiction.[6]

ENTERING THE PLAIN OF JEZREEL

As Jesus and his disciples descended from the highlands of Samaria into the luxurious and fertile plains of Jezreel, they saw before them Israel's Garden of Eden.

This valley or plain is often referred to by its Greek name, Esdraelon, but in the Bible it is called Jezreel. It is a triangle with its western point at a pass near modern Haifa on the Mediterranean, and the wider portion extends eastward about eighteen miles. On that front, the plain breaks up into "finger valleys" and these descend eastward down to the River Jordan.

---

[5] 2 Kings 6:26-29.
[6] Genesis, chapter 37.

Jezreel is famous for its many battles, both ancient and modern. For the most part, it has a flat valley floor, and this lends itself to the use of chariots during ancient times, as well as mechanical weapons in modern times. This favorable terrain has attracted military strategists in every age.

Overlooking the valley along the southern side of the plain is the famous fortress city of Meggido. This is where the great battle of Armageddon will begin in the not too distant future. Both ancient and modern scriptures describe that coming event in considerable detail.[7]

Jezebel and Ahab had their winter palace in this rich valley,[8] and the owner of a nearby vineyard was murdered so Ahab could seize his property.[9]

It was here that Elijah suddenly appeared after the great famine and ordered the lecherous priests of Jezebel and Ahab to meet him on nearby Mount Carmel. Only the 400 priests of King Ahab showed up, but they got to see fire coming down from heaven to consume Elijah's sacrifice. Then they were slain by the infuriated people who realized that these false priests had lured them into committing heinous crimes against God.[10]

It was also here that the wicked Jezebel was finally crushed to death under the wheels of Jehu's chariot and afterwards had her body torn to bits by famished dogs.[11]

As Jesus and his disciples came near the northern side of the valley, they were not far from Endor, where Saul had gone to see a witch just before his great last battle with the Philistines.

---

[7]W. Cleon Skousen, *Prophecy and Modern Times*, Salt Lake City: Deseret Book Company, 1979, pp. 87-91.
[8]1 Kings 21:1.
[9]1 Kings ch. 21.
[10]1 Kings, ch. 18.
[11]2 Kings 9:33:37.

The witch made contact with a familiar spirit who pretended to be the prophet Samuel. This familiar spirit had little difficulty predicting that Saul would lose the battle and be killed. Toward the end of the conflict, Saul tried to save his life by retreating to the nearby mountains of Gilboah, while his three sons tried to protect him by fighting a rear guard action. Before long, however, Saul saw that his three sons had been killed, and he therefore climbed up to a secluded spot and committed suicide by falling on his sword.[12]

On this north side of the valley there were two other famous sites. One was Mount Tabor, which is located at a place where the valley seems to push back the Galilean mountains several miles to the north. This puts Mount Tabor about six miles to the east of Nazareth.

Mount Tabor is where Deborah, the prophetess, induced Barak to challenge the Canaanites, who had put the Israelites under heavy tribute. The Canaanites sent Sisera and nine hundred iron chariots from Hazor to Mount Tabor to defeat the Israelites. However, when a heavy rain brought the mired chariots to a standstill, Sisera fled for his life. A woman named Jael invited Sisera into her husband's tent to rest. While he was asleep she drove a tent stake through his head. Later, Deborah sang a famous song of praise to the bravery of all those who brought about this great victory of the Israelites, and special mention was made of Jael.[13]

The other site of historic importance was the place where Gideon undertook to wage war against thousands of Midianites and Amalekites who raided Israel each year at harvest time, and seized their grain and wine. This battle is said to have taken place around the Hill Moreh which modern scholars identify with a mountain which is now called "Little Hermon." It is not far from Mount Tabor.

It was here that the Lord ordered Gideon to reduce his army of 32,000 to 300! The Lord then told Gideon to attack during the night by blowing trumpets and waving torches. In the darkness, the

---

[12]1 Samuel, chapters 28 and 31.
[13]Judges, chapters 4 and 5.

sleepy-eyed Midianites and Amalekites mistook one another for Israelites and slaughtered one another by the thousands. The remnant finally fled in terror back toward their own country.[14]

JESUS AND HIS DISCIPLES ENTER GALILEE

It is most likely that Jesus and his disciples would not have gone as far east as Mount Tabor and the Hill Moreh, but perhaps they could have seen them in the distance.

As they came down the pass from Dothan, their most direct route would have been to follow the road that led almost straight north across the valley and up into the mountains of Nazareth.

We learn that as the little band trudged along the mountain road, Jesus did not stop off at his home town. As they passed by Nazareth, he simply said:

"A prophet hath no honour in his own country."[15]

Then the scripture continues:

"So Jesus came again into Cana of Galilee, where he made the water wine."[16]

As nearly as we can tell, Jesus had decided to encourage his disciples to return to their homes while he went on to Cana where he had performed his first miracle and where his mother may have still been visiting. Meanwhile, the disciples who were Galileans could join their families and report the marvelous things they had witnessed during their absence the previous weeks.

It is clear that Jesus was welcomed as a distinguished Galilean luminary when it became known that he had returned. John says:

---

[14]Judges, chapter 7.
[15]John 4:44.
[16]John 4:46.

"When he was come into Galilee, the Galilaeans received him, having seen all the things that he did at Jerusalem at the feast: for they also went unto the feast."[17]

JESUS HEALS A NOBLEMAN'S SON

Because the word spread rapidly after people learned that Jesus was in the vicinity, he did not enjoy his rest at Cana for long. One man who eagerly sought after Jesus was a certain "nobleman" who belonged to the court of Herod Antipas, and made his home in Capernaum.[18] The scripture says:

"When he heard that Jesus was come out of Judaea into Galilee, he went unto him [in Cana], and besought him that he would come down, and heal his son: for he was at the point of death."[19]

But Jesus did not respond to every casual request for a healing. Special blessings of this sort were for the benefit of believers whose faith deserved to be rewarded. He was especially determined not to heal people just to satisfy the curiosity of sign-seekers. Jesus therefore spoke rather abruptly to the nobleman to test him and said:

"Except ye see signs and wonders, ye will not believe."[20]

The nobleman refused to argue about it. He simply said in pleading tones:

"Sir, come down ere my child die."[21]

Jesus was touched. Here indeed was genuine faith, and therefore Jesus sent a signal across the distance from Cana to Capernaum and spoke to the millions of intelligences in the dying body of the nobleman's son. Those intelligences heard the Master's voice and the healing process began. Jesus then said to the nobleman:

---

[17]John 4:45.
[18]Adam Clarke, *Bible Commentary*, New York: Phillips and Hunt, 1884, vol. 5, p. 328.
[19]John 4:47.
[20]John 4:48.
[21]John 4:40.

"Go thy way; thy son liveth.

"And the man believed the word that Jesus had spoken unto him, and he went his way.

The nobleman's manifest faith was soon rewarded as he approached Capernaum. John says:

"As he was now going down, his servants met him, and told him, saying, Thy son liveth.

"Then inquired he of them the hour when he began to amend. And they said unto him, Yesterday at the seventh hour the fever left him.

"So the father knew that it was at the same hour, in the which Jesus said unto him, Thy son liveth: and himself believed, and his whole house."[22]

John then closes this remarkable event with an editorial footnote. He says:

"This is again the second miracle that Jesus did, when he was come out of Judea into Galilee."[23]

Of course, Jesus had performed many healings in Jerusalem and Judea, so Bible scholars generally agree that John's intent was to say that this was the second miracle he had performed in Cana and he did it after coming out of Judea into Galilee.[24]

JESUS RETURNS TO NAZARETH

It is amazing how rapidly the report of a miraculous healing can travel. The news of the healing of the nobleman's son had already reached the Savior's hometown when he finally decided to visit Nazareth. No doubt the people were especially astonished when

[22]John 4:50-53.
[23]John 4:54.
[24]Adam Clarke, *Bible Commentary*, vol. 5:32.

they heard that Jesus could heal the son of the nobleman in Capernaum while he was still in Cana.

The record indicates that the local people in Nazareth were anxious to see some of that wonder-working talent of the carpenter's son put on a display for the home folks. The first chance they had to see him was at the local synagogue. The Bible says:

"And he came to Nazareth, where he had been brought up: and, as his custom was, he went into the synagogue on the sabbath day, and stood up for to read.

"And there was delivered unto him the book of the prophet Esaias. And when he had opened the book, he found the place where it was written,

"The Spirit of the Lord is upon me, because he hath anointed me to preach the gospel to the poor; he hath sent me to heal the brokenhearted, to preach deliverance to the captives, and recovering of sight to the blind, to set at liberty them that are bruised,

"To preach the acceptable year of the Lord.

"And he closed the book, and he gave it again to the minister, and sat down."[25]

Every person in that synagogue assembly knew that Jesus had just read the first-person account of what the Messiah said he would do when he came upon the earth. It was puzzling. What was the carpenter's son trying to tell them?

"And the eyes of all them that were in the synagogue were fastened on him.

"And he began to say unto them, This day is this scripture fulfilled in your ears."[26]

---

[25]Luke 4:16-20.
[26]Luke 4:20-21.

This was even more puzzling. They still could not quite grasp what was going on here.

"And all bare him witness, and wondered at the gracious words which proceeded out of his mouth. And they said, Is not this Joseph's son?"[27]

Now Jesus perceived what was going on in their minds. These people had grown up with Jesus. They had seen him in moments of distress, fatigue, and no doubt some minor illnesses. They may have even seen him wince with pain when a hammer hit a thumb instead of a nail. They had seen him undergo many of the same travails and temptations they had gone through themselves.

So why did Jesus read this Messianic scripture from Isaiah? Was he trying to tell his own people, right there in Nazareth, that he was something very special, very different? Jesus answered what was in their minds before they asked him:

"And he said unto them, Ye will surely say unto me this proverb, Physician, heal thyself: whatsoever we have heard done in Capernaum, do also here in thy country."[28]

This was a double-headed challenge. If he was so special and could heal other people, why had they seen him indisposed and going through the ordinary travails of life like common people?

Furthermore, laying that aside, how about a demonstration of what he could do to heal some of his former neighbors and friends, the way he had healed the nobleman's son in Capernaum?

Before responding to their challenge, Jesus expressed one of the great disappointments of both prophets and leaders who hope they will enjoy support from those who know them best. But it seldom works out that way, so Jesus said sadly:

---

[27]Luke 4:22.
[28]Luke 4:23.

"Verily I say unto you, No prophet is accepted in his own country."[29]

At that point Jesus began to cite some scriptures demonstrating that God decides who will be healed. Some he heals, some he doesn't. Healing is God's business. Therefore, it is not a matter of simply providing a healing every time someone demands it. The important point is whether or not it is the desire of God to heal a particular person at that time. Jesus reminded them that there were:

"Many lepers...in Israel in the time of Eliseus [Elisha] the prophet; and none of them was cleansed, saving Naaman the Syrian."[30]

That did it.

It seemed plain to the people in his own synagogue at Nazareth that he was citing all these scriptures just to give him an excuse for not performing any miracles for those who really knew him. It was becoming vividly plain that he was fooling a lot of the people, but he was not going to fool them.

The scripture says:

"And all they in the synagogue, when they heard these things, were filled with wrath,

"And rose up, and thrust him out of the city, and led him unto the brow of the hill whereon their city was built, that they might cast him down headlong."[31]

This is the first time Jesus had ever encountered actual violence. It is obvious that he was handled roughly, perhaps even brutally. The intent was to throw him over the cliff headfirst and kill him.

---

[29]Luke 4:24.
[30]Luke 4:27.
[31]Luke 4:28-29.

And all of this was because he wouldn't show them a miracle. What his would-be murderers didn't know was the fact that they were about to witness a miracle after all—a rather amazing miracle—so amazing that they wouldn't even know when it happened.

As we have previously seen, this miracle is called the veiling of the eyes. Jesus now did the same thing he had done at the temple during the Passover.[32] So there he was, poised on the edge of the cliff ready to be pushed off, when suddenly the scripture says:

"He passing through the midst of them went his way."[33]

What a gratifying thing it must have been to the angels in heaven to see the consternation of this murderous mob when they finally came to their senses and nobody could figure out where Jesus had gone. Who has him? Did he escape? That's impossible!

The answer was simple: They asked for a miracle. They got one.

JESUS GOES TO CAPERNAUM

It will be observed that while Jesus was in Cana and Nazareth, he was alone. However, when he arrived in Capernaum Jesus was ready to launch forth in a massive missionary effort, and he needed his disciples to help him. He started with some of those who had been with him from the beginning.

It must have been a surprise to his former missionary companions when Jesus suddenly appeared on the shore of Galilee with a great crowd of people following him. The scripture says:

"And it came to pass, that, as the people pressed upon him to hear the word of God, he stood by the lake of Gennesaret [the Sea of Galilee],

---

[32]John 2:23-24.
[33]Luke 4:16-30.

"And saw two ships standing by the lake: but the fishermen were gone out of them, and were washing their nets.

And he entered into one of the ships, which was Simon's [Peter's], and prayed him that he would thrust out a little from the land. And he sat down, and taught the people out of the ship."[34]

The problem with an enthusiastic crowd is getting them to stand back far enough so the teacher can talk to the whole group and not just to the few who bunch up around him. Pushing Peter's boat out a short distance from the shore was an ideal way to allow all of the people to hear him.

ANOTHER MIRACLE AT CAPERNAUM

"Now when he had left speaking, he said unto Simon, Launch out into the deep, and let down your nets for a draught.

"And Simon answering said unto him, Master, we have toiled all the night, [the usual time for fishing] and have taken nothing: nevertheless at thy word I will let down the net."[35]

It has been said that when reason and revelation conflict, always follow the revelation. This is what Peter did.

"And when they had this done, they inclosed a great multitude of fishes: and their net brake.

"And they beckoned unto their partners, which were in the other ship, that they should come and help them. And they came, and filled both the ships, so that they began to sink."[36]

Peter had been with Jesus long enough to recognize a miracle when he saw one. He fell to his knees and exclaimed:

"Depart from me; for I am a sinful man, O Lord.

---

[34]Luke 5:1-3.
[35]Luke 5:4-5.
[36]Luke 5:6-7.

"For he was astonished, and all that were with him, at the draught of the fishes which they had taken:

"And so was also James, and John, the sons of Zebedee, which were partners with Simon."[37]

Having made his point, Jesus said:

"Fear not; from henceforth thou shalt catch men.

"And when they had brought their ships to land, they forsook all, and followed him."[38]

With these staunch followers who would later become apostles, Jesus was ready to launch his ministry in Galilee.

*   *   *   *

TOPICS FOR REFLECTION AND DISCUSSION

1. What are some of the advantages which result from becoming famous? What are some of the disadvantages? In what way was Jesus subject to both?

2. Why has Bible history been so harsh in describing the lives of Ahab and Jezebel? What happened to Jezebel? Name four miraculous events in the life of Joseph who was sold into Egypt.

3. Would a witch be able to contact Samuel the prophet for Saul? Then whom did she contact? Describe the last hour of Saul's life. Why do you think God reduced Gideon's army from 32,000 to 300? Why would 32,000 have gotten in the way?

4. When Jesus returned to Galilee, what did he say about the people of Nazareth? Where did he go first? What did he apparently tell his disciples to do for the next little while?

---

[37]Luke 5:8-10.
[38]Luke 5:10-11.

5. What was the first miracle Jesus performed after returning to Galilee? Whom did he heal? How could this be done when Jesus was in Cana and the person being healed was in Capernaum? What did this healing of a Gentile do for the reputation of Jesus?

6. Where did Jesus first appear when he returned to Nazareth? What did he read to the people? What was significant about these passages? Did the people tell him of their suspicions or did he perceive it?

7. What made the people of Nazareth think Jesus was a false prophet? What would have been wrong with the performing of a miracle just to satisfy their curiosity? How can you explain the violent reaction of these people to their frustrations? How did Jesus save his life? Did he do the same thing on other occasions?

8. When Jesus showed up on the shores of the Sea of Galilee, was he alone? When he saw Peter, what was the first thing he asked him to do? Later what did he tell Peter to do? Was it reasonable? Then why did Peter do it? When there is a conflict between reason and revelation, which should prevail?

9. How impressive was the miracle which Jesus performed for Peter and his fellow fishermen? How would it be possible for a net to contain so many fish that it would cause a boat to begin sinking?

10. What was Peter's reaction to all of this? What did Jesus reply? Having acquired several stalwart helpers, what was Jesus now prepared to do?

*   *   *   *

CHAPTER 11

A FLOOD OF MIRACLES IN GALILEE

After Jesus had gathered about him his four fishermen, Peter, Andrew, James and John, he launched forth on one of the most spectacular demonstrations of the miraculous power of God since the days of Moses. It all began on a sabbath day at Capernaum on the northeast corner of the Galilee where Peter lived.[1] The scripture says:

"And they went into Capernaum; and straightway on the sabbath day he entered into the synagogue, and taught."[2]

The important message here is that he taught. When Jesus was twelve years old he taught, completely astonishing the most learned men at the temple.[3] Eighteen years later, he had a mission to teach ALL the people. And what he had to say was impressive. Luke says:

"And they were astonished at his doctrine: for he taught them as one that had authority, and not as the scribes."[4]

JESUS CASTS OUT A GROUP OF EVIL SPIRITS

At some point in the devotional exercises, Jesus went from preaching to practice. It was the result of a man in the congregation having some kind of seizure. Luke says:

"And there was in their synagogue a man with an unclean spirit; and he cried out...."[5]

---

[1]Matthew 8:14; Mark 1:29; Luke 4:38.
[2]Mark 1:21.
[3]Luke 2:47.
[4]Mark 1:22.
[5]Mark 1:23.

But it turned out that the man wasn't possessed by just one evil spirit. There was a host of them occupying his mortal tabernacle. This became apparent when these fallen angels of Satan used the afflicted man's voice to cry out:

"Let *us* alone; what have we to do with thee, thou Jesus of Nazareth? art thou come to destroy us? I know thee who thou art, the Holy One of God."[6]

Notice the admission that there are many evil spirits in this afflicted man. They said: "Let US alone; what have WE to do with thee."

Jesus addressed the one spirit who seemed to be the spokesman for the rest, and said:

"Hold thy peace, and come out of him."[7]

The unclean spirits recognized Jesus, and the knew they had to obey him, but before giving up the body they had invaded, these minions of Satan savagely wrenched the afflicted man and tossed him about. Mark says:

"And when the unclean spirit [note the singular, the one who seemed to be in charge] had torn him, and cried with a loud voice, he came out of him."[8]

The group of evil spirits seem to have followed their leader as Jesus ordered him to depart. As the afflicted man sank back in relief, the people in the synagogue were astonished. With their own ears they had heard Jesus speak directly to the evil spirits and confound them with a voice of authority which those spirits had felt compelled to obey. Among themselves, they whispered:

---

[6]Mark 1:24 (emphasis added).
[7]Mark 1:25.
[8]Mark 1:26.

"What thing is this? what new doctrine is this? for with authority commandeth he even the unclean spirits, and they do obey him."[9]

As the congregation of the synagogue dispersed to their homes, one can well imagine the sensational report they carried to their neighbors. The scripture tells us what happened after that:

"And immediately his fame spread abroad throughout all the region round about Galilee."[10]

JESUS HEALS THE MOTHER OF PETER'S WIFE

But this was not the only miracle Jesus performed that day. Luke says:

"He arose out of the synagogue, and entered into Simon's house. And Simon's wife's mother was taken with a great fever; and they besought him for her.

"And he stood over her, and rebuked the fever; and it left her: and immediately she arose and ministered unto them."[11]

Both of these healings occurred on the sabbath, and later on the jealous leaders of the Pharisees would raise a great furor over the Savior doing a "work" on the sabbath. However, on this occasion there was no challenge, but the prevalent teaching of the rabbis is reflected in the fact that others at the synagogue who had sick among them restrained themselves and did not approach Jesus for a healing blessing until the sabbath had ended at sunset. Once the sabbath was over, however, they descended on him in a multitude. Luke describes it as follows:

"Now when the sun was setting, all they that had any sick with divers diseases brought them unto him; and he laid his hands on *every one* of them, and healed them."[12]

---

[9]Mark 1:27.
[10]Mark 1:21-28.
[11]Luke 4:38-39.
[12]Luke 4:40 (emphasis added).

It was typical of Jesus to take the time to heal every individual who came for a blessing. We believe he had done this a few weeks earlier when he was healing the beggars at the temple. Apparently, not a single person who needed a blessing was neglected or left without one. Luke continues:

"And devils also came out of many, crying out, and saying, Thou art Christ the Son of God. And he rebuking them suffered them not to speak: for they knew that he was Christ."[13]

This is truly ironic. Here were the fallen angels of Satan bearing testimony that Jesus is the Christ. In all probability they remembered the great Jehovah from his resounding victory during the war in heaven.[14] There is nothing to indicate that they had lost their memories of the preexistence, and just as he had cast them out of heaven, so now he cast them out of afflicted bodies they had pirated here on earth.

HEALING WITH A WORD

Matthew emphasizes that Jesus healed those who were sick or physically afflicted simply "with his word."[15]

We have already discussed in chapter 7 the "key to miracles" as set forth in both ancient and modern scriptures. It is fascinating how the millions of intelligences associated with the particles of matter in our bodies will respond to the word of the Savior and restructure themselves to achieve the healing process when they are commanded to do so. Truly, here is one of the great secrets to God's omnipotent power.

The next verse indicates what a tremendous burden Jesus took upon himself as he set out to heal "every one" who came to him for a blessing. It appears that Jesus was giving these blessings and healings far into the night. When morning came, many were still

---

[13]Luke 4:40-41.
[14]Moses 4:3.
[15]Matthew 8:16.

lingering about, and when Jesus tried to retreat into the wilderness, they saw where he went and followed him. Mark says:

"And in the morning, rising up a great while before day, he went out, and departed into a solitary place, and there prayed."[16]

But not for long. Even though it was very early, the crowds were already beginning to assemble, no doubt bringing additional sick with them, and demanding that the disciples ask Jesus to come forth. Of course, when the followers of Jesus found he was not in his quarters, they knew he had gone to commune with his Father in prayer. Therefore, Mark says:

"Simon and they [the disciples] that were with him followed after him. And when they had found him, they said unto him, All men seek for thee."[17]

The Savior's reply verifies that those who had followed Simon Peter were the disciples rather than the crowd. He said to them:

"Let *us* go into the next towns, that I may preach there also: for therefore came I forth."[18]

This ministry was to the whole region, not just Capernaum. We get the impression from Luke that if the local people could have had their way they would have made Jesus the exclusive and permanent fixture of their own community. On this occasion, they apparently saw Jesus and his disciples leaving because it says:

"The people sought him, and came unto him, and stayed him, that he should not depart from them."[19]

---

[16]Mark 1:35.
[17]Mark 1:36-37.
[18]Mark 1:38.
[19]Luke 4:42.

Then Jesus told the people, as he had previously explained to his disciples, that he must continue his ministry to other communities. Luke quotes Jesus as saying to them:

"I must preach the kingdom of God to other cities also: for therefore am I sent."[20]

THE MINISTRY OF MIRACLES ATTRACTS CROWDS FROM ALL OVER THE COUNTRY

As Jesus began his circuit throughout Galilee, it is almost incomprehensible what he accomplished during the next few months. Matthew describes it as follows:

"And Jesus went about all Galilee, teaching in their synagogues, and preaching the gospel of the kingdom, and healing all manner of sickness and all manner of disease among the people *WHICH BELIEVED ON HIS NAME.*"[21]

It is interesting that in the Inspired Version the scripture indicates that Jesus did not go about performing miracles in a promiscuous manner. It was only those who "believed on his name," who received the blessing.

Now we learn how extensive this "ministry of miracles" turned out to be. Matthew says:

"And his fame went throughout all Syria [east of the Jordan River]: and they brought unto him all sick people that were taken with divers diseases and torments, and those which were possessed with devils, and those which were lunatick, and those that had the palsy; and he healed them."[22]

We pause to consider those who were "lunatick." In some cases it would appear that the evil spirits completely destroyed the free

---

[20]Luke 4:43.
[21]JST Matthew 4:23.
[22]Matthew 4:24.

agency of those they possessed so that their behavior became violent and irrational, and they appeared to be lunatics.

This tells us that once these dark spirits gain control of a body, they are completely incapable of functioning in a mortal tabernacle. The scripture says that some possessed persons cast themselves into the fire, cut themselves on sharp rocks, or fell into the water and were nearly drowned.[23]

Of course, it is not always possible to distinguish between those who are possessed and those who are suffering from a genuine mental illness. But, in either case, the afflicted person is entitled to a priesthood blessing. Where it is determined that an individual is suffering from a mental illness, the individual should be blessed and compassionately nursed back to health and strength like any other person who is ill.[24]

THE HEALING OF A LEPER

Once the people learned what Jesus was doing, it seemed that neither distance nor difficulty would prevent them from bringing their sick and afflicted to be healed. Matthew says:

"And there followed him great multitudes of people from Galilee, and from Decapolis [the ten Greek cities beyond the Jordan], and from Jerusalem, and from Judaea, and from beyond Jordan."[25]

As Jesus moved through Galilee blessing the sick and teaching his doctrine, the number of healings must have grown into thousands. The Gospel writers describe some of the more notable miracles to illustrate what was happening from day to day throughout this ministry. One involved the healing of a leper.

Leprosy was the most dreaded of all ancient diseases. One authority describes the disease as follows:

---

[23]Mark 9:22.
[24]Doctrine and Covenants 42:43.
[25]Matthew 4:25.

"Leprosy was nothing short of a living death, a corrupting of all the humors, a poisoning of the very springs of life; a dissolution, little by little, of the whole body, so that one limb after another actually decayed and fell away....The disease, moreover, was incurable by the art and skill of man....The leper, thus fearfully bearing about the body—the outward and visible tokens of sin in the soul—was treated throughout as a sinner, as one in whom sin had reached its climax."[26]

It was such a person as this who came before Jesus and worshipped him, saying: "If thou wilt, thou canst make me clean!"[27]

Mark says:

"And Jesus, moved with compassion, put forth his hand, and touched him, and saith unto him, I will; be thou clean.

"And as soon as he had spoken, immediately the leprosy departed from him, and he was cleansed."[28]

It is impossible to imagine the astonishment of those who witnessed this miracle. It was the most dramatic of all the miracles except raising the dead. Suddenly the scabs scaled away, the running sores were resuscitated, and the great areas of inflamed, decayed flesh became firm and healthy.

As it turned out, this was such a sensational demonstration of the Savior's healing power that it was bound to create a problem for him. Jesus knew that the moment word reached the nearby city that he could even heal lepers, he would be mobbed. And so he said to the man:

"See thou say nothing to any man: but go thy way, shew thyself to the priest, and offer for thy cleansing those things which Moses commanded, for a testimony unto them.

---

[26]Quoted by Talmage in *Jesus the Christ,* pp. 200-201.
[27]Matthew 8:2.
[28]Mark 1:41-42.

"But he went out, and began to publish it much, and to blaze abroad the matter, insomuch that Jesus could no more openly enter into the city, but was without in desert places: and they came to him from every quarter."[29]

Ordinarily, Jesus did not admonish those who were healed to keep it a secret, but in this instance it would have been helpful. However, it was too much to expect. The former leper spread the glorious news that Jesus had healed him, and Jesus was mobbed just as he had anticipated. The crowd swarmed in upon him until it was impossible for him to enter the city and find an orderly place where he could teach the people.[30]

Meanwhile, we observe that Jesus did not tell the leper to join some Christian community or go to a Christian bishop for friendship and comfort. The structuring of Christ's church did not take place until after his resurrection. Therefore, Jesus told the former leper to seek out the priest at his local synagogue and go through the cleansing ceremonies which were required of lepers according to the law of Moses.[31]

DID JESUS HAVE THE POWER TO FORGIVE SINS?

The next miracle which the Gospel writers felt was important was the healing of a man suffering from palsy. This was after Jesus had completed one circuit of his ministry requiring "many days,"[32] and now he was back in Capernaum. Once more the people thronged about him, bringing their sick and afflicted to be healed. Luke says one man was paralyzed with palsy and therefore some friends carried him to Jesus in a bed. However, the crowd was so packed in around the place where Jesus was staying that they couldn't get near him. Therefore Luke says:

[29]Mark 1:44-45.
[30]Ibid.
[31]Leviticus 14:1-57.
[32]JST Mark 2:1.

"They went upon the housetop, and let him down through the tiling with his couch into the midst before Jesus."[33]

The Savior was very impressed with the faith of the men who had taken such extreme measures to get the sick man into the room that Luke says:

"When he saw their faith, he said unto him, Man, thy sins are forgiven thee."[34]

In the Inspired Version or the Joseph Smith translation, we get a somewhat fuller text. It quotes Jesus as having said:

"Son, be of good cheer. Thy sins be forgiven thee; *go thy way and sin no more.*"[35]

As the sick man heard these words, there no doubt flashed into his memory those offenses that might have related directly to his affliction, or the Savior might have been referring to his sins in general. In any event, the man was instantly healed and Jesus wanted him to show his appreciation by forsaking his sins—whatever they may have been—and purifying his life.

But there was something Jesus had said as he healed this man that created a sudden consternation of righteous indignation among the learned scribes who were watching. They began mumbling among themselves and decided that, although it was acceptable for Jesus to heal, it was blasphemy for him to pretend he could forgive sins. However, before they could accuse him, Jesus read what was in their hearts, and said:

"Wherefore is it that ye think evil in your hearts?

"For whether is it not easier to say, Thy sins be forgiven thee, than to say, Arise, and walk?

---

[33]Luke 5:19.
[34]Luke 5:20.
[35]JST Matthew 9:2 (emphasis added).

"But I said this that ye may know that the Son of man hath power on earth to forgive sins."[36]

Then Jesus turned to the sick man to demonstrate that he not only had the power to forgive sins, but also the power to heal the consequences of sin if the individual had sufficient faith and repentance to warrant it. In this case, he said to the man:

"Arise, take up thy bed, and go unto thy house.

"And he immediately arose and departed to his house."[37]

Matthew did not want to leave any doubt as to the impact which this miracle had upon the multitude as they saw this man, who had been helplessly paralyzed, walking out before them and carrying his couch or mattress with him. Matthew says:

"When the multitudes saw it, they marvelled, and glorified God, which had given such power unto men."[38]

JESUS RECRUITS A TAX COLLECTOR

Shortly after this miracle, Jesus was being surrounded by such crowds that Mark says he decided to go to the seashore.[39] It was his custom to get in a small boat and push out from shore a few yards so he could teach the whole crowd and not just a few clustered around him. On this occasion, Mark says that he "taught" the multitude, but he does not indicate what Jesus said.[40]

Afterwards, Jesus and his disciples were continuing on their way when suddenly Jesus encountered one of those who had been foreordained to be one of the special witnesses. Luke says:

---

[36]JST Matthew 9:4-6.
[37]JST Matthew 9:7-8.
[38]JST Matthew 9:9.
[39]Mark 2:13.
[40]Ibid.

"He went forth, and saw a publican, named Levi, sitting at the receipt of custom: and he said unto him, Follow me.

"And he left all, rose up, and followed him."[41]

From this passage we learn that the new disciple was a "publican," or a tax collector. Mark and Luke called him "Levi," but in Matthew's gospel narration, he refers to this disciple as "Matthew." Since Matthew was speaking of himself, we assume that this is the name he preferred, and even Mark and Luke subsequently refer to this disciple as "Matthew."[42]

Levi or Matthew felt so honored to be called into the service of the Savior that he prepared a great feast for Jesus and his disciples. Understandably, he invited to this feast his friends and professional colleagues who were also publicans, or tax collectors. It is clear from the scriptures that public officials of this profession were looked upon as "sinners," and no doubt many of them were. In fact, when some of them came to John the Baptist to be baptized, he commanded them, saying, "Exact no more than that which is appointed you."[43]

As Jesus and his disciples came to the feast, the scribes and Pharisees felt the Savior and his followers were contaminating themselves. Luke says:

"[They] murmured against his disciples, saying, Why do ye eat and drink with publicans and sinners?"[44]

How Jesus handled this complaint is very interesting. He neatly disposed of the whole issue by saying simply that it was part of his mission to mingle with sinners and the spiritually ill so he could call them to repentance. Luke says:

---

[41]Luke 5:27-28.
[42]Mark 3:18; Luke 6:15.
[43]Luke 3:13.
[44]Luke 5:30.

"And Jesus answering said unto them, They that are whole need not a physician; but they that are sick.

"I came not to call the righteous, but sinners to repentance."[45]

Of course, the self-righteous Pharisees immediately identified themselves as those who needed no physician, so they missed the point that Jesus was calling all sinners to repentance, including the Pharisees.

But Jesus let it go at that. After all, he and his disciples were guests at a feast, and since his brief answer seemed to have pacified the critics, he knew he could deal with the wickedness of the Pharisees at a later date.

HOW VALID IS A PHARISEE BAPTISM?

Everywhere he went, Jesus preached that the people must repent and be baptized in order to enter the kingdom of God. This offended many of those who had already been circumcised and had gone through the traditional ritual baths so as to receive an "ablution," and overcome any stigma of being "unclean."[46] They therefore said to Jesus:

"Why will ye not receive us with our baptism, seeing we keep the whole law?

"But Jesus said unto them, Ye keep not the law. If ye had kept the law, ye would have received me, for I am he who gave the law.

"I receive not you with your baptism, because it profiteth you nothing.

"For when *that which is new* is come, the old is ready to be put away."[47]

---

[45]Luke 5:27-32.
[46]Isaiah 1:16.
[47]JST Matthew 9:18-21 (emphasis added).

To reform Judaism was not the purpose of the Savior. Its fabric was too weak and its doctrines apostate. The fresh new gospel principles would not wear well with it. The Savior's new kingdom must have a new structure, new ordinances and a new covenant. As Jesus explained it:

"No man putteth a piece of new cloth unto an old garment, for that which is put in to fill it up taketh from the garment, and the rent is made worse.

"Neither do men put new wine into old bottles: else the bottles break, and the wine runneth out, and the bottles perish: but they put new wine into new bottles, and both are preserved."[48]

He taught the same principles when he later appeared as a resurrected being among the Nephites. Even those who had been baptized under the law of Moses had to be baptized again in order to receive "the new covenant" and enter the church of Jesus Christ.[49]

The baptism required by Jesus supersedes all other baptisms. As we mentioned earlier, when the gospel was restored in our own day there were some who wanted to join the church but felt their baptisms by the clergy of a previous church should suffice. To these the Savior said:

"Behold, I say unto you that all old covenants have I caused to be done away in this thing; and this is a new and an everlasting covenant, even that which was from the beginning.

"Wherefore, although a man should be baptized an hundred times it availeth him nothing, for you cannot enter in at the strait gate by the law of Moses, neither by your dead works.

---

[48]Matthew 9:16-17.
[49]3 Nephi 19:11-12.

"For it is because of your dead works that I have caused this last covenant and this church to be built up unto me, even as in days of old.

"Wherefore, enter ye in at the gate, as I have commanded, and seek not to counsel your God."[50]

FULFILLING ISAIAH'S GREAT PROPHECY

The Savior's "ministry of miracles" in Galilee began the fulfillment of a famous prophecy by Isaiah. In the same chapter where he said: "Unto us a child is born, unto us a son is given," Isaiah prophesied that the great mission of the Messiah would be centered in Galilee. Speaking of the land of Zebulun and Naphtali, he said:

"The people that walked in darkness have seen a great light: they that dwell in the land of the shadow of death, upon them hath the light shined."[51]

Around 721 B.C., when the Assyrians came down to conquer the northern ten tribes of Israel, Galilee was virtually devastated. In a literal sense, the shadow of death was on this region for two or three years. It continued until the remnant, consisting of a few thousand survivors, was carried off to Assyria.[52]

Nevertheless, Isaiah had looked down the future corridor of time and beheld that this same territory would become radiant with the light of the gospel as Jesus made it the major center of his ministry in the meridian of time.

When Jesus performed his great ministry of miracles, most of the Galileans did not realize that one of Isaiah's most famous prophecies concerning the Messiah was being literally fulfilled in their day.

---

[50]D&C: Section 22:1-4.
[51]Isaiah 9:1-2.
[52]Skousen, *The Fourth Thousand Years*, pp. 497-499.

ANOTHER MIRACLE IN JERUSALEM

Before long it was time to return to Jerusalem for another feast. It is generally presumed that this was the Feast of the Passover, but it could have been one of the other special feast days.

In any event, Jesus came quietly and unannounced into the sacred precincts of the temple area. At the sheep market there was a pool where the sheep were washed for the sacrifices. It was apparently a mineral spring with curative properties called the Pool of Bethesda. A rather large building with five porches had been constructed nearby and underground pressure made the water bubble up at certain intervals.

There was a tradition that the first person in the pool after the water was "troubled" would be cured. Therefore, the handicapped and sick sat around, hoping to be first. Now we come to one of the most interesting and instructive stories in the Bible. It says:

"And a certain man was there, which had an infirmity thirty and eight years.

"When Jesus saw him lie, and knew that he had been now a long time in that case, he saith unto him, Wilt thou be made whole?

"The impotent man answered him, Sir, I have no man, when the water is troubled, to put me into the pool: but while I am coming, another steppeth down before me.

"Jesus saith unto him, Rise, take up thy bed, and walk.

"And immediately the man was made whole, and took up his bed, and walked: and on the same day was the sabbath.

"The Jews therefore said unto him that was cured, It is the sabbath day: it is not lawful for thee to carry thy bed."[53]

---

[53]John 5:5-10.

Notice that they ignored the exciting news that this man had been cured after 38 years of impotent helplessness. They were obsessed with the possibility that this man had committed a technical violation of one of the trivial laws which the Pharisees themselves had contrived as ironclad rules for keeping the sabbath day holy. When they accused the former cripple, he said:

"He that made me whole, the same said unto me, Take up thy bed, and walk.

"Then asked they him, What man is that which said unto thee, Take up thy bed, and walk?

"And he that was healed wist not who it was: for Jesus had conveyed himself away, a multitude being in that place.

"Afterward Jesus findeth him in the temple, and said unto him, Behold, thou art made whole: sin no more, lest a worse thing come unto thee.

"The man departed, and told the Jews that it was Jesus, which had made him whole.

"And therefore did the Jews persecute Jesus, and sought to slay him, because he had done these things on the sabbath day."[54]

This whole scenario is so ugly and evil it is virtually incomprehensible. No wonder the Lord revealed to his prophets centuries earlier that no people on earth were as wicked as the chief priests who conspired to kill Christ even after he had demonstrated so openly and conclusively the miraculous power of God that was within him.[55]

Now Jesus wanted to get something else on the record. It was as though he wanted to say: "If you are offended because I healed a cripple on the sabbath day, then hear this!"

---

[54]John 5:11-16.
[55]2 Nephi 10:3-6.

JESUS TELLS THEM GOD IS HIS FATHER

"But Jesus answered them, *MY* Father worketh hitherto, and I work.

"Therefore the Jews sought the more to kill him, because he not only had broken the sabbath, but said also that God was his Father, making himself equal with God."[56]

For most of the fifth chapter of John, Jesus bears testimony of himself and pronounces a stinging indictment against the wicked men who stood before him.

1. Jesus said he only does what he has seen his Father do (verse 19).

2. The Father loves the Son and they will see Jesus do even greater things than he has done already (verse 20).

3. He said that as the Father can raise the dead, so can the Son raise the dead (verse 21).

4. In fact, the Father has given all judgment into the hands of the Son (verse 22).

5. Therefore if they do not honor the Son, then they are dishonoring the Father who sent him (verse 23).

6. He said that when John came bearing witness that Jesus was the Son of God and the promised Messiah, they rejoiced in the expectation of his coming (verse 33-35).

7. However, now that John's promise was fulfilled and the Son had actually come, they "believe it not" (verse 38).

---

[56]John 5:17-18 (emphasis added).

8. Jesus said the greatest witness of all concerning his divinity was the miraculous powers that they had seen manifested in him (verse 36).

9. Had they studied the words of the prophets they would have recognized that Jesus was the one they prophesied about. He said, "they are they which testify of me" (verse 39).

10. Then Jesus concluded by pronouncing a solemn judgment as to the reason they would not accept what he had told them. He said it was because "ye have not the love of God in you" (verse 42).

So, having left this motley crowd of wicked Israelites with a testimony and a rebuke, Jesus returned to Galilee.

JESUS HEALS A MAN WITH A WITHERED HAND

Shortly after he returned to Galilee, Jesus went into a synagogue on the sabbath day and healed the withered hand of a man just as he had healed the crippled man at the Pool of Bethesda in Jerusalem. There was an immediate uproar. The scripture says:

"And the Pharisees went forth, and straightway took counsel with the Herodians against him, how they might destroy him."[57]

And all of this because he had healed a man on the sabbath day!

By this time, Jesus was coming to the conclusion of this phase of his ministry in Galilee. It would appear to have taken many months, perhaps even more than a year.

Now he was ready to call his twelve apostles.

* * * *

TOPICS FOR REFLECTION AND DISCUSSION

1. Why do you think Jesus performed so many of his miracles in the various synagogues? Why do you think the evil spirit in the man at

---

[57]Mark 3:6.

the synagogue in Capernaum referred to himself as "us," yet Jesus gave the command to "him"?

2. When an evil spirit uses the voice of his victim to talk, what does this tell us about the free agency of the man who is possessed? Does an evil spirit know how to function in a mortal tabernacle? Do we have any evidence of this?

3. In one place it says Jesus healed people by laying "his hands on every one of them," and in another place it says he healed them "by his word." Are both correct? How did Jesus heal "by his word"?

4. Did people have "to believe on him" as the Messiah before he healed them?

5. Did Jesus have the power to forgive sins? Could he heal an affliction which was the result of sin?

6. Are some people victims of "guilt by association"? Was this true of Matthew? In what way? Was it also true of Jesus? Do you know some other people who are exceptionally good people but have been victims of this type of social injustice?

7. Why were the Nephites who were baptized into the church under the law of Moses required to be baptized again in order to be members of the church of Jesus Christ?

8. Many churches accept the baptisms of other churches. Does the Lord accept the baptisms of churches other than his own?

9. What kind of people rejected the miracles of Jesus when he performed them on the sabbath? What did Jacob say about them? (2 Nephi 10:3-4)

10. Into whose hands has the Father given all judgment? How do you account for the fact that the wicked rejoiced in the message of John but still rejected Jesus when he appeared on the scene? What did Jesus say his critics lacked?

*   *   *   *

CHAPTER 12

WHO WERE THE TWELVE APOSTLES ORDAINED BY JESUS?

Matthew tells us that after Jesus had completed what we have called his Galilean "ministry of miracles," he attempted to return home. But huge crowds followed him. According to the Gospel writers, he was virtually mobbed by these crowds. As we have already indicated, Matthew says:

"And there followed him great multitudes of people from Galilee, and from Decapolis, and from Jerusalem, and from Judaea, and from beyond Jordan."[1]

Mark gives us a similar picture. He says:

"Jesus withdrew himself with his disciples to the sea: and a great multitude from Galilee followed him, and from Judaea, And from Jerusalem, and from Idumea, and from beyond Jordan; and they about Tyre and Sidon, a great multitude, when they had heard what great things he did, came unto him....

"For he had healed many; insomuch that they pressed upon him for to touch him, as many as had plagues."[2]

JESUS PREPARES TO ORGANIZE THE TWELVE

The Savior had now reached a point in his ministry where he needed to ask the Father to help him do three important things:

---

[1]Matthew 4:25.
[2]Mark 3:7-10.

First, he must select from among the body of his disciples those who were foreordained to serve as the first Quorum of Twelve apostles.

Second, these must be ordained to their high callings as apostles. For some of them, this calling would eventually lead to their martyrdom.

Third, the apostles must be taught the rules for the perfecting of the Christian way of life. These are set forth in the famous "Sermon on the Mount," the greatest sermon ever recorded.

Of course, by this time, Jesus had surrounded himself with hundreds of followers, perhaps even thousands. And from all of these he must select twelve to be his apostles.

It is interesting that before he made his final selection he completely separated himself from both his disciples and the crowds. Luke says:

"He went out into a mountain to pray, and continued all night in prayer to God.

"And when it was day, he called unto him his disciples: and of them he chose twelve...."[3]

Mark says he not only selected them at this time but he also "ordained" them.[4] As Jesus would later say:

"Ye have not chosen me, but I have chosen you, and ordained you."[5]

Of course, they had been ordained to the priesthood earlier so they could assist the Savior in baptizing the many new converts,[6] but

---

[3]Luke 6:;12-13.
[4]Mark 3:14.
[5]John 15:16.
[6]JST John 4:3, compare with KJT John 4:2.

now they were ordained to the high and holy calling of apostles, which means "special witnesses."[7]

The place where all of this took place is not positively known, but tourists visiting the Holy Land are shown a hill which could very well have been the place. Today, it is called "The Mount of Beatitudes." It is on the northwestern coast of the Sea of Galilee, not far from Capernaum. This hill or mount has a beautiful view of the nearby sea, and a Catholic convent maintains a quiet garden of trees and flowers where it is believed the Savior met with the twelve.

Mark lists the names of the twelve who were ordained at this time, as follows:

"And Simon he surnamed Peter; And James the son of Zebedee, and John the brother of James; and he surnamed them Boanerges, which is, The sons of thunder: And Andrew, and Philip, and Bartholomew, and Matthew, and Thomas, and James the son of Alphaeus, and Thaddaeus, and Simon the Canaanite, And Judas Iscariot, which also betrayed him."[8]

In this chapter we hope to get better acquainted with the Savior's first Quorum of the Twelve. We know more about Peter than any of the rest, so we will begin with him.

THE APOSTLE WHO IS SAID TO HAVE BEEN CRUCIFIED

Simon was the name of the apostle who headed the list. It is interesting that the first time Jesus met him, the Savior gave him the Aramaic name of Cephas, or Petra in Greek. This term means a "rock," and because the Greek form of Petra became popular, we refer to this apostle as "Peter." Sometimes the Gospel writers refer to him by both his given name and the new name given to him by Jesus. Hence, we read in some passages: "Simon Peter."[9]

---

[7]Doctrine and Covenants, 107:23.
[8]Mark 3:16-19.
[9]Matthew 16:16; Luke 5:8; John 6:68.

Peter had a brother named Andrew, who was also ordained as an apostle. These two brothers were the sons of Jonas,[10] and they followed the family tradition of making a living as fishermen. Their partners in the fishing business were James and John, the sons of Zebedee, and the four seemed to have prospered since they owned their own boats and hired others to help them.

Peter's early life was spent in the place of his birth, called Bethsaida, on the northern coast of the Sea of Galilee.[11] However, by the time Jesus called him to become a "fisher of men," Peter and his family were living in another nearby fishing village called Capernaum. There he apparently had his own home, where he lived with his wife and his wife's mother.[12]

In the beginning, Peter and his brother, Andrew, had responded to the call of John the Baptist, and they went down to the Jordan River to be baptized. It was while they were there that Andrew heard the Baptist call Jesus "the Lamb of God." Andrew ran immediately to find Peter and said, "We have found the Messiah." Both of them thereupon became disciples of Jesus, and went with him to the wedding in Cana.[13]

A little later on, they returned to their fishing enterprises, where they were when Jesus came and gave them their official call. He said they were to become fishers of men. At the same time, Jesus called James and John.[14]

As the Savior's group of disciples gradually increased, Peter, James and John noticed that they were selected from among the disciples to be present on special occasions. For example, they were the only disciples allowed to see the daughter of Jairus raised from the dead.[15]

---

[10]John 1:42.
[11]John 1:44; 12:21.
[12]Matthew 8:14; Mark 1:29; Luke 4:38.
[13]John 1:36-42; 2:1-2.
[14]Luke 5:1-10.
[15]Luke 8:51; Mark 5:37.

A little later on, they were selected to go up to the Mount of Transfiguration with the Savior.[16]

Like most faithful Jews of that period, Peter was raised and schooled as a Pharisee. However, when the council of rulers in Jerusalem called Peter and his associates "unlearned and ignorant men," they simply meant they had not received formal training in the schools of the rabbis. What amazed the council was that these unschooled fishermen could have such wisdom as well as the power to heal a crippled beggar at the temple.[17]

As mentioned above, Simon Peter was a married man before he was called to the ministry, and he and his partners had been successful in the fishing business. When Peter said he had "left all" to follow the Savior, the substantial extent of his personal sacrifices could not be denied.[18]

Little did this humble Galilean fisherman realize that someday he would be the president of the Savior's church.[19] He would be the one to introduce the stewardship principles and lay the foundation for a Zion society.[20] He became one of the greatest missionaries of all time. One sermon converted 3,000 in a single day,[21] and another sermon converted 5,000.[22] Although arrested, he sometimes had ministering angels to help him escape.[23] He healed the sick,[24] and raised the dead.[25]

It was Peter who introduced the gospel to the gentiles by baptizing a Roman commander and a great number of his friends. Later, he and Paul took the gospel to Rome.[26]

---

[16]Luke 9:28; Mark 9:2; Mark 5:37.
[17]Acts 3:10.
[18]Mark 10:28.
[19]Acts 1:15.
[20]Acts 2:44-45.
[21]Acts 2:41.
[22]Acts 4:4.
[23]Acts 12:6-7.
[24]Acts 5:15.
[25]Acts 9:36-41.
[26]1 Peter 5:13.

In the end, Peter was crucified. This is verified by Tertullion, an early Christian historian. Another famous Christian writer, named Origen, states that, in deference to the crucifixion of Christ, Peter asked to be crucified with his head downwards.[27]

THE APOSTLE WHO WAS BEHEADED BY HEROD AGRIPPA

We now come to the first counsellor in the presidency of the apostolic church of Jesus Christ. He was James, who was a partner in the fishing business along with John, Peter and Andrew. The name "James" is the English translation for the Hebrew name "Jacob."[28]

Right after the Savior called Peter and Andrew to leave their fishing business and become his disciples, he saw their partners James and John mending their nets nearby, and asked them to follow him also. Matthew says they left their ships and fishing gear with their father, and immediately followed Jesus.[29]

Mark tells us that James and John were sometimes called "Boanerges" (Bow-an-ER-gees) which means "Sons of Thunder." This is believed by most authorities to refer to the fact that when Jesus was resisted by some hostile Samaritans, James and John wanted Jesus to assert his divine power immediately and call down fire from heaven to consume them.[30]

It is interesting that when the apostles were being led up to Jerusalem for the last time, they heard Jesus speak of the kingdom he was going to set up. James and John,[31] or the mother of James and John,[32] asked that as soon as Jesus established his kingdom, he assign them to sit on his right hand and on his left. The Savior side-stepped the question and said that was something the Father would decide.

---

[27]Encyclopedia Britannica, Scholars edition [11th] under "Peter."
[28]Peloubet's *Bible Dictionary*, under "James."
[29]Matthew 4:21-22.
[30]Luke 9:54.
[31]Mark 10:41.
[32]Matthew 20:20.

It is interesting that many commentaries suggest that the two brothers were talking about the kingdom of God in heaven, but we now know they were talking about the earthly kingdom that they were expecting Jesus to set up in the immediate future.

Matthew comments on this incident, and says:

"And when the ten heard it, they were moved with indignation against the two brethren. But Jesus called unto them and said....whosoever will be great among you, let him be your minister; And whosoever will be chief among you, let him be your servant."[33]

As a rule, we do not read of James doing things alone. He is nearly always mentioned in association with Peter and John. As indicated earlier, he was with Peter and John when Jesus raised the daughter of Jairus,[34] and was chosen along with Peter and John to accompany Jesus up into the Mount of Transfiguration.[35]

As Jesus completed his ministry and began talking about the destruction of Jerusalem, it was James, along with Peter, John and Andrew, who came to Jesus "privately," and asked: "When shall these things be?" As a result, we received the great sermon in Matthew, chapter 24, in which Jesus prophetically describes the highlights of the next two thousand years.

James was also invited by Jesus to accompany Peter and John into the olive vineyard to stand watch while the Savior went to plead with the Father to remove the cup of the crucifixion from him.[36]

Unfortunately, all three missed most of what happened because they fell asleep and had to be roused by Jesus between each of the Savior's prayers.[37]

---

[33]Matthew 20:24-27.
[34]Mark 5:37; Luke 8:51.
[35]Matthew 17:1; Mark 9:2; Luke 9:28.
[36]Mark 14:33-36.
[37]Mark 14:36-40.

By this time the scripture says the apostles had begun to doubt that he was the Messiah because of the weakness and sorrow he was exhibiting,[38] and when Jesus allowed himself to be crucified without setting up the great kingdom which Daniel had predicted,[39] they felt certain the Savior had misled them.

Like all of the other apostles, James had never understood the Savior's statement that he would rise the third day,[40] and therefore he was truly amazed—and even frightened—when the resurrected Jesus suddenly stood in their midst.[41]

James was on the Mount of Olives at the time of the Ascension[42], and was in the conference that selected Matthias to replace Judas Iscariot.[43] At that time he, and all the rest of the apostles were residing together in a house with an "upper room,"[44] which appears to be the rather sumptuous residence of the parents of Mark.[45]

On the Day of Pentecost he witnessed the miraculous powers that were so spectacular that it attracted a huge crowd. He was also present when Peter's sermon converted 3,000 in a single day.[46] A little later he was present when a second missionary sermon by Peter converted 5,000.[47]

The greatest enemy of James turned out to be Herod Agrippa. Herod Agrippa was part Jew and part Edomite or Arabian. His father and mother had both been murdered by his grandfather, Herod the Great, because of jealousy. Nevertheless, when Claudius became the

---

[38]JST Mark 14:36.
[39]Daniel 2:44.
[40]John 20:9.
[41]Luke 24:36-40.
[42]Luke 24:48-53.
[43]Acts 1:22-26.
[44]Acts 1:13.
[45]Acts 12:12-13; Edersheim, *The Life and Times of Jesus*, vol. 2, p. 485.
[46]Acts 2:41.
[47]Acts 4:4.

emperor of Rome in 41 A.D. he made Herod Agrippa the ruler of the entire region.

To curry favor with the Jewish rulers, Herod Agrippa launched a persecution of the Christians, and initiated this campaign of terrorism by having James beheaded with a sword.[48]

Peter was also captured but an angel rescued him, and Herod ordered the jailers put to death for allowing him to escape.[49] Shortly after that, Herod was struck down by the Lord with a loathsome disease and the scripture says:

"He was eaten of worms, and gave up the ghost."[50]

THE ONLY APOSTLE WHO NEVER DIED

Everything we have said about James applies to his younger brother, John—except, of course, for the execution of James by Herod Agrippa.

John had an exceptionally close and affectionate relationship with the Savior which earned him the title of "John the Beloved."[51]

This is demonstrated in the following incident:

"Now there was leaning on Jesus' bosom one of his disciples, whom Jesus loved. Simon Peter therefore beckoned to him, that he should ask who it should be of whom he spake.

"He then lying on Jesus' breast saith unto him, Lord, who is it? Jesus answered, He it is, to whom I shall give a sop, when I have dipped it. And when he had dipped the sop, he gave it to Judas Iscariot, the son of Simon."[52]

---

[48]Acts 12:2.
[49]Acts 12:19.
[50]Acts 12:23.
[51]John 13:23; 19:26; 20:2; 21:7, 20.
[52]John 13:23-26.

Some time before the Ascension, John was granted a remarkable dispensation by the Savior which greatly troubled Peter. It all came about when John said to the Savior:

"Lord, give unto me power over death, that I may live and bring souls unto thee."[53]

Peter wanted this spelled out in a little more detail, and so he said to Jesus:

"Lord, and what shall this man do?

"Jesus saith unto him, If I will that he tarry till I come, what is that to thee? follow thou me."[54]

In John's gospel, we have the following:

"Then went this saying abroad among the brethren, that disciples should not die; yet Jesus said *not* unto him, He shall not die; but, If I will that he tarry till I come, what is that to thee."[55]

We get a much deeper insight into John's status from then until now when we discover that three of the Savior's disciples in America made the same request as John.

From the book of 3 Nephi we learn that John and all individuals who are translated—such as the people of Enoch, the three Nephites, and the people of Salem under Melchizedek—must go through the "death" process before they are resurrected. However, it is done in the "twinkling of an eye." As Jesus said to the three Nephites who had made the same request as John:

"Ye shall never taste of death; but ye shall live to behold all the doings of the Father unto the children of men, even until all things

---

[53]Doctrine and Covenants 7:2.
[54]John 21:21-22.
[55]John 21:23.

shall be fulfilled according to the will of the Father, when I shall come in my glory with the powers of heaven.

"And ye shall never endure the pains of death; but when I shall come in my glory ye shall be changed in the twinkling of an eye from mortality to immortality; and then shall ye be blessed in the kingdom of my Father.

"And again, ye shall not have pain while ye shall dwell in the flesh, neither sorrow save it be for the sins of the world; and all this will I do because of the thing which ye have desired of me, for ye have desired that ye might bring the souls of men unto me, while the world shall stand."[56]

So John is still ministering to the children of men in his own special way, and preparing them to receive the fullness of the gospel of Christ. We have a statement from one of God's modern servants that individuals such as John, and other translated beings, do not live on the earth, even though they minister to its inhabitants from time to time. The place where they reside is a much more pleasant place than our earth. Concerning the residence of translated beings, we read:

"Many have supposed that the doctrine of translation was a doctrine whereby men were taken immediately into the presence of God, and into an eternal fullness, but this is a mistaken idea. Their place of habitation is that of the terrestrial order, and a place prepared for such characters He held in reserve to be ministering angels unto many planets, and who as yet have not entered into so great a fullness as those who are resurrected from the dead."[57]

Since John, like the Three Nephites, was promised that he would not go through the death process until the Lord comes in glory, we are led to conclude that this has not yet happened. He is the one apostle who, as yet, has never died.

---

[56] 3 Nephi 28:7-9.
[57] *Teachings of the Prophet Joseph Smith*, p. 170.

ANDREW, PETER'S PATIENT BROTHER

The known facts about Andrew, the brother of Peter, are remarkable in a number of ways.

To begin with, he started out as a disciple of John the Baptist, but was the first of all the disciples to gain a testimony of Jesus when John pointed out the Savior to him. He immediately sought out his brother, Peter, and exclaimed:

"We have found the Messias, which is, being interpreted, the Christ [the anointed one]. And he brought him to Jesus."[58]

Originally, both Andrew and Peter were from the fishing village of Bethsaida,[59] but by the time Jesus called them to the ministry, they were living in an adjoining fishing village called Capernaum. We learn that the families of both Peter and Andrew occupied the same house, and it was in this joint dwelling that Jesus healed Peter's mother-in-law on the Sabbath day.[60]

At the time Jesus fed the five thousand, he asked:

"Whence shall we buy bread that these may eat?...One of his disciples, Andrew, Simon Peter's brother, saith unto him, There is a lad here, which hath five barley loaves, and two small fishes: but what are they among so many?"[61]

It will be recalled that Jesus blessed this humble meal and had it distributed among the five thousand men plus all the women and children. When they had eaten, they gathered up twelve baskets that were not consumed. What an astonishing experience that was for Andrew and the rest of the Savior's disciples.

---

[58]John 1:41-42.
[59]John 144.
[60]Mark 1:29.
[61]John 6:5-9.

We should also mention that Andrew seems to have been closely associated with the three men who were already being selected for special experiences by the Savior. For example, when Jesus had finished his ministry and told his disciples that Jerusalem would soon be destroyed, it was Andrew who went "privately" with Peter, James and John to ask the Savior,

"When shall these things be?"[62]

As we mentioned earlier, it was this inquiry that produced the Savior's discourse covering more than 2,000 years of prophetic history and which is recorded in Matthew, chapter 24.

One final note concerning Andrew. Even though he was a business partner with Peter, James and John, he is never mentioned as complaining when the other three were selected to accompany the Savior on special occasions such as the raising of the daughter of Jairus, the revelations on the Mount of Transfiguration, or the special guard duty at the Garden of Gethsemane. He seems to have been perfectly and humbly satisfied with whatever role the Savior assigned to him.

PHILIP

Now we come to the remainder of the Quorum of the Twelve. Most of these are mentioned only briefly, but we will relate what few facts the scriptures disclose, beginning with Philip.

We know that Philip was from Bethsaida, the original home town of Peter and Andrew.[63]

We also know that the day after Jesus made contact with Andrew and Peter, he came across Philip as the Savior was traveling from the site of his baptism toward Galilee.[64] This conclusion is based on the

---

[62]Matthew 24:3.
[63]John 1:44.
[64]John 1:43-44.

fact that Jesus had gone all the way up to Cana by the next day,[65] and so we assume he came across Philip along the way.

We also learn that it was Philip who is credited with having found another future apostle named Nathanael—who is associated with Philip in other scriptures under the name of Bartholomew.[66]

Philip was present at the feeding of the five thousand.[67] And after the Savior cleansed the temple during the last week of his life, when certain Greek converts wanted to see Jesus, they first approached Philip who took Andrew with him to tell Jesus of their request.[68]

Later, at the Last Supper, it was Philip who was bold enough to say to the Savior: "Lord, show us the Father and it sufficeth us."[69] The Savior's response to that question occupies thirteen verses!

NATHANAEL OR BARTHOLOMEW

The story of Nathanael begins with the following verses:

"Philip findeth Nathanael, and saith unto him, We have found him, of whom Moses in the law, and the prophets, did write, Jesus of Nazareth, the son of Joseph. And Nathanael said unto him, Can there any good thing come out of Nazareth? Philip saith unto him, Come and see.

"Jesus saw Nathanael coming to him, and saith of him, Behold an Israelite indeed, in whom is no guile! Nathanael saith unto him, Whence knowest thou me? Jesus answered and said unto him, Before that Philip called thee, when thou wast under the fig tree, I saw thee.

"Nathanael answered and saith unto him, Rabbi, thou art the Son of God; thou art the King of Israel. Jesus answered and said unto

---

[65]John 2:1.
[66]Matthew 10:3; Luke 6:14.
[67]John 6:5-7.
[68]John 12:21-22.
[69]John 14:8.

him, Because I said unto thee, I saw thee under the fig tree, believest thou? thou shalt see greater things than these....Hereafter ye shall see heaven open, and the angels of God ascending and descending upon the Son of man."[70]

Nathanael was from Cana and both he and Philip appear to have been with Jesus at Cana when he performed his first miracle.[71]

After the Savior's resurrection, Nathanael was one of the seven apostles who was served breakfast by Jesus on the shore of the Galilee.[72]

John never refers to this apostle by any other name except Nathanael. The other Gospel writers never refer to Nathanael but always associate Philip with an apostle named Bartholomew.[73] Authorities tend to agree that both names refer to the same apostle.[74]

THOMAS DIDYMUS, THE TWIN

Thomas was sometimes referred to as "Didymus," which, in the Greek, means "a twin."[75] Thomas seems to have been a little on the dour or pessimistic side. On the way up to see Lazarus at the request of Mary and Martha, Jesus said Lazarus was already dead. When Thomas heard this, he gloomily remarked, "Let us also go, that we may die with him."[76]

At the Last Supper when Jesus said, "I go to prepare a place for you," Thomas asked, "Lord, we know not whither thou goest; and how can we know the way?" At that point, nothing Jesus might have said would have satisfied Thomas, and so the Savior's response was

---

[70]John 1:45-51.
[71]John 2:11.
[72]John 21:2.
[73]Matthew 10:3; Mark 3:18; Luke 6:14; Acts 1:13.
[74]Peloubet's *Bible Dictionary*, under "Bartholomew."
[75]John 11:16.
[76]John 11:14-16.

rather obscure as he simply said, "I am the way, the truth, and the life."[77]

After the resurrection, Thomas would not accept the testimony of the ten apostles who said they had seen Jesus, nor the women who said they had seen him, nor the testimony of the two disciples who had walked and talked with Jesus on the way to Emmaus.[78] However, Thomas was overwhelmed when Jesus suddenly appeared before all of the apostles eight days later while Thomas was present. Thomas virtually collapsed, saying, "My Lord and my God!"[79]

A little later, when Jesus appeared on the shores of Galilee and invited seven of the apostles to dine with him, Thomas was one of them.[80]

MATTHEW, THE TAX COLLECTOR

Matthew was originally called Levi, but after his conversion he preferred to be called Matthew, "the son of Alphaeus".[81] He served as a tax collector at Capernaum, and is believed to have been in the service of Herod Antipas or the Roman government.[82]

Soon after he received his call, Matthew held a feast at his home, and invited many of his professional friends. Jesus was criticized by the Pharisees for associating with these "publicans" who were considered sinful men.[83] Jesus told these critics it was his calling and mission to teach sinful men.

It is said that Matthew wrote his gospel some 30 years after the Savior's resurrection, and made frequent reference to Old Testament citations to prove to his fellow Jews that Jesus was indeed the Christ, the long awaited Messiah.[84]

---

[77]John 14:2-6.
[78]John 20:25.
[79]John 20:27-28.
[80]John 21:2.
[81]Mark 2:14.
[82]Peloubet's *Bible Dictionary*, under "Matthew".
[83]Matthew 9:9-13; Mark 2:14-17; Luke 5:27-32.
[84]Peloubet's *Bible Dictionary*, under "Matthew."

JAMES, THE SON OF ALPHAEUS

This apostle may be identical with James the Less, but nothing further is known of either man. This James is in all of the lists of the apostles, but no specific event is connected with him. However, since he is always described as "the son of Alphaeus", it would appear that he was the brother of Matthew.[85]

LEBBAEUS THADDAEUS

We are told that this man's proper name was Lebbaeus, and his surname was Thaddaeus.[86] This apostle appears in the lists of the apostles by either one or both of these names.[87] He is referred to by John as "Judas...not Iscariot".[88]

At the Last Supper, this apostle was puzzled by the Savior's statements that he was going away. Nevertheless, Jesus said he would later manifest himself to his disciples, but not unto the world. Judas, "who was not Iscariot," wondered how this could be done. Jesus said he would personally appear to some and even reveal the Father.[89]

SIMON THE CANAANITE

Sometimes Simon is referred to as a Zealot, which carries the same connotation as a Canaanite.[90] The term refers to a person who is a strong believer in all the details of the Mosaic ritual. Except for his appearance in the lists of the apostles, Simon is not identified with any particular event.[91]

JUDAS ISCARIOT

This man is believed to have come from the community of Kerioth in Judea. If so, he would be the only apostle who was not

---

[85]Compare Mark 2:14 with Matthew 10:3, Mark 3:18; Luke 6:15; Acts 1:13.
[86]Matthew 10:3.
[87]Matthew 10:3; Mark 3:18; Luke 6:16; Acts 113.
[88]John 14:22.
[89]John 14:22-23; Doctrine and Covenants 130:3.
[90]Luke 6:15; Acts 1:13.
[91]Matthew 10:3; Mark 3:18.

a Galilean.[92] His treachery toward the Savior began when Judas took the initiative to go to the chief priests and ask how much they would pay him to betray Jesus into their hands. The bribe was 30 pieces of silver.[93]

On the night Judas led the guards to Gethsemane, he kissed Jesus to identify him in the darkness for the guards.[94] Later, he regretted what he had done and tried to get the chief priests to take the money back, but they refused.[95]

Judas then committed suicide. It says that when he fell "headlong, he burst asunder in the midst, and all his bowels gushed out."[96]

When Jesus was reporting to the Father in his great high priest's prayer, he said this concerning the twelve apostles:

"And none of them is lost, but the son of perdition."[97]

This is highly significant.

After the resurrection, Peter told the Jews who assented to the crucifixion of Christ that they could be forgiven because they did it in ignorance.[98] Then what about Judas Iscariot? Why did the Savior call him "perdition," which means that his sin could not be forgiven? We note that Jesus specifically referred to him as "lost."

It is my opinion that we do not have the whole story of Judas Iscariot. The Savior would never have passed judgment on him as a son of perdition unless there was a lot more to his betrayal than we have been told. In the end, we may find that the roots of his crime

---

[92]Talmage, *Jesus the Christ*, p. 125-6.
[93]Matthew 26:14-16.
[94]Luke 22:47.
[95]Matthew 27:3.
[96]Acts 1:18.
[97]John 17:12.
[98]Acts 3:17-19.

against the Lord extended clear back into the pre-existence, as was the case with Cain.[99]

CONCLUSION

Once Jesus had chosen and ordained his twelve apostles, he was ready to begin explaining to them the Beatitudes.

Then he could tutor these chosen servants of God on the further beatification of the human spirit as set forth in the Sermon on the Mount.

* * * *

TOPICS FOR REFLECTION AND DISCUSSION

1. What serious problem confronted the Savior when he returned from his "ministry of miracles?" What did he do to get off by himself? Then what three things did he ask the Father to help him do?

2. Can you name eight of the twelve apostles? What four apostles were recruited from Capernaum? Which apostles were formerly the disciples of John the Baptist?

3. Which three apostles did Jesus seem to favor all during his ministry? Can you think of a reason?

4. What five things do you remember in the life of Peter that are the most outstanding in your mind? On a scale of one to ten, where would you place Peter as a leader?

5. Name three things in the life of James that are the most memorable to you. Who had him executed by a sword? What happened to the ruler who was responsible for his death?

6. Which of the apostles had the reputation of being more loved than any of the others? Was he Peter's first or second counsellor?

---

[99]Moses 5:24.

7. What special request did John make of the Savior prior to the Ascension? Why did this seem to bother Peter? Has John died yet? From all we have been told, where does he actually reside? Will he eventually go through the death process before he is resurrected?

8. Why would we expect Andrew to complain a little? Did he? At the Last Supper, who asked Jesus to show the apostles the Savior's Father? John calls one of the apostles Nathanael. What do the other gospel writers call him?

9. Based on the available scriptures, how would you describe the personality of the apostle Thomas? Why was he sometimes called Didymus? When Jesus said Lazarus was already dead, what dour comment did Thomas make? After doubting that Jesus was resurrected, what did he say when Jesus suddenly appeared before him?

10. No one knows exactly why Judas Iscariot was chosen as an apostle. At the last supper what did Jesus call him? Did Judas ever try to give back the 30 pieces of silver to the rulers? How did Judas die?

*   *   *   *

CHAPTER 13

THE SERMON ON THE MOUNT

Part One

Jesus had the highest aspirations for the human family. He wanted mankind to become beautiful people and perfect themselves in righteousness.

However, Jesus knew that the dangerous pathway that winds and twists up through the Second Estate is steep, and the road is rocky. The main problem is "human nature."

Of course, we "inherited" our human nature. It is carefully structured on a foundation of God-given instincts, specifically designed to help us survive.

In a sense these survival instincts are built-in resources which turn out to be powerful desires, emotions and demands that our physical bodies constantly impose upon us.

For example, they demand that we eat. They demand that we drink. They demand that we be comfortable—not too much heat, not too much cold, not too hard, and not too soft. They demand that we satisfy certain appetites. They demand that we satisfy certain tastes and abhor others. They demand that we seek out certain pleasant smells but treat others with disdain. They demand that others like us. They demand that we avenge ourselves on those who don't like us. They demand that we satisfy our sexuality. They demand that we get things, and get them in quantity. The list goes on and on.

These instincts begin before birth and most of them last until we die.

HOW DO OUR GOD-GIVEN INSTINCTS
BECOME THE ENEMY OF GOD?

The problem with all of these instincts is that, while they are important for our survival, they get in the way of spiritual growth and longterm happiness. Therefore, every human being is confronted with a dilemma. God gives us a set of survival instincts, and then tells us to subdue them in order to achieve eternal life.

Consequently, all through our earth-life, there is a war going on between the spirit and the flesh.

The prophets have left no doubt about the reality of this war. The righteous King Benjamin declared:

"The natural man is an enemy to God, and has been from the fall of Adam, and will be, forever and ever, unless he yields to the enticings of the Holy Spirit, and putteth off the natural man and becometh a saint through the atonement of Christ the Lord, and becometh as a child, submissive, meek, humble, patient, full of love, willing to submit to all things which the Lord seeth fit to inflict upon him, even as a child doth submit to his father."[1]

The apostle Paul adds his admonition:

"Let not sin therefore reign in your mortal body, that ye should obey it in the lusts thereof.

"Neither yield ye your members as instruments of unrighteousness unto sin: but yield yourselves unto God, as those that are alive from the dead, and your members as instruments of righteousness unto God.

"For sin shall not have dominion over you."[2]

---

[1]Mosiah 3:19, B. of M.
[2]Romans 6:12-14.

So a primary purpose of the Sermon on the Mount was to give the children of the Father a series of beacon lights to guide them through the storms of mortal life and help them overcome the element of sin or "instinctive rebellion" in the flesh. As Paul indicates, the Lord's purpose is to have us survive but not to allow sin to have *dominion* over us.

THIS SERMON HAD YET ANOTHER PURPOSE FOR THE APOSTLES

In order to prepare his twelve apostles for their great mission, Jesus had to impress upon them the fact that the gospel is for everybody. He knew that from their earliest childhood, these men had been taught the fundamental principle of the Pharisees that God's plan of salvation is a very exclusive affair. After all, were not the Jews the final remnant of the children of Israel whom God had called his chosen people?[3]

Jesus had the task of gradually expanding the understanding of the apostles to appreciate that Israel was not chosen as the only favored people of God, but that they were chosen as the leaders to bring the whole human race to God. Or at least as many as would listen.

As a result, Jesus had been broadening his focus. In fact, only recently it must have come as a genuine culture shock to the Savior's disciples when they saw Jesus including in his ministry the "harlots and publicans" as well as the "good people." And what was even more astonishing, he had called a "publican," named Matthew, to be one of the apostles![4]

Jesus wanted his apostles to know that the gospel of redemption can pick up the Father's precious children wherever it finds them. They may be in palaces, at the common market, or herding sheep among the hills. They can even be in the filth of the gutter or in the deepest dregs of human depravity. They can still be transformed into blessed people.[5]

---

[3]Deuteronomy 7:6; 14:2.
[4]Luke 5:27.
[5]See, for example, King Lamoni—Mosiah 17:28; Alma 19:35-36; or Alma the Elder—Mosiah 17:2;

The secret is "to come unto Christ."

It is on this theme that Jesus introduced one of the most inspiring parts of the Sermon on the Mount—the Beatitudes, or how to bless and sublimate the human spirit.

THE BEATITUDES

At the very beginning of this part of his great sermon, Jesus addressed himself to the lonely, the depressed, the sad and the despondent. His first beatitudes were for those who feel they have failed and have no hope. To them, Jesus said:

"Blessed are the poor in spirit, for theirs is the kingdom of God.[6]

"Blessed are they that mourn: for they shall be comforted."[7]

When I was a child, these promises were beyond my comprehension. I thought of the millions of people who are lonely and depressed and who live out their lives in sadness and never even hear of the kingdom of God. And I thought of other millions who mourn away their lives and are never comforted.

But what I didn't know in those childish years was the fact that four important words are missing from the King James version of the Bible.

Those four words are, "who come unto me."[8]

Now that we have the complete text of this famous sermon, we know that each of the Beatitudes is predicated upon the Savior's gracious and loving invitation, "come unto me."

18:1; Mosiah 25:19; 26:8-9; or Alma the Younger—Mosiah 27:8, 18-24, B. of M.

[6]Matthew 5:3.

[7]Matthew 5:4.

[8]After his resurrection, Jesus gave this sermon to the Nephites whereby we obtained the correct text (3 Nephi, chapters 12-14). Although the words, "who come unto me," are stated only in the first Beatitude, they are implied for all of them. See Appendix E in volume 2.

NINE MAJOR STEPS IN BEATIFYING
THE HUMAN SPIRIT

As we carefully study the Beatitudes, we notice that they follow the same pattern as the first principles of the gospel outlined in the Articles of Faith.

The first principle of the gospel is faith, and coupled with it is the first beatitude where Jesus promises the discouraged, the depressed, and the poor in spirit an opportunity to inherit the kingdom of heaven if they will just come unto him.

The second principle of the gospel is repentance, and coupled with it is the second beatitude, which reaches out to those who are mourning over their mistakes or even the catastrophe which they may have made of their lives. There is no remedy comparable to the relief and joy which Jesus can offer, and therefore Jesus says that if they will come unto him, they can be comforted.

The third principle of the gospel is the ordinance of baptism for the remission of sins. And it is interesting that the third Beatitude contains the Savior's marvelous promise which he makes to those who are sufficiently meek and humble to take this decisive step. He said, "Blessed are the meek for they shall inherit the earth."[9]

In the scripture meekness is associated with the willingness of a person to accept the sacred ordinances required by the Lord, which begin with baptism.[10]

And we observe that the Lord says that all those who are sufficiently meek to come unto him and be baptized shall "inherit the earth." This is a glorious promise. It turns out that the destiny of the earth is to become a celestialized planet on which those who attain the celestial glory will dwell. To one of his prophets the Lord said:

---

[9]Matthew 5:5.

[10]Mosiah and Jesus say that those who take this step and thereafter endure to the end, will "inherit the earth."

"It is decreed that the poor and the meek of the earth shall inherit it. Therefore...it must be prepared for the celestial glory...that [those] of the celestial kingdom may possess it forever and ever."[11]

The fourth principle of the gospel is receiving the gift of the Holy Ghost under the hands of someone holding the higher priesthood. In connection with this principle, Jesus provided a special beatitude for those who are about to have the Holy Ghost confirmed upon them. He said:

"Blessed are those who hunger and thirst after righteousness [and come unto Christ] *for they shall be filled with the Holy Ghost.*"[12]

A fifth principle of the gospel has to do with forgiveness, and there is a fifth beatitude to go with it. Once a person has "come unto Christ," the mercy of God becomes available to the new convert, and he or she receives a forgiveness of sins through the atonement. However, the fifth beatitude clearly states that the Lord expects the new member of God's kingdom to be as merciful to others as God has been to him or her. Jesus said:

"And blessed are the merciful, for they SHALL obtain mercy."[13]

This beatitude suggests an interesting gospel principle, namely, that even when a person is baptized and confirmed, that individual's sins are forgiven only as he or she is able to forgive others. Mark records this teaching by the Savior as follows:

"If ye do not forgive, neither will your Father which is in heaven forgive your trespasses."[14]

The sixth beatitude is designed for the those who strive to attain one of the highest levels of refined spirituality in the kingdom of God. To those who come unto Christ, Jesus said:

---

[11]Doctrine and Covenants 88:17-20.
[12]Matthew 5:6 plus 3 Nephi 12:6, B. of M. Once again we have a number of important words left out of the King James translation, but these were restored in the Nephite version.
[13]Matthew 5:7.
[14]Mark 11:26.

"Blessed are the pure in heart, for they shall see God."[15]

Nearly every instinct tends to corrupt the purity of the heart. It runs the gamut of anger, coveting, greed, lust, stealing, lying, assault, jealousy, dishonesty, and even homicide. Those who constantly restrain these corruptive proclivities have a special promise from the Savior. He said: "They shall see God."

The seventh beatitude is for those sweet and gentle souls who have the rare ability to pour oil on troubled waters. Whether in a family, the neighborhood, the community or the nation, Jesus made a very special promise to those who have the talent and inclination to quiet the stormy turbulence of contention.

He said:

"Blessed are the peacemakers, for they shall be called the children of God."[16]

The Lord has said that contention is of the devil,[17] but the Almighty is a God of peace.[18]

It follows that those who spread the spirit of peace are "the children of God."

The eighth beatitude is for the Savior's spiritual warriors. These are they who enter the front-line trenches and valiantly fight God's war against the forces of evil. Jesus said:

"Blessed are they which are persecuted for righteousness' sake: for theirs is the kingdom of heaven."[19]

The kingdom of heaven truly belongs to those who wage God's great battle on earth just as it was waged during the war in heaven.

---

[15]Matthew 5:8.
[16]Matthew 8:9.
[17]3 Nephi 11:29, B. of M.
[18]1 Corinthians 14:33.
[19]Matthew 5:10.

Persecution means ridicule, slander, false accusations, imprisonment, deportation, expulsion, and being outlawed, burned at the stake, flogged, kidnapped and tortured.

Persecution becomes prosecution when political or military oppression enters in. It then becomes oppression "by principalities and powers." This is what happened to Peter, James and Paul. As we saw in the previous chapter, tradition has it that Peter was crucified upside-down, and James was officially executed. Later, Paul was beheaded. For all of the Savior's disciples who are persecuted for righteousness' sake, Jesus said, "Theirs is the kingdom of heaven."

The ninth beatitude is a twin to the eighth.

It is as though Jesus wanted to single out those who are not only persecuted but are blatantly reviled and trashed by the scandal-mongers. To be reviled by one's enemies is to be expected, but to have one's friends and family indoctrinated with "official" and "creditable" or "proven" false accusations of the most evil and bizarre dimensions is a laceration of the soul that can be more painful than a flogging or a martyrdom.

To all of these, Jesus said:

"Blessed are ye when men shall revile you and persecuteyou, and say all manner of evil against you falsely, for my sake. Rejoice, and be exceeding glad: for great is your reward in heaven."[20]

This is the Savior's beatitude for those who risk both martyrdom and disgrace for the sake of Jesus Christ.

So these are the nine beautiful blessings Jesus pronounced on those who would strive to beautify their spirits. The righteous are promised they will be able to:

belong to the kingdom of heaven...
enjoy the comforting words of the Savior himself...

---

[20]Matthew 5:11-12.

be a resident of God's Celestialized earth...
be filled with the Holy Ghost...
enjoy God's richest mercy...
have the thrill of seeing God...
be called the children of God...
possess a portion of the kingdom of heaven...
be exceedingly glad over the Father's great reward.

RIGHTEOUS LEADERS ARE ALWAYS IN SHORT SUPPLY

Now Jesus desired to launch into the main portion of the Sermon on the Mount by telling the disciples how precious they are to God.

The Lord has said, "There are many called, but few are chosen,"[21] which means that righteous leaders have always been too few. This would suggest that on the executive level of the Godhead, the greatest challenge is managing billions of human beings with relatively few valiant leaders.

Moses knew about this. He said that in the pre-earth life, God planned the extent of various nations and the duration of the major empires in accordance with the supply of leaders available.[22] These leaders were not only selected in the pre-earth life, but they were foreordained.[23]

Moses says that even in the pre-existence, these valiant spirits were called "Israel,"[24] a name that has rich significance. Israel means "soldier of God,"[25] or "one who prevails with God."[26]

So how does God perceive those who have been chosen and ordained before the foundation of this world to be his leaders?

---

[21]Doctrine and Covenants 121:34.
[22]Deuteronomy 32:7-8.
[23]Alma 13:6; Ephesians 1:4, 11; 1 Peter 1:2.
[24]Deuteronomy 32:8.
[25]Quoting Gesenius In Peloubet's *Bible Dictionary*, under "Israel."
[26]Genesis 32:28, LDS Bible Dictionary under "Israel."

YE ARE THE SALT OF THE EARTH

Jesus said:

"Ye are the salt of the earth: but if the salt have lost his savor, wherewith shall it be salted? it is thenceforth good for nothing, but to be cast out, and to be trodden under foot of men."[27]

Here was the Savior's first challenge to his disciples. If they are to be valiant leaders in the cause of righteousness, he needed disciples capable of influencing the whole world. Their savor must spread its flavor to all humanity. Salt has two attributes. It seasons and it preserves. Jesus would soon send these men out as ordained apostles and they would need rich endowments of those qualities which characterized the virtues of salt.

It is interesting that salt, as such, never loses its savor, but it can be leeched out by moisture or be corrupted by mixing it with foreign substances. In either case, the residue is good for nothing but to be cast out and trodden under foot like common dirt. Disciples without savor, whether by leaching or by corruption, could not provide the useful service needed by the Lord.

YE ARE THE LIGHT OF THE WORLD

Jesus also needed leaders who would radiate a spirit of enthusiasm, hope, conviction, and self-confidence. There was to be action, preaching, teaching, proselyting. Therefore, he said:

"Ye are the light of the world. A city that is set on an hill cannot be hid.

"Neither do men light a candle, and put it under a bushel, but on a candlestick; and it giveth light unto all that are in the house.

"Let your light so shine before men, that they may see your good works, and glorify your Father which is in heaven."[28]

---

[27]Matthew 5:13.
[28]Matthew 5:14-16.

These passages make it vividly clear that the Savior is pleading with his disciples to be valiant, to be noble, to be exemplary, and to give the Father the righteous leaders he needs to light the gospel flame in the hearts of men and women throughout the world.

JESUS CAME TO FULFILL THE CARNAL LAW

Now Jesus wanted to tell these "soldiers of God" something about himself and his mission. He said:

"Think not that I am come to destroy the law, or the prophets: I am not come to destroy, but to fulfil.

"For verily I say unto you, Till heaven and earth pass, one jot or one tittle shall in no wise pass from the law, till all be fulfilled."[29]

The law Jesus came to fulfill was the Carnal Law. This was the law which Paul said was "added" to the original gospel out of necessity.[30]

There never would have been any Carnal Law if the Israelites had not apostatized and worshipped the golden calf. The Carnal Law was added to teach these rebellious and obstreperous people the rhythm of obedience so the Savior could be born among them, and so they could qualify for the great blessings God had in store for them.[31]

But the Lord despised the Carnal Law. He told Isaiah that all of those tedious rituals and ceremonies that had been added were an "abomination" which he "hated." The Lord said, "They are a trouble unto me; I am weary to bear them."[32]

But they did point the way to the coming of Christ. As Paul said, it was a "schoolmaster to bring them to Christ."[33] Now that Christ had come, their purpose had been fulfilled. Jesus said that once his

---

[29]Matthew 5:17-18.
[30]Galatians 3:19.
[31]Galatians 3:24.
[32]Isaiah 1:14.
[33]Galatians 3:24.

mission had been completed the Carnal Laws were to be eliminated.[34]

THE ORIGINAL GOSPEL PRINCIPLES
AND ORDINANCES GIVEN TO THE ANCIENT
PATRIARCHS WERE STILL IN FORCE

However, Jesus pointed out that the original gospel laws given to the ancient patriarchs constitute a permanent part of the government of God's kingdom and they must still be obeyed and taught to the people from generation to generation. This original gospel law included the Ten Commandments. Jesus said:

"Whosoever therefore shall break one of these least commandments, and shall teach men so, he shall be called the least in the kingdom of heaven: but whosoever shall do and teach them, the same shall be called great in the kingdom of heaven."[35]

THE TEN COMMANDMENTS

In their abbreviated form, the Ten Commandments might be stated as follows:

1. Thou shalt have no other gods before me.[36]
2. Thou shalt not worship or attribute God's power to images or false gods.[37]
3. Oaths in the name of God shall not be taken in vain.[38]
4. Keep the sabbath day holy.[39]
5. Honor thy father and thy mother.[40]
6. Thou shalt not kill.[41]
7. Thou shalt not commit adultery.[42]

---

[34]3 Nephi 9:19-20, B. of M.
[35]Matthew 5:19.
[36]Exodus 20:3.
[37]Exodus 20:4-6.
[38]Exodus 20:7.
[39]Exodus 20:8.
[40]Exodus 20:12.
[41]Exodus 20:13.
[42]Exodus 20:14.

8. Thou shalt not steal.[43]
9. Thou shalt not lie.[44]
10. Thou shalt not covet and scheme to take away thy neighbor's possessions.[45]

YOUR RIGHTEOUSNESS MUST EXCEED THAT OF THE SCRIBES AND PHARISEES

Jesus wanted his followers to live all of the commandments and gospel principles on a higher plane than had been customary in the past. Naturally, the tendency of the Jews was to use their leaders as a criterion of godliness, but Jesus said that was not good enough.

In the Savior's day, the scribes and Pharisees held themselves up as the epitome of true godliness and the most dedicated adherents to the commandments of God. However, Jesus said:

"I say unto you, That except your righteousness shall exceed the righteousness of the scribes and Pharisees, ye shall in no case enter into the kingdom of heaven."[46]

In a way, this was shocking because Jesus was saying that these robed and respected rabbis who occupied the highest seats in the synagogues and the Sanhedrin would not have a place in the kingdom of heaven. Of course, he was referring to their status at the time he was speaking. Like everyone else, they were still candidates for heaven if they would just humble themselves and enter the waters of baptism. But this turned out to be extremely difficult for the graduates of the rabbinical schools. Christ's conversation with the venerable Nicodemus illustrated the point.

THOU SHALT NOT KILL...BUT I SAY UNTO YOU....

Jesus began selecting specific examples of the ancient law which he wanted interpreted on a much higher level than in the past. He said:

---

[43]Exodus 20:15.
[44]Exodus 20:16.
[45]Exodus 20:17.
[46]Matthew 5:20.

"Ye have heard that it was said by them of old time, Thou shalt not kill; and whosoever shall kill shall be in danger of the judgment:

"But I say unto you, That whosoever is angry with his brother without a cause shall be in danger of the judgment: and whosoever shall say to his brother, Raca [despised one], shall be in danger of the council: but whosoever shall say, Thou fool, shall be in danger of hell fire."[47]

Murders are nearly always crimes of passion. Feelings of anger, hatred, revenge or covetous greed often lie at the root of deliberate, premeditated killing.

Jesus wanted to make it a law of Christian godliness that his disciples would strictly avoid any provocative or insulting language that might arouse emotions of intense anger or murderous thoughts in the mind of another.

IF THY BROTHER HATH OUGHT AGAINST THEE....

A good place to begin the process of eliminating bad personal feelings, or even bitter feuds, is within the family.

Jesus knew how frail human nature is, and one of these frailties is rushing off to church to worship the Lord without first asking ourselves if we are really prepared to come before the Lord. Jesus gave an example:

"If thou bring thy gift to the altar, and there rememberest that thy brother hath ought against thee, leave there thy gift before the altar, and go thy way; first be reconciled to thy brother, and then come and offer thy gift."[48]

Bringing a gift to the altar was usually associated with the fulfilling of a covenant with God, much as the payment of tithes and fast offerings in our own day. Jesus suggested that in order to sanctify

---

[47]Matthew 5:21-22.
[48]Matthew 5:23-24.

an offering and make it acceptable to God, the hostile feelings between brothers or neighbors should be taken care of first.

WHAT IS REQUIRED WHEN ONE HAS COMMITTED AN OFFENSE AGAINST ANOTHER?

Jesus then related a situation which had far broader implications than a casual reading of the text might suggest. As we pointed out earlier, the Savior taught that when a serious offense has been committed against someone, it is important to seek forgiveness in this life "while thou art in the way with him."[49] This means attempting to be reconciled and forgiven by the person who has been offended while we are both together in this life. Only then can we expect forgiveness by the Lord.

Amulek, the great student of the prophet Alma, set forth the Savior's teachings concerning this important principle which is emphasized in the Sermon on the Mount. Amulek said:

"For behold, *THIS LIFE* is the time for men to prepare to meet God; yea, behold the day of this life is the day for men to perform their labors.

"And now, as I said unto you before, as ye have had so many witnesses, therefore, I beseech of you that ye do not procrastinate the day of your repentance until the end; for after this day of life, which is given us to prepare for eternity, behold, if we do not improve our time while in this life, then cometh the night of darkness wherein there can be no labor performed.

"Ye cannot say, when ye are brought to that awful crisis, that I will repent, that I will return to my God."[50]

---

[49]Matthew 5:25.
[50]Alma 34:32-34 (emphasis added), B. of M.

THE UNFORGIVEN OFFENDER MUST PAY IN THE
NEXT WORLD TO THE UTTERMOST FARTHING

This explains why Jesus literally pleaded with everyone to take advantage of the gospel and the atonement while they are in this life. He said:

"For behold, I, God, have suffered these things for all, that they might not suffer if they would repent;

"But if they would not repent, they must suffer even as I;

"Which suffering caused myself, even God, the greatest of all, to tremble because of pain, and to bleed at every pore, and to suffer both body and spirit—and would that I might not drink the bitter cup, and shrink."[51]

When we understand the reality of these passages, it makes the Savior's words in the Sermon on the Mount much more meaningful. Let us repeat the full text of what he said:

"Agree with thine adversary quickly, *while thou art in the way with him*; lest at any time the adversary deliver thee to the judge, and the judge deliver thee to the officer, and thou be cast into prison.

"Verily I say unto thee, Thou shalt by no means come out thence, *till thou hast paid the uttermost farthing*."[52]

This is not only true of a person who is thrown into prison for an offense in this life; it is equally true for an unforgiven offense in the next life. Notice that Amulek warned that one who does not repent after hearing the gospel, and "dies in his sins" will find that in the next life "there can be no labor performed" for him. This means the Savior cannot plead before the Father on behalf of that person as he does for those who have repented and endeavored to endure to the end.[53] Having rejected the gospel, he must suffer for his own sins.[54]

---

[51]Doctrine and Covenants 19:16-18 (emphasis added).
[52]Matthew 5:25-26 (emphasis added).
[53]Doctrine and Covenants 45:3-5.

As the newly ordained twelve apostles and his most loyal disciples sat on the mount listening to these profound teachings from Jesus, it must have challenged their hearts and minds as they reflected on the high standards of discipleship Jesus was laying before them.

In the next chapter we will continue the Savior's gospel themes set forth in this famous sermon.

* * * *

TOPICS FOR REFLECTION AND DISCUSSION

1. Name six of the basic instincts with which all human beings are born. What is their fundamental purpose? Where did we get these instincts? At what point do they become an "enemy to God"? Who can prevent this from happening?

2. How is the Sermon on the Mount related to the problem of dealing with our instincts? Do you think this famous sermon is given adequate study? Describe the kind of world we would have if mankind lived according to its principles. What major problems would it eliminate?

3. Is it "lineage" or "obedience" that makes people "chosen"? Where and when did the original choosing take place? What did God call those who were called to be his leaders during the Second Estate? What does this term mean? Who is Jesus trying to reach with the gospel message? Why was this a surprise to the apostles?

4. How would you define a "beatitude"? Can you identify the first five principles of the gospel that completely coincide with the first five beatitudes? Can a person who is baptized and confirmed gain a forgiveness of his sins if he refuses to forgive those who have trespassed against him?

5. What does it mean to "hunger and thirst after righteousness"?

---

[54]Doctrine and Cpovenants 19:17.

What did Jesus promise those who eagerly seek after a deeper understanding of gospel principles? On a scale of one to ten, to what extent do you feel you qualify for this blessing?

6. Why does the Lord say it is important for each of us to learn how to forgive those who trespass against us? Name three of the main instincts that tend to corrupt the purity of our hearts. Think of one occasion when you witnessed a "peacemaker" successfully handling a contentious situation.

7. Have God's people in both ancient and modern times suffered great persecution? Give an example of each. To what end does tradition say persecution ultimately led Peter, James, and Paul? Why is it such a hardship to a righteous servant of God when his friends and even his own family begin to believe falsehoods being spread about him?

8. Why do you believe so many are called by the Lord to be great leaders, but so few are chosen? The Doctrine and Covenants 121:35-36 explains why they are not chosen. What else does the Lord say? Can you think of some notable examples?

9. Name two ways in which men and women called into God's service are like the salt of the earth. What are two things salt will do? There are two things that can make salt good for nothing. What are they? Name two ways in which righteous leaders are God's light to the world. What are some of the qualities of light that a valiant servant of God should emulate?

10. What is the Carnal Law? Why was it added to the original laws of the gospel? Why does God "hate" the Carnal Law? Did Jesus come to destroy it or to fulfill it? Are the Ten Commandments part of the Gospel Law or the Carnal Law? How long do you think it would take you to memorize the basic idea in each of the Ten Commandments? Would you seriously attempt to do it?

*   *   *   *

CHAPTER 14

THE SERMON ON THE MOUNT

Part Two

The Sermon on the Mount has sometimes been referred to as a string of pearls. Each topic is a sermonette all by itself. Others have thought of it as the "Christian Constitution." Certainly, it sets before us the principles for the structuring of an ideal Christian life.

Jesus continued selecting some of the ancient laws, and demonstrated how they should be interpreted on a higher plane than in the past.

THOU SHALT NOT COMMIT ADULTERY:
BUT I SAY UNTO YOU....

Jesus opened his next gospel theme by saying:

"Ye have heard that it was said by them of old time, Thou shalt not commit adultery:

"But I say unto you, That whosoever looketh on a woman to lust after her hath committed adultery with her already in his heart."[1]

Lust is defined as being, among other things, a bodily appetite "conducive to unrestrained sexual gratification." Lust is a selfish desire to possess and exploit another. A lustful person therefore seeks to debauch or despoil the virtue of another, and will concoct elaborate schemes to snare his victim for personal gratification.

---

[1]Matthew 5:27-28.

The tragedy is aggravated by the fact that once the passion of lust is aroused, the assault may occur against an innocent person, or even a child.

Some assaults on women are also motivated by lust mixed with a stunted personality complex that harbors an arrogant, chauvinistic aspiration to dominate. Under God's law, the crime of rape carried the possibility of a maximum penalty—death.[2]

God's mandate applies as much to lustful women as it does to lustful men.[3]

Lust is sometimes aroused by pornographic literature, obscene movies and stage plays, the telling of dirty stories, and individuals cultivating sexual fantasies that involve committing adultery or fornication in one's heart.[4]

THE DIFFERENCE BETWEEN LOVE AND LUST

Note the fundamental difference between love and lust. Lust is a passion to possess someone for selfish exploitation. Love is just the opposite. It is a rapture of anxiety to give, to sustain, to share, and to sacrifice for the object of one's affection. Lust is venal, carnal, sordid, and ugly. Love is elevating, inspiring, virtuous, compassionate, and beautiful.

God gave each person an inborn inclination to be attracted to someone of the opposite sex, but the resulting relationship can only be a happy one if it is based on genuine, wholesome love, not cheap, sordid lust.

In the Sermon on the Mount, the Savior's words of solemn warning are particularly applicable to modern times when the depravity of public morals is beginning to duplicate the degradation of Sodom and Gomorrah. Jesus anticipated this and warned that the circumstances which would characterize our day would be as evil as

---

[2]Deuteronomy 22:25.
[3]Proverbs 5:3-5.
[4]Matthew 5:28.

human debauchery in Noah's day.[5] And the wickedness in Noah's day so offended God that he destroyed every human being on the face of the earth except Noah and his family.[6] There will also be a cleansing at the Second Coming of Christ.[7]

A modern scripture reflects the anxiety of the Savior not only to avoid immoral acts, but to cleanse one's mind of lustful thoughts. He said:

"Let virtue garnish thy thoughts unceasingly; then shall thy confidence wax strong in the presence of God; and the doctrine of the priesthood shall distil upon thy soul as the dews from heaven.

"The Holy Ghost shall be thy constant companion, and thy scepter an unchanging scepter of righteousness and truth; and thy dominion shall be an everlasting dominion, and without compulsory means it shall flow unto thee forever and ever."[8]

IF THY RIGHT EYE OFFEND THEE, PLUCK IT OUT.
IF THY RIGHT HAND OFFEND THEE, CUT IT OFF.

Jesus said to his disciples:

"And if thy right eye offend thee, pluck it out, and cast it from thee: for it is profitable for thee that one of thy members should perish, and not that thy whole body should be cast into hell.

"And if thy right hand offend thee, cut if off, and cast it from thee: for it is profitable for thee that one of thy members should perish, and not that thy whole body should be cast into hell."[9]

The modern reader would not know what Jesus meant if he had not explained it at a later date. Both Matthew and Mark give the Savior's meaning to these two verses. We use the Joseph Smith

---

[5]Matthew 24:37.
[6]Genesis 7:21-23.
[7]Matt. 24:39-40.
[8]Doctrine and Covenants 121:45-46.
[9]Matthew 5:29-30.

translation, or Inspired Version, to show the way Matthew originally wrote it:

"And a man's *HAND* is his FRIEND, and his *FOOT* also; and a man's *EYE*, are they of his *OWN HOUSEHOLD*."[10]

In the Inspired Version, Mark records a similar interpretation of these passages by the Savior. He says:

"Therefore, if thy hand offend thee, cut it off; or if thy *BROTHER* offend thee and confess not and forsake not [his sins], he shall be cut off. It is better for thee to enter into life maimed, than having two hands, to go into hell.

"For it is better for thee to enter into life without thy *BROTHER*, than for thee and thy brother to be cast into hell; into the fire that never shall be quenched, where their worm dieth not, and the fire is not quenched.

"And again, if thy foot offend thee, cut it off; for he that is thy *STANDARD*, by whom thou *WALKEST*, if he become a transgressor, he shall be cut off....

"Therefore, let every man stand or fall, by himself, and not for another; or not trusting another."[11]

Matthew and Mark both record the advice of the Savior indicating that when a person finds that his best friend, his brother, his teacher—or anyone else on whom he depends for guidance—is falling away, that person should completely separate himself from that denigrating influence. He may love the offender, but must abhor the offense. As Alexander Pope wrote in his *Essay on Man*, "vice is a monster...yet seen too oft...we first endure, then pity, then embrace."[12]

---

[10]Matthew 18:7-9.

[11]JST Mark 9:40-44, compare KJT.

[12]*Bartlett's Familiar Quotations*, p. 409.

This next provision was not included by the Savior when he gave this sermon to the Nephites. No doubt this was because the Nephites were not acquainted with the Jewish custom of referring to a teacher, a relative or a friend—upon whom a person depended for guidance—as an *eye* or a *hand*. He knew the Jews would understand the metaphor, whereas the Nephites would not.

JESUS EMPHASIZES THE SANCTITY OF MARRIAGE

The marriage relationship is of supreme importance to God, as he indicated in the very beginning. The family is the nuclear unit of society and when a man and woman enter into a covenant they are looked upon by the Lord as "one flesh."[13]

But with the passing of time, many factors tend to erode the unity of the family, and can lead to the most serious and devastating consequence—divorce. Many divorces are caused by a man being attracted to a secretary, a flirtatious neighbor, or a covetous adventurer anxious to capture someone else's husband who happens to be well off. But whatever may be the cause, the Lord knows that divorce usually creates far more problems than the parties ever imagined. Therefore Jesus discouraged divorce and, even though the fault may sometimes rest upon the wife, the Lord placed the major responsibility for the security and perpetuating of the family on the husband. Here are his comments:

"It hath been said, Whosoever shall put away his wife, let him give her a writing of divorcement: But I say unto you, That whosoever shall put away his wife, saving for the cause of fornication, causeth her to commit adultery: and whosoever shall marry her that is divorced committeth adultery."[14]

These passages emphasize the sanctity of marriage in the eyes of God, and the responsibility of married couples to work out their problems if at all possible. However, priesthood leaders are authorized to evaluate situations where the relationship in a marriage is not tenable, and where the circumstances are sufficiently

---

[13]Genesis 2:24.
[14]Matthew 5:31-32.

compelling to dissolve the marriage. The same authority that joined the couple in a union for time and all eternity, can sever the union and have it no longer recognized in heaven.[15]

OATH-TAKING AND PROFANITY

Jesus then presented the next law he wanted his disciples to incorporate in their lives. This had to do with oath-taking and profanity. He said:

"Ye have heard that it hath been said by them of old time, Thou shalt not forswear thyself, but shalt perform unto the Lord thine oaths:

"But I say unto you, Swear not at all; neither by heaven; for it is God's throne:

"Nor by the earth; for it is his footstool: neither by Jerusalem; for it is the city of the great King.

"Neither shalt thou swear by thy head, because thou canst not make one hair white or black.

"But let your communication be, Yea, yea; Nay, nay: for whatsoever is more than these cometh of evil."[16]

From the beginning the Lord made the taking of an oath a very sacred commitment because an oath is a solemn contract made in the name of God.[17] This is done when we enter into holy covenants, when we swear to tell the truth in court, and when the oath is administered to those who are being sworn into a high and important office. In the eyes of God, an oath is not only very sacred, but God commands that it shall not be taken in vain.[18]

---

[15]Matthew 16:19.
[16]Matthew 5:33-37.
[17]Deuteronomy 6:13.
[18]Exodus 20:7.

In the days of the Savior the Jewish people were accustomed to using oaths in their commercial transactions or to emphasize a casual commitment. They would swear by the earth, or the heavens, by the heart or the head, that a particular product was of a certain quality or that a specific service would be performed. It was this kind of swearing or oath-taking that Jesus had in mind when he said: "Swear not at all." Then he listed all the things by which they had been swearing and pointed out how foolish and meaningless this cheap and casual forswearing really was.

Jesus said their representations or commitments should be simply "Yea, yea," or "Nay, nay."[19] In other words, describe your product or the service you are promising to perform and let that be the end of the matter.

Some Christians, such as the Quakers, took this passage to mean that a person should never take an oath. To accommodate the people who held to this view, the judicial oath was changed to say, "Do you swear or *affirm*...."

SPEECH POLLUTION

Jesus was also concerned about the common practice of what we might call speech pollution. This is getting in the habit of replacing "Yea, yea" and "Nay, nay," with expletives in the form of swearing, obscenities or profanity.

A few years ago certain radical elements on many university campuses set out to launch a carefully orchestrated campaign to use obscene and indecent shock words to drive a wedge between the adult generation and the youth. Even before the campaign was launched, J. Edgar Hoover became aware of this drive to widen the so-called generation gap. He therefore published a stirring pamphlet warning parents of the coming assault on youth.

But the warning went unheeded, and the "dirty word" campaign succeeded far beyond the wildest expectations of the sponsors. On some campuses rallies were held with several thousand students

---

[19]Matthew 5:37.

shouting in unison various four-letter shock words. The object was
to show contempt for university standards and local municipal laws.
Many times radical faculty members joined with the students. They
called it a revolt against prudish Victorian propriety, but it was
expressly designed to expand the generation gap.

Vulgar and obscene talk gained tremendous momentum.
Virtually overnight the entertainment media took advantage of the
permissive climate to introduce the most lurid and salacious smut
language into plays, movies and popular literature. What had
formerly been considered the language of the gutter and the lowest
level of culture became commonplace.

Parents found their children participating in this new trend along
three different levels. It usually began with the "hell-and-damn"
syndrome. Then it moved on to the obscenities with four-letter words
formerly confined to mule skinners and harbor riffraff. Finally, there
was profanity with the taking of the Lord's name in vain.

Winifred Smith tells of hearing her 15-year-old granddaughter
using some rough language with her friends, so she tried an
experiment. She gave her a gift of fifty one-dollar bills with the
provision that every time she used a bad word she had to return a
dollar. Then she put the granddaughter on her honor to keep track
of her language and the money she must return. With this girl, the
results were miraculous. In a very pragmatic way, Grandma Smith
had suddenly made it seem most desirable to use good language.[20]

IT HAS BEEN SAID "AN EYE FOR AN EYE" BUT....

The scriptures plainly said:

"As he hath done, so shall it be done to him;

"Breach for breach, eye for eye, tooth for tooth: as he hath
caused a blemish in a man, so shall it be done to him again."[21]

---

[20]Robert E. Wells, *The Mount and the Master*, Deseret Book, p.122.
[21]Leviticus 24:19-20.

Was this to be taken literally or figuratively?

There had been a dispute between the Pharisees and the Sadducees as to whether or not this scripture was to be taken literally. The Sadducees felt this scripture meant there should be an eye for an eye, lash for lash, burn for burn, and the victim should be allowed to wreak vengeance on the offender by "doing unto him as he had been done by."[22]

However, the Pharisees pointed out that Moses had taught that no one needed to lose his eye or suffer physical punishment if the offender would redeem the injury by the payment of money or by working out some kind of compensation which was acceptable to the victim. Even the scripture made provision for such an arrangement so that the offender could give monetary "satisfaction" to the injured person.[23]

Notice that the purpose of this law was not revenge but to balance the scale of justice between the parties. There were never any fines paid to the court or the government. Damages went to the victim.

Under modern law, fines are almost invariably paid to the city, the county, the state or the federal government. If the victim wants any remedy he must sue for damages in a civil court. But as everyone knows, by the time a criminal has paid his fines to the court, he is usually depleted of funds or consigned to a prison where he is earning nothing. As a result, modern justice penalizes the offender, but does virtually nothing for the victim. To this extent true justice is robbed.

The Lord's law was much more just, because the object was to get satisfaction for the injured party, not to pay the salaries and expenses of the local judiciary.

---

[22]Skousen, *The Third Thousand Years*, op. cit., p. 356.
[23]For example, see Exodus 22:22,30.

THE LUST FOR DAMAGES

But now let's look at the other side of the coin. Should the victim of an injury rush off to court every time he or she suffers the slightest hurt? That was the tendency of the people in the days of the Savior. This being the case, consider the astonishing new doctrine which Jesus taught his disciples:

"Ye have heard that it hath been said, An eye for an eye, and a tooth for a tooth:

"But I say unto you, That ye resist not evil: but whosoever shall smite thee on thy right cheek, turn to him the other also.

"And if any man will sue thee at the law, and take away thy coat, let him have thy cloak also.

"And whosoever shall compel thee to go a mile, go with him twain.

"Give to him that asketh thee, and from him that would borrow of thee turn not thou away."[24]

Because these passages are often misunderstood, let us carefully consider each part.

First of all, the Savior told his disciples he did not want them violently protesting every misfortune that might happen to them and demanding a pound of flesh for every injury. He wanted them to develop a superior moral capacity to turn the other cheek.[25] This is not easy. It is not even natural. The inborn instinct is to strike back, to retaliate. But now Jesus was calling for the refinement of the human spirit to the highest level of tolerance and patient endurance. But how MUCH endurance? How about rights? How about damages?

---

[24]Matthew 5:38-42.
[25]Matthew 5:39.

Here is the way the Lord describes what he expects of his disciples if they wish to be like their Master:

"If men will smite you, or your families, once, and ye bear it patiently and revile not against them, neither seek revenge, ye shall be rewarded."[26]

Then the Lord goes on to say that if there is additional affliction and it is still borne without striking back, it is counted an even greater achievement.[27]

The Lord wanted to reverse the trend of vengeance and contention with a flood of friendly persuasion and Godly patience by going the second mile, the third mile, and, if necessary, the seventh mile.

However, this principle must not be pressed beyond rational expectations. A person has his rights. Even from the very first abuse, a person is "justified" in the eyes of the Lord in standing up for his or her rights. In fact, they are guaranteed under the Lord's law of equity and justice. So the Lord says:

"But if ye bear it *not* patiently, it shall be accounted unto you as being meted out as a just measure unto you."[28]

In other words, if you want to stand your ground and demand your rights from the very beginning, it will be considered a righteous and just demand. Nevertheless, there is an abundance of overflowing blessings for the individual or family who, in the interest of pouring oil on troubled waters, tries to reduce a prevailing friction in human relations and avoid the contention and quarrels that may lead to violence or even war.

But notice how the Lord closes this discussion. He says:

---

[26]Doctrine and Covenants 98:23.
[27]Doctrine and Covenants 93:25-3.
[28]Doctrine and Covenants 98:24.

"Nevertheless, thine enemy is in thine hands; and if thou rewardest him according to his works thou art justified; if he has sought thy life, and thy life is endangered by him, thine enemy is in thine hands and thou art justified."[29]

This is in harmony with the teachings of the Book of Mormon which says that in trying to be patient it must not be overlooked that when life or liberty are put in jeopardy, there is a responsibility to protect both. It says:

"For the Lord had said unto them, and also unto their fathers, that: Inasmuch as ye are not guilty of the first offense, neither the second, ye shall *not* suffer yourselves to be slain by the hands of your enemies.

"And again, the Lord has said that: Ye shall defend your families even unto bloodshed. Therefore for this cause were the Nephites contending with the Lamanites, to defend themselves, and their families, and their lands, their country, and their rights, and their religion."[30]

In fact, it was a capital offense for a man to refuse to defend his country and his people in time of war or threatened attack.[31]

From the above it will be seen that the principle of "turning the other cheek" has been grossly misunderstood. Some people have thought it was a Christian doctrine to refuse to defend one's country or to protect one's life and liberty.

Jesus himself stated to his apostles in the latter part of his ministry that since times and circumstances were changing, they were no longer to go forth without purse or scrip, and without a sword. They were entering into a period of severe persecution and therefore he said:

---

[29]Doctrine and Covenants 98:31.
[30]Alma 43:46-47 (emphasis added).
[31]Alma 51:15.

"When I sent you without purse, and scrip, and shoes, lacked ye any thing? And they said, Nothing.

"Then said he unto them, But now, he that hath a purse, let him take it, and likewise his scrip: and he that hath no sword, let him sell his garment, and buy one."[32]

Peter responded to this suggestion, but little did he know that he would be using his sword that very night![33]

THE CHRISTIAN SENSE OF CHARITY AND GENEROSITY

Now Jesus came to the cornerstone of a Zion society. The apostles did not know it during these early days of their ministry, but after Christ's resurrection he would establish among his disciples the foundation for the kind of society that made Enoch famous. It would be a marvelous association of people in which there would be "no poor among them."[34] The key to this achievement is the principle of generous discipleship which Jesus shared with his followers:

"Give to him that asketh thee, and from him that would borrow of thee turn not thou away."[35]

Of course, generosity must necessarily be tempered with prudence, and a person can neither lend nor give that which he does not already possess. Nevertheless, when everyone in a community or society has a genuine concern for those in need, it is possible to build a Zion society where poverty is completely eliminated in a remarkably short period of time.

The Savior's disciples in America achieved this in a single generation.[36] This is because they were willing to live under the laws of a Zion society as revealed to Enoch and Moses. The ancient

---

[32]Luke 22:35-36.
[33]John 18:10.
[34]Moses 7:18.
[35]Matthew 5:42.
[36]4 Nephi 1:2-3.

Israelites were not willing to live under those heavenly principles,[37] but the Nephites did. Here is how the scripture describes it:

"And it came to pass in the thirty and sixth year, the people were all converted unto the Lord, upon all the face of the land, both Nephites and Lamanites, and there were no contentions and disputations among them, and every man did deal justly one with another.

"And they had all things common among them; therefore there were not rich and poor, bond and free, but they were all made free, and partakers of the heavenly gift."[38]

The exciting thing about all of this is that Moses was told that this same law of Zion would be lived in its perfection as the Israelites gathered in the latter days.[39] The fullness of the great gathering and the setting up of a Zion society is yet in the future.

CHARGE NO INTEREST ON LOANS TO THE POOR

One of the provisions under the law of Zion, as given to Moses, was that the whole community was expected to help every family enjoy the security of an inheritance with their own home and their own plot of ground. This was facilitated by the fact that newly married couples, immigrants, or those who were considered "poor" or limited in resources were granted loans by their more prosperous neighbors without having to pay any interest. The Lord said:

"And if thy brother be waxen poor, and fallen in decay with thee; then thou shalt relieve him: yea, though he be a stranger, or a sojourner; that he may live with thee.

"Take thou no usury of him, or increase: but fear thy God; that thy brother may live with thee.

---

[37]Deuteronomy 31:29.
[38]4 Nephi 1:2-3.
[39]Deuteronomy 30:8.

"Thou shalt not give him thy money upon usury, nor lend him thy victuals for increase."[40]

The significance of this law may be better appreciated when we stop to realize that in modern times a home purchased on a long term loan will require the purchaser to pay for the home two to three times its original cost, because of the interest.

THE CHRISTIAN COMMUNITY UNDER THE APOSTLES

The Jewish Christians set up a number of Zion communities under the apostles, and were well on the way to achieving exactly what the Nephites accomplished in America, until the Romans launched a series of bitter persecutions against both the Christians and Jews so that they were soon disorganized and scattered.

SHARING PROBLEMS IN COMMON

Concerning the Christian community near Jerusalem, the scripture says:

"And all that believed were together, and had all things common;

"And sold their possessions and goods, and parted them to all men, as every man had need."[41]

It turned out that they didn't have their "things" in common, but rather their problems. There was no pooling of property. Each person decided what he could sell to help the poor, but kept the remaining property as a stewardship so it could be improved to further help the poor. This concept of stewardship and helping one another was described as follows:

"And the multitude of them that believed were of one heart and of one soul: neither *said* any of them that ought of the things which he possessed was his own; but they had all things common....

---

[40]Leviticus 25:35-37.
[41]Acts 2:44-45.

"Neither was there any among them that lacked: for as many as were possessors of lands or houses sold them, and brought the prices of the things that were sold,

"And laid them down at the apostles' feet: and distribution was made unto every man according as he had need."[42]

LOVE AND PRAY FOR YOUR ENEMY

Finally we come to the most difficult commandment of all. The Savior said:

"Ye have heard that it hath been said, Thou shalt love thy neighbour, and hate thine enemy.

"But I say unto you, Love your enemies, bless them that curse you, do good to them that hate you, and pray for them which despitefully use you, and persecute you;

"That ye may be the children of your Father which is in heaven: for he maketh his sun to rise on the evil and on the good, and sendeth rain on the just and on the unjust.

"For if ye love them which love you, what reward have ye? do not even the publicans the same?

"And if ye salute your brethren only, what do ye more than others? do not even the publicans so?"[43]

In all of this there emerges a very important question: HOW do you love your enemy? It is not difficult to pray for one's enemy, or even to ask God to bless him with a repentant heart so that he ceases to be your enemy; but how to LOVE one's enemy, there is the rub.

An enemy is defined in many different ways. The dictionary says an enemy may be one who cherishes harmful designs against another, one who is hostile or extremely unfriendly, a declared

[42]Acts 4:32-35 (emphasis added).
[43]Matthew 5:43-47.

opponent or adversary, an assailant, a backbiter or slanderer, a military antagonist, a stiff competitor, or a traitor.

Obviously, there are many different kinds of enemies, and they must be dealt with in several different ways. Perhaps we could classify them in three different groups.

First, there is the human relations enemy. This is the most common kind. Such an enemy may arise from a personality conflict, an off-handed, unkind remark, spreading gossip or tale-bearing, perceiving the individual as being a social or business threat, perhaps mutual resentment because of adverse political views or even different religious views.

This type of "enemy" can be cultivated with kindness and tolerance easier than the next two groups. Sometimes it simply requires getting better acquainted with the other person to make the hostility barrier diminish and eventually disappear. Watching for an opportunity to do a favor for an adversary nearly always alleviates tensions and opens doors for better relations. Seeking to develop a true sense of understanding and love can bring some surprising results.

The next group is more challenging. This is where you or your family have suffered a significant injury by someone. The injury may be physical, economic, or even an injury to one's position in a profession or social status. Even *wanting* to love this kind of enemy takes a lot of prayer and introspection. But since this problem arises in every congregation or neighborhood, the Lord has suggested the following procedure to see if the feelings of those who have been injured can be resolved. Both in the New Testament and modern scripture, the Savior has said:

"Moreover if thy brother shall trespass against thee, go and tell him his fault between thee and him alone: if he shall hear thee, thou hast gained thy brother.

"But if he will not hear thee, then take with thee one or two more, that in the mouth of two or three witnesses every word may be established.

"And if he shall neglect to hear them, tell it unto the church: but if he neglect to hear the church, let him be unto thee as an heathen man and a publican."[44]

Although this three-step attempt to love someone who has been an offender does not always work, it succeeds often enough to make it very worthwhile.

Finally, we come to the third and most difficult group of all. These are the wretched wicked. They are the enemies of the community, sometimes preying upon the whole of society. This type of enemy is in a mental state of anarchy and revolt. We call it the criminal mind. This type of person enjoys his or her greatest satisfaction in getting away with deceit and treachery.

This type of enemy does not respond to kindness and love the way both of the other groups usually do. This last group considers kindness a weakness. It is interpreted as stupidity that deserves to be exploited by the criminal. To love this kind of enemy requires a different approach.

Professional penologists have learned that the criminal mind must discover certain strict and undeviating legal barriers beyond which he or she cannot go. The criminal must discover that he or she cannot go beyond these limits without inviting serious consequences. This is called establishing fixed parameters with visible firmness.

The next step is to establish a sense of fairness—a feeling that he or she is being treated fairly even though the program is administered with firmness. The incorrigible criminal may not respond to the firmness-fairness therapy, but the majority do. Once the criminal has demonstrated a desire to cooperate and get back on track, then the element of love and kindness can be carefully administered in measured doses.

However, at no time must the criminal get the impression you feel sorry for him or her. Nor must the criminal get the impression

---

[44]Matthew 18:15-17; Doctrine and Covenants 42:88-92.

that you accept any kind of excuse for what happened. It is very important that the offender face up to what was done. The Lord calls it "confession of sins." Penologists call it "reality therapy."

So we learn from the Lord what he means by loving our enemies. We must love them enough to want to help them. We must pray for them, and work with them. However, there is no requirement that we drown them with love. Wisdom must be used. Love is a very sacred and precious attribute and it must be administered carefully and wisely. It must not be cheapened or squandered. The best kind of love is reciprocal love, and that is the ultimate goal—to change an enemy into a loving friend.

STRIVE FOR PERFECTION

As we have just seen, of all the virtues which qualify a person to be perfect—like unto our Heavenly Father—the foremost is a sincere sympathy and a feeling of kindness for those in need. Jesus emphasized this Godly quality over and over again. As he would later say, "Inasmuch as ye do it unto the least of these my brethren, ye do it unto me."[45]

Jesus wanted to associate the quality of generosity with the perfection of his Father. Therefore he encouraged his disciples never to become discouraged, whether people appreciated their generosity or not. He said:

"Be ye therefore perfect, even as your Father which is in heaven is perfect."[46]

Thus we conclude this segment of the Sermon on the Mount which includes some of the most profound principles of the gospel. As we have seen, he wanted his disciples to attain the highest possible level of human perfection during earth life. In our next chapter we will conclude the Savior's instructions to his disciples.

*   *   *   *

---

[45]Matt. 25:41.
[46]Matthew 5:48.

TOPICS FOR REFLECTION AND DISCUSSION

1. Because we live in an age of salacious literature and movies as well as hard-core pornography, how would you advise a young person to live and think above it? What is the real difference between love and lust? Can you tell from your own feelings which is which?

2. Among the Jews, what was the offending eye that should be plucked out? What was an offending hand that should be cut off? Why didn't the Savior use this same metaphor when he gave the Sermon on the Mount to the Nephites?

3. Name three reasons why the Lord has urged parents to weather the storms of life and avoid getting a divorce if at all possible. When a crisis is occurring in a family, where should they go for assistance? Do the servants of the Lord have a vested interest in helping troubled couples work out their problems?

4. Name three times when a sacred oath is appropriate. Because the use of profanity and obscenities has become the routine lifestyle of so many people, what successful device have you employed to avoid this type of evil?

5. Can you describe what the scriptures mean by "an eye for an eye?" Is this to be taken literally? Under God's law, who received the fines or damages? Would that procedure be more just today?

6. How would you interpret the Savior's admonition to "turn the other cheek"? Does this work successfully in most day-to-day relations? At what point do you feel the Savior would consider you justified in resisting evil? What is the Savior's ultimate purpose in having his righteous Saints absorb persecution and abuse as they have done in the past? In the end, who wins?

7. Why do you think the Lord attributes a high degree of godliness to people who are compassionate toward those in need? When a person comes to borrow, why do you think the Lord said, "Turn him not away"? Even if one cannot spare any funds, is it possible to help in other ways?

8. Describe the highlights of those righteous societies of the past that loved their neighbors as themselves. Is it possible to actually eliminate poverty where those principles are practiced?

9. Can you think of a person who really thinks of you as an enemy? Have you ever prayed for that person? Do you think you could generate a love for that person even if he or she did not reciprocate?

10. Jesus is the only perfect person who ever lived on the earth. Then why do you think Jesus commanded us to "be perfect even as our Father in Heaven is perfect"? Can you pay a perfect tithing? Can you fulfill home teaching assignments perfectly? What other phases of life can be approached with a high degree of perfection?

*   *   *   *

CHAPTER 15

THE SERMON ON THE MOUNT

Part Three

As we have already mentioned, the best way to help the poor is to do it in an organized way, but since that would not come until later, Jesus told his disciples how to help the poor for the present through almsgiving. The most important single factor connected with almsgiving is the attitude of the person giving the alms.

GIVE ALMS IN SECRET
AND YOU WILL BE REWARDED OPENLY

Jesus said:

"Take heed that ye do not your alms before men, to be seen of them: otherwise ye have no reward of your Father which is in heaven.

"Therefore when thou doest thine alms, do not sound a trumpet before thee, as the hypocrites do in the synagogues and in the streets, that they may have glory of men. Verily I say unto you, They have their reward. But when thou doest alms, let not thy left hand know what thy right hand doeth:

"That thine alms may be in secret: and thy Father which seeth in secret himself shall reward thee openly."[1]

---

[1]Matthew 6:1-4.

PRAY IN SECRET AND
YOU WILL BE REWARDED OPENLY

It was in this same spirit that Jesus wanted to emphasize the importance of a person's attitude when he or she comes before the Lord in prayer. He said:

"And when thou prayest, thou shalt not be as the hypocrites are: for they love to pray standing in the synagogues and in the corners of the streets, that they may be seen of men. Verily I say unto you, They have their reward."[2]

Obviously, their reward was the praise they were seeking by having people see how religious and devoted they were. So, having loved to pray standing in the synagogues and in the corners of the streets, they perceived the admiring glances of those who saw them and that was their reward.

Now Jesus wanted to emphasize that the best prayer—from the standpoint of the individual—is not a public prayer. Said he:

"But thou, when thou prayest, enter into thy closet, and when thou hast shut thy door, pray to thy Father which is in secret; and thy Father which seeth in secret shall reward thee openly."[3]

Jesus knew that in a time of crisis, it is in the quiet solitude of some private place that a person pours out his heart in prayer.

DO NOT USE VAIN REPETITIONS

There is also a rut into which most people tend to find themselves. That is where a person uses the same words to ask a blessing on the food, the same blessing in the morning, and the same blessing at night. There are even some who believe that the constant repeating of a certain prayer can have some special influence on God. None of these approaches fit the parameters of meaningful prayers set forth by Jesus. He said:

---

[2]Matthew 6:5.
[3]Matthew 6:6.

"But when ye pray, use not vain repetitions, as the heathen do: for they think that they shall be heard for their much speaking.

"Be not ye therefore like unto them: for your Father knoweth what things ye have need of, before ye ask him."[4]

A good rule that may help to prevent falling into a rut of habitual repetition is to think in advance of those specific things for which one feels especially thankful at that very moment. Then think of the specific things that are very critical to you or to those close to you, and earnestly petition for your Heavenly Father's help. This will make every prayer different, appropriate, and more likely to be heard.

THE LORD'S PRAYER

To illustrate what he was trying to teach the apostles, Jesus gave them an example of a righteous prayer. He said:

"After this manner therefore pray ye: Our Father which art in heaven, Hallowed be thy name.

"Thy kingdom come. Thy will be done in earth, as it is in heaven.

"Give us this day our daily bread.

"And forgive us our debts, as we forgive our debtors.

"And lead us not into temptation, but deliver us from evil: For thine is the kingdom, and the power, and the glory, for ever. Amen."[5]

What a beautiful prayer. So simple. So direct. So explicit.

FORGIVE TRESPASSES

Jesus felt it was important to comment on one element of this prayer. He wanted to talk to them about one of the most universal

---

[4]Matthew 6:7-8.
[5]Matthew 6:9-13.

human frailties—the inability of even "good" people to forgive one another. Therefore he said:

"If ye forgive men their trespasses, your heavenly Father will also forgive you:

"But if ye forgive not men their trespasses, neither will your Father forgive your trespasses."[6]

FAST IN SECRET AND YOU WILL BE REWARDED OPENLY

The principle of fasting has deep significance beyond the veil. It is easy to pray and ask for something, but the mere asking does not fully demonstrate how badly a person truly wants it or actually needs it.

Fasting is one of the ways we can show the Lord the importance of those things for which we are praying. Fasting permits us to go before the Lord in a spirit of sacrifice. It indicates humility and a contrite heart. It is a quiet and sacred way to communicate to the Lord the urgent importance of the thing for which we are fasting.

But fasting, like praying, is recognized by others as a quality of saintliness. Jesus knew that many people fast and pray for the wrong reason. They want to be recognized and admired for their seeming saintliness. Therefore, he said:

"Moreover when ye fast, be not, as the hypocrites, of a sad countenance: for they disfigure their faces, that they may appear unto men to fast. Verily I say unto you, They have their reward.

"But thou, when thou fastest, anoint thine head, and wash thy face;

"That thou appear not unto men to fast, but unto thy Father which is in secret: and thy Father, which seeth in secret, shall reward thee openly."[7]

---

[6]Matthew 6:14-15.
[7]Matthew 6:16-18.

STRIVE TO LAY UP TREASURES IN HEAVEN

Now Jesus shifted to another human frailty: Greed. To want things, to want to improve things, to want to beautify things, is not evil. But they need to be wanted, improved, and beautified for the right reason. The prophet Jacob, son of Lehi, saw the balance between wanting things and having the right reason for seeking them. He said:

"But before ye seek for riches, seek ye for the kingdom of God.

"And *after* ye have obtained a hope in Christ ye shall obtain riches, if ye seek them; and ye will seek them for *the intent to do good*—to clothe the naked, and to feed the hungry, and to liberate the captive, and administer relief to the sick and the afflicted."[8]

Some people discover that they have a remarkable skill for the assembling of wealth. Part of it seems to be a gift, a special insight, and the other part is the willingness to work hard at it. Of course, sometimes it is just good fortune. But acquiring wealth is no virtue in and of itself. Jacob knew that. He gave the key to true wealth when he said we should seek riches with which to do good. In that way a person accumulates riches in heaven.

Jesus endorsed this entire principle by saying:

"Lay not up for yourselves treasures upon earth, where moth and rust doth corrupt, and where thieves break through and steal.

"But lay up for yourselves treasures in heaven, where neither moth nor rust doth corrupt, and where thieves do not break through nor steal:

"For where your treasure is, there will your heart be also."[9]

---

[8]Jacob 2:18-19 (emphasis added), B. of M.
[9]Matthew 6:19-21.

NO MAN CAN SERVE TWO MASTERS

Jesus later mentions that if a person has made his covenants with the Lord and is seeking riches with which to do good, it is absolutely essential that he never lose sight of which of his goals is the most important.

One will sometimes hear a wealthy person say, "I am not going to help the poor just now because I am saving my money in order to make more money. Then I can help the poor all the more!" Of course, saving money to make more money is a correct principle, but saving money while ignoring the crying needs of the poor makes it rather obvious which master the man is actually serving. Therefore the Lord said:

"No man can serve two masters: for either he will hate the one, and love the other; or else he will hold to the one, and despise the other. Ye cannot serve God and mammon."[10]

The Lord is saying, in effect, "Keep your priorities straight!"

BUT WHAT ABOUT THE SERVANTS OF MAMMON?

Jesus knew that the accumulation of wealth always carries with it a massive accumulation of political and economic power. More often than not, this power is used for evil and selfish purposes rather than to do good. So where do the disciples of Christ fit into such an environment?

Jesus gave his disciples a lesson in tactical strategy. He said:

"And I say unto you, Make to yourselves friends of the mammon of unrighteousness; that, when ye fail, they may receive you into everlasting habitations."[11]

This is stated even more clearly in a modern revelation where the Lord said:

---

[10]Matthew 6:24.
[11]Luke 16:9.

"And now, verily I say unto you, and this is wisdom, make unto yourselves friends with the mammon of unrighteousness, and they will not destroy you.

"Leave judgment alone with me, for it is mine and I will repay."[12]

Some day the Savior will take on Satan at full strength and in direct confrontation, but that time is not yet. Therefore it is wisdom, the Lord says, to plough around the servants of Satan so as to avoid giving them an excuse to destroy the Lord's disciples or frustrate the Savior's work.

Just as Paul did not rail out against Caesar when he was taken to Rome, but respected him in his office despite the evil of his personal life, so also today, the leaders of the church steer a steady course in spite of all the evil in high places. They continue to denounce evil in principle but do not rail against the leaders and their evil ways or allow the church to become embroiled in their many snares. Nevertheless, church history will demonstrate that there have been a few close calls.

So the Savior's advice was both wise and timely.

TAKE NO THOUGHT OF THE MORROW

One of the most basic lessons of life on this earth is to prepare for the exigencies of the future. As Solomon said to the slothful and lazy in his day:

"Go to the ant, thou sluggard; consider her ways, and be wise: which having no guide, overseer, or ruler, provideth her meat in the summer, and gathereth her food in the harvest."[13]

All of the apostles had been trained in this tradition, and therefore it must have come as a shock to them as they received the following commandment from Jesus:

---

[12]Doctrine and Covenants 82:22-23.
[13]Proverbs 6:6-8.

"I say unto you, Take no thought for your life, what ye shall eat, or what ye shall drink, nor yet for your body, what ye shall put on....Behold the fowls of the air...your Heavenly Father feedeth them....Consider the lilies of the field...Solomon in all his glory was not arrayed like one of these....

"Take therefore no thought for the morrow: for the morrow shall take thought for the things of itself. Sufficient unto the day is the evil thereof."[14]

At no time did Jesus give a command such as this to the general membership of the church. It was only to those who had the full-time responsibility of governing the affairs of his entire ministry that he asked for such a complete commitment and a total consecration of their time and talent based on pure faith.

This was clearly demonstrated when he repeated this same sermon to the Nephites after his resurrection. He selected twelve disciples from among the multitude of 2,500 people[15] assembled at the temple in Bountiful, and in the midst of his sermon, he turned away from the multitude, and the scripture says:

"He looked upon the twelve whom he had chosen, and said unto them....Take no thought for your life, what ye shall eat, or what ye shall drink...." etc.[16]

After repeating everything he had previously told his Jewish apostles, the scripture says:

"He turned again to the multitude,"[17] and continued his sermon to the end.

So it is clear that this commandment to "take no thought of the morrow" was directed only to his leaders. However, we observe that under certain circumstances, the Savior even suspended this

---

[14]Matthew 6:25-34.
[15]3 Nephi 17:25, B. of M.
[16]3 Nephi 13:25-26, B. of M.
[17]3 Nephi 14:1, B. of M.

commandment to his leaders. As we have previously mentioned, it was just as he was coming to the end of his ministry, and the crisis of the crucifixion lay directly before him that Jesus said to the eleven faithful apostles who were still with him:

"When I sent you without purse, and scrip, and shoes, lacked ye any thing? And they said, Nothing.

"Then said he unto them, But *NOW*, he that hath a purse, let him take it, and likewise his scrip."[18]

Even so, the scriptures are clear that after the resurrection, the apostles returned to their previous commitment, and there was no paid ministry among them. As Paul wrote to the Corinthians:

"What is my reward then? Verily that, when I preach the gospel, I may make the gospel of Christ without charge."[19]

CONCERNING THE JUDGING OF OTHERS

At this point let us insert something Jesus will be saying a little later. It fits in with the Savior's comments about forgiving. Let us consider what Jesus had to say about judging other people, particularly for the purpose of condemning them. Based on the best translation available, he said:

"Judge not unrighteously, that ye be not judged; but judge righteously.

"For with what judgment ye judge, ye shall be judged: and with what measure ye mete, it shall be measured to you again...

"Why is it that thou beholdest the mote that is in thy brother's eye, but considerest not the beam that is in thine own eye?

---

[18]Luke 22:35-36.
[19]1 Corinthians 9:18.

"Or how wilt thou say to thy brother, Let me pull out the mote out of thine eye; and, behold, a beam is in thine own eye?"[20]

We generally think of God judging us and forgiving us, but here we discover that how he judges us will depend to a large extent upon ourselves. It is rather startling to be told that we will be judged and forgiven by the same measurement we have used to judge and forgive others.

BEWARE WHAT IS FED INTO THE MIND BY THE EYE

What we feed into our minds either by what we view or what we read has a lot to do with how we think, how we feel, and what we do. It is said that the idea in the mind is the parent of the subsequent act, and it is amazing how many ideas come to us through the eye. Therefore Jesus wisely said:

"The light of the body is the eye: if therefore thine eye be single, thy whole body shall be full of light.

"But if thine eye be evil, thy whole body shall be full of darkness. If therefore the light that is in thee be darkness, how great is that darkness!"[21]

This is just another way of saying "as we see, so we do." Filling the mind with the writings of the prophets and the precepts of the Lord builds strong fibers of character and elevates our sights to match the visions of eternity. The best thing about it is that the teachings of scripture are all light—bright, beautiful, inspiring light.

GIVE NOT THAT WHICH IS HOLY UNTO THE UNWORTHY

There is a sacred responsibility placed on the servants of the Lord to use good judgment and teach the sacred principles of the gospel only as the Spirit dictates. One who ministers the gospel will soon learn that EXCEPT FOR THE MESSAGE Of REPENTANCE, the Spirit

---

[20]JST Matthew 7:2-5, compare KJT Matthew 1-5.
[21]Matthew 6:22-23.

will not tarnish sacred principles by lavishing them on those who are depraved and debauched. Therefore, Jesus said:

"Give not that which is holy unto the dogs, neither cast ye your pearls before swine, lest they trample them under their feet, and turn again and rend you."[22]

ASK AND YE SHALL RECEIVE

One of the great disappointments of the Lord occurs when his choice servants lose their spiritual curiosity. They become satisfied with a little when they could have a lot. They stop hungering and thirsting after righteousness and an increased knowledge of heavenly things.

This happened to the twelve apostles in Jerusalem. Jesus wanted to tell them about the great body of Christians in America, but they wouldn't ask. He gave them the strongest hint which should have awakened a sense of wonderment in their minds, but it did not. When Jesus visited his saints in America he told them how disappointed he was when his apostles would not ask about his "other sheep." Jesus said:

"This much did the Father command me, that I should tell unto them: That other sheep I have which are not of this fold; them also I must bring, and they shall hear my voice; and there shall be one fold, and one shepherd.

"And now, because of stiffneckedness and unbelief they understood not my word; therefore I was commanded to say no more of the Father concerning this thing unto them."[23]

The Father yearns to reveal the secrets of heaven to his righteous servants. Therefore Jesus said:

"Ask, and it shall be given you; seek, and ye shall find; knock, and it shall be opened unto you:

---

[22]Matthew 7:6.
[23]3 Nephi 15:16-18, B. of M.

"For every one that asketh receiveth; and he that seeketh findeth; and to him that knocketh it shall be opened.

"Or what man is there of you, whom if his son ask bread, will he give him a stone?

"Or if he ask a fish, will he give him a serpent?

"If ye then, being evil, know how to give good gifts unto your children, how much more shall your Father which is in heaven give good things to them that ask him?"[24]

SEARCHING THE SCRIPTURES
FOR THE HIDDEN TREASURES

Many times God reveals precious truths but hides them in his scriptures so the casual reader will not immediately comprehend them. These are the Godly mysteries that the Spirit reveals only to the mind of the diligent and prayerful student. This is what the Lord called hungering and thirsting after righteousness.[25] Furthermore, it is precisely what King Benjamin meant when he said:

"Open your ears that ye may hear, and your hearts that ye may understand, and your minds that the MYSTERIES of God may be unfolded to your view."[26]

And this is what the Lord meant when he said:

"If thou shalt ask, thou shalt receive revelation upon revelation, knowledge upon knowledge, that thou mayest know the MYSTERIES and peaceable things—that which bringeth joy, that which bringeth life eternal."[27]

From passages such as these we gain a new insight into what God calls a "mystery." It is something he has revealed and hidden

---

[24]Matthew 7:7-11.
[25]Matthew 5:6.
[26]Mosiah 2:9 (emphasis added), B. of M.
[27]Doctrine and Covenants 42:61 (emphasis added).

away in the scripture, but we haven't found it yet. In contrast to the "revealed" mysteries, there are things the Lord has not yet found it expedient to reveal. Subjects that fall into this latter category are unprofitable and sometimes misleading to speculate about.

THE GOLDEN RULE

And now we come to the most perfect yet simple rule for Godly conduct ever devised. We often call it the Golden Rule. Jesus said:

"Therefore all things whatsoever ye would that men should do to you, do ye even so to them: for this is the law and the prophets."[28]

This rule requires the most vigorous self discipline. It is not an easy rule to live by, but of all the rules, it is the most rewarding. Any person who masters this mode of life is living on the level of the prophets of God.

THE BROAD WAY AND THE NARROW WAY

There are two roads that stand open before every human being who reaches the age of accountability. The gift of happiness as well as salvation come only to those who get on the right road.

Jesus wanted all who heard his message to enter in at the "strait gate," which means a restricted, narrow passageway. In the gospel this refers to repentance, baptism for the remission of sins and the laying on of hands for the gift of the Holy Ghost. This is the only way to get on the right road—the road leading to exaltation and eternal life.

But there is a "wide gate" that requires no commitments, no repentance, no covenant, and no effort. A person stumbling through life without a purpose and without developing a searching, seeking mind will inevitably wander into the wide gate and then stagger down the broad way until he reaches the portals of despair where Satan awaits him.

---

[28]Matthew 7:12.

In the most urgent anxiety, Jesus said:

"Enter ye in at the strait gate: for wide is the gate, and broad is the way, that leadeth to destruction, and many there be which go in thereat:

"Because strait is the gate, and narrow is the way, which leadeth unto life, and few there be that find it."[29]

From the perspective of our Heavenly Father, the saddest part of this last verse is the word, "few."

BEWARE OF FALSE PROPHETS

The most tragic influence down through the ages has been exerted by the servants of Satan who have risen among the people as "angels" of light. These are the false prophets, the false messiahs, the false politicians, the false teachers, the wicked miscreants dressed in godly raiment. Jesus lumped them all together as "false prophets" and said:

"Beware of false prophets, which come to you in sheep's clothing, but inwardly they are ravening wolves."[30]

But how can these treacherous instruments of deceptive subterfuge be detected? Jesus said the best way is to test them by their fruits. This method has an accuracy rating of 100 percent. He said:

"Ye shall know them by their fruits. Do men gather grapes of thorns, or figs of thistles?

"Even so every good tree bringeth forth good fruit; but a corrupt tree bringeth forth evil fruit.

"A good tree cannot bring forth evil fruit, neither can a corrupt tree bring forth good fruit.

---

[29]Matthew 7:13-14.
[30]Matthew 7:15.

"Every tree that bringeth not forth good fruit is hewn down, and cast into the fire.

"Wherefore by their fruits ye shall know them."[31]

NOT EVERYONE THAT SAITH, "LORD, LORD," SHALL ENTER THE KINGDOM OF HEAVEN

Of course, one of the most popular nostrums sold by the false prophets has always been the promise that getting into heaven is not a climb, it's a glide. You just put a dollar on the plate, say "Lord, Lord," and coast in. To all such, Jesus said:

"Not every one that saith unto me, Lord, Lord, shall enter into the kingdom of heaven; but he that doeth the will of my Father which is in heaven."[32]

Doing the will of the Father is not a slide or a glide but an upward climb of repentance, commitment, service, sacrifice, and struggle. The effort is one of endurance—to the end! But the reward is celestial, glorious and eternal.

CONCERNING THOSE WHO ARE NOT VALIANT

When the Lord comes in glory, nothing will be more heartbreaking than the sorrows of those who have thought they were disciples of Christ, and then find they are not. Concerning these, Jesus said:

"Many will say to me in that day, Lord, Lord, have we not prophesied in thy name? and in thy name have cast out devils? and in thy name done many wonderful works?

"And then will I profess unto them, I never knew you: depart from me, ye that work iniquity."[33]

---

[31]Matthew 7:16-20.
[32]Matthew 7:21.
[33]Matthew 7:22-23.

THE HOUSE BUILT ON A ROCK

"Therefore whosoever heareth these sayings of mine, and doeth them, I will liken him unto a wise man, which built his house upon a rock:

"And the rain descended, and the floods came, and the winds blew, and beat upon that house; and it fell not: for it was founded upon a rock."[34]

THE HOUSE BUILT ON SAND

"And every one that heareth these sayings of mine, and doeth them not, shall be likened unto a foolish man, Which built his house upon the sand:

"And the rain descended, and the floods came, and the winds blew, and beat upon that house; and it fell: and great was the fall of it."[35]

JESUS TAUGHT AS ONE HAVING AUTHORITY

The supreme achievement of Jesus, as he completed his Sermon on the Mount, was the tremendous impact that it had on the hearts and minds of those who heard it. The scripture says:

"And it came to pass, when Jesus had ended these sayings, the people were astonished at his doctrine:

"For he taught them as one having authority, and not as the scribes."[36]

PREPARING FOR AN EXPANDED MINISTRY

Having selected, ordained and trained his twelve apostles, Jesus prepared to launch into his second tour of Galilee.

---

[34]Matthew 24-25.
[35]Matthew 7:26-27.
[36]Matthew 7:28-29.

However, let us first complete our discussion of the Sermon on the Mount by comparing the three versions of this famous sermon which are available to us. We will do this in the next chapter.

* * * *

TOPICS FOR REFLECTION AND DISCUSSION

1. Why did Jesus need to establish among his disciples a completely new standard of godliness? What did he say about the Scribes and the Pharisees? What did he say about people who rush off to worship in church without first being prepared to come before the Lord?

2. Explain: "Let not thy left hand know what thy right hand doeth."

3. In what way did Jesus associate charity with becoming perfect like the Father? Why is charity better administered in an organized way than through individual almsgiving?

4. Why do you think Jesus urged us to have private prayers or secret prayers? Do you ever find yourself praying repetitiously? What is one way to prevent this from occurring? Read the Lord's prayer and see if you can find ten significant elements.

5. Is it really justice to have God judge us by the way we have judged others? Is it really justice to have God forgive us in terms of how we have forgiven others? Why is this scary?

6. How can earthly treasures be the means of laying up a store of heavenly treasures? Under what conditions is it right in the sight of God to seek riches? Is it good or evil to make friends with the servants of mammon? Why does the Lord call this "wisdom"?

7. Why does Jesus call the eye the light of the whole body? Is it true that from the time of childhood upward, "what we see is what we do"?

8. Why does the Lord say we miss a lot because we do not ask? Can you think of three important revelations that Joseph Smith received

as a result of asking? Can you think of three revelations subsequent prophets received as a result of asking?

9. Give an example in your own life when it "paid off" to follow the Golden Rule.

10. What are the two roads that lie before us after we reach the age of accountability? What is the "strait gate"? What is the difference between the word "strait" and the word "straight"? What POSITIVE test did Jesus give to detect a false prophet or a false teacher? After we hear the gospel, what must follow if we are to gain our salvation?

*   *   *   *

CHAPTER 16

COMPARING THREE VERSIONS OF THE SERMON ON THE MOUNT

There is a tremendous advantage in having three versions of the Sermon on the Mount for scriptural study.

Many of the verses are virtually identical, but a glance through these pages will reveal some very significant changes or additions which provide insights as well as choice segments of new knowledge that were not available in the original Bible version.

In this parallel presentation of these three versions, the following background may prove helpful.

THE KING JAMES VERSION

There were several efforts to translate the Bible into English before a committee was appointed by King James of England to employ the oldest available manuscripts, as well as any existing translations, and produce a version of the Bible which the people could use as an "authorized" text.

This text was completed in 1611 and published as the "authorized version."

Subsequent studies of additional manuscripts were published by scholars claiming they had improved on the Bible and therefore published various "revised" versions. However, it turns out that these are not usually revisions of the King James version, but additions from various compilations of questionable validity.

One of the best treatments of the historical background of both the "authorized version" and the "Revised Version" is the work of J. Reuben Clark, Jr. His book is entitled, *Why the King James Version.* It was published in 1956 by the Deseret Book Company of Salt Lake City.

J. Reuben Clark, Jr. came to the conclusion that we are not only very fortunate to have the King James Version, but it is far and away the best substantive text for scriptural study.

THE INSPIRED VERSION

The apostle Peter spoke of the latter-days when there would be a "restitution of all things which God hath spoken by the mouth of all his holy prophets since the world began."[1]

The beginning of this remarkable "restitution" commenced in 1820 and has been rapidly unfolding ever since. One of the great treasures to come into our possession was a review of the King James Version of the Holy Bible by Joseph Smith, the prophet of the new dispensation.

This is not a revision of the whole Bible, but sets forth major changes as they were revealed to Joseph Smith prior to his martyrdom in 1844. It is usually referred to as the "Joseph Smith Translation," but could more accurately be called the "Inspired Version," or "Joseph Smith's Revision."

In the following pages we are only presenting the changes and additions which were given by direct revelation to Joseph Smith while reviewing the Sermon on the Mount. It will be quickly recognized that many important insights and some elements of new knowledge were made available through Joseph Smith's review of this famous scripture.

[1]Acts 3:21.

THE BOOK OF MORMON VERSION

Following the Savior's resurrection he appeared to his "other sheep" in America whom he had mentioned to his apostles.[2]

During his brief ministry to the American Christians, Jesus repeated much of what he had taught the Jews, including the Sermon on the Mount.

However, the text of the Sermon on the Mount was very carefully recorded in America at the time it was given, so we have several advantages in studying this version. Much of the text is identical with the New Testament, but where there are changes or additions, or even deletions, we see the value of this more complete version which was recorded in the ancient American scripture, and restored in our own day and time as part of The Book of Mormon.

---

[2]John 10:16.

Comparing Three Versions of the Sermon on the Mount

King James	Joseph Smith Translation	Book of Mormon
Matt. 5	Matt. 5	3 Nephi 12
1. And seeing the multitudes, he went up into a mountain: and when he was set, his disciples came unto him: 2. And he opened his mouth, and taught them, saying,	1. And Jesus, seeing the multitudes, went up into a mountain; and when he was set down, his disciples came unto him; 2. And he opened his mouth, and taught them saying, 3. Blessed are they who shall believe on me; and again, more blessed are they who shall believe on your words, when ye shall testify that ye have seen me and that I am. 4. Yea, blessed are they who shall believe on your words, and come down into the depth of humility, and be baptized in my name; for they shall be visited with fire and the Holy Ghost, and shall receive a remission of their sins.	1. And it came to pass that v Jesus had spoken these w unto Nephi, and to those had been called, (now number of them who had called, and received powe authority to baptize, was tw and behold, he stretched his hand unto the multitude cried unto them, saying: Ble are ye if ye shall give heed the words of these twelve w I have chosen from among to minister unto you, and t your servants; and unto th have given power that they baptize you with water; after that ye are baptized water, behold, I will baptize with fire and with the ' Ghost; therefore blessed a if ye shall believe in me an baptized, after that ye have me and know that I am.

BLESSED ARE THEY WHO JOIN THE CHURCH OF JESUS CHRIST

		2. And again, more blessec they who shall believe in words because that ye testify that ye have seen me that ye know that I am. blessed are they who **believe** in your words, come down into the dept humility and be **baptizec** they shall be visited with and with the **Holy Ghost** shall receive a remission of sins.

BLESSED ARE THE POOR IN SPIRIT WHO JOIN THE CHURCH
AND COME UNTO CHRIST

ssed [are] the poor in spirit: heirs is the kingdom of n.	5. Yea, blessed are the poor in spirit, **who come unto me**; for theirs is the kingdom of heaven.	3. Yea, blessed are the poor in spirit **who come unto me,** for theirs is the kingdom of heaven.

BLESSED ARE THEY THAT MOURN (WHO COME UNTO CHRIST)

ssed [are] they that mourn: ey shall be comforted.	6. And again, blessed are they that mourn; for they shall be comforted.	4. And again, blessed are all they that mourn, for they shall be comforted.

BLESSED ARE THE MEEK (WHO COME UNTO CHRIST)

ssed [are] the meek: for hall inherit the earth.	7. And blessed are the meek; for they shall inherit the earth.	5. And blessed are the meek, for they shall inherit the earth.

BLESSED ARE THEY WHO HUNGER AND THIRST AFTER
RIGHTEOUSNESS (AND COME UNTO CHRIST)

ssed [are] they which do er and thirst after ousness: for they shall be	8. And blessed are all they that do hunger and thirst after righteousness; for they shall be filled with the Holy Ghost.	6. And blessed are all they who do hunger and thirst after righteousness, for they shall be filled with the Holy Ghost.

BLESSED ARE THE MERCIFUL (WHO COME UNTO CHRIST)

ssed [are] the merciful: for hall obtain mercy.	9. And blessed are the merciful; for they shall obtain mercy.	7. And blessed are the merciful, for they shall obtain mercy.

BLESSED ARE THE PURE IN HEART (WHO COME UNTO CHRIST)

ssed [are] the pure in heart: y shall see God.	10. And blessed are all the pure in heart; for they shall see God.	8. And blessed are all the pure in heart, for they shall see God.

BLESSED ARE THE PEACEMAKERS (WHO COME UNTO CHRIST)

sed [are] the peacemakers: ey shall be called the n of God.	11. And blessed are all the peacemakers; for they shall be called the children of God.	9. And blessed are all the peacemakers, for they shall be called the children of God.

BLESSED ARE THE PERSECUTED (WHO ENDURE FOR THE SAVIOR'S SAKE)

10. Blessed [are] they which are persecuted for righteousness' sake: for theirs is the kingdom of heaven.	12. Blessed are all they that are persecuted for my name's sake; for theirs is the kingdom of heaven.	10. And blessed are all the are persecuted for my r sake, for theirs is the kingc heaven.

BLESSED ARE THEY WHO ARE REVILED FOR THE SAVIOR'S SAKE

11. Blessed are ye, when [men] shall revile you, and persecute [you], and shall say all manner of evil against you falsely, for my sake.	13. And blessed are ye when men shall revile you, and persecute you, and shall say all manner of evil against you falsely, for my sake.	11. And blessed are ye men shall revile you persecute, and shall s manner of evil agains falsely, for my sake;
12. Rejoice, and be exceeding glad: for great [is] your reward in heaven: for so persecuted they the prophets which were before you.	14. For ye shall have great joy, and be exceeding glad; for great shall be your reward in heaven; for so persecuted they the prophets which were before you.	12. For ye shall have gre and be exceedingly gla great shall be your rew heaven; for so persecute the prophets who were you.

YE ARE THE SALT OF THE EARTH

13. Ye are the salt of the earth: but if the salt have lost his savour, wherewith shall it be salted? it is thenceforth good for nothing, but to be cast out, and to be trodden under foot of men.	15. Verily, verily, I say unto you, I give unto you to be the salt of the earth; but if the salt shall lose its savor, wherewith shall the earth be salted? the salt shall thenceforth be good for nothing, but to be cast out, and to be trodden under foot of men.	13. Verily, verily, I say unt I give unto you to be the the earth; but if the saf lose its savor wherewitl the earth be salted? The sa be thenceforth good for ne but to be cast out and trodden under foot of me

YE ARE THE LIGHT OF THE WORLD

14. Ye are the light of the world. A city that is set on an hill cannot be hid. 15. Neither do men light a candle, and put it under a bushel, but on a candlestick; and it giveth light unto all that are in the house.	16. Verily, verily, I say unto you, I give unto you to be the light of the world; a city that is set on a hill cannot be hid. 17. Behold, do men light a candle and put it under a bushel? Nay, but on a candlestick; and it giveth light to all that are in the house.	14. Verily, verily, I say ur you, I give unto you to be light of this people. A city set on a hill cannot be hi 15. Behold, do men light candle and put it under a bushel? Nay, but on a candlestick, and it giveth to all that are in the hous

YE ARE THE LIGHT OF THE WORLD (continued)

t your light so shine before that they may see your works, and glorify your · which is in heaven.	18. Therefore, let your light so shine before this world, that they may see your good works, and glorify your Father who is in heaven.	16. Therefore let your light so shine before this people, that they may see your good works and glorify your Father who is in heaven.

I CAME NOT TO DESTROY THE LAW

ink not that I am come to y the law, or the prophets: ot come to destroy, but to	19. Think not that I am come to destroy the law, or the prophets: I am not come to destroy, but to fulfill.	17. Think not that I am come to destroy the law or the prophets. I am not come to destroy but to fulfil;
r verily I say unto you, Till n and earth pass, one jot · tittle shall in no wise pass he law, till all be fulfilled.	20. For verily I say unto you, heaven and earth must pass away, but one jot or tittle shall in no wise pass from the law, until all be fulfilled.	18. For verily I say unto you, one jot nor tittle hath not passed away from the law, but in me it hath all been fulfilled.

KEEP THE COMMANDMENTS

hosoever therefore shall one of these least andments, and shall teach o, he shall be called the n the kingdom of heaven: hosoever shall do and [them], the same shall be great in the kingdom of n.	21. Whosoever, therefore, shall break one of these least commandments, and shall teach men so to do, he shall in no wise be saved in the kingdom of heaven; but whosoever shall do and teach these commandments of the law until it be fulfilled, the same shall be called great, and shall be saved in the kingdom of heaven.	19. And behold, I have given you the law and the commandments of my Father, that ye shall believe in me, and that ye shall repent of your sins, and come unto me with a broken heart and a contrite spirit. Behold, ye have the commandments before you, and the law is fulfilled.

YOUR RIGHTOUSNESS MUST EXCEED THAT OF SCRIBES AND PHARISEES

r I say unto you, That t your righteousness shall d [the righteousness] of the s and Pharisees, ye shall in e enter into the kingdom ven.	22. For I say unto you, except your righteousness shall exceed that of the Scribes and Pharisees, ye shall in no case enter into the kingdom of heaven.	20. Therefore come unto me and be ye saved; for verily I say unto you, that except ye shall keep my commandments, which I have commanded you at this time, ye shall in no case enter into the kingdom of heaven.

CONCERNING THE COMMANDMENT NOT TO KILL

21. Ye have heard that it was said by them of old time, Thou shalt not kill; and whosoever shall kill shall be in danger of the judgment: 22. But I say unto you, That whosoever is angry with his brother without a cause shall be in danger of the judgment: and whosoever shall say to his brother, Raca, shall be in danger of the council: but whosoever shall say, Thou fool, shall be in danger of hell fire.	23. Ye have heard that it hath been said by them of old time, that, Thou shalt not kill; and whosoever shall kill, shall be in danger of the judgment of God. 24. But I say unto you, that whosoever is angry with his brother, shall be in danger of his judgment; and whosoever shall say to his brother, Raca, or Rabcha, shall be in danger of the council; and whosoever shall say to his brother, Thou fool, shall be in danger of hell fire.	21. Ye have heard that been said by them of ol and it is also written befo that thou shalt not ki whosoever shall kill sha danger of the judgment o 22. But I say unto yo whosoever is angry w brother shall be in dange judgment. And whosoeve say to his brother, Raca, s in danger of the counc whosoever shall say, Tho shall be in danger of hell

**WHAT IS REQUIRED WHEN ONE HAS COMMITTED
AN OFFENSE AGAINST ANOTHER**

23. Therefore if thou bring thy gift to the altar, and there rememberest that thy brother hath ought against thee; 24. Leave there thy gift before the altar, and go thy way; first be reconciled to thy brother, and then come and offer thy gift.	25. Therefore, if ye shall come unto me, or shall desire to come unto me, or if thou bring thy gift to the altar, and there rememberest that they brother hath aught against thee, 26. Leave thou thy gift before the altar, and go thy way unto thy brother, and first be reconciled to thy brother, and then come and offer thy gift.	23. Therefore, if ye shall unto me, or shall desire to unto me, and remembere thy brother hast aught . thee-- 24. Go thy way unto thy b and first be reconciled brother, and then come u with full purpose of hear will receive you.

THE UNFORGIVEN OFFENDER MUST PAY TO THE UTTERMOST FARTHING

25. Agree with thine adversary quickly, whiles thou art in the way with him; lest at any time the adversary deliver thee to the judge, and the judge deliver thee to the officer, and thou be cast into prison. 26. Verily I say unto thee, Thou shalt by no means come out thence, till thou hast paid the uttermost farthing.	27. Agree with thine adversary quickly, while thou art in the way with him; lest at any time thine adversary deliver thee to the judge, and the judge deliver thee to the officer, and thou be cast into prison. 28. Verily I say unto thee, thou shalt by no means come out thence, until thou hast paid the uttermost farthing.	25. Agree with thine adv quickly while thou art way with him, lest at an he shall get thee, and tho be cast into prison. 26. Verily, verily, I say unt thou shalt by no means out thence until thou ha the uttermost senine. Anc ye are in prison can ye pa one senine? Verily, verily unto you, Nay.

CONCERNING ADULTERY

have heard that it was y them of old time, Thou ot commit adultery:	29. Behold, it is written by them of old time, that thou shalt not commit adultery.	27. Behold, it is written by them of old time, that thou shalt not commit adultery;
it I say unto you, That ever looketh on a woman after her hath committed ry with her already in his	30. But I say unto you, that whosoever looketh on a woman to lust after her, hath committed adultery with her in his heart already.	28. But I say unto you, that whosoever looketh on a woman, to lust after her, hath committed adultery already in his heart.
	31. Behold, I give unto you a commandment, that ye suffer none of these things to enter into your heart, for it is better that ye should deny yourselves of these things, wherein ye will take up your cross, than that ye should be cast into hell.	29. Behold, I give unto you a commandment, that ye suffer none of these things to enter into your heart;
		30. For it is better that ye should deny yourselves of these things, wherein ye will take up your cross, than that ye should be cast into hell.

THE OFFENDING EYE

d if thy right eye offend pluck it out, and cast [it] hee: for it is profitable for hat one of thy members l perish, and not [that] thy body should be cast into	32. Wherefore, if thy right eye offend thee, pluck it out and cast if from thee; for it is profitable for thee that one of thy members should perish, and not that thy whole body should be cast into hell.	

THE OFFENDING HAND

d if thy right hand offend ut it off, and cast [it] from or it is profitable for thee e of thy members should , and not [that] thy whole hould be cast into hell.	33. Or if thy right hand offend thee, cut it off and cast it from thee; for it is profitable for thee that one of thy members should perish and not that thy whole body should be cast into hell.	
	34. And now this I speak, a parable concerning your sins; wherefore, cast them from you, that ye may not be hewn down and cast into the fire.	

CONCERNING DIVORCE

31. It hath been said, Whosoever shall put away his wife, let him give her a writing of divorcement:	35. It hath been written that, Whosoever shall put away his wife, let him give her a writing of divorcement.	31. It hath been writte▮ whosoever shall put aw▮ wife, let him give her a ▮ of divorcement.
32. But I say unto you, That whosoever shall put away his wife, saving for the cause of fornication, causeth her to commit adultery: and whosoever shall marry her that is divorced committeth adultery.	36. Verily, verily, I say unto you that whosoever shall put away his wife, saving for the cause of fornication, causeth her to commit adultery; and whosoever shall marry her that is divorced, committeth adultery.	32. Verily, verily, I say unt▮ that whosoever shall put▮ his wife, saving for the ca▮ fornication, causeth h▮ commit adultery; and ▮ shall marry her who is di▮ committeth adultery.

CONCERNING OATHS OTHER THAN TO GOD

33. Again, ye have heard that it hath been said by them of old time, Thou shalt not forswear thyself, but shalt perform unto the Lord thine oaths:	37. Again, it hath been written by them of old time, Thou shalt not forswear thyself, but shall perform unto the Lord thine oaths.	33. And again it is written shalt not forswear thyself shalt perform unto the Lo▮ thine oaths;
34. But I say unto you, Swear not at all; neither by heaven; for it is God's throne:	38. But I say unto you, swear not at all; neither by heaven, for it is God's home; nor by the earth, for it is his footstool; neither by Jerusalem, for it is the city of the great King; neither shalt thou swear by thy head, because thou canst not make one hair white or black.	34. But verily, verily, I say you, swear not at all; neit▮ heaven, for it is God's thr▮
35. Nor by the earth; for it is his footstool: neither by Jerusalem; for it is the city of the great King.		35. Nor by the earth, for i▮ footstool;
36. Neither shalt thou swear by thy head, because thou canst not make one hair white or black.	39. But let your communication be Yea, yea; Nay, nay; for whatsoever is more than these cometh of evil.	36. Neither shalt thou sw▮ thy head, because thou c▮ not make one hair black ▮ white;
37. But let your communication be, Yea, yea; Nay, nay: for whatsoever is more than these cometh of evil.		37. But let your communi▮ be Yea, yea; Nay, nay; fo▮ whatsoever cometh of m▮ than these is evil.

THE ROLE OF THE PEACEMAKER: TURN THE OTHER CHEEK

e have heard that it hath said, An eye for an eye, tooth for a tooth:	40. You have heard that it hath been said, An eye for an eye, and a tooth for a tooth.	38. And behold, it is written, an eye for an eye, and a tooth for a tooth;
ıt I say unto you, That ye not evil: but whosoever smite thee on thy right , turn to him the other	41. But I say unto you, that ye resist not evil; but whosoever shall smite thee on thy right cheek, turn to him the other also.	39. But I say unto you, that ye shall not resist evil, but whosoever shall smite thee on thy right cheek, turn to him the other also;
ıd if any man will sue thee law, and take away thy let him have [thy] cloak ıd whosoever shall compel ı go a mile, go with him	42. And if any man will sue thee at the law, and take away thy coat, let him have it; and if he sue thee again, let him have thy cloak also. 43. And whosoever shall compel thee to go a mile, go with him a mile; and whosoever shall compel thee to go with him twain, thou shalt go with him twain.	40. And if any man will sue thee at the law and take away thy coat, let him have thy cloak also; 41. And whosoever shall compel thee to go a mile, go with him twain.

BE GENEROUS TO THOSE IN NEED

ve to him that asketh thee, ɔm him that would borrow e turn not thou away.	44. Give to him that asketh of thee; and from him that would borrow of thee, turn not thou away.	42. Give to him that asketh thee, and from him that would borrow of thee turn not away.

LOVE THINE ENEMIES

ı have heard that it hath ʂaid, Thou shalt love thy ɔour, and hate thine ɣ.	45. Ye have heard that it hath been said, Thou shalt love thy neighbour, and hate thine enemy.	43. And behold it is written also, that thou shalt love thy neighbor and hate thine enemy;

LOVE THINE ENEMIES (continued)

44. But I say unto you, Love your enemies, bless them that curse you, do good to them that hate you, and pray for them which despitefully use you, and persecute you;	46. But I say unto you, love your enemies; bless them that curse you; do good to them that hate you; and pray for them which despitefully use you and persecute you;	44. But I say unto you, lov enemies, bless them that you, do good to them tha you, and pray for them despitefully use you persecute you;
45. That ye may be the children of your Father which is in heaven: for he maketh his sun to rise on the evil and on the good, and sendeth rain on the just and on the unjust.	47. That ye may be the children of your Father who is in heaven; for he maketh his sun to rise on the evil and on the good, and sendeth rain on the just and on the unjust.	45. That ye may be the ch of your Father who is in h for he maketh his sun to r the evil and on the good.
46. For if ye love them which love you, what reward have ye? do not even the publicans the same?	48. For if ye love only them which love you, what reward have you? Do not even the publicans the same?	
47. And if ye salute your brethren only, what do ye more [than others]? do not even the publicans so?	49. And if ye salute your brethren only, what do ye more than others? Do not even the publicans the same?	

BE YE PERFECT

48. Be ye therefore perfect, even as your Father which is in heaven is perfect.	50. Ye are therefore commanded to be perfect, even as your Father who is in heaven is perfect.	46. Therefore those which were of old time, were under the law, in m all fulfilled.
		47. Old things are done and all things have be new.
		48. Therefore I would t should be perfect even a your Father who is in hea perfect.

WHEN THOU DOEST ALMS

Matt. 6	Matt. 6	3 Nephi 13
ke heed that ye do not your before men, to be seen of ; otherwise ye have no rd of your Father which is aven. ierefore when thou doest ·] alms, do not sound a et before thee, as the crites do in the synagogues n the streets, that they may glory of men. Verily I say you, They have their ·d. r when thou doest alms, let iy left hand know what thy hand doeth: at thine alms may be in :: and thy Father which in secret himself shall d thee openly.	1. And it came to pass that as Jesus taught his disciples, he said unto them, Take heed that ye do not your alms before men, to be seen of them; otherwise ye have no reward of your Father who is in heaven. 2. Therefore, when thou doest alms, do not sound a trumpet before thee, as the hypocrites do, in the synagogues and in the streets, that they may have glory of men. Verily I say unto you, they have their reward. 3. But when thou doest alms, let it be unto thee as thy left hand not knowing what thy right hand knowing what thy right hand doeth; 4. That thine alms may be in secret; and thy Father who seeth in secret, himself shall reward thee openly.	1. Verily, verily, I say that I would that ye should do alms unto the poor; but take heed that ye do not your alms before men to be seen of them; otherwise ye have no reward of your Father who is in heaven. 2. Therefore, when ye shall do your alms do not sound a trumpet before you, as will hypocrites do in the synagogues and in the streets, that they may have glory of men. Verily I say unto you, they have their reward. 3. But when thou doest alms let not thy left hand know what thy right hand doeth; 4. That thine alms may be in secret; and thy Father who seeth in secret, himself shall reward thee openly.

WHEN THOU PRAYEST

l when thou prayest, thou not be as the hypocrites for they love to pray ng in the synagogues and corners of the streets, that nay be seen of men. Verily unto you, They have their d.	5. And when thou prayest, thou shalt not be as the hypocrites; for they love to pray standing in the synagogues and in the corners of the streets, that they may be seen of men; for, verily, I say into you, they have their reward.	5. And when thou prayest thou shalt not do as the hypocrites, for they love to pray, standing in the synagogues and in the corners of the streets, that they may be seen of men. Verily I say unto you, they have their reward.

PRAY IN SECRET

6. But thou, when thou prayest, enter into thy closet, and when thou hast shut thy door, pray to thy Father which is in secret; and thy Father which seeth in secret shall reward thee openly.	6. But thou, when thou prayest, enter into thy closet, and when thou hast shut thy door, pray to thy Father which is in secret; and thy Father which seeth in secret shall reward thee openly.	6. But thou, when thou p▸ enter into thy closet, and thou hast shut thy door, ▸ thy Father who is in secre thy Father, who seeth in ▸ shall reward thee openly.

USE NOT VAIN REPETITIONS

7. But when ye pray, use not vain repetitions, as the heathen [do]: for they think that they shall be heard for their much speaking. 8. Be not ye therefore like unto them: for your Father knoweth what things ye have need of, before ye ask him.	7. But when ye pray, use not vain repetitions, as the hypocrites do; for they think that they shall be heard for their much speaking. 8. Therefore be ye not like unto them; for your Father knoweth what things ye have need of, before ye ask him.	7. But when ye pray, u▸ vain repetitions, as the he▸ for they think that they s▸ heard for their much spea▸ 8. Be not ye therefore lik▸ them, for your Father kn▸ what things ye have ne▸ before ye ask him.

THE LORD'S PRAYER

9. After this manner therefore pray ye: Our Father which art in heaven, Hallowed be thy name. 10. Thy kingdom come. Thy will be done in earth, as [it is] in heaven. 11. Give us this day our daily bread. 12. And forgive us our debts, as we forgive our debtors. 13. And lead us not into temptation, but deliver us from evil: For thine is the kingdom, and the power, and the glory, for ever. Amen.	9. Therefore after this manner shall ye pray, saying, 10. Our Father who art in heaven, Hallowed be thy name. 11. Thy kingdom come. Thy will be done on earth, as it is done in heaven. 12. Give us this day, our daily bread. 13. And forgive us our trespasses, as we forgive those who trespass against us. 14. And suffer us not to be led into temptation, but deliver us from evil. 15. For thine is the kingdom, and the power, and the glory, forever and ever, Amen.	9. After this manner the▸ pray ye: Our Father who▸ heaven, hallowed be thy ▸ 10. Thy will be done on e▸ it is in heaven. 11. And forgive us our de▸ we forgive our debtors. 12. And lead us not ▸ temptation, but deliver u▸ evil. 13. For thine is the king▸ and the power, and the ▸ forever. Amen.

FORGIVE TRESPASSES

or if ye forgive men their ısses, your heavenly Father ılso forgive you: ıut if ye forgive not men ,respasses, neither will your r forgive your trespasses.	16. For if ye forgive men their trespasses, who trespass against you, your heavenly Father will also forgive you; but if ye forgive not men their trespasses, neither will your heavenly Father forgive you your trespasses.	14. For, if ye forgive men their trespasses your heavenly Father will also forgive you; 15. But if ye forgive not men their trespasses neither will your Father forgive your trespasses.

CONCERNING FASTING

loreover when ye fast, be ıs the hypocrites, of a sad .enance: for they disfigure ′aces, that they may appear men to fast. Verily I say you, They have their ′d. ıt thou, when thou fastest, ,t thine head, and wash thy ıhat thou appear not unto :o fast, but unto thy Father ı is in secret: and thy ır, which seeth in secret, ıeward thee openly.	17. Moreover, when ye fast, be not as the hypocrites, of a sad countenance for they disfigure their faces, that they may appear unto men to fast. Verily I say unto you, they have their reward. 18. But thou, when thou fastest, anoint thy head and wash thy face, that thou appear not unto men to fast, but unto thy Father who is in secret; and thy Father who seeth in secret, shall reward thee openly.	16. Moreover, when ye fast be not as the hypocrites, of a sad countenance, for they disfigure their faces that they may appear unto men to fast. Verily I say unto you, they have their reward. 17. But thou, when thou fastest, anoint thy head, and wash thy face; 18. That thou appear not unto men to fast, but unto thy Father, who is in secret; and thy Father, who seeth in secret, shall reward thee openly.

LAY NOT UP TREASURES UPON EARTH

ay not up for yourselves ıres upon earth, where and rust doth corrupt, and ıe thieves break through ıeal:	19. Lay not up for yourselves treasures upon earth, where moth and rust doth corrupt, and where thieves break through and steal.	19. Lay not up for yourselves treasures upon earth, where moth and rust doth corrupt, and thieves break through and steal;

LAY UP TREASURES IN HEAVEN

20. But lay up for yourselves treasures in heaven, where neither moth nor rust doth corrupt, and where thieves do not break through nor steal:	20. But lay up for yourselves treasures in heaven, where neither moth nor rust doth corrupt, and where thieves do not break through nor steal.	20. But lay up for yours treasures in heaven, w neither moth nor rust corrupt, and where thieve not break through nor stea
21. For where your treasure is, there will your heart be also.	21. For where your treasure is, there will your heart be also.	21. For where your treasu there will your heart be als

THE LIGHT OF THE EYE

22. The light of the body is the eye: if therefore thine eye be single, thy whole body shall be full of light.	22. The light of the body is the eye; if therefore thine eye be single to the glory of God, thy whole body shall be full of light.	22. The light of the body i eye; if, therefore, thine ey single, thy whole body sha full of light.
23. But if thine eye be evil, thy whole body shall be full of darkness. If therefore the light that is in thee be darkness, how great [is] that darkness!	23. But if thine eye be evil, thy whole body shall be full of darkness. If therefore the light which is in thee be darkness, how great shall that darkness be!	23. But if thine eye be evi whole body shall be fu darkness. If, therefore, the that is in thee be darkness, great is that darkness!

NO MAN CAN SERVE TWO MASTERS

24. No man can serve two masters: for either he will hate the one, and love the other; or else he will hold to the one, and despise the other. Ye cannot serve God and mammon.	24. No man can serve two masters, for either he will hate the one, and love the other; or else he will hold to the one and despise the other. Ye cannot serve God and Mammon.	24. No man can serve masters; for either he will the one and love the othe else he will hold to the one despise the other. Ye ca serve God and Mammon.

INSTRUCTION TO THE TWELVE:
TAKE NO THOUGHT WHAT YE SHALL EAT OR DRINK

25. Therefore I say unto you, Take no thought for your life, what ye shall eat, or what ye shall drink; nor yet for your body, what ye shall put on. Is not the life more than meat, and the body than raiment?	25. And again, I say unto you, go ye into the world, and care not for the world; for the world will hate you, and will persecute you, and will turn you out of their synagogues.	25. And now it came to pa that when Jesus had spoke these words he looked up the twelve whom he had chosen, and said unto ther Remember the words whi

INSTRUCTION TO THE TWELVE:
TAKE NO THOUGHT WHAT YE SHALL EAT OR DRINK
(continued)

ehold the fowls of the air:
ey sow not, neither do they
nor gather into barns; yet
heavenly Father feedeth
. Are ye not much better
they?

Which of you by taking
ght can add one cubit unto
ature?

nd why take ye thought for
ent? Consider the lilies of
ield, how they grow; they
ot, neither do they spin:

nd yet I say unto you, That
Solomon in all his glory
not arrayed like one of
e.

Vherefore, if God so clothe
grass of the field, which to
s, and to morrow is cast into
oven, [shall he] not much
[clothe] you, O ye of little

herefore take no thought,
ng, What shall we eat? or,
t shall we drink? or,
rewithal shall we be
ed?

For after all these things do
Gentiles seek:) for your
enly Father knoweth that ye
need of all these things.
?

26. Nevertheless, ye shall go
forth from house to house,
teaching the people; and I will
go before you.

27. And your heavenly Father
will provide for you, whatsoever
things ye need for food, what ye
shall eat; and for raiment, what
ye shall wear or put on.

28. Therefore I say unto you take
no thought for your life, what ye
shall eat or what ye shall drink;
nor yet for your bodies, what ye
shall put on. Is not the life more
than meat, and the body than
raiment?

29. Behold the fowls of the air,
for they sow not, neither do they
reap, nor gather into barns; yet
your heavenly Father feedeth
them. Are ye not much better
than they? How much more will
he not feed you?

30. Wherefore take no thought
for these things, but keep my
commandments wherewith I
have commanded you.

31. For which of you by taking
thought can add one cubit unto
his stature.

32. And why take ye thought for
raiment? Consider the lilies of
the field, how they grow; they
toil not, neither do they spin.

have spoken. For behold, ye
are they whom I have chosen to
minister unto this people.
Therefore I say unto you, take
no thought for your life, what ye
shall eat, or what ye shall drink;
nor yet for your body, what ye
shall put on. Is not the life more
than meat, and the body than
raiment?

26. Behold the fowls of the air,
for they sow not, neither do they
reap nor gather into barns; yet
your heavenly Father feedeth
them. Are ye not much better
than they?

27. Which of you by taking
thought can add one cubit unto
his stature?

28. And why take ye thought for
raiment? Consider the lilies of
the field how they grow; they
toil not, neither do they spin;

**INSTRUCTION TO THE TWELVE:
TAKE NO THOUGHT WHAT YE SHALL EAT OR DRINK
(continued)**

	33. And yet I say unto you, that even Solomon, in all his glory, was not arrayed like one of these.	29. And yet I say unto you even Solomon, in all his g was not arrayed like on these.
	34. Therefore, if God so clothe the grass of the field, which to-day is, and tomorrow is cast into the oven, how much more will he not provide for you, if ye are not of little faith.	30. Wherefore, if God so c the grass of the field, w today is, and tomorrow is into the oven, even so wi clothe you, if ye are not of faith.
	35. Therefore take no thought saying, What shall we eat, or What shall we drink? or, Wherewithal shall we be clothed?	31. Therefore take no thou saying, What shall we eat? What shall we drink? Wherewithal shall we clothed?
	36. Why is it that ye murmur among yourselves, saying, We cannot obey thy word because ye have not all these things, and seek to excuse yourselves, saying that, After all these things do the Gentiles seek.	32. For your heavenly Fa knoweth that ye have need these things.
	37. Behold, I say unto you, that your heavenly Father knoweth that ye have need of all these things.	

SEEK YE FIRST THE KINGDOM OF GOD

33. But seek ye first the kingdom of God, and his righteousness; and all these things shall be added unto you.	38. Wherefore, seek not the things of this world but seek ye first to build up the kingdom of God, and to establish his righteousness, and all these things shall be added unto you.	33. But seek ye first the kingdom of God and his righteousness, and all these things shall be added unto

APOSTLES TOLD TO TAKE NO THOUGHT OF THE MORROW

ake therefore no thought e morrow: for the morrow take thought for the things elf. Sufficient unto the day e evil thereof.	39. Take, therefore, no thought for the morrow; for the morrow shall take thought for the things of itself. Sufficient unto the day shall be the evil thereof.	34. Take therefore no thought for the morrow, for the morrow shall take thought for the things of itself. Sufficient is the day unto the evil thereof.

JESUS TURNS BACK TO THE MULTITUDE

Matt. 7	Matt. 7	3 Nephi 14
	1. Now these are the words which Jesus taught his disciples that they should say unto the people.	1. And now it came to pass that when Jesus had spoken these words he turned again to the multitude, and did open his mouth unto them again, saying:

JUDGE NOT

dge not, that ye be not d.	2. Judge not unrighteously, that ye be not judged; but judge righteous judgment.	2. Verily, verily, I say unto you, Judge not, that ye be not judged.

THE MOTE IN THY BROTHER'S EYE

r with what judgment ye , ye shall be judged: and what measure ye mete, it be measured to you again.	3. For with what judgment ye shall judge, ye shall be judged; and with what measure ye mete, it shall be measured to you again.	2. For with what judgment ye judge, ye shall be judged; and with what measure ye mete, it shall be measured to you again.
d why beholdest thou the that is in thy brother's but considerest not the that is in thine own eye?	4. And again, ye shall say unto them, Why is it that thou beholdest the mote that is in thy brother's eye, but considerest not the beam that is in thine own eye?	3. And why beholdest thou the mote that is in thy brother's eye, but considerest not the beam that is in thine own eye?
how wilt thou say to thy er, Let me pull out the out of thine eye; and, ld, a beam [is] in thine eye?	5. Or how wilt thou say to thy brother, Let me pull out the mote out of thine eye; and canst not behold a beam in thine own eye?	4. Or how wilt thou say to thy brother: Let me pull the mote out of thine eye--and behold, a beam is in thine own eye?

THE MOTE IN THY BROTHER'S EYE (continued)

5. Thou hypocrite, first cast out the beam out of thine own eye; and then shalt thou see clearly to cast out the mote out of thy brother's eye.	6. And Jesus said unto his disciples, Beholdest thou the Scribes, and the Pharisees, and Priests, and the Levites? They teach in their synagogues, but do not observe the law, nor the commandments; and all have gone out of the way, and are under sin. 7. Go thou and say unto them, Why teach ye men the law and the commandments, when ye yourselves are the children of corruption? 8. Say unto them, ye hypocrites, first cast out the beam out of thine own eye and then shalt thou see clearly to cast out the mote out of thy brother's eye.	5. Thou hypocrite, first ca beam out of thine own ey then shalt thou see clea cast the mote out o brother's eye.

CAST NOT YOUR PEARLS BEFORE SWINE

6. Give not that which is holy unto the dogs, neither cast ye your pearls before swine, lest they trample them under their feet, and turn again and rend you.	9. Go ye into the world, saying unto all, Repent, for the kingdom of heaven has come nigh unto you. 10. And the mysteries of the kingdom ye shall keep within yourselves; for it is not meet to give that which is holy unto the dogs; neither cast ye your pearls unto swine, lest they trample them under their feet. 11. For the world cannot receive that which ye, yourselves, are not able to bear; wherefore ye shall not give your pearls unto them, lest they turn again and rend you.	6. Give not that which is unto the dogs, neither ca your pearls before swine they trample them under feet, and turn again and you.

ASK AND IT SHALL BE GIVEN

, and it shall be given you; and ye shall find; knock, shall be opened unto you:	12. Say unto them, Ask of God; ask, and it shall be given you; seek, and ye shall find; knock, and it shall be opened unto you.	7. Ask, and it shall be given unto you; seek, and ye shall find; knock, and it shall be opened unto you.
r every one that asketh eth; and he that seeketh th; and to him that eth it shall be opened.	13. For every one that asketh, receiveth; and he that seeketh, findeth; and unto him that knocketh, it shall be opened.	8. For every one that asketh, receiveth; and he that seeketh, findeth; and to him that knocketh, it shall be opened.
what man is there of you, if his son ask bread, will e him a stone?	14. And then said his disciples unto him, they will say unto us, We ourselves are righteous, and need not that any man should teach us. God, we know, heard Moses and some of the prophets; but us he will not hear.	9. Or what man is there of you, who, if his son ask bread, will give him a stone?
r if he ask a fish, will he im a serpent?		10. Or if he ask a fish, will he give him a serpent?
ye then, being evil, know o give good gifts unto your en, how much more shall Father which is in heaven good things to them that im?	15. And they will say, We have the law of our salvation, and that is sufficient for us. 16. Then Jesus answered and said unto his disciples, thus shall ye say unto them, 17. What man among you, having a son, and he shall be standing out, and shall say, Father, open thy house that I may come in and sup with thee, will not say, Come in my son; for mine is thine, and thine is mine? 18. Or what man is there among you, who, if his son ask bread, will give him a stone? 19. Or if he ask a fish, will he give him a serpent? 20. If ye then, being evil, know how to give good gifts unto your children, how much more shall your Father who is in heaven give good things to them that ask him?	11. If ye then, being evil, know how to give good gifts unto your children, how much more shall your Father who is in heaven give good things to them that ask him?

THE GOLDEN RULE

12. Therefore all things whatsoever ye would that men should do to you, do ye even so to them: for this is the law and the prophets.	21. Therefore, all things whatsoever ye would that men should do unto you, do ye even so to them; for this is the law and the prophets.	12. Therefore, all t whatsoever ye would tha should do to you, do ye e to them, for this is the la the prophets.

ENTER IN AT THE STRAIT GATE

| 13. Enter ye in at the strait gate: for wide [is] the gate, and broad [is] the way, that leadeth to destruction, and many there be which go in thereat: | 22. Repent, therefore, and enter ye in at the strait gate; for wide is the way that leadeth to destruction, and many there be who go in thereat. | 13. Enter ye in at the strai for wide is the gate, and br the way, which leade destruction, and many the who go in thereat; |
| 14. Because strait [is] the gate, and narrow [is] the way, which leadeth unto life, and few there be that find it. | 23. Because strait is the gate, and narrow is the way that leadeth unto life, and few there be that find it. | 14. Because strait is the and narrow is the way, ▾ leadeth unto life, and few be that find it. |

BEWARE OF FALSE PROPHETS

| 15. Beware of false prophets, which come to you in sheep's clothing, but inwardly they are ravening wolves. | 24. And, again, beware of false prophets, who come to you in sheep's clothing; but inwardly they are ravening wolves. | 15. Beware of false prop who come to you in sh clothing, but inwardly the ravening wolves. |

YE SHALL KNOW THEM BY THEIR FRUITS

| 16. Ye shall know them by their fruits. Do men gather grapes of thorns, or figs of thistles?

17. Even so every good tree bringeth forth good fruit; but a corrupt tree bringeth forth evil fruit. | 25. Ye shall know them by their fruits; for do men gather grapes of thorns, or figs of thistles?

26. Even so every good tree bringeth forth good fruit; but a corrupt tree bringeth forth evil fruit. | 16. Ye shall know them by their fruits. Do men gathe grapes of thorns, or figs of thistles?

17. Even so every good tre bringeth forth good fruit; I corrupt tree bringeth forth fruit. |

YE SHALL KNOW THEM BY THEIR FRUITS
(continued)

good tree cannot bring evil fruit, neither [can] a ɔt tree bring forth good	27. A good tree cannot bring forth evil fruit; neither a corrupt tree bring forth good fruit.	18. A good tree cannot bring forth evil fruit, neither a corrupt tree bring forth good fruit.
very tree that bringeth not good fruit is hewn down, ast into the fire.	28. Every tree that bringeth not forth good fruit, is hewn down, and cast into the fire.	19. Every tree that bringeth not forth good fruit is hewn down, and cast into the fire.
herefore by their fruits ye know them.	29. Wherefore by their fruits ye shall know them.	20. Wherefore, by their fruits ye shall know them.

NOT EVERYONE THAT SAITH, LORD, LORD...

ɔt every one that saith unto ord, Lord, shall enter into ingdom of heaven; but he oeth the will of my Father ɪ is in heaven.	30. Verily I say unto you, it is not every one that saith unto me, Lord, Lord, that shall enter into the kingdom of heaven; but he that doeth the will of my Father who is in heaven.	21. Not every one that saith unto me, Lord, Lord, shall enter into the kingdom of heaven; but he that doeth the will of my Father who is in heaven.
	31. For the day soon cometh, that men shall come before me to judgment, to be judged according to their works.	

CONCERNING THOSE WHO ARE NOT VALIANT

lany will say to me in that Lord, Lord, have we not hesied in thy name? and in ame have cast out devils? in thy name done many lerful works?	32. And many will say unto me in that day, Lord, Lord, have we not prophesied in thy name; and in thy name cast out devils; and in thy name done many wonderful works?	22. Many will say to me in that day: Lord, Lord, have we not prophesied in thy name, and in thy name have cast out devils, and in thy name done many wonderful works?
nd then will I profess unto , I never knew you: depart me, ye that work iniquity.	33. And then will I say, Ye never knew me; depart from me ye that work iniquity.	23. And then will I profess unto them: I never knew you; depart from me, ye that work iniquity.

THE HOUSE BUILT ON ROCK

24. Therefore whosoever heareth these sayings of mine, and doeth them, I will liken him unto a wise man, which built his house upon a rock: 25. And the rain descended, and the floods came, and the winds blew, and beat upon that house; and it fell not: for it was founded upon a rock.	34. Therefore, whosoever heareth these sayings of mine and doeth them, I will liken him unto a wise man who built his house upon a rock, and the rains descended, and the floods came, and the winds blew, and beat upon that house, and it fell not; for it was founded upon a rock.	24. Therefore, whoso h these sayings of mine and them, I will liken him wise man, who built his upon a rock-- 25. And the rain descende the floods came, and the blew, and beat upon that and it fell not, for it was fo upon a rock.

THE HOUSE BUILT ON SAND

26. And every one that heareth these sayings of mine, and doeth them not, shall be likened unto a foolish man, which built his house upon the sand: 27. And the rain descended, and the floods came, and the winds blew, and beat upon that house; and it fell: and great was the fall of it.	35. And every one that heareth these sayings of mine, and doeth them not, shall be likened unto a foolish man, who built his house upon the sand; and the rains descended, and the floods came, and the winds blew, and beat upon that house, and it fell; and great was the fall of it.	26. And every one that he these sayings of mine and them not shall be likened i foolish man, who built his upon the sand— 27. And the rain descende the floods came, and the blew, and beat upon that h and it fell, and great was th of it.

JESUS TAUGHT AS ONE HAVING AUTHORITY

28. And it came to pass, when Jesus had ended these sayings, the people were astonished at his doctrine: 29. For he taught them as [one] having authority, and not as the scribes.	36. And it came to pass when Jesus had ended these sayings with his disciples, the people were astonished at his doctrine; 37. For he taught them as one having authority from God, and not as having authority from the Scribes.	

CHAPTER 17

THE SECOND TOUR
THROUGH GALILEE

Having completed our discussion of the Sermon on the Mount, let us now remind ourselves where we are in the story of the Savior's life. It will be recalled that as Jesus returned to the area of Capernaum—after his ministry of miracles throughout Galilee—a huge crowd followed him right down to the shores of the sea. In order to escape from these adoring multitudes, many of whom he had healed, Jesus retreated into a nearby mountain.

After praying to the Father all night he called some of his disciples to him. From among these he chose twelve and ordained them apostles. Then he carefully instructed all of the disciples in the sacred lecture which we have just reviewed called the Sermon on the Mount.

As we mentioned earlier, whenever Jesus retreated to a mountain to pray, or to have a quiet conversation with his disciples, the people respected his desire to be alone and did not attempt to follow him.

However, on this occasion Jesus was gone all night and probably much of the next day. One would suppose that after such a long time, the crowd would have dispersed and gone to their homes, but not so.

When Jesus and his disciples came down from the mountain, there was the adoring multitude, patiently waiting. Matthew says:

"When he was come down from the mountain, great multitudes followed him."[1]

---

[1]Matthew 8:1.

THE SERMON ON THE PLAIN

At this point, Luke picks up the narrative and says that Jesus decided to reward these patient people by first healing any additional sick who had appeared on the scene, and then telling the people nearly everything he had told his apostles on the mount.

This second discourse on the Christian way of life is called the "Sermon on the Plain." The "plain" has reference to the rather smooth meadow land along the shores of the Galilee. Luke says:

"And he came down with them, and stood in the plain, and the company of his disciples, and a great multitude of people out of all Judaea and Jerusalem, and from the sea coast of Tyre and Sidon, which came to hear him, and to be healed of their diseases;

"And they that were vexed with unclean spirits: and they were healed.

"And the whole multitude sought to touch him: for there went virtue out of him, and healed them all."[2]

After he had healed those with diseased or crippled bodies, Luke says Jesus looked out upon this vast audience and said:

"Blessed be ye poor: for yours is the kingdom of God...."[3]

Thus began an abbreviated version of the Sermon on the Mount. But now it was the Sermon on the plain. Luke describes in general what Jesus told the people,[4] and we notice that it included nearly all the highlights of those thing he had told the apostles on the mount. The only important difference was that Jesus left out his instructions to the apostles in which he said, "Take no thought of the morrow."

As we mentioned in chapter 15, when the resurrected Christ went to minister to his other sheep in America he also left out this part

---

[2]Luke 6:17-19.
[3]Luke 6:20.
[4]Luke 6:20-49.

while addressing the general congregation. However, when he turned to his twelve special disciples, he told them to "take no thought of the morrow" just as he had his Jewish apostles.[5]

JESUS HEALS ANOTHER LEPER

As Jesus finished his Sermon on the Plain, he began his journey toward nearby Capernaum. The vast throng crowded and pushed right along with him. But before Jesus had gone far, a wretched creature full of running sores, with filthy clothes and a foul breath, fell at his feet pleading with him. The man was a leper. Mark described the healing of a leper, but under different circumstances (p. 195). Assuming that we are now talking about a different leper, here is his story. The leper said:

"Lord, if thou wilt, thou canst make me clean.

"And Jesus put forth his hand, and touched him, saying, I will; be thou clean. And immediately his leprosy was cleansed."[6]

Leprosy was such a horrible disease that sometimes the rotting flesh and even the joints of the extremities were sloughed off. To be healed of such a disease was virtually unthinkable. No doubt the crowd was horrified as Jesus touched the crouching figure. It was believed that touching a leper was the way the disease was spread. That is why lepers had to go about crying "Unclean! Unclean!"[7] But suddenly this man was clean. His clothes were still filthy and stained from the sores, but his flesh was clean. Truly, this was unbelievable.

"And Jesus saith unto him, See thou tell no man; but go thy way, shew thyself to the priest, and offer the gift that Moses commanded, for a testimony unto them."[8]

This was the same advice he had given the previous leper during the first tour through Galilee (p. 197).

---

[5]Compare 3 Nephi 13:25 with 14:1.
[6]Matthew 8:2-3.
[7]Leviticus 13:45.
[8]Matthew 8:4; Leviticus, chap. 14.

As we have mentioned before, one cannot help but wonder why Jesus would tell some of those he healed to keep their miraculous blessing a secret. It may have been done so that the immediate bystanders would hear him and thereby witness that he was not seeking to promote himself or publicize his healing powers. If this were the case, it may have been his way of refuting the jealous religious leaders who tried to brush aside his miracles by saying they were merely publicity stunts.

THE FIRST ROMAN TO BE BLESSED WITH A MIRACLE

As Jesus came into Capernaum, he was met by the leaders of the local synagogue. They came at the request of the commander of the Roman garrison in the town. We do not know this officer's name, but he was highly respected by the Jews. Amazingly, he had paid for the building of their synagogue, and had the reputation among the Jews of being a good and just man even though he was a Roman.

Jesus was told that this Roman centurion (commander of a hundred soldiers) had a servant suffering terribly from palsy. In fact, even while the Jewish delegation was talking to Jesus, the centurion came to the Savior in person "beseeching him."[9] Jesus offered to go to his house, but the Roman commander astonished Jesus by saying:

"Lord, I am not worthy that thou shouldest come under my roof: but *speak the word only, and my servant shall be healed.* For I am a man under authority, having soldiers under me: and I say to this man, Go, and he goeth; and to another, Come, and he cometh; and to my servant, Do this, and he doeth it."[10]

Jesus said to the multitude nearest him:

"Verily I say unto you, I have not found so great faith, no, not in Israel."[11]

---

[9]Matthew 8:5.
[10]Matthew 8:8-9.
[11]Matthew 8:10.

Then, as he contemplated the faith of this pagan soldier, and compared it with the blindness of this multitude of his own people who would mostly reject him in the end, he said:

"I say unto you, That many shall come from the east and west, and shall sit down with Abraham, and Isaac, and Jacob, in the kingdom of heaven.

"But the children of the kingdom shall be cast out into outer darkness: there shall be weeping and gnashing of teeth."[12]

Jesus turned to the centurion and said, "Go thy way; and as thou hast believed, so be it done unto thee."[13]

When the centurion returned to his home he was elated to discover that his servant was "healed in the selfsame hour."[14]

JESUS RAISES THE DEAD FOR THE FIRST TIME

By the next day or soon thereafter, Jesus had left the vicinity of Capernaum and had traveled, with many people following him, to a town below Nazareth in the Jezreel valley called Nain. The people did not know it, but they were about to behold a miracle which, so far as we know, Jesus had never performed before. The scripture says:

"Now when he came nigh to the gate of the city, behold, there was a dead man carried out, the only son of his mother, and she was a widow: and much people of the city was with her.

"And when the Lord saw her, he had compassion on her, and said unto her, Weep not.

---

[12]Matthew 8:11-12.
[13]Matthew 8:13.
[14]Ibid.

"And he came and touched the bier: and they that bare him stood still. And he said, Young man, I say unto thee, Arise.

"And he that was dead sat up, and began to speak. And he delivered him to his mother."[15]

Truly, this seemed to be the ultimate in miracles. The multitude whispered among themselves that indeed God had been good to send such a man among them. The news that Jesus had raised the dead swept through the country like the east wind. The scripture says:

"And this rumour of him went forth throughout all Judaea, and throughout all the region round about."[16]

JESUS IS MINISTERED TO BY A SINFUL WOMAN

A sophisticated and learned Pharisee named Simon thought he would invite Jesus to dinner and perhaps study this famous stranger at closer range. To the chagrin of the Pharisee, right in the middle of the dinner, a woman who was well-known as "a sinner," came quietly into the room, knelt before Jesus, and began anointing and kissing his feet.

Simon immediately thought to himself that if Jesus were a prophet he would never have permitted this sinful woman to touch him. But he had barely let this thought creep into his mind when Jesus read his thoughts and said:

"Simon, I have somewhat to say unto thee....

"Seest thou this woman? I entered into thine house, thou gavest me no water for my feet: but she hath washed my feet with tears, and wiped them with the hairs of her head.

"Thou gavest me no kiss: but this woman since the time I came in hath not ceased to kiss my feet.

---

[15]Luke 7:12-15.
[16]Luke 7:17.

"My head with oil thou didst not anoint: but this woman hath anointed my feet with ointment.

"Wherefore I say unto thee, Her sins, which are many, are forgiven; for she loved much: but to whom little is forgiven, the same loveth little.

"And he said unto her, Thy sins are forgiven."[17]

Those at the table were electrified by this last statement. Was Jesus pretending to be God? He had told this woman he was forgiving her sins! As Jesus went his way, he must have left Simon and his guests mumbling among themselves and discussing the whole situation in confused excitement.

WHO WAS THE SINFUL WOMAN?

Scholars have wondered who this woman was. Some have speculated that she might have been Mary, the sister of Martha, who is later described as anointing the feet of Jesus at the home of another man named Simon.[18] However, this is a pure coincidence. Mary, the sister of Martha, was a righteous woman. She was no sinner.

Some have also thought this woman might have been Mary Magdalene who was the first to see Jesus after his resurrection. Luke himself provides the best evidence that the "sinful woman" was not Mary Magdalene. As we shall mention in a moment, just two verses after Luke discussed the incident of the "sinful woman," he began listing several righteous women who had ministered to the needs of Jesus and the apostles. The name of Mary Magdalene leads the list. It is difficult to believe that he would have failed to identify the sinful woman and then mention Mary Magdalene two verses later as being among some of the most notable women in Galilee.

JESUS AND THE TWELVE TOUR GALILEE AGAIN

Now, for the second time, Jesus made a tour of Galilee and no doubt duplicated the same marvelous miracles he had performed

---

[17]Luke 7:40, 44-48.
[18]Matthew 26:6-13.

earlier. Throughout the tour there were multiple instances of healing the sick, casting out devils, and earnestly preaching, at every opportunity, the gospel of the kingdom.

We can well imagine that these were arduous and difficult days, but there were caring people who did what they could to provide the basic comforts of life for Jesus and his apostles. We are told that sometimes Jesus was ministered to by converts who were women of wealth and prominence, while others who ministered to him were those he had healed. Luke says:

"He went throughout every city and village, preaching and shewing the glad tidings of the kingdom of God: and the twelve were with him,

"And certain women, which had been healed of evil spirits and infirmities, Mary called Magdalene, out of whom went seven devils,

"And Joanna the wife of Chuza Herod's steward, and Susanna, and many others, which ministered unto him of their substance."[19]

The fact that Jesus had healed Mary Magdalene of her infirmities and had cast out seven tormenting evil spirits, is no reflection on the character of this choice young woman. In fact, the Savior paid her one of the highest compliments possible by granting her the privilege of being the first person on earth to see him after his resurrection.[20]

SEVERAL HIGHLIGHTS OF
THIS SECOND GALILEAN TOUR

It was on this tour that Jesus taught some of his most famous parables, which we shall consider later.

It was also on this tour that, among his many miracles, he healed a man who was deaf and blind. This led the people to say among themselves, "Is not this the Son of David [the Messiah]?"[21]

---

[19]Luke 8:1-3.
[20]John 20:11-18.
[21]Matthew 12:23.

This greatly alarmed the Pharisees who could not deny the miracles but said it was all a trick which Jesus did by the power of the devil. By using this strategy, the Pharisees didn't have to deny the miracles, but simply dismissed Jesus as a charlatan and a tool of Satan. And who wants to support the miracles of the devil?

There was another group that said Jesus did not have to be accepted until God had sent a sign from heaven verifying that he was the Messiah. It is interesting that the marvelous miracles Jesus had been performing were not equated with a "sign from heaven."

Of course, as we pointed out in Chapter 5, the people had been warned by some of their most learned leaders that unless a miracle worker overthrew the Romans, he did not have the full credentials of the great Messiah.

Jesus decided to dispose of these two groups of assailants before their agitation festered into an eruption of violent hostility. To the Pharisees, and their "devil theory," he said:

"Every kingdom divided against itself is brought to desolation; and every city or house divided against itself shall not stand:

"And if Satan cast out Satan, he is divided against himself; how shall then his kingdom stand?"[22]

Then Jesus referred to some of the more faithful Jewish religious leaders who were acknowledged to have succeeded in liberating a number of afflicted individuals from the power of evil spirits. Jesus had made the point that since the devil would not cast out his own evil spirits, then who had given their more righteous religious leaders the power to cast them out? Obviously it would have to be the power of God. So Jesus said:

"And if I by Beelzebub cast out devils, by whom do your children cast them out? Therefore they shall be your judges."[23]

---

[22]Matthew 12:25-26.
[23]Matthew 12:27.

And it follows, of course, that if these miracles are being performed by the power of God then they must acknowledge that Jesus has come into their midst as an emissary of the Almighty. So Jesus said:

"But if I cast out devils by the Spirit of God, then the kingdom of God is come unto you."[24]

In terms of sophisticated polemics, no Pharisee could match this amazing Galilean. No matter which way they turned, he cornered them.

Next he turned to the sign-seekers. What he had to say to them exposed some of their evil ways with a direct accusation. Their big mistake was when they said:

"Master, we would see a sign from thee."[25]

Jesus decided to tell the multitude what he knew about people who "seek signs." He said:

"An evil and adulterous generation seeketh after a sign."[26]

This put a label on these sign-seekers that they were not anxious to discuss any further. Jesus knew them better than they thought.

EVIL SPIRITS SOMETIMES TRY TO RETURN

This entire discussion about miracles and the source of Christ's power came about as a result of a miracle in which Jesus had cast an evil spirit from a man who was blind and deaf. The man was instantly healed.

But now Jesus had something to say to all those who had been healed by having evil spirits cast out of them. He said:

[24]Matthew 12:28.
[25]Matthew 12:38.
[26]Matthew 12:39.

"When the unclean spirit is gone out of a man, he walketh through dry places, seeking rest, and finding none, he saith, I will return unto my house whence I came out....

"Then goeth he, and taketh to him seven other spirits more wicked than himself; and they enter in, and dwell there: and the last state of that man is worse than the first."[27]

This message was for those who had just been healed. It is true that nature abhors a vacuum, and if the departure of the evil spirits had left a vacancy in the spiritual tabernacle of a person, he or she had better fill it up to overflowing with the Spirit of the Lord. A spiritual vacancy is an open invitation to the evil spirits to return, and Jesus therefore said, "the state of that man is worse than the first."[28]

THE FAMILY OF JESUS ARRIVES

While Jesus was in an enclosure and the crowd was swarming in about him, Jesus learned that his mother and brothers were outside and wanted to see him. His mother loved him, but his brothers were unbelievers,[29] and so the Savior decided to make a point about "relatives" before he met with his family. Jesus said:

"Who is my mother? and who are my brethren?

"And he stretched forth his hand toward his disciples, and said, Behold my mother and my brethren!

"For whosoever shall do the will of my Father which is in heaven, the same is my brother, and sister, and mother."[30]

The Savior's love for the human family is universal. He wanted them to know that they were just as precious to him as his immediate relatives. Having made his point, he no doubt welcomed his family into the arena where he was teaching.

---

[27]Luke 11:24-26.
[28]Luke 11:26.
[29]John 7:5.
[30]Matthew 12:48-50.

JESUS LAYS DOWN THE LAW OF THE SABBATH

One additional event of interest is believed to have happened during this period when Jesus was on his second tour of Galilee.

This incident happened on a sabbath day. His disciples were hungry, and as they walked through a field of ripened grain, they plucked some of it up and, after rubbing the chaff from the heads of wheat, they ate the kernels.[31]

There must have been a few Pharisee spies in the vicinity because they immediately accused the Savior's disciples of violating the sabbath day by threshing out kernels of wheat and eating them.[32]

Jesus tried to reach their hearts by reasoning with their minds. He first cited David who, when he was hungry, ate the priest's shew bread in the tabernacle.[33] Had he been so inclined he could even have pointed out that the priests worked in the temple on the sabbath but were never accused of violating the Mosaic law.

But the larger question was simply who established the law of the sabbath in the first place? He told them they had in their midst someone greater than the temple, even the Son of Man, and he is the Lord of the sabbath![34] Should not the Lord of the sabbath decide whether or not it is acceptable to do good on the sabbath day?

THE LORD OF THE SABBATH PRACTICES
THE LAW OF THE SABBATH

From this point on, Jesus tantalized his critics by deliberately performing miracles on the sabbath day. A short time after the above incident, Matthew says:

"He went into their synagogue:

---

[31]Luke 6:1.
[32]Luke 6:2.
[33]Luke 6:3-4.
[34]Luke 6:5.

"And, behold, there was a man which had his hand withered. And they asked him, saying, Is it lawful to heal on the sabbath days? that they might accuse him.

"And he said unto them, What man shall there be among you, that shall have one sheep, and if it fall into a pit on the sabbath day, will he not lay hold on it, and lift it out?

"How much then is a man better than a sheep? Wherefore it is lawful to do well on the sabbath days.

"Then saith he to the man, Stretch forth thine hand. And he stretched it forth; and it was restored whole, like as the other.

"Then the Pharisees went out, and held a council against him, how they might destroy him."[35]

Next comes the best part of all. Right while the Pharisees were plotting to find some basis for killing him, Matthew says:

"But when Jesus knew it, he withdrew himself from thence: and great multitudes followed him, and he healed them all."[36]

To withdraw from his accusers and take the crowd with him was sufficient to outrage these plotters, but to go right ahead and use the sabbath to heal every person in sight was like pouring salt into an open wound.

THE BEGINNING OF PARABLES

Later on, Jesus went down to the shore of the Galilee and was followed by the multitude. The crowd was crushing in upon him and so the scripture says:

---

[35]Matthew 12:9-14.
[36]Matthew 12:15.

"And great multitudes were gathered together unto him, so that he went into a ship, and sat; and the whole multitude stood on the shore."[37]

It was in this setting that Jesus began his series of stories especially designed for those with listening ears.

He first told the "Parable of the Sower," and the apostles were disturbed by this new method of teaching. Apparently they were in the boat with Jesus, and the scripture says:

"And the disciples came, and said unto him, 'Why speakest thou to them in parables?'[38] Jesus answered:

"Because it is given unto you to know the mysteries of the kingdom of heaven, but to them it is not given."[39]

The Savior was simply saying that the gospel of Jesus Christ is very precious and it involves significant moral, spiritual and intellectual obligations. Some people are ready for this outreach and some are not. The parables are designed to teach those whose hearts are humble and whose minds are ready for these powerful new dimensions of truth.

For all those who are not ready, the parable remains a simple story, with its hidden meaning carefully obscured.

As we mentioned, the Savior's first parable was about a sower, and it was designed to answer an important question.

WHY DOESN'T EVERYONE ACCEPT THE GOSPEL?

Jesus wanted to give his answer in a gentle but completely accurate way, and so he told the story of a sower who scattered his seeds of grain in different kinds of soil and in a variety of circumstances. Some went by the way side where the fowls ate them

---

[37]Matthew 13:2.
[38]Matthew 10:11 (see Appendix B in volume 2).
[39]Matthew 13:11.

up. Some fell among stones, some among thorns, and finally some fell in good rich soil where they grew and produced a harvest.

In the interest of brevity, here is the interpretation of this parable which Jesus later gave to his apostles:

"Hear ye therefore the parable of the sower.

"When any one heareth the word of the kingdom, and understandeth it not, then cometh the wicked one, and catcheth away that which was sown in his heart. This is he which received seed by the way side.

"But he that received the seed into stony places, the same is he that heareth the word, and anon [thereafter] with joy received it. Yet he hath not root in himself, but dureth for a while: for when tribulation or persecution ariseth because of the word, by and by he is offended.

"He also that received seed among the thorns is he that heareth the word; and the care of this world, and the deceitfulness of riches, choke the word, and he becometh unfruitful.

"But he that received seed into the good ground is he that heareth the word; and understandeth it; which also beareth fruit, and bringeth forth, some an hundredfold, some sixty, some thirty."[40]

WHY NOT SEPARATE THE GOOD PEOPLE FROM THE BAD?

Throughout the earth, there seems to be an intermingling of the "good" people with the "bad." Of course, these are relative terms, but wouldn't it be better if God separated the good from the bad?

To answer this query, Jesus taught the "Parable of the Tares."

"The kingdom of heaven [on earth] is likened unto a man which sowed good seed in his field:

---

[40]Matthew 13:18-23.

"But while men slept, his enemy came and sowed tares among the wheat, and went his way.

"But when the blade was sprung up, and brought forth fruit, then appeared the tares also.

"So the servants of the householder came and said unto him, Sir, didst not thou sow good seed in thy field? from whence then hath it tares?

"He said unto them, An enemy hath done this. The servants said unto him, Wilt thou then that we go and gather them up?

"But he said, Nay; lest while ye gather up the tares, ye root up also the wheat with them.

"Let both grow together until the harvest: and in the time of harvest I will say to the reapers, Gather ye together first the tares, and bind them in bundles to burn them: but gather the wheat into my barn."[41]

It is interesting that wheat and tares look exactly alike when they are growing up together. It is not until the heads of grain appear that they can be easily distinguished. There are two lessons to be drawn from this parable.

First, the righteous must not pray for the premature destruction of the tares, because many of the righteous, and those who are capable of becoming righteous, would be destroyed in the process.

Secondly, people are different than tares in that the seed of a tare is doomed to grow up to be a tare, whereas people can be changed during a lifetime from a tare into the Lord's choice wheat.

---

[41]Matthew 13:24-30.

HOW CAN SO FEW BE EXPECTED TO DO SO MUCH?

"Another parable put he forth unto them, saying, The kingdom of heaven [on earth] is like to a grain of mustard seed, which a man took, and sowed in his field:

"Which indeed is the least of all seeds: but when it is grown, it is the greatest among herbs, and becometh a tree, so that the birds of the air come and lodge in the branches thereof."[42]

This parable reminds us of the saying, "Out of a tiny acorn the mighty oak doth grow."

HOW GOD SWEETENS THE BREAD OF LIFE AMONG MANKIND

Jesus next wanted to emphasize the tremendous influence of one righteous person. He said:

"The kingdom of heaven [on earth] is like unto leaven, which a woman took, and hid in three measures of meal, till the whole was leavened."[43]

Only a tiny fragment of leaven can make a world of difference. Abraham was such a fragment, so was Moses and so were the rest of the prophets. Each in their way made a "world of difference." The Savior expects the same of his disciples in every age.

THE APOSTLES GET TO ASK QUESTIONS

At this point the scripture says, "Then Jesus sent the multitude away, and went into the house."[44] It was then that the apostles were able to ask questions.

During this discussion, Jesus wanted his disciples to comprehend the immeasurable value of the gospel. Some of them would be asked

---

[42]Matthew 13:31-32.
[43]Matthew 13:33.
[44]Matthew 13:36.

to die for it. He wanted them to catch the Father's vision of the great plan of salvation. He said:

"Again, the kingdom of heaven is like unto treasure hid in a field; the which when a man hath found, he hideth, and for joy thereof goeth and selleth all that he hath, and buyeth that field.

"Again, the kingdom of heaven is like unto a merchant man, seeking goodly pearls:

"Who, when he had found one pearl of great price, went and sold all that he had, and bought it."[45]

WHY DOESN'T THE GOSPEL NET JUST BRING IN GOOD PEOPLE?

No doubt the apostles had noticed that among the new converts an occasional renegade would creep into the ranks. Why couldn't a more restrictive arrangement be made so that only "good" people would be brought up in the gospel net?

While it is true that the gospel sometimes attracts people who are only half converted, and others who become backsliders, Jesus left no doubt that the members of his kingdom have a basic duty to:

"Succor the weak, lift up the hands which hang down, and strengthen the feeble knees."[46]

Nevertheless, Jesus wanted his disciples to know that in the end there will be a complete separation of the sheep and the goats. He emphasized the point in the following parable:

"Again, the kingdom of heaven is like unto a net, that was cast into the sea, and gathered of every kind:

"Which, when it was full, they drew to shore, and sat down, and gathered the good into vessels, but cast the bad away.

---

[45]Matthew 13:44-46.
[46]Doctrine and Covenants 81:5.

"So shall it be at the end of the world: the angels shall come forth, and sever the wicked from among the just."[47]

As this personal interview with the apostles came to an end, Jesus said:

"Have ye understood all these things? They say unto him, Yea, Lord."[48]

Jesus then told them to treasure up all of these things so that in time of need they could use them to an advantage, both "the old and the new."

"And it came to pass, [that] when Jesus had finished these parables, he departed thence."[49]

The apostles would never have guessed what was about to happen next.

* * * *

TOPICS FOR REFLECTION AND DISCUSSION

1. Had you ever before heard of the Sermon on the Plain? What did Jesus do just before he taught the Sermon on the Plain? Was this sermon given just to the apostles or to the whole multitude of the Savior's followers? To whom had he said, "take no thought of the morrow?"

2. Why was it considered so dangerous for Jesus to touch a leper as he undertook to heal him? Describe the nature of the disease which the people in the days of Jesus called leprosy. Why would this healing be more spectacular than healing the blind or raising the dead?

3. We have reached a point where Jesus tells many of those who were healed to keep it a secret. Have you wondered what purpose

---

[47]Matthew 13:47-49.
[48]Matthew 13:51.
[49]Matthew 13:53.

Jesus might have had in mind when he did this? What was your conclusion?

4. Why did the Jews petition Jesus to heal the servant of the Roman centurion in Capernaum? What did the Roman centurion do that led Jesus to say that his faith exceeded that of the Jews?

5. When Jesus raised the dead for the first time, where did it take place? Was it in the open where the people could see him do it or in a private house? Was the dead person a boy or a grown man? What was the reaction of the Jews throughout the region when they heard that Jesus had raised a person from the dead?

6. How do you account for the statement that a distinguished Pharisee would invite Jesus to dinner when the Pharisees were among his strongest critics? What happened during the meal that shocked the Pharisee?

7. How did the Pharisees explain the many miracles that Jesus performed on his second tour of Galilee? How did this allow them to accept the reality of his miracles but still deny their divinity?

8. When evil spirits have been cast out, do they sometimes try to repossess their victims? Why do you think Jesus said it would be more difficult to drive them out the next time? Whom does Jesus consider his "family"? How would you define "the law of the sabbath"? When Jesus confounded his critics, what did they plot to do?

9. In what way was the Parable of the Sower a parable of "soils and circumstances"? What should be our attitude toward a person who enters the kingdom but doesn't seem to be converted?

10. Why doesn't the Lord separate the wheat from the tares right now? Will he ultimately separate them?

*   *   *   *

CHAPTER 18

THE APOSTLES NEARLY DROWN

Evil Spirits Enter 2,000 Swine
A Girl is Raised from the Dead
The Apostles Depart on Their Mission

After telling this initial series of parables, Jesus took ship with his apostles to visit the eastern shore of the Galilee. But some of the multitude saw him leaving and decided to follow. There were fishing villages all along the coast, so the Savior's craft had not gone far before "other little ships" joyfully hastened along with it.[1]

As the wind filled the sail of the Savior's boat and picked up speed, the exhausted Jesus fell asleep in the prow of the ship. However, it was not long before it became apparent that a storm was brewing. No doubt the "other little ships" hurried back to safety. The wind rose higher and very shortly the sea had been whipped into a turmoil of boiling whitecaps.

A number of the apostles were experienced sailors, and they knew these storms on the Galilee could be deadly. As the waves rose higher and washed over the sides of the ship, it began floundering and the apostles knew it was taking in more water than they could bail out. As the disciples became terrified, the scripture says:

"And they were filled with water, and were in jeopardy.

"And they came to him, and awoke him, saying, Master, master, we perish. Then he arose, and rebuked the wind and the raging of the water; and they ceased, and there was a calm.

---

[1]Mark 4:36.

"And he said unto them, Where is your faith? And they being afraid wondered, saying one to another, What manner of man is this! for he commandeth even the winds and water, and they obey him."[2]

The Savior's challenge to their faith was probably designed to elevate their self confidence. After all, within a few weeks they would be on their own missions and performing miracles themselves.

AN ENCOUNTER WITH EVIL SPIRITS

As the boat landed on the eastern shore, it was beached in an area inhabited by the people called the Gadarenes or Gergesenes. However, the place where the Savior and the apostles disembarked was some distance from the city.

To their surprise, two wild men suddenly came running out to meet them from the tombs of the dead nearby. Matthew was there, and he says they "were exceeding fierce, so that no man might pass by that way."[3]

Luke indicates that only one of these men reached the Savior. The man acted as though he were crazy. He was naked and dirty, his hair was disheveled, and he was covered with cuts and bruises.[4]

No doubt the disciples were fearful this wild man might hurt the Savior as he rushed toward him, but Jesus recognized that the man was possessed by one or more evil spirits. He therefore commanded the devils to depart out of him. The man fell at the feet of Jesus and the evil spirit within him cried out:

"What have I to do with thee, Jesus, thou Son of God most high? I beseech thee, torment me not....

---

[2]Luke 8:23-25.
[3]Matthew 8:28.
[4]Luke 8:27, 29.

"And Jesus asked him, saying, What is thy name? And he said, Legion: because many devils were entered into him."[5]

Jesus explained to his disciples on another occasion that when a person allows an evil spirit to enter into him, that minion of Satan will often invite other evil spirits to join him.[6] In this case there were so many devils in the man that the spirit speaking for them said they were "legion."

The spokesman for all these spirits then used the voice of the man to plead with Jesus not to terminate the pleasure they were having in tormenting this pitiful creature whose body they had taken over. They especially sought Jesus not to send them back into "the deep," referring perhaps to the desolate regions or "the dry places," where evil spirits are constantly "seeking rest and findeth none."[7]

JESUS GRANTS A STRANGE REQUEST

However, when the evil spirit who acted as spokesman for the host of devils saw that Jesus was determined to drive them out, he asked if they might enter into the bodies of a large herd of swine nearby. Mark says the number was about 2,000![8]

Of course, no Jews would be raising swine, but the Gadarenes belonged to a district called the Decapolis where there were ten cities of Greeks and mixed nationalities. In this region swine meat was a delicacy. A herd of 2,000 swine was no doubt a major part of the collective wealth of the entire community.

In response to the devil's plea, Jesus finally consented. Luke says:

"Then went the devils out of the man, and entered into the swine: and the herd ran violently down a steep place into the lake, and were choked.

---

[5]Luke 8:28, 30.
[6]Matthew 12:43-45.
[7]Matthew 12:43.
[8]Mark 5:13.

"When they that fed them saw what was done, they fled, and went and told it in the city and in the country.

"Then they went out to see what was done; and came to Jesus, and found the man, out of whom the devils were departed, sitting at the feet of Jesus, clothed and in his right mind."[9]

They might have also observed that this poor fellow was so grateful to Jesus that he wanted to become the Savior's disciples and follow him wherever he went, but Jesus said:

"Return to thine own house, and shew how great things God hath done unto thee. And he went his way, and published throughout the whole city how great things Jesus had done unto him."[10]

JESUS IS ASKED TO LEAVE IMMEDIATELY

Meanwhile, the people of the community, and especially those who owned the swine, were in a great state of alarm. Here was a Jew with a group of Jewish followers who healed a crazy man and then had 2,000 of their choice pigs run down the cliff and drown themselves in the sea. This practically wiped out the profits of a whole season. For the Gadarenes this was too much for their simple souls to endure. Luke says:

"Then the whole multitude of the country of the Gadarenes round about besought him to depart from them; for they were taken with great fear: and he went up into the ship, and returned back again."[11]

As the Savior's ship approached the western shore of the Galilee, the people recognized it, and the word spread rapidly. When he landed Luke says:

---

[9]Luke 8:33-35.
[10]Luke 8:39.
[11]Luke 8:37.

"...the people gladly received him: for they were all waiting for him."[12]

THE RULER OF THE LOCAL SYNAGOGUE
ASKS JESUS TO SAVE HIS DAUGHTER

In this crowd waiting for the Savior's return was a ruler of the local synagogue. His name was Jairus. He frantically made his way to Jesus and humbly fell at his feet. He pleaded with the Savior to come to his house where his twelve-year-old daughter, his only child, was dying. Jesus consented, but as he moved forward the crowd surged around him so that he was "thronged" or impeded by the multitude.

A WOMAN WITH AN "ISSUE OF BLOOD"
TOUCHES JESUS AND IS HEALED

In the midst of all this, Jesus suddenly said:

"Who touched me? When all denied, Peter and they that were with him said, Master, the multitude throng thee and press thee, and sayest thou, Who touched me?

"And Jesus said, Somebody hath touched me: for I perceive that virtue is gone out of me."[13]

It turned out that there was a woman in the crowd who had suffered many years from an "issue of blood." She felt that if she could just touch the Savior, she would be healed. And she was. But she was frightened and amazed when she realized Jesus knew she had touched him and wanted to know who it was. Then Luke says:

"And when the woman saw that she was not hid, she came trembling, and falling down before him, she declared unto him before all the people for what cause she had touched him and how she was healed immediately.

---

[12]Luke 8:40.
[13]Luke 8:45-46.

"And he said unto her, Daughter, be of good comfort: thy faith hath made thee whole; go in peace."[14]

JESUS BRINGS A TWELVE-YEAR-OLD
GIRL BACK FROM THE DEAD

Following this slight delay, Jesus prepared to hasten to the house of Jairus where his daughter was dying. Apparently Jairus was standing nearby, because the scripture says:

"While he yet spake, there cometh one from the ruler of the synagogue's house, saying to him, Thy daughter is dead; trouble not the Master.

"But when Jesus heard it, he answered him, saying, Fear not: believe only, and she shall be made whole.

"And when he came into the house, he suffered no man to go in, save Peter, and James, and John, and the father and the mother of the maiden.

"And all wept, and bewailed her: but he said, Weep not; she is not dead, but sleepeth.

"And they laughed him to scorn, knowing that she was dead."[15]

With Jesus this was a very sacred moment. Just as he would do for Lazarus later on, he was no doubt praying fervently to the Father for permission to raise this little girl from the dead.[16] Jesus had always said, "The Son can do nothing of himself."[17] But once Jesus had been assured by his Father that he could proceed, here is what Luke says happened:

"And he put them all out, and took her by the hand, and called, saying, Maid, arise.

---

[14]Luke 8:47-48.
[15]Luke 8:49-53.
[16]John 11:41.
[17]John 5:19.

"And her spirit came again, and she arose straightway: and he commanded to give her meat.

"And her parents were astonished: but he charged them that they should tell no man what was done."[18]

Once again we remind ourselves that Jesus openly requested that his greatest miracles be kept secret so that all who witnessed them would know he was not doing it for show or self-aggrandizement, but was performing a sacred act.

JESUS RISKS VISITING NAZARETH
A SECOND TIME

As Jesus continued his ministry he came near Nazareth and decided to visit his hometown even though they had tried to kill him the last time he was there.[19] The reason the people had become outraged then was because he would not perform some spectacular miracle. He had told them they didn't have enough faith. Therefore they dragged him to the top of a cliff and would have thrown him over if he hadn't miraculously disappeared from among them.[20]

Jesus may have sent his disciples to their respective homes for a rest while he visited Nazareth, just as he had done the first time he went there. We conclude this from the fact that there is no reference to them as Jesus approached "his own country." As he entered Nazareth, Jesus came on very quietly. He made his first appearance in the local synagogue and entered into their conversation concerning the prophets and the scriptures. Matthew says:

"They were astonished, and said, Whence hath this man this wisdom, and these mighty works?

"Is not this the carpenter's son? is not his mother called Mary? and his brethren, James, and Joses, and Simon, and Judas?

---

[18]Luke 8:54-56.
[19]Luke 4:29.
[20]Luke 4:30.

"And his sisters, are they not all with us? Whence then hath this man all these things?

"And they were offended in him. But Jesus said unto them, A prophet is not without honour, save in his own country, and in his own house.

"And he did not many mighty works there because of their unbelief."[21]

But while he did not do any "*mighty* works...because of their unbelief," he did do some works. As he moved among the people he laid his hands on some who were sick and administered to them just as the elders do today. And they were healed.[22]

THE TWELVE APOSTLES ARE SENT
FORTH TWO BY TWO

It was about this time that Jesus assembled his twelve apostles and prepared them to go by themselves on their first mission. Up to now they had simply been companions of the Savior. It had been he who took the lead, answered all the hard questions, and dealt with everything from the dead to demons. Now they would get their own baptism of fire as they undertook to get their first taste of what Christ would later ask them to do for the rest of their lives.

It is at this point that we have each of the twelve carefully identified:

"Now the names of the twelve apostles are these; The first, Simon, who is called Peter, and Andrew his brother; James the son of Zebedee, and John his brother;

"Philip, and Bartholomew; Thomas, and Matthew the publican; James the son of Alphaeus, and Lebbaeus, whose surname was Thaddaeus;

---

[21]Matthew 13:54-58.
[22]Mark 6:5.

"Simon the Canaanite [taken from the Greek for Zelote, a Jewish faction], and Judas Iscariot, who also betrayed him."[23]

THE APOSTLES RECEIVE GUIDELINES
FOR THEIR MISSION

To these carefully chosen ambassadors, Jesus gave approximately 40 guidelines. He already knew that eleven of them would eventually qualify to return to the Father, but one would become a son of perdition.

Later, at his great Passover sermon,[24] the Savior would enlarge on some of these instructions to make certain they were properly understood. A few of these are included in the following list:

1. Remember, you did not choose me, I chose you and ordained you.[25]

2. You are to go forth two by two.[26]

3. Do not spend time among the Gentiles for the present.[27]

4. Nor should you spend time with the Samaritans on this mission.[28]

5. Your assignment is exclusively to the lost sheep of Israel.[29]

6. Call the people to repentance.[30]

7. Tell them, the kingdom of heaven is near.[31]

---

[23]Matthew 10:2-4.
[24]John, chapters 13 to 16.
[25]John 15:16.
[26]Mark 6:7; Luke 10:1.
[27]Matthew 10:5.
[28]Ibid.
[29]Matthew 10:6.
[30]Mark 6:12.
[31]Matthew 10:7.

8. Heal the sick.[32]

9. Cleanse the lepers.[33]

10. Raise the dead—when the Spirit instructs you to do so.[34]

11. Cast out devils.[35]

12. Preach and teach without compensation. Freely you received, freely give.[36]

13. Take neither gold, silver, money or scrip.[37]

14. Take sandals and only one coat.[38]

15. Take no shoes[39] nor "staves."[40] However, Mark specifically says that one staff was permissible.[41]

16. When you reach a place, inquire who is the most worthy, and establish your residence there so the people will know where to find you up to the time you depart.[42]

17. When you go to a house (tracting?), identify yourself and describe your mission. Matthew calls it a "salute."[43]

18. If you are received at a house, leave your blessing. If not, retain your blessing.[44]

---

[32]Matthew 10:8.
[33]Ibid.
[34]John 5:19; 11:41. Matthew 10:8.
[35]Matthew 10:8.
[36]Ibid.
[37]Matthew 10:9-10.
[38]Mark 6:9.
[39]Just sandals, Ibid.
[40]Matthew 10:10.
[41]Mark 6:8.
[42]Matthew 10:11; Mark 6:10.
[43]Matthew 10:12.
[44]Matthew 10:13.

19. If you are hated and rejected, shake off the dust from your feet as a witness against them when the judgment comes.[45]

20. You should realize that you are being sent forth as a sheep among wolves.[46]

21. Therefore you are commanded to be as wise as serpents in dealing with your adversaries, but harmless as doves.[47]

22. Beware of those evil men who, at the slightest pretense, will have you scourged in the synagogues.[48]

23. If you are arrested, let the Holy Spirit guide you in what you will say at the time of your defense. Do not try to devise some clever defense on your own.[49]

24. The gospel will expose deceit and hypocrisy so that you can expect brother to testify against brother.[50]

25. You can also expect to be hated of all classes of men.[51]

26. Nevertheless, he that endureth to the end shall be saved.[52]

27. When they persecute you in one city, flee unto another, for you will not have gone over all the cities of Israel "till the Son of man be come"—obviously referring to missionary work far in the distant future.[53]

---

[45]Matthew 10:14-15.
[46]Matthew 10:16.
[47]Ibid.
[48]Matthew 10:17.
[49]Matthew 10:19-20.
[50]Matthew 10:21.
[51]Matthew 10:22.
[52]Ibid.
[53]Matthew 10:23.

28. Fear not the plots against you by evil and designing men, for all of their hidden secrets shall be revealed.[54]

29. When I reveal to you the secret combinations and the hidden machinations of evil men, declare it from the housetops. Let the hidden devices of evil men be known.[55]

30. "Fear not him who can destroy the body [persecute you to death] but fear him who can destroy both body and soul."[56] Only God can destroy both body and soul. No doubt this shaft of eternal truth was aimed directly at Judas Iscariot.

He would be the only apostle who would become a son of perdition. Only he would be resurrected without any degree of glory.[57] As a "son of perdition," he would never be forgiven.[58] Therefore, having defiled his God-given tabernacles—both the body and the spirit—he would ultimately lose them.[59] We are told that as the light of Christ is withdrawn from the resurrected body it will cease to abound.[60]

31. Constantly remember that the Father is mindful of you in all your tribulations. Not even a sparrow falls without his knowledge, and of course you are more precious than many sparrows.[61]

32. Bear your testimony! If you confess me before the world, I will confess you before your Father.[62]

---

[54]Matthew 10:26.
[55]Matthew 10:27.
[56]Matthew 10:28.
[57]Doctrine and Covenants 76:38; 88:32.
[58]Doctrine and Covenants 76:34.
[59]Doctrine and Covenants 93:35.
[60]Doctrine and Covenants 88:50.
[61]Matthew 10:29-31.
[62]Matthew 10:32.

33. Those who become frightened and deny me, I will deny them before the Father.[63]

34. Remember that the gospel does not bring peace but raises up a standard of truth and righteousness that separates families, communities and nations. The righteous will discover enemies arising in their own households.[64]

35. Teach that one who hears the gospel and then becomes ambivalent and elects to unite with his hostile family or other opponents of the gospel, is not worthy of the Savior or the gospel.[65]

36. Teach also that he who will not take up his cross and follow the Savior is not worthy of the Savior.[66]

37. He that puts his own life at a premium over the gospel and his eternal life will lose it, but he who gives his whole life for the cause of the Savior and his righteousness shall find life—eternal life.[67]

38. He who receives you and your message receives me, and he who receives me receives the Father.[68]

39. All who receive you as my messengers will receive the same reward as my messengers, whether it be a prophet or a righteous man, which would include the apostles.[69]

40. Whoever will help you, even with a cup of water, will in no wise lose their reward.[70]

---

[63]Matthew 10:33.
[64]Matthew 10:34-36.
[65]Matthew 10:37.
[66]Matthew 10:38.
[67]Matthew 10:39.
[68]Matthew 10:40.
[69]Matthew 10:41.
[70]Matthew 10:42.

EIGHTEEN MONTHS LATER SOME OF
THESE INSTRUCTIONS WERE CHANGED

We have already mentioned that the instructions to go forth without purse or scrip, staves or sword, and without even an extra cloak, or emergency food rations, was changed about eighteen months later because circumstances had changed.

At the Last Supper, Jesus instructed the apostles to provide the means to protect their lives and prepare for their needs before going out on their missions.[71]

A similar transition occurred in modern times. When the gospel was first restored in its fullness, the Lord said:

"Let no man among you...take purse or scrip, that goeth forth to proclaim this gospel of the kingdom."[72]

As circumstances changed, the missionaries were instructed to provide for their families before leaving on missions, and to have the means from their own resources—or those of friends and relatives—to provide for their basic needs while serving in the field.

JESUS CONTINUES HIS PERSONAL
MINISTRY ALONE

It is generally estimated that Jesus was about half way through his ministry when the twelve were sent on their mission.[73] It is further estimated that they were gone for approximately three months.[74]

It would be interesting to know which of the apostles labored with Judas Iscariot. Up to this time there is no evidence in the record of any signs of defection, so perhaps his behavior and experiences

---

[71]Luke 22:35-36.
[72]Doctrine and Covenants 84:86.
[73]Clark, *Our Lord of the Gospels*, op. cit. p. 259.
[74]Ibid. p. 264.

during the apostolic mission were similar to those of the rest of the twelve.

Meanwhile, Jesus continued his own ministry in the towns and villages of Galilee. Matthew says:

"And it came to pass, when Jesus had made an end of commanding his twelve disciples, he departed thence to teach and to preach in their cities."[75]

JOHN THE BAPTIST SENDS TWO DISCIPLES TO JESUS

It may have been while the apostles were on their missions that John the Baptist sent two of his disciples to visit Jesus.

From all the circumstances it would appear that John was having serious difficulty with some of his disciples. As we have mentioned earlier, some of them had become converted to John, but not to his message concerning the identity of the Messiah. This seems to have been more or less characteristic of the Pharisees who became his disciples. The Inspired Version of the scripture says:

"...many received John as a prophet, but they believed not on Jesus."[76]

It would appear that some of John's disciples who "believed not on Jesus" had visited the Baptist in prison and expressed their doubts concerning the Nazarene.

All John could do was bear his fervent testimony, but when this apparently failed, he had only one final solution: Send them to Jesus. Matthew says John had already "heard in the prison the works of Christ" and all the miracles he was performing, so he apparently felt it would strengthen their appreciation of the Savior if they saw him in action. Therefore, he sent two of his doubting disciples to Jesus so they could address their questions to him.

---

[75]Matthew 11:1.
[76]JST John 4:2.

The scripture says:

"When the men were come unto him, they said, John Baptist hath sent us unto thee, saying, Art thou he that should come? or look we for another?"[77]

Some Bible students have wondered if perhaps John had become despondent in prison and had begun to question Christ's divinity. However, it requires very little reflection to appreciate that it was the disciples of John who had the problem, not John himself. John had already expressed his heartfelt testimony concerning Jesus. Furthermore, he had enjoyed the companionship of angels to affirm the divine purpose in both of their missions.[78]

Perhaps it was natural for John's disciples to make their questions sound as though they were coming from John instead of themselves. In any event, after Jesus had listened to their questions he made no attempt to answer them. Instead, he turned about and continued his ministry of miracles. The scripture says:

"And in that same hour he cured many of their infirmities and plagues, and of evil spirits; and unto many that were blind he gave sight."[79]

Finally he turned back to John's disciples. Now he was ready to respond to their query. He said:

"Go your way, and tell John what things ye have seen and heard; how that the blind see, the lame walk, the lepers are cleansed, the deaf hear, the dead are raised, to the poor the gospel is preached.

"And blessed is he, whosoever shall not be offended in me."[80]

---

[77]Luke 7:20.
[78]JST Matthew 4:11; compare KJT Matthew 4:12.
[79]Luke 7:21.
[80]Luke 7:20-23.

This last comment was for the special benefit of these doubting disciples. Jesus had given these two men a display of miraculous power that would corroborate John's testimony with overwhelming evidence concerning the divinity of Christ. They had seen Jesus cure blind people, make the lame stand up and walk, turn the putrid, ugly sores of lepers into healthy flesh, and bless the deaf so they suddenly could hear.[81]

In the final analysis, there was no doubt about it. This Jesus was doing everything Isaiah had predicted the Messiah would do, including the preaching of the gospel to the meek and the poor.[82]

It would be interesting to learn what happened when these two disciples returned to John and told them what they had seen.

THE SAVIOR'S BRILLIANT TRIBUTE TO JOHN THE BAPTIST

Barely were John's disciples out of sight, when Jesus turned to the multitude who had been watching. Luke says:

"He began to speak unto the people concerning John, What went ye out into the wilderness for to see? A reed shaken with the wind?

"But what went ye out for to see? A man clothed in soft raiment? Behold, they which are gorgeously apparelled, and live delicately, are in kings' courts.

"But what went ye out for to see? A prophet? Yea, I say unto you, and much more than a prophet.

"This is he, of whom it is written, Behold, I send my messenger before thy face, which shall prepare thy way before thee.

"For I say unto you, Among those that are born of women there is not a greater prophet than John the Baptist."[83]

---

[81]Luke 7:22.
[82]Isaiah 61:1-3.
[83]Luke 7:24-28.

It was only a short time after Jesus expressed this affectionate tribute to John the Baptist that this noble prophet of God was dead.

* * * *

TOPICS FOR REFLECTION AND DISCUSSION

1. When the apostles awakened Jesus to prevent them from drowning, why do you think Jesus said, "Where is your faith"? Who greeted Jesus and the apostles when they landed? When Jesus commanded the evil spirits to come forth, what request did they make? Did Jesus grant it? What happened? Then what did the people of that area ask Jesus to do?

2. When Jesus returned to the western shore, why did the ruler of the synagogue ask Jesus to hurry to his house? As Jesus tried to get through the crowd in response to this request, what stopped him? By the power of whose faith was the woman healed? What had happened to the ruler's daughter while Jesus was delayed by the woman who was healed by touching him? Who were the six people in the room when Jesus raised the daughter of Jairus from the dead?

3. How do you account for the Savior's willingness to return to Nazareth when these people had tried to kill him on an earlier visit? When he discussed the scriptures with the people at the local synagogue, why were the people offended?

4. Did Jesus do any "mighty works" in Nazareth? What kind of "works" did he do?

5. When Jesus assembled the twelve to prepare them for their mission, how many specific instructions did he give them? Had any of the twelve volunteered for their work? What would appear to be the advantage in going forth to preach "two by two"?

6. When the apostles were received in a house, what did Jesus say they were to leave with that family? Why did the Savior say their message of peace would create hatred toward themselves and cause brother to oppose brother? Does that happen today?

7. Did Jesus say the evil designs of men and the secret combinations were to be denounced or kept secret? What did Jesus say the apostles should expect as they taught the gospel and then exposed the schemes of evil men?

8. What do you think it meant to "take up the cross" and follow Jesus? Did they go without purse or scrip? In what way does this policy test the faith of the people? Why were some of these instructions changed at the Last Supper?

9. Why did John send two of his disciples to visit Jesus? Why didn't he immediately answer their questions? What did Jesus say they should tell John? Do you think these answers were for John the Baptist or for his disciples?

10. How did Jesus rate John the Baptist in comparison with all the other prophets? Since Mary is described as the "cousin" of Elisabeth, what relation would Jesus be to John the Baptist?

*   *   *   *

CHAPTER 19

MURDER OF JOHN THE BAPTIST

The Feeding of 5,000
Jesus Walks on the Water

There is an element of historical irony in the fact that it was while the apostles were enjoying the final, glorious days of their marvelous mission that a plot was brewing to kill John the Baptist.

THE FINAL DAYS OF JOHN THE BAPTIST

It was Josephus, the famous Jewish historian, who identified the fortress where John was imprisoned and ultimately executed. He says it was the fortress of Macherus located on the border between Perea and the kingdom of Aretas, the father of the first wife of Herod Antipas.[1]

The Macherus fortress was located on the eastern side of the Dead Sea and was perched on a high cliff overlooking the acrid waters (1,292 feet below sea level) which spread out for a distance of twelve miles far below. The dungeon of this fortress is said to have provided the most formidable prison in the land.

Several centuries after the days of John the Baptist, pilgrims to the Holy Land attempted to establish the tradition that it was in Samaria that John was imprisoned and killed. In fact, modern tourists are still told that story.

However, we know this entire territory of Samaria, which was west of the Jordan, had been placed under the exclusive control of Pontius Pilate. This Roman governor was extremely jealous of his

---

[1]Josephus, *Antiquities of the Jews*, Book 18, ch. 5:1-2.

jurisdiction. He would never have allowed an outsider such as Herod Antipas to maintain a palace in his domain or execute a resident of his kingdom without his consent.

So far as I know there is nothing in the known history of John the Baptist that gives any credence to the story that modern tourists are being told about John the Baptist being imprisoned and executed in Samaria.

HERODIAS PLOTS TO HAVE HER HUSBAND BEGUILED INTO KILLING JOHN THE BAPTIST

It appears that after John had been in prison for approximately eighteen months the following tragic sequence of events took place.

"Herod on his birthday made a supper to his lords, high captains, and chief estates of Galilee;

"And when the daughter of the said Herodias came in, and danced, and pleased Herod and them that sat with him, the king said unto the damsel, Ask of me whatsoever thou wilt, and I will give it thee.

"And he sware unto her, Whatsoever thou shalt ask of me, I will give it thee, unto the half of my kingdom."[2]

Up to this point the plot was working perfectly. Herod Antipas had committed himself, so the trap was laid. The daughter of Herodias therefore ran back to her mother to get further instructions:

"And she went forth, and said unto her mother, What shall I ask? And she said, The head of John the Baptist.

"And she came in straightway with haste unto the king, and asked, saying, I will that thou give me by and by in a charger the head of John the Baptist.

---

[2]Mark 6:21-23.

"And the king was exceeding sorry; yet for his oath's sake, and for their sakes which sat with him, he would not reject her.

"And immediately the king sent an executioner, and commanded his head to be brought: and he went and beheaded him in the prison,

"And brought his head in a charger, and gave it to the damsel: and the damsel gave it to her mother."[3]

PROFILE OF HEROD ANTIPAS

Probably no one has expressed a deeper insight into the malevolent implications of this deliberate murder of John the Baptist than Robert Matthews. In his book, *A Burning Light,* he wrote the following:

"It is interesting that Herod, the king, should be outmaneuvered by his wife and by a dancing girl.

"His appetite and lust for the girl's bodily charms snared him into a compromising situation for which he was afterwards very sorry.

"The whole caper was brought about in the first place because of his libidinous desire for Herodias, whom he had spirited away from Philip, and whom it was not lawful for him to have.

"It was bodily lust and passion that had caused him to forsake his [first] wife, the daughter of Aretas, for Herodias, and now it was more of the same that made him vulnerable to the scheming of Herodias in her plan to make him destroy the very man he had previously protected.

"Herodias, above all others, knew what kind of a man Herod was....

"Herod had shown himself to be a man of much passion, with fleeting moments of good intentions, but with little self-

---

[3]Mark 6:24-28.

control....Herodias herself had beguiled him in their days at Rome, and now she again played upon his weaknesses."[4]

HEROD ANTIPAS NEVER FORGAVE HIMSELF FOR MURDERING JOHN THE BAPTIST

Nevertheless, Herod Antipas never forgave himself for the execution of John the Baptist. One cannot help but ask: Why didn't he back out and refuse to have John beheaded when he discovered that the whole setup was a trick?

It turns out that in ancient times, the failure of a ruler to fulfill a commitment or a solemn promise was like abdicating his throne. The scandalous news that a sovereign had reneged on a promise was enough to shatter public confidence in a royal dynasty. Notice that the scripture says:

"The king was exceeding sorry; yet for his oath's sake, and for their sakes which sat with him, he would not reject her."[5]

Herodias knew this was the way her husband had been trained, and she felt she could gamble on Herod Antipas fulfilling his pledge if her sensuous daughter could extract a promise from him.

As we shall see later, the specter of John haunted Herod Antipas the rest of his life. When he heard of all of the miraculous things Jesus was doing, Herod Antipas feared that somehow this man might be John the Baptist who had returned to life to avenge himself. In the fevered anguish of his mind he said of Jesus:

"[He] is John, whom I beheaded: he is risen from the dead."[6]

Although Herod Antipas did not realize it, he was dealing with two great men, not just one. In fact, he had encountered two of the greatest men who ever walked the earth.

---

[4]Matthews, *A Burning Light*, op. cit. 96-97.
[5]Mark 6:26.
[6]Mark 6:16.

THE END OF THE STORY FOR
HEROD ANTIPAS AND HERODIAS

Just a few years later, after both John and the Savior had fulfilled their missions, Herod Antipas found his incestuous wife concocting yet another plot, and this one cost him his kingdom.

Herodias was a shrewd, cunning and ambitious woman. When she learned that her brother, Herod Agrippa—who ruled Judaea and Samaria—had been honored by Rome with the title of "king," she immediately wanted her husband, Herod Antipas—who ruled Galilee and Perea—to be designated a king as well. She pestered her husband until he finally agreed to go to Rome and seek the coveted title of king.

But Herod Antipas was not given the title of king. Instead, charges of treason were levelled against him by his nephew, Herod Agrippa, and this resulted in Herod Antipas being disinherited. In the end, Herod Agrippa, who was not only the nephew of Herod Antipas, but the brother of Herodias, asked the Roman emperor to intervene in his behalf. As a result, he triumphantly took over both Galilee and Perea, which had been the domain of Herod Antipas and Herodias. The Roman emperor also decided that in order to avoid the possibility of a civil war between these two Herodians, he would order Herod Antipas to be exiled for life to Lyons in faraway Gaul.

When Herodias saw that her vicious and greedy ambitions had virtually destroyed her husband, she felt sufficiently guilty to volunteer to go into exile with him.

In contemplating the history of these descendants of Herod the Great, we cannot resist measuring the madness and sadness of their grotesque and tragic lives, compared to the noble serenity and majesty of the lives of Jesus and John.

THE RETURN OF THE APOSTLES COINCIDES
WITH THE DEATH OF JOHN THE BAPTIST

As we have previously indicated, John came to his tragic death just as the apostles were returning from their missions.

The record is clear that even though the missions of the twelve were of relatively short duration, they had enjoyed tremendous success. Mark says:

"And they went out, and preached that men should repent.

"And they cast out many devils, and anointed with oil many that were sick, and healed them."[7]

They had seen the Savior do all of these things so many times it had become routine. But now these men found themselves in the same role with the same power. It must have been awesome. Even though they may not have completely understood the operation of their priesthood authority over evil spirits as well as the intelligences in matter, it must have been thrilling indeed to heal the sick, cast out devils, and duplicate many of the astonishing things they had seen the Savior do.

The date for completing their missions seems to have been predetermined since the apostles all returned at about the same time. And, as it is with all missionaries, they had some amazing things to share with the Savior and with one another. As the scripture says:

"The apostles gathered themselves together unto Jesus, and told him all things, both what they had done, and what they had taught."[8]

The excitement of this reunion is reflected in the words of Mark when he says:

"There were many coming and going, and they had no leisure so much as to eat."[9]

This appears to have been the situation when the disciples of John the Baptist brought the tragic news from Macherus prison. Matthew says that after John was executed, his disciples "...took up

---

[7]Mark 6:12-13.
[8]Mark 6:30.
[9]Mark 6:31.

the body [of their beloved prophet] and buried it, and went and told Jesus."[10]

We can only imagine the churning currents of emotional distress that gripped the mind of Jesus as the joy in seeing the returning apostles was shattered by the desolating sorrow that came with the news of John's execution. Jesus said to the twelve:

"Come ye yourselves apart into a desert [uninhabited] place, and rest a while."[11]

JESUS LEAVES THE MULTITUDE AND TAKES HIS APOSTLES TO A QUIET PLACE

The place Jesus had in mind was a pleasant spot across the northern end of the Sea of Galilee near a low mountain, not far from the town of Bethsaida.[12]

This small community is believed to have been located just east of the place where the headwaters of the Jordan flow into the Sea of Galilee. It had the same name as another town near Capernaum.

Happily, it was springtime,[13] and the scripture refers to the meadows surrounding this mountain which were covered with new green grass.[14] It is also likely that the tiny spring flowers, for which the Holy Land is famous, were beginning to bloom.

Because the boat trip was only about eight miles, the Savior and the twelve probably arrived at their destination fairly early in the day. During the first part of the trip they may have noticed a multitude of people hastening along the shore as they tried to follow the boat and see where Jesus was going.[15]

---

[10]Matthew 14:12.
[11]Mark 6:31.
[12]Luke 9:10.
[13]John 6:4.
[14]Matthew 14:19.
[15]Matthew 14:13.

It is clear that the Savior and his apostles reached their destination in time to seclude themselves high on the mountain before the crowd arrived. In this quiet place, the apostles were able to express their most tender feelings toward Jesus, while at the same time trying to cheer him with details of the spiritual triumph they had experienced during their missions.

Meanwhile, the multitude of several thousand eager followers had located the Savior's anchored ship and patiently waited for Jesus and his apostles to reappear. As we have mentioned before, the crowds always respected the privacy of Jesus whenever he retired to the upper heights of a mountain to pray or to confer with his disciples.

JESUS PREACHES TO 5,000 MEN IN ADDITION TO MANY WOMEN AND CHILDREN

When Jesus saw this vast, worshipful multitude which Matthew describes as "about five thousand men, beside women and children,"[16] he immediately "began to teach them many things."[17]

Nothing could have healed the wounds of sorrow in the Savior's heart more speedily than a chance to preach the gospel.

THE SETTING FOR A NEW KIND OF MIRACLE

Nevertheless, as the afternoon wore on, and the sun was beginning to set, the apostles became apprehensive. They finally interrupted the Savior to say:

"This is a desert [meaning uninhabited] place, and now the time is far passed:

"Send them away, that they may go into the country round about, and into the villages, and buy themselves bread: for they have nothing to eat."[18]

---

[16]Matthew 14:21.
[17]Mark 6:34.
[18]Mark 6:35-36.

No doubt they expected him to heartily agree with this suggestion, but instead, he said:

"Give ye them to eat."[19]

This was comparable to having a football stadium filled with people, and hearing the Savior say to his twelve astonished apostles, "Give ye them to eat."

They were dumbfounded. They finally asked:

"Shall we go and buy two hundred pennyworth of bread, and give them to eat?"[20]

Jesus looked at Philip and said:

"Whence shall we buy bread that these may eat?"[21]

John adds: "And this he said to prove him: for he himself knew what he would do."[22]

THE MIRACLE OF MULTIPLYING SUBSTANCES

It is doubtful there was two hundred pennyworth of bread in all of Bethsaida or even in the tiny villages surrounding it. At the prevailing wage in those days, it would take a man six months to earn the money to buy that much bread.

"He saith unto them, How many loaves have ye?"[23]

Andrew, the brother of Simon Peter said:

---

[19]Mark 6:37.
[20]Mark 6:37.
[21]John 6:5.
[22]John 6:6.
[23]Mark 6:38.

"There is a lad here, which hath five barley loaves, and two small fishes: but what are they among so many?"[24]

What the apostles did not know was the fact that Jesus had already decided to use this occasion to demonstrate a very remarkable type of miracle. It is called the multiplying of substances.

Just as the intelligences in the molecular structure of water could be instructed to change into a high grade of wine, so the intelligences in the surrounding environment could be instructed to duplicate the structure of five barley loaves and two small fishes.

THE PROPHETS HAD DONE THIS IN ANCIENT TIMES

This same type of miracle was performed for the widow who gave Elijah her last morsel of food. As a reward she found her barrel of meal replenished and her cruse of oil miraculously filled so she had sufficient to feed herself, her son, and Elijah for over three years.[25]

The miracle of multiplying substances was also granted to Elisha who fed a hundred men with 20 small loaves.[26]

Of course, Jesus had only five barley loaves and two small fishes with which to feed around twelve to fifteen thousand people. If any of us had been there, no doubt we would have been as amazed as the apostles when they saw what Jesus did. The scripture says:

"And he commanded them to make all sit down by companies upon the green grass.

"And they sat down in ranks, by hundreds, and by fifties."[27]

---

[24]John 6:9.
[25]1 Kings 17:16.
[26]2 Kings 4:42-43.
[27]Mark 6:39-40.

Notice the discipline of these people under the law of Moses. Any Jewish congregation would automatically know that if they were to be organized in an orderly manner for some special purpose, it would be in "ranks of hundreds and fifties."[28]

JESUS FEEDS THE MULTITUDE

"And when he had taken the five loaves and the two fishes, he looked up to heaven, and blessed, and brake the loaves, and gave them to his disciples to set before them; and the two fishes divided he among them all.

"And they did all eat, and were filled."[29]

It is apparent that Jesus not only multiplied the substance of the five loaves and two fishes, but the miracle included *baked* bread and *cooked* fish. Furthermore, we read that Jesus had not only supplied enough heavenly food to satisfy the hunger of this huge crowd, but more besides. And it was not to be wasted. Jesus said to his disciples:

"Gather up the fragments that remain, that nothing be lost.

"Therefore they gathered them together, and filled twelve baskets with the fragments of the five barley loaves, which remained over and above unto them that had eaten."[30]

We notice that this was enough extra food to give each of the apostles a full basket. We assume this food was promptly placed in the boat because it says:

"And straightway he constrained his disciples to get into the ship, and to go to the other side before [him] unto Bethsaida [another Bethsaida near Capernaum], while he sent away the people."[31]

---

[28]Deuteronomy 1:15.
[29]Mark 6:41-42.
[30]John 6:12-13.
[31]Mark 6:45.

JESUS REMAINS BEHIND

But after the apostles had left, Jesus discovered that saying good night to this crowd of well-fed, happy and adoring people presented a major problem. These people had plans of their own. John says:

"Those men, when they had seen the miracle that Jesus did, said, This is of a truth that prophet that should come into the world.

"When Jesus therefore perceived that they would come and take him by force, to make him a king, he departed again into a mountain himself alone."[32]

At Nazareth, Jesus had disappeared from the midst of a multitude who were going to kill him.[33] Now he disappeared from among a multitude who wanted to proclaim him their King-Messiah.

THE APOSTLES WITNESS ANOTHER MIRACLE

Meanwhile, it had grown very dark and the disciples aboard their ship found themselves in very serious trouble because of a great wind that had suddenly come up and whipped the sea into foaming billows of turbulent waves.

The wind was too wild to use the sails and so the apostles were frantically rowing toward the lights on the distant shore over toward Bethsaida and Capernaum. By this time it was past three A.M., which meant the apostles had been rowing six or seven hours.[34]

John was in that boat and he says that after they had strained at the oars for 20 to 30 furlongs (a little over four miles)[35] an amazing thing happened.

In the darkness they could barely make out an object not far from the boat. As it gradually came closer, they finally perceived it was a

---

[32]John 6:14-15.
[33]Luke 4:29-30.
[34]Matthew 14:24-25.
[35]John 6:19.

man. He was walking among the waves on the water, and he was walking faster than they could row the boat. It looked as though he would pass them.[36]

This was unreal. The scripture says the apostles were so frightened they "cried out" thinking it was an apparition or some kind of ghostly spirit.

"But he saith unto them, It is I; be not afraid."[37]

PETER ASPIRES TO WALK ON THE WATER AND JOIN JESUS

It would be interesting to know what was surging through the mind of Peter as he looked out and saw his beloved Master walking on the water, unhindered by either the howling wind or the billowing waves. But no matter how shocked he might have been when he first saw the Savior, it did not take him long to decide that he would like to get out of the boat and do the same thing. Matthew was also a witness to all of this and says:

"Peter...said, Lord, if it be thou, bid me come unto thee on the water.

"And he said, Come. And when Peter was come down out of the ship, he walked on the water, to go to Jesus."[38]

Peter was a fisherman of long experience and as he walked away from that boat in the midst of a tempestuous sea, he no doubt began to suddenly realize that there was nothing beneath him but black, foaming water. The thought no sooner entered his head than he began to sink. He knew that almost in an instant, with his heavy clothing sucking up the water, he could be drowned. In a voice of terror, he cried out:

"Lord, save me!

---

[36]Mark 6:48.
[37]John 6:20.
[38]Matthew 14:28-29.

"And immediately Jesus stretched forth his hand, and caught him, and said unto him, O thou of little faith, wherefore didst thou doubt?

"And when they were come into the ship, the wind ceased."[39]

This near disaster was not only frightening to Peter but to all of the apostles. Nevertheless, as this scripture indicates, once Peter and Jesus had climbed back into the boat, everything suddenly became very calm. Not long before, the apostles had been caught in a similar storm and when the boat was on the verge of sinking, they awakened Jesus and he rebuked the wind and water.[40] Now, on this black night, he had calmed the storm again. The scripture continues:

"... they that were in the ship came and worshipped him, saying, Of a truth thou art the Son of God!"[41]

Finally the boat reached a wharf at a small fishing village not far from the two communities of Capernaum and "the other" Bethsaida. This fishing village was called Gennesaret.[42]

As these disciples stepped ashore, it must have been a relief to feel the security of the good firm earth under their feet again.

What a day and night of miracles this had been for the Savior's twelve apostles. They thought they had experienced marvels and wonders during their missionary journeys, but there had never been anything equal to this.

* * * *

TOPICS FOR REFLECTION AND DISCUSSION

1. When John the Baptist was thrown into prison, approximately where was the place of incarceration located? Who was Herodias?

---

[39]Matthew 14:30-32.
[40]Matthew 8:24-27.
[41]Matthew 14:33.
[42]Matthew 14:34.

What was the occasion when the daughter of Herodias danced for Herod Antipas? What pledge did Herod Antipas make to her that he later regretted?

2. Who told the daughter of Herodias to ask Herod Antipas for the head of John the Baptist? When Herod Antipas found he had been tricked, why didn't he refuse to have John the Baptist beheaded? What caused Herod Antipas to later identify Jesus with John the Baptist?

3. What were the apostles doing at about the time John was executed? What were the circumstances when they first heard about it? What impact did John's execution have on the Savior? Who brought him word of the execution? Where did Jesus say he wanted to go? Did he walk?

4. As soon as Jesus and his apostles anchored their boat, where did they go? Did the multitude follow them? How did they know where Jesus was? Did they attempt to go up where Jesus and the apostles were meeting together?

5. Why were the apostles so astonished when they came down from the mountain? How many people do Bible scholars estimate were in this crowd?

6. As Jesus came down among this vast multitude, what did he begin to do? At dusk who suggested that the crowd be encouraged to hurry to their homes? What was the Savior's response?

7. Why did the Savior's command to his apostles seem so ridiculous? How much food did the apostles find in the possession of a lad?

8. What miracle did Jesus perform with this small amount of food? What do we call this type of miracle? How much food was left over? Apparently who got it?

9. Then what did Jesus tell his apostles to do? What did Jesus say he would do after they were gone? Why did he have trouble doing it? What did the crowd want to do with Jesus? How did he escape from them?

10. About how far did the apostles row their boat in the storm? What was their reaction when they saw Jesus walking on the water near them? What did Peter say to the Savior? Then what happened? Would you have dared to try to walk on the water if the Savior had invited you to leave the boat and come to him? When Peter and Jesus entered the boat, what happened to the wind and the sea? Where did the boat finally land?

* * * *

CHAPTER 20

JESUS TESTS THE FAITH
OF HIS DISCIPLES

And Many Desert Him

As we noted at the close of the previous chapter, the Savior's
sailing boat finally glided into the port of Gennesaret. So far as we
know, it had now been over twenty-four hours since Jesus and his
apostles had been able to get any sleep.

One would have thought that after a strenuous night of rowing,
as well as the strain of the previous day, the Savior and his apostles
would have sought for a quiet place to rest and recuperate. But they
were not allowed that luxury.

The scripture says:

"And when they were come out of the ship, straightway they
knew him,

"And ran through that whole region round about, and began to
carry about in beds those that were sick, where they heard he was."[1]

MEANWHILE THE THOUSANDS WHOM JESUS
HAD FED WERE STILL LOOKING FOR HIM

It will be recalled that after Jesus had fed the 5,000 men as well
as the additional thousands of women and children, he was
compelled to escape in the darkness and ascend a nearby mountain
lest these people take him by force and make him their king.

[1]Mark 6:54-55.

After a sacred hour of prayer to his Father, Jesus had come down from the mountain without being detected. He had then disappeared in the darkness as he strode out onto the Sea of Galilee and walked among the turbulent waves until he reached the apostles who were rowing their boat through the storm. After the Savior's encounter with Peter, he helped the apostle back into the boat and immediately the wind and the waves became calm.

Then, as we have already seen, Jesus and his apostles tied up at the wharf in Gennesaret on the west shore. Of course, the thousands of people Jesus had fed knew nothing about this, and they were still patiently waiting for him to come down from the mountain. John describes their dilemma. He says:

"The day following...the people which stood on the other side of the sea saw that there was none other boat there, save that one whereinto his disciples were entered, and that Jesus went not with his disciples into the boat, but that his disciples were gone away alone....

"When the people therefore saw that Jesus was not there, neither his disciples, they also took shipping, and came to Capernaum, seeking for Jesus."[2]

The scripture would suggest that this multitude was not successful in finding Jesus when they first arrived in Capernaum. To begin with, he had arrived at the port of Gennesaret which was south of Capernaum on the west shore. Furthermore, he did not stay in Gennesaret long, but left almost immediately on a new kind of healing mission. It would be awhile before the people saw Jesus in Capernaum again.

PEOPLE HEALED BY MERELY TOUCHING JESUS OR HIS CLOTHING

In the early part of the Savior's ministry it seemed that Jesus healed people by touching them.[3] However, just before he gave his

---

[2]John 6:22-24.
[3]For example, Matthew 8:15; Mark 1:41.

Sermon on the Plain, he moved through the crowd, and all who had the faith to be healed would receive their great blessing by merely touching Jesus or the clothing he was wearing.[4] The scripture says that as each person touched him "virtue" would go out of him.[5] As we mentioned earlier, a woman with an "issue of blood," touched him and the same thing happened.[6]

In the past, the instant healing of people who took the initiative to touch Jesus—or the hem of his garment—seemed rather rare. Now it became an established pattern. As Jesus moved through Gennesaret and then out into the surrounding countryside, it was astonishing what happened.

Mark says:

"And whithersoever he entered into villages, or cities, or country, they laid the sick in the streets, and besought him that they might touch if it were but the border of his garment: and as many as touched him were made whole."[7]

JESUS RETURNS TO CAPERNAUM

It is not clear how long Jesus was away healing the sick, but in due time he returned to Capernaum where he was in the synagogue teaching the local people when some of the thousands who had been miraculously fed heard he had returned.[8] John says:

"And when they had found him on the other side of the sea, they said unto him, Rabbi, when camest thou hither?

"Jesus answered them and said, Verily, verily, I say unto you, Ye seek me, not because ye saw the miracles, but because ye did eat of the loaves, and were filled."[9]

---

[4]Luke 6:19.
[5]Ibid.
[6]Mark 5:25-34.
[7]Mark 6:56.
[8]John 6:59.
[9]John 6:25-26.

We observe that Jesus made no attempt to satisfy their curiosity by telling them how he had arrived undetected "on the other side of the sea," but went right to the heart of their real problem, which was their failure to be converted by what he had done for them.

They had not come seeking salvation for their souls, but food for their stomachs, which they knew he could miraculously provide.

Therefore Jesus said:

"Labour not for the meat which perisheth, but for that meat which endureth unto everlasting life, which the Son of man shall give unto you: for him hath God the Father sealed.

"Then said they unto him, What shall we do, that we might work the works of God?"[10]

Obviously, the "works of God" which they wanted to possess was that marvelous, miraculous power to make great quantities of food out of what appeared to be the thin air. They were asking how they might perform these same great "works of God."

Jesus answered, "This is the work of God, that ye believe on him whom he hath sent."[11]

These Galileans were no doubt Pharisees, and they perceived that Jesus was asking them to believe in him as an emissary of the Father. They also realized that he was shifting the topic of conversation away from their original question of how to get the divine power to make food. Some could see that he wanted them to believe in him as a messenger of God.

This presented to them a completely new problem. They had seen him provide bread miraculously, but to accept him as God's spokesman required that they have some kind of "sign from heaven."

---

[10]John 6:27-28.
[11]John 6:29.

Obviously, the Savior's heavenly power to perform miracles had not converted them. Therefore they said:

"What sign shewest thou then, that we may see, and believe thee? what dost thou work?

"Our fathers did eat manna in the desert; as it is written, He gave them bread from heaven to eat."[12]

THOSE WHO HAD BEEN MIRACULOUSLY FED BECOME SIGN SEEKERS

What they were saying was simply that the miracle of providing bread for twelve to fifteen thousand people was not equal to the miracle performed by Moses who gave the Israelites manna from heaven for a full forty years. They were demanding more evidence that Jesus possessed heavenly credentials comparable to those of Moses.

Of course, what they did not realize, and apparently did not have the spiritual curiosity to discover, was the exciting reality that this miracle-working servant of God standing before them was the great Jehovah of the Old Testament through whom the Father provided the manna for Moses and the Israelites.

Jesus decided to share this heavenly secret with them. He said:

"Verily, verily, I say unto you, Moses gave you *not* that bread from heaven; but my Father giveth you the true bread from heaven."[13]

He first wanted to have them understand that Moses had no power within himself to provide the manna which came from heaven for forty years. It came from God, and now the Father had sent the true bread from heaven which the manna merely represented. Whether they appreciated it or not, the Father had sent his Son to provide them the sustaining nourishment of salvation for all eternity.

---

[12]John 6:30-31.
[13]John 6:32.

But all of this heavenly symbolism went completely over their heads. From here on these unbelieving Pharisees were going to get what we might refer to as "the Nicodemus treatment."

Jesus perceived that they were so intent on gaining the power of God to make food, that they were resisting his attempt to reach them with the meat, the bread, or even the milk of the gospel.

So Jesus started using the code phrases of the gospel just as he did with the spiritually blind Nicodemus. To these people who refused to comprehend or even to make humble inquiry so they could begin to comprehend, he said:

"For the bread of God is he which cometh down from heaven, and giveth life unto the world."[14]

Once more, they anxiously demanded:

"Lord, evermore give us this bread!"[15]

Obviously, they were still thinking of their stomachs, so Jesus resorted to his missionary device of last resort. He boldly bore his testimony to them, just as he had to Nicodemus.[16] Jesus said:

"I AM THE BREAD OF LIFE: he that cometh to me shall never hunger; and he that believeth on me shall never thirst."[17]

Then Jesus said something which would stand against these unbelieving Pharisees at the last judgment. He said:

"Ye also have seen me, and believe not!"[18]

---

[14]John 6:33.
[15]John 6:33-34.
[16]JST John 3:18.
[17]John 6:35.
[18]John 6:36.

JESUS SAID HIS TRUE DISCIPLES WERE
FOREORDAINED TO RECOGNIZE HIM WHEN HE CAME

The Savior elected to describe to this congregation why he was not discouraged even though most of them refused to recognize him in his divine role. He said:

"All that the Father giveth me shall come to me....

"And this is the Father's will...that of all which he hath given me I should lose nothing."[19]

But apparently most of the people were not listening. They were murmuring among themselves about his statement that "I am the bread of life which came down from heaven." How could he be the "bread of life" sent down from heaven? They said among themselves:

"Is not this Jesus, the son of Joseph, whose father and mother we know? how is it then that he saith, I came down from heaven?"[20]

JESUS TESTS HIS FOLLOWERS AND MANY DESERT HIM

Jesus perceived their thoughts and decided to cleanse this flock of doubters with some meaty doctrine that would send them fluttering away in all directions like a flock of frightened birds.

John said Jesus did this because he "knew from the beginning who they were that believed not."[21] With this foreknowledge the Savior began talking about his flesh and blood which would be represented later in the emblems of the sacrament. In the Christian culture, partaking of the sacrament is often described as partaking of the flesh and blood of the Savior who died for us. But this multitude of doubters were incapable of giving a spiritual interpretation to what Jesus now said, and a literal interpretation of his words was shocking in the extreme.

---

[19]John 6:37-39.
[20]John 6:42.
[21]John 6:64.

He declared:

"I am the living bread which came down from heaven: if any man eat of this bread, he shall live for ever: and the bread that I will give is my flesh, which I will give for the life of the world."[22]

Now came the thunderbolt:

"Verily, verily, I say unto you, Except ye eat the flesh of the Son of man, and drink his blood, ye have no life in you.

"Whoso eateth my flesh, and drinketh my blood, hath eternal life; and I will raise him up at the last day....

"As the living Father hath sent me, and I live by the Father: so he that eateth me, even he shall live by me.

"This is that bread which came down from heaven: not as your fathers did eat manna, and are dead: he that eateth of this bread shall live for ever."[23]

The spiritual blindness of those listening to Jesus produced the same impact on their minds as it did on the mind of Nicodemus.

Even some of the Savior's disciples were so disturbed they said among themselves:

"This is an hard saying; who can hear it?"[24]

Jesus intended his words to be a "hard saying," hard enough to make his listeners ask questions and want to know more. But they did neither. Had they been humble enough to ask the meaning of this latest metaphor they would have learned that he was talking about the sacrament that would be instituted at his last supper, wherein the bread represented his body that would suffer for them,

---

[22]John 6:51.
[23]John 6:53-58.
[24]John 6:60.

and the wine or water represented his blood that would be spilt for them.

When Jesus perceived what they were thinking, he said:

"Does this offend you?

"What and if ye shall see the Son of man ascend up where he was before?"[25]

In other words, the Father is not offended by the Savior's teachings. This crowd of critics may be offended, but what will these doubters say when they see the Son return to the Father to sit on his right hand where he was before? This would not happen unless the Father approved of him.

Then Jesus told them why they were so dull-witted and hard of hearing. He said:

"It is the spirit that quickeneth; the flesh profiteth nothing: the words that I speak unto you, they are spirit, and they are life."[26]

Jesus was administering a sharp reprimand to these particular disciples. He was warning them that if they had been listening with the Spirit they would have understood what he was saying in its spiritual sense. But since they were not in tune with the Spirit, they were confounded just like the others.

Jesus knew these disciples had reached a fork in the road. The Spirit was sorting them out at that very moment and Jesus saw that many lacked sufficient spirituality to choose the strait and narrow road and survive as his disciples. Therefore he said:

"There are some of you that believe not....

---

[25]John 6:61-62.
[26]John 6:63.

"Therefore said I unto you, that no man can come unto me, except it were given unto him of my Father."[27]

To those of the Savior's disciples who had not cultivated the Spirit, this statement was offensive just as his previous comments had been. Therefore John writes:

"From that time many of his disciples went back, and walked no more with him."[28]

WHAT ABOUT THE TWELVE APOSTLES?

Now Jesus turned directly to his twelve apostles. They had not asked any questions either. A spiritual thirst for knowledge is a critical ingredient of the gospel.[29] In the Sermon on the Mount, Jesus had told these apostles:

"Ask, and it shall be given you; seek, and ye shall find; knock, and it shall be opened unto you.

"For every one that asketh receiveth; and he that seeketh findeth; and to him that knocketh it shall be opened to him."[30]

It must have been disturbing to him that they were silent. As we have already mentioned, it was similar to a future day when Jesus would say:

"Other sheep I have, which are not of this fold: them also I must bring, and they shall hear my voice; and there shall be one fold, and one shepherd."[31]

None of the apostles asked, "What sheep," or "Where are they?" As a result, Jesus was forbidden by the Father to tell the apostles

[27]John 6:64-65.
[28]John 6:66.
[29]Matthew 5:6.
[30]Matthew 7:7-8.
[31]John 10:16.

about the Christians in America or about the Savior's ministry to the "lost" Ten Tribes after his resurrection.[32]

So, on this occasion when many of the Savior's disciples were fleeing from him, Jesus confronted the twelve who stood silent before him. He challenged them, and said:

"Will ye also go away?

"Simon Peter answered him, Lord, to whom shall we go? thou hast the words of eternal life.

"And we believe and are sure that thou art that Christ, the Son of the living God."[33]

Peter did not know it, but it was this fervent testimony of the Savior that would one day qualify him to become the president of the Savior's church. Because of this testimony, which was revitalized after the resurrection, he would eventually be considered worthy to receive all the keys and authority necessary to set up the full structure of the church upon the earth in the meridian of time.

In addition to the twelve apostles, there were also other choice disciples who remained faithful during this difficult time of testing. Later, two of these were identified by name. One was Joseph, surnamed Justus, and the other was Matthias.[34] The scripture says these two were among the disciples who were with the apostles from "the baptism of John" until the Savior ascended into heaven.[35] These were among those who had passed the test.

Matthias was later selected to replace Judas Iscariot in the quorum of the twelve apostles.[36]

---

[32]3 Nephi 15:13-18, 16:1-4, B. of M.
[33]John 6:67-69.
[34]Acts 1:23.
[35]Acts 1:22.
[36]Acts 1:26.

JUDAS REMAINED WITH JESUS
BUT ONLY TO BETRAY HIM

As Jesus looked carefully at each of the apostles, he said:

"Have not I chosen you twelve and one of you is a devil?"[37]

This must have been both shocking and puzzling to the apostles. Later, when John wrote his Gospel text, he knew from subsequent events what Jesus meant:

"He spake of Judas Iscariot the son of Simon: for he it was that should betray him, being one of the twelve."[38]

The Savior's reference to Judas as a "devil" [meaning a false accuser][39] is later fortified and amplified when Jesus refers to him as a "son of perdition,"[40] which means one who can never be forgiven,[41] but will be cast out with Satan and his angels.[42]

The scripture also makes a similar reference to Cain as "perdition."[43] This might suggest that both Judas and Cain had a history extending back into the pre-existence which has not yet been revealed. What has been said of them clearly implies that it was foreknown where their secret loyalties lay.

THE TRUE NATURE OF CLEANLINESS

Barely had Jesus watched many of his former followers depart when he was challenged by certain Pharisees and scribes who had come from Jerusalem to spy on him.

They challenged Jesus and his disciples for not following the traditional requirements of ceremonial washing before eating. In fact

---

[37]John 6:70.
[38]John 6:71.
[39]See *Webster's Unabridged Dictionary* under "Devil."
[40]John 17:12.
[41]3 Nephi 29:7.
[42]Doctrine and Covenants 76:43-44.
[43]Moses 5:22-24.

there were all kinds of ceremonial washings of cups, pots, kettles, and tables that had become part of the ritual required by the rabbis. In the absence of these ceremonial procedures, the members of a household were considered "unclean."

Jesus decided it was time to teach a lesson about true cleanliness, so he said:

"Well hath Esaias prophesied of you hypocrites, as it is written, This people honoureth me with their lips, but their heart is far from me.

"Howbeit in vain do they worship me, teaching for doctrines the commandments of men."[44]

Since the days of Moses the rulers of the Jews had introduced a vast array of burdensome ceremonies and rituals which were truly "the commandments of men."

In their anxiety to follow all the trivial details of these rituals they had ignored or neglected the substantive commandments of God. So Jesus said:

"Laying aside the commandment of God, ye hold the tradition of men, as the washing of pots and cups: and many other such like things ye do....

"Full well ye reject the commandment of God, that ye may keep your own tradition."[45]

Then he decided to give them a specific example of a very important commandment they had grossly violated:

"Moses said, Honour thy father and thy mother; and, Whoso curseth father or mother, let him die the death:

---

[44]Mark 7:6-7; Isaiah 29:13.
[45]Mark 7:8-9.

"But ye say, If a man shall say to his father or mother, It is Corban, that is to say, a gift, by whatsoever thou mightest be profited by me; he shall be free."[46]

This somewhat obscure statement was well understood by the Jews. They were accustomed to saying that all of the material things they could spare had been given to God as a contribution and therefore they were free of any obligation to their parents. Jesus drove his point home by saying:

"And ye suffer him [who gives gifts to God] no more to do ought for his father or his mother;

"Making the word of God of none effect through your tradition, which ye have delivered: and many such like things do ye."[47]

Jesus could scarcely have singled out a more striking example of the disgraceful way in which many Jews were twisting the law so as to excuse the neglect of their aged parents.

THE NATURE OF GODLY CLEANLINESS

Then he turned to the multitude to teach them a basic principle of Godly cleanliness. He said:

"Hearken unto me every one of you, and understand:

"There is nothing from without a man, that entering into him can defile him [spiritually]: but the things which come out of him, those are they that defile the man."[48]

Jesus then turned and went into a nearby house and his disciples followed after him. They were not sure they understood what Jesus meant so they asked him about it. He said:

---

[46]Mark 7:10-11.
[47]Mark 7:12-13.
[48]Mark 7:14-15.

"Do ye not perceive, that whatsoever thing from without entereth into the man, it cannot defile him;

"Because it entereth not into his heart, but into the belly, and goeth out into the draught, purging all meats?

"And he said, That which cometh out of the man, that defileth the man."[49]

Both the Jews and his disciples understood the word, "defile" to mean the contamination of the soul before God. Jesus wanted to clearly distinguish between cleanliness of the body and cleanliness of the spirit.

The spies from Jerusalem had accused Jesus and his disciples of offending God by failing to cater to all of the ceremonies and rituals of the rabbis. Jesus wanted his disciples to appreciate what really offended God and tainted their souls, so he said:

"For from within, out of the heart of men, proceed evil thoughts, adulteries, fornications, murders,

"Thefts, covetousness, wickedness, deceit, lasciviousness, an evil eye, blasphemy, pride, foolishness:

"All these evil things come from within, and defile the man."[50]

Very well, so he is talking about defiling of the heart or the spirit, but the disciples were nevertheless concerned that the manner in which Jesus had expressed himself was very offensive to the learned dignitaries from Jerusalem.

The Savior gave them a very definitive answer. He said:

"Every plant, which my heavenly Father hath not planted, shall be rooted up.

---

[49]Mark 7:18-20.
[50]Mark 7:21-23.

"Let them alone: they be blind leaders of the blind. And if the blind lead the blind, both shall fall into the ditch."[51]

The Savior wanted to make it clear that neither he nor his Father had any regard for these burdensome, manmade rabbinical traditions. They were stumbling blocks to the people and blinded them to the things that God had said were important. He said the learned men who had invented all this trivia would end up in the ditch and their precious traditions would be rooted up and cast off forever.

* * * *

TOPICS FOR REFLECTION AND DISCUSSION

1. Why were the thousands whom Jesus had fed so perplexed when they couldn't find Jesus after the apostles left without him? What did they finally do? Did they find him immediately after returning to Capernaum? Why not?

2. Where was Jesus when he first began his latest ministry of healing based on the people merely touching him or his garments? As each person touched the Savior, why would he feel "virtue" go out of him? Up to this time had this been an exceptional type of miracle or a regular pattern?

3. When Jesus returned to Capernaum, what did the people (who had been miraculously fed) ask him to explain? Did he ever tell them? What did he say was the real reason they wanted to find him?

4. The people whom Jesus had fed said they wanted to have the power to "work the works of God." What did they mean? Whom did Jesus say was responsible for sending the Israelites the manna that fed them in the wilderness for forty years? Now what bread did he say was being sent by that same person? Did Jesus ever come right out and plainly state he was that bread, even the bread of life?

---

[51]Matthew 15:13-14.

5. Why didn't Jesus become discouraged when so many people seemed deaf to what he was saying and blind to what they were seeing? What doctrine did Jesus preach which caused many of the Savior's disciples to abandon him? What did Peter say when Jesus asked if the apostles were going to leave also?

6. What reward did Peter eventually receive for his faithfulness? Other disciples besides the apostles remained with Jesus. Do the scriptures identify any of them by name? Can you recall one of them? What did he become?

7. Did Jesus ever call one of his apostles a "devil"? Did John identify him by name? What is a son of perdition? What is their punishment?

8. By the time of Christ's ministry, how had the commandments of God been corrupted by the commandments of men? How had the people twisted the law and excused themselves from caring for their elderly parents? How would you define "corbin"?

9. How would you define Godly cleanliness? What is the main source of evil for which a person will be judged? Can the human spirit become "unclean" before the Lord?

10. What did Jesus say would happen to the rituals and inventions of men which had been added to the commandments of God? What did he say would happen to those who had burdened the law of God with these corruptions?

* * * *

CHAPTER 21

AT DECAPOLIS JESUS
FEEDS 4,000

The Savior's next field of labor was in northern Galilee near the borders of the Gentile region of Tyre and Sidon.

Jesus and his apostles were invited to stay at the home of one of the disciples, and as soon as Jesus had been assigned a room, he asked to be alone. Whether this was for physical rest or for meditation and prayer, we are not told. The scripture simply says that he went into the house and requested that "no man should know it."[1]

But the word spread rapidly, as it did wherever he went, and Mark says his presence in that region "could not be hid."[2]

Before long, a certain "woman of Canaan" (whom Mark calls a Syrophenician) came to him and said in a pleading voice:

"Have mercy on me O Lord, thou Son of David; my daughter is grievously vexed with a devil."[3]

The scripture says:

"He answered her not a word."[4]

Except for the Roman centurion, and possibly one or two others, Jesus had restricted his ministry to the house of Israel.

---

[1]Mark 7:24.
[2]Ibid.
[3]Matthew 15:22.
[4]Matthew 15:23.

Therefore, when Jesus did not immediately respond, the woman went to the apostles. Finally, the disciples said to the Savior:

"Send her away, for she crieth after us."[5]

Jesus apparently turned to the woman to test her faith, and said:

"I am not sent but unto the lost sheep of the house of Israel."[6]

But this humble and distraught Gentile woman behaved as nobly as any Israelite. The scripture says:

"Then came she and worshipped him, saying, Lord, help me.

"But he answered and said, It is not meet to take the children's bread, and to cast it to dogs."[7]

To modern ears this seems like a very harsh utterance to come from the lips of the Savior, but it was a common phrase which meant that the good food prepared for the children should not be tossed to the pet dog under the table.[8] It was a metaphor used by both Jews and Gentiles to denote something sacred that should not be carelessly cast to the unholy or the unworthy.

But this good woman was not to be denied. True, she was not of the chosen seed of Israel, but she said:

"Yet the dogs eat of the crumbs which fall from their masters' table."[9]

Just as with the Roman centurion, Jesus was deeply impressed with this marvelous manifestation of faith by this non-Israelite. He therefore said:

---

[5]Ibid.
[6]Matthew 15:24.
[7]Matthew 15:25-26.
[8]Edersheim, *The Life and Times of Jesus*, vol. 2, p. 41.
[9]Matthew 15:27.

"O woman, great is thy faith: be it unto thee even as thou wilt. And her daughter was made whole from that very hour."[10]

Although the Father's original plan called for the preaching of the gospel to the Israelites first, and then to the Gentiles,[11] nevertheless, these two incidents of the Roman centurion and the Canaanite woman clearly demonstrate that blessings come through faith, regardless of lineage.

JESUS MAKES THE MOST UNIQUE JOURNEY IN NEW TESTAMENT HISTORY

Now Jesus took his disciples and made a journey which began on the borders of Tyre and Sidon near the Mediterranean Sea and went all the way to the ten Greek cities of Decapolis on the east side of the Jordan River. And all of this without a single comment by the apostles as to what happened along the way.

It is assumed that he did his usual preaching and healing as he proceeded toward this new destination. However, it may have been more or less repetitious of what they had reported before, and therefore the apostles made no special mention of the teachings or events on this journey.

After traversing the entire breadth of Galilee, they finally came to the next field of labor.

JESUS VISITS THE REGION OF DECAPOLIS

Decapolis was the last remnant of the once mighty Greek empire of Syria and Palestine that was once ruled by the house of the Greek Seleucids, descendants of one of the most famous generals of Alexander the Great. This region was called Decapolis, meaning "ten cities."

---

[10]Matthew 15:28.
[11]Smith, *Teachings of the Prophet Joseph Smith*, p. 15.

The Roman historian, Pliny the Young, (c. 63-113 A.D.) listed the ten cities as Seythopolis, Hippos, Gidara, Pella, Philadelphia, Gerasa, Dion, Canatha, Damascus, and Raphana.

It is interesting that none of the apostles indicate that Jesus visited any of these cities on this journey even though their inhabitants included Jews as well as Greeks and other nationalities.

However, the Gospel writers do say that when Jesus went along the eastern shore of the Galilee—which is part of the district of Decapolis—the crowds surged forth to hear him.

It is not likely that many non-Jewish people were among those who came out to see Jesus, especially the Greeks, because in this region he was in bad repute among them.

It will be recalled that Jesus had ministered in this general area several months earlier, and he was blamed for causing the death of 2,000 swine when they broke away from their herders and rushed madly down the steep slopes into the sea where they were drowned.

Swine meat was considered a delicacy by the Greek population, and this loss of a whole season's supply of swine was such a serious financial disaster that the rulers of the area begged Jesus to leave.[12]

Now he was back.

JESUS WENT INTO A MOUNTAIN
AND THE PEOPLE GATHERED TO HIM

It is interesting that Jesus did not seek the people, they sought him. And they no doubt had to send out scouts to locate him, because he was in a remote and secluded place. The scripture says:

"And Jesus...came nigh unto the sea of Galilee; and went up into a mountain, and sat down there.

---

[12]Matthew 8:32-34.

"And great multitudes came unto him, having with them those that were lame, blind, dumb, maimed, and many others, and cast them down at Jesus' feet; and he healed them:

"Insomuch that the multitude wondered, when they saw the dumb to speak, the maimed to be whole, the lame to walk, and the blind to see: and they glorified the God of Israel."[13]

However, there was one man who seemed to be a difficult case. Just as Jesus would later tell his followers that some evil spirits cannot be cast out without much prayer and fasting, so now Jesus decided to follow a special procedure in healing this man who was deaf and suffered from an impairment of speech.

Mark says:

"And they bring unto him one that was deaf, and had an impediment in his speech; and they beseech him to put his hand on him.

"And he took him aside from the multitude, and put his fingers into his ears, and he spit, and touched his tongue;

"And looking up to heaven, he sighed, and saith unto him, *EPHPHATHA*, that is, Be opened.

"And straightway his ears were opened, and the string of his tongue was loosed, and he spake plain.

"And he charged them that they should tell no man: but the more he charged them, so much the more a great deal they published it;

"And were beyond measure astonished, saying, He hath done all things well: he maketh both the deaf to hear, and the dumb to speak."[14]

---

[13]Matthew 15:29-31.
[14]Mark 7:32-37.

THE FEEDING OF 4,000 MEN
PLUS WOMEN AND CHILDREN

The mountain where Jesus had chosen to perform this vast quantity of miracles was so remote, and the demonstration of his power so inspiring, that the people stayed to listen and watch for three whole days.

They had water nearby, but no food whatsoever. In this extremity, something had to be done. Therefore the scripture says:

"Then Jesus called his disciples unto him, and said, I have compassion on the multitude, because they continue with me now three days, and have nothing to eat: and I will not send them away fasting, lest they faint in the way."[15]

Jesus and his disciples had also been without food for three days, so they undoubtedly felt as faint from fasting as the multitude.

Matthew continues:

"And his disciples say unto him, Whence should we have so much bread in the wilderness, as to fill so great a multitude?

"And Jesus saith unto them, How many loaves have ye? And they said, Seven, and a few little fishes.

"And he commanded the multitude to sit down on the ground."[16]

Here, on the eastern side of the Sea of Galilee, Jesus was about to perform the same miracle of the "multiplication of substances" as that which he had used to provide food for twelve to fifteen thousand on the northeastern shores of the Galilee a few weeks before.

---

[15]Matthew 15:32.
[16]Matthew 15:33-35.

So Matthew says:

"And he took the seven loaves and the fishes, and gave thanks, and brake them, and gave to his disciples, and the disciples to the multitude."[17]

Just as before, the miracle included bread already baked, and fish already cooked.

"And they did all eat, and were filled: and they took up of the broken meat that was left seven baskets full.

"And they that did eat were four thousand men, beside women and children."[18]

It is on the basis of this last verse that various scholars have estimated that this miraculous meal from heaven may have fed as many as ten to twelve thousand people.

JESUS AND THE APOSTLES TAKE SHIP
FOR THE WESTERN SIDE OF GALILEE

After Jesus had finished feeding the huge crowd on the mountain, he invited the people to depart to their homes. Then he prepared to take his disciples and leave the district of Decapolis by crossing the Sea of Galilee to the western shore.

Matthew wrote:

"And he sent away the multitude, and took ship, and came into the coasts of Magdala."[19]

On this journey, the Savior's little ship had crossed the Galilee at its widest expanse. Magdala is believed to have been four miles up the coast from the city of Tiberias where Herod the Great had built a beautiful Roman spa. The warm mineral springs in this area were

---

[17]Matthew 15:36.
[18]Matthew 15:37-38.
[19]Matthew 15:39.

famous, and Herod had provided it with several magnificent marble baths to attract the most sophisticated and wealthy patrons.

But Magdala was less favored. It was a traditional Jewish marketing community, specializing in the harvest of fish from the Sea of Galilee.

THE SAVIOR'S RECEPTION WHEN
HE REACHED THE WESTERN SHORE

Seldom did Jesus encounter hostile and taunting crowds when he first arrived in a new area. Usually those who welcomed him were families who had heard about his healing powers, and they therefore hurried to meet him with their sick and afflicted.

However, at Magdala it was the more self-righteous Pharisees and Sadducees who rushed to the wharf to ridicule Jesus. They brought with them an assortment of corrupt and tainted minds along with their chronically sick spirits. Jesus wished he could have nurtured and healed them, but it soon became apparent that he first had to listen to their taunts.

Matthew witnessed the scene and afterwards wrote:

"The Pharisees also with the Sadducees came, and tempting desired him that he would shew them a sign from heaven.

"He answered and said unto them, When it is evening, ye say, It will be fair weather: for the sky is red.

"And in the morning, It will be foul weather to day: for the sky is red and lowering. O ye hypocrites, ye can discern the face of the sky; but can ye not discern the signs of the times?"[20]

Jesus was scolding these high minded "learned men" for their poverty in scriptural scholarship. They could read the weather better than they could read the writings of the prophets who described the signs of the times for their day. In their day Jesus had come healing

---

[20]Matthew 16:1-3.

the sick, straightening crooked limbs, curing the blind, the deaf and the dumb. In fact, for over a year it had been widely known that on several occasions he had raised the dead.

But these proud and pompous cynics were unconvinced. They demanded some kind of spectacular "sign from heaven." Isaiah had seen Jesus under these circumstances in prophetic vision, and had written concerning him as follows:

"He is despised and rejected of men; a man of sorrows, and acquainted with grief: and we hid as it were our faces from him; he was despised, and we esteemed him not."[21]

It is rather singular that the Pharisees and Sadducees were united in their mutual disdain for Jesus. These two sects were mortal enemies who, from time to time, had even engaged in open warfare against each other. But in fulfilling Isaiah's prophecy they stood shoulder to shoulder. And they had something else in common—venal immorality. Therefore, Jesus said to them:

"An evil and adulterous generation seeketh after a sign; and there shall no sign be given unto it, but the sign of the prophet Jonas [Jonah].

"For as Jonas was three days *and three nights* in the whale's belly, so likewise shall the Son of man be buried in the heart of the earth."[22]

Having disposed of their demands for "signs," Jesus prepared to depart.

THE COMING DESTRUCTION OF MAGDALA

No doubt these scholarly critics would have been totally amazed if Jesus had shared with them his prophetic knowledge of the afflictions coming to this region very shortly. In less than three decades, Magdala would fall under the sledge hammer attacks of the

---

[21]Isaiah 53:3.
[22]Matthew 12:39-40 (emphasis added); 16:4.

Roman legions sent in by Titus. History tells us 6,700 Jews were slain, 6,000 of the strongest were sent to Nero to dig the Corinthian canal, and 30,400 were auctioned off as slaves.[23]

JESUS PROCEEDS NORTHWARD

Now Jesus was ready to go north, where the next important highlights of his mission would soon take place.

To have walked from Magdala to Bethsaida and Capernaum—located on the northwest corner of the Galilee—would have been a tedious journey. Therefore Mark tells us:

"And entering into the ship again [they] departed to the other side [the north side where Bethsaida and Capernaum were situated].

"Now the disciples had forgotten to take bread, neither had they in the ship with them more than one loaf."[24]

While the disciples were contemplating their pangs of hunger, Jesus said something which gave them an opportunity to bring up the subject of food. Jesus said:

"Take heed, beware of the leaven of the Pharisees, and of the leaven of Herod.

"And they reasoned among themselves, saying, It is because we have no bread."[25]

JESUS DENOUNCES THE DISCIPLES' CLAMOR FOR BREAD

At this stage of the Savior's ministry he had a crushing burden on his mind. Every hour increased the dark shadow of the terrible ordeal he would have to endure within that very year. Therefore, when he perceived what his disciples were thinking, he became impatient. Here he had tried to warn them against the fermenting leaven of false

---

[23]Berrett, *Discovering the World of the Bible*, p. 353. See also pp. 163, 165.
[24]Mark 8:13-14.
[25]Mark 8:15-16.

teachings and beliefs of the Pharisees and Sadducees, and all they could think about was bread.

He could not help but express his exasperation when he said:

"Why reason ye, because ye have no bread? perceive ye not yet, neither understand? have ye your heart yet hardened?

"Having eyes, see ye not? and having ears, hear ye not? and do ye not remember?

"When I brake the five loaves among five thousand, how many baskets full of fragments took ye up? They say unto him, twelve.

"And when the seven [loaves were blessed and distributed] among four thousand, how many baskets full of fragments took ye up? And they said, Seven.

"And he said unto them, How is it that ye do not understand?"[26]

We can sympathize with the hungry disciples, but we can also appreciate the desperate anxiety of Jesus who sensed the compelling necessity to prepare these humble Galileans for the monumental task of taking over the administration of the kingdom of God within a few months.

To Jesus it was distressing and vexing that he had barely mentioned the metaphor of "leaven" and the disciples immediately began thinking of their growling stomachs. They had completely missed the vital warning which he was trying to plant in their minds concerning the fermented doctrinal evils of the Pharisees and Sadducees.

The boat soon reached the northern coast of the lake and landed at Bethsaida, near Capernaum. Apparently Jesus and his disciples obtained some nourishment there because they didn't mention the subject again.

---

[26]Mark 8:17-21.

HEALING A BLIND MAN BY STAGES

While they were still in Bethsaida the scripture says;

"And they bring a blind man unto him, and besought him to touch him."[27]

It will be recalled that earlier many people had been healed by touching the Savior, or by the Savior touching them. It had become a routine procedure. But that is not what Jesus did in the case of this blind man. The apostles must have been surprised when they saw him leading the man out of town. The scripture says:

"And he took the blind man by the hand, and led him out of the town; and when he had spit on his eyes, and put his hands upon him, he asked him if he saw ought.

"And he looked up, and said, I see men as trees, walking."[28]

It was obvious that this man's blindness was being healed gradually, a little at a time. In all probability, this was not because of the obstinate nature of his affliction as much as it was the desire of the Savior to have him appreciate the great blessing he was receiving. Mark continues:

"After that he put his hands again upon his eyes, and made him look up: and he was restored, and saw every man clearly.

"And he sent him away to his house, saying, Neither go into the town, nor tell it to any in the town."[29]

We do not have the rest of the story, but based on the results of the Savior's admonition to people he had healed in the past, this man probably ran into town as fast as his legs could carry him, and spread the word of his miraculous cure in all directions.

---

[27]Mark 8:22.
[28]Mark 8:23-24.
[29]Mark 8:25-26.

JESUS PREPARES HIS APOSTLES TO SHARE IN ONE OF THE MOST IMPORTANT EVENTS OF HIS ENTIRE MINISTRY

It must have been astonishing to the Savior's apostles and disciples as he led them back and forth across the land, over the sea, up the mountains, and from town to town without the slightest vestige of advanced notification or any announced plan of needed preparation.

However, a brief review of the remarkable things which occurred in each new field of labor demonstrates that Jesus was being led by the Spirit to achieve the Father's will.

The apostles had no way of knowing that one of the most glorious events some of them would ever experience lay just ahead. The details are in the next chapter.

*   *   *   *

TOPICS FOR REFLECTION AND DISCUSSION

1. When the Canaanite woman came to Jesus to plead with him to heal her daughter, why do you think the Savior did not answer her at first, either one way or the other? What did his disciples want him to do with her? Why?

2. In what way did this Canaanite woman act out her part as nobly as an Israelite? When Jesus said the children's bread should not be cast to the dogs, was the woman offended? In their culture, what did this metaphor mean?

3. In what way did Jesus indicate by his blessings that faith is more important than lineage? Why was the Savior's trip from the land of Tyre and Sidon to Decapolis unique? Did Jesus visit any of the cities in the area of Decapolis? Where did he go?

4. Why weren't the Greeks likely to attend the Savior's convocations on the mountain? How many days did the huge multitude of men, women, and children, go without food? Did they have any fresh water?

5. Did Jesus or the apostles initiate the idea of getting food for the people? Had Jesus and the apostles also been fasting for three days in spite of all the preaching and teaching they were doing?

6. When Jesus asked how many loaves the apostles had, what did they answer? And how many fish? By the miraculous multiplication of substances, how many people is it estimated that Jesus fed on this occasion? How many baskets of food were left over?

7. When Jesus and the apostles arranged for a ship to take them across the Sea of Galilee, where did they land? Can you locate Magdala on the map? What was the name of the famous Roman spa just a few miles to the south? What was the principal industry in Magdala?

8. What kind of people usually met the Savior when he arrived at a new place? What kind of people met him at Magdala? What did they seek as proof that Jesus was sent from God? What did Isaiah say that describes the treatment of the Savior during this period?

9. What kind of people are always "seeking signs"? What sign did Jesus say their generation would get which would verify the divinity of Christ? As Jesus departed northward by ship, what did he say that made his disciples think of food? What was the Savior's reaction to their clamor for bread?

10. After the boat landed near Bethsaida, what unusual thing did Jesus do with a certain blind man? Do you think the gradual healing process was absolutely necessary, or do you think it was done to help the blind man appreciate the miracle of being healed? Did the Savior tell the man to keep his healing a secret? Had people honored this request in the past?

*   *   *   *

CHAPTER 22

HEAVENLY EVENTS ON THE MOUNT OF TRANSFIGURATION

After healing the blind man at Bethsaida, Jesus appears to have guided his disciples past Capernaum and then proceeded along the north shore of the sea until he came to the place where the Jordan River flows into the upper Galilee. The party then journeyed up along the stream northward for about twenty miles, traveling through a beautiful valley.

The headwaters of the Jordan River consist of two separate crystal clear streams, both of which are fed by the melting snow seeping down from the heights of Mount Hermon. This mountain is over 9,000 feet above sea level and looms over north Galilee like a huge Davidic lion guarding the valley below.

The larger of these two streams gushes forth from a spring in a limestone cave at the foot of Mount Hermon. The oasis that immediately surrounds this area is such a lush and beautiful assortment of trees, ferns and flowers that visitors who come there are reluctant to leave.

A GARDEN OF EDEN DISCOVERED BY THE TRIBE OF DAN

The tribe of Dan discovered this place, but it was so far from the inheritances of the other tribes that they felt sorry for Dan.

Actually, the tribe of Dan had originally been assigned a territory west of Jerusalem that included the Sorek Valley.

This is the valley leading down from Jerusalem to the plains of Samaria stretching along the seacoast, and occupied in earlier days by the Philistines.

The problem for the tribe of Dan was the fact that whenever the Philistines made an attack on the Israelites, to put them under tribute, the Philistines would charge up the Sorek Valley and the Danites would be the first ones to take the full brunt of the battle until troops arrived from the other tribes.

Understandably, the Danites soon grew weary of this arrangement, and that is how they happened to send an expedition north to find a better place. What they discovered was one of the most beautiful spots in all Palestine.

During the Savior's life, this area was part of the Roman empire that had been assigned to Philip, the fifth son of Herod the Great. So Philip built a small but luxurious city near the headwaters of the Jordan and called it Caesarea-Philippi in honor of the emperor and himself.

It was to this place[1] that Jesus now led his twelve apostles as a prelude to an upcoming event that would be one of the foremost experiences in the Savior's entire ministry. Not since the forty days of spiritual beatification in the wilderness would there be anything to compare with it.

JESUS ASKS HIS APOSTLES WHO THEY THINK HE IS

After reaching their destination, Luke says the Savior and his disciples found a private place where they could pray together.[2] Then the scripture says:

"He asked his disciples, saying, Whom do men say that I the Son of man am?

---

[1]Mark 8:27.
[2]Luke 9:18.

"And they said, Some say that thou art John the Baptist: s o m e, Elias; and others, Jeremias, or one of the prophets."[3]

It is rather astonishing to find that some of the people would think Jesus was John the Baptist. We recall that this was the result of a story which was being spread around by Herod Antipas.

As we have noted in a previous chapter, John the Baptist was beheaded by Herod Antipas, and now this dissolute descendant of King Herod was terrified by the possibility that Jesus might be the reincarnation of John. Perhaps John had returned as Jesus to avenge himself. It was widely known that Herod Antipas harbored this fear.[4]

Then Jesus asked:

"But whom say ye that I am?

"And Simon Peter answered and said, Thou art the Christ, the Son of the living God."[5]

This was the second time the testimony of the disciples had been put to the test. The first time was when the doctrine of the sacrament was misinterpreted by the Savior's followers and many of them deserted him. It will be recalled that Jesus then turned to the twelve and said: "Will ye also go away?" Before anyone else could answer, Peter had said:

"Lord to whom shall we go? Thou hast the words of eternal life. And we believe and are sure that thou art the Christ, the son of the living God."[6]

Now at Caesarea-Philippi we have Peter once more speaking up ahead of his fellow disciples and declaring with the deepest conviction: "Thou art the Christ, the Son of the living God."

---

[3]Matthew 16, 13-14.
[4]Mark 6:14.
[5]Matthew 16:15-16.
[6]John 6:68-69.

Jesus thereupon turned to Peter and said:

"Blessed art thou, Simon bar-jona: for flesh and blood hath not revealed it unto thee, but my Father which is in heaven.

"And I say also unto thee, That thou art Peter, and upon this rock I will build my church; and the gates of hell shall not prevail against it.

"And I will give unto thee the keys of the kingdom of heaven: and whatsoever thou shalt bind on earth shall be bound in heaven: and whatsoever thou shalt loose on earth shall be loosed in heaven."[7]

THE ROCK ON WHICH CHRIST
HAS BUILT HIS CHURCH

Throughout the intervening centuries there has been a great debate as to the identity of the "rock" on which the Savior would build his church. Some had thought Jesus meant Peter.

It turns out that the rock on which Jesus built his church was the Savior himself. Here are several passages in the scriptures which clearly indicate what the Savior meant:

"And now my sons, remember, remember that it is upon the *rock of our Redeemer, who is Christ, the Son of God*, that ye must build your foundation."[8]

"Build upon my *rock*, which is my gospel [of Jesus Christ]; Deny not the spirit of revelation, nor the spirit of prophecy, for wo unto him that denieth these things."[9]

"I give unto you a commandment, that you rely upon the things which are written; for in them are all things written concerning the foundation of my church, my gospel, and my *rock*. Wherefore, if you

---

[7]Matthew 16:17-19.
[8]Helaman 5:12, B. of M.
[9]Doctrine and Covenants 11:24-25.

shall build up my church, upon the foundation of my gospel and my rock, the gates of hell shall not prevail against you."[10]

"I say unto you, this is my gospel; and remember that they shall have faith in *me* or they can in nowise be saved; and upon this *rock* I will build my church; yea, upon this *rock* ye are built, and if ye continue, the gates of hell shall not prevail against you."[11]

From all of these sources we learn that the "rock" on which the Lord would build his church, was not Peter or any other man, but Jesus Christ, the Son of God.

Therefore, all things associated with the Savior are part of that "rock" on which he has built his church. These include *faith* in the Lord Jesus Christ, accepting the *gospel* of Jesus Christ, studying the *scriptures* about Jesus Christ, and accepting, as Peter did, the *revelations* from the Holy Ghost that Jesus Christ is indeed the Son of God, the Savior of the world.

This is the point Jesus made with his saints in America when they did not know the name by which the church would be called. He said:

"And they said unto him: Lord, we will that thou wouldst tell us the name whereby we shall call this church; for there are disputations among the people concerning this matter....[The Savior answered] Whatsoever ye shall do, ye shall do it in my name; therefore ye shall call the church in my name."[12]

THE PERSONALITY OF PETER

Some have assumed that because Peter was the first to speak out on both of the above occasions and quick to defend the Savior at Gethsemane, he seemed to be "impulsive."

---

[10]Doctrine and Covenants 18:3-5.
[11]Doctrine and Covenants 33:12-13.
[12]3 Nephi 27:3-7, B. of M.

It is more likely that he was a man of strong convictions and that he was quick, courageous, and bold in defending them. The true spirit of Peter throughout his ministry is reflected in his advice to the members of the church after he was designated the chief of the apostles. He said:

"Be ready always to give an answer to every man that asketh you a reason of the hope that is in you."[13]

Peter wanted the members of the kingdom to be good students; students of the doctrines, principles, and precepts; students of Biblical history, secular history, and current history. As this knowledge is developed, Peter wanted the Savior's followers to organize a presentation on each principle, and then carefully articulate it to others so that they might feel the excitement and joy that comes with knowing about God's plan of salvation. In a modern revelation the Lord reflects the same spirit and mandates the same command as that which emanates from the epistle of Peter.[14]

I have a very high regard for Peter. In a modern business, Peter would probably have been an executive. In the military, he would probably have been a general. In God's kingdom he was about to be made the president of the church and the Savior's principal prophet, seer and revelator for that dispensation.

JESUS SENSES A GROWING DANGER

By this time Jesus knew that the principalities and powers of Satan were tightly combined and getting ready to roar out against him. Therefore every precaution had to be taken so that the murderous hatred which the devil was stirring up in the hearts of the people would not erupt too soon and at the wrong place.

In order to keep matters at a low key and avoid anything provocative, the scripture says:

---

[13]1 Peter 3:15.
[14]Doctrine and Covenants 88:77-80.

"Then charged he his disciples that they should tell no man that he was Jesus the Christ."[15]

This was a temporary restriction on the apostles, but, as we shall see, the Savior continued bearing testimony of himself.

JESUS SEEKS TO SHARE HIS GREAT BURDEN WITH HIS DISCIPLES

At this point, Jesus determined to take the twelve apostles into his confidence. He wanted them to appreciate, to some degree, the terrifying agonies that lay ahead for him. The scripture says:

"From that time forth began Jesus to shew unto his disciples, how that he must go unto Jerusalem, and suffer many things of the elders and chief priests and scribes, and be killed, and be raised again the third day."[16]

However, the twelve were not psychologically prepared for this shocking reality. Right at the time the Savior was suffering the utmost anguish and needing the compassionate understanding of his closest friends, these men could not grasp the final tragic requirements of the Savior's earthly mission, *even when he told them.*

In fact, Peter determined to reassure the Savior. Matthew was at the scene, and says:

"Peter took him, and began to rebuke him, saying, Be it far from thee, Lord: this shall not be unto thee."[17]

Nothing Peter could have said at this particular moment could have been worse than this well-intentioned declaration of protective allegiance and fidelity. Jesus was seeking sympathy and understanding for the terrible thing he must endure, and here was the chief of his apostles declaring that he would never let it happen. In absolute exasperation, Jesus said:

---

[15]Matthew 16:20.
[16]Matthew 16:21.
[17]Matthew 16:22.

"Get thee behind me, Satan! Thou art an offence unto me: for thou savourest not the things that be of God, but those that be of men."[18]

It would be interesting to know what was going through the mind of Jesus during these critical hours. As we shall see later, it was not part of the plan to have the apostles become aware that Jesus would be crucified and resurrected the third day until after these events had occurred. And yet Jesus seems to have felt compelled to talk about it with his friends, even though he knew the apostles would not understand what he was saying and would soon forget it.

Luke later explained it by saying:

"And they understood none of these things; and this saying was hid from them, neither knew they the things which were spoken."[19]

We also recall the statement of Mark when he said:

"But they understood not that saying, and were afraid to ask him."[20]

Under these circumstances, we are led to wonder why Jesus would even bring up the subject.

Perhaps if all the facts were known, we would discover that Jesus was desperately lonely in these last few months of his mortal life. It almost seems as though he took advantage of the non-comprehending minds of his apostles to articulate some of the terrible internal tensions that were boiling within him, even though he knew his words were falling on deaf ears.

John later assures us that the only reason the apostles were able to include the words of the Savior in their writings was because the

---

[18]Matthew 16:23.
[19]Luke 18:31-34.
[20]Mark 9:32.

Holy Ghost revealed to them what Jesus had said.[21] By heavenly design the memory of all of these things had been tuned out of their minds until the Holy Ghost restored them.

JESUS SHARES HIS CONCERN FOR
HIS APOSTLES WHOM HE LOVED

Apparently Jesus decided that since his disciples had no comprehension of what would be required of him, at least he could warn them of the trials and sacrifices that would be required of *them*. Therefore, he said:

"If any man will come after me, let him deny himself, and take up his cross, and follow me.

"For whosoever will save his life shall lose it: and *whosoever will lose his life for my sake* shall find it."[22]

James, who was with the Savior on the Mount, would be executed in less than a decade. The other faithful apostles would endure imprisonment, flogging, hunger, thirst and cold. And several of them would suffer martyrdom, including Peter. In the most earnest tones, Jesus urged them to stay true to the faith, saying:

"For what is a man profited, if he shall gain the whole world, and lose his own soul? or what shall a man give in exchange for his soul?

"For the Son of man shall come in the glory of his Father with his angels; and then he shall reward every man according to his works."[23]

But then, after indicating that some of them might lose their lives for the Savior's sake, Jesus made this puzzling statement:

---

[21]John 14:26.
[22]Matthew 16:24-25 (emphasis added).
[23]Matthew 16:26-27.

"Verily I say unto you, There be some standing here, which shall not taste of death, till they see the Son of Man coming in his kingdom."[24]

Although Jesus used the word, "some," we know of only one of the twelve who was translated. This was John the Beloved,[25] who, like Enoch, did not taste of death.[26]

It will be recalled that we have already discussed this episode in chapter 12.

THE GLORIOUS EVENTS ON THE MOUNT OF TRANSFIGURATION

On a certain afternoon or early evening, Jesus invited Peter, James and John to go with him into a nearby mountain to pray.[27]

On at least one other occasion, Jesus had selected Peter, James and John to accompany him and witness a great manifestation of God's power. The previous occasion was when Jesus raised the daughter of Jairus from the dead. The scripture says that as he went into the room where the dead girl was lying, He "suffered no man to follow him save Peter...James...and John."[28]

There is no indication that the other nine apostles were jealous or offended by the Savior's decision to exclude them from witnessing this great miracle of raising the twelve-year-old girl from the dead. Nor does there appear to be any jealousy or resentment when Jesus selected these same three apostles to go with him up into the Mount of Transfiguration.

---

[24]Matthew 16:28.
[25]Doctrine and Covenants, Section 7.
[26]Hebrews 11:5.
[27]Luke 9:28.
[28]Mark 5:37.

WHERE WAS THE MOUNT
OF TRANSFIGURATION?

The events which occurred on the Mount of Transfiguration were so sacred and memorable that it is important to identify the location of the mountain if possible.

Matthew says the Savior and his disciples were in Caesarea-Philippi six days prior to the time that the transfiguration took place.[29] Luke, who was not present, recorded it as eight days.[30] In any event, we know where the Savior and his apostles were staying just before this glorious event took place.[31]

The circumstances would indicate that the "high mountain" mentioned by Matthew was Mount Hermon, since Caesarea-Philippi lies at the base of this mountain among its lower foothills. Many authorities have reached this conclusion.[32]

However, for centuries, the older Christian churches have assumed that the mount of transfiguration was Mount Tabor, and several beautiful chapels have been built on top of this mountain to commemorate the sacred event.

But the choice of Mount Tabor as the site of the transfiguration presents some problems. For example, Mount Tabor is not a "high" mountain compared to Mount Hermon. Mount Tabor is only 1,843 feet above sea level compared to an altitude of 9,200 for Mount Hermon.

Furthermore, Mount Tabor is located at the end of the Esdraelon valley, below the southern tip of the Sea of Galilee. This is a long distance from Caesarea-Philippi which is located twenty miles *north* of the Galilee. The writer has visited both sites many times and is persuaded, along with many others, that the transfiguration must have taken place on Mount Hermon.

---

[29]Matthew 16:13, 17:1.
[30]Luke 9:28.
[31]Mark 8:27.
[32]Hastings' *Dictionary of the Bible*, under "Hermon."

PETER, JAMES AND JOHN
WITNESS THE UNBELIEVABLE

When Jesus took the three apostles into the "high mountain," they would never have suspected what was about to happen to them.

The higher regions of Mount Hermon are snowcapped most of the year, so it would be unreasonable to assume that Jesus would climb clear to the top. Nevertheless, it is likely that he took the apostles high enough to be sure there would be no danger of herdsmen or hunters accidentally intruding upon their place of prayer.

It seems apparent from the scripture that by the time they had reached their destination, the three apostles were totally exhausted. As soon as Jesus went off a short distance to pray, the three tired apostles fell sound asleep.[33]

What awakened them was a dazzling, brilliant light directly in front of them. At first they must have thought they had died and gone to heaven. The scripture says Jesus stood:

"...transfigured before them: and his face did shine as the sun, and his raiment was white as the light.

"And, behold, there appeared unto them Moses and Elias [Elijah] talking with him."[34]

We can well imagine the thrill of these three apostles when they learned the actual identity of these two famous prophets who stood before them in transcendent glory. We know they somehow learned who they were because of Peter's words which we shall quote in a moment.

---

[33]Luke 9:32.
[34]Matthew 17:2-3.

For approximately 1,400 years, Moses had existed as a translated being, following his ministry on earth. The scripture says the "Lord took him."[35] He had probably dwelt with Enoch on a partially glorified planet where he and Melchizedek—and the multitudes of their people who were translated with them—were taken to serve God as ministering angels. Commenting on this remarkable body of God's servants, Joseph Smith said:

"By faith Enoch was translated, that he should not see death....Many have supposed the doctrine of translation was a doctrine whereby men were taken immediately into the presence of God...but this is a mistaken idea. Their place of habitation is that of the terrestrial order...to be held in reserve to be ministering angels unto many planets."[36]

Long after Enoch, two great servants of God, Moses and Elijah (called Elias in the New Testament) were translated. This also happened to Melchizedek and the whole city of Salem.[37]

Of all of these translated beings, Moses and Elijah had been held in reserve for this historic moment when they could confer their respective keys of authority upon Peter, James and John. Joseph Smith learned that the conferring of these keys upon the three apostles was one of the principal purposes for the appearance of Moses and Elijah on the mount at the time of the transfiguration.[38]

Moses held the priesthood keys for the gathering of Israel.[39]

Elijah held the priesthood keys for the sealing power of the priesthood on behalf of both the living and the dead.[40]

Peter, James and John had to be given these keys so they could fulfill their mighty missions in their dispensation.

---

[35]JST Deuteronomy 34:6.
[36]*Teachings of the Prophet Joseph Smith*, p. 170.
[37]JST Genesis 14:32-34.
[38]*Teachings of the Prophet Joseph Smith*, p. 158.
[39]Doctrine and Covenants 110:11.
[40]Doctrine and Covenants 110:13-16.

It will be recalled that barely a week before, Jesus had promised Peter that he would receive these keys.[41]

At the time Peter and his two counsellors received these keys, they were suddenly transfigured and glorified when the Savior, Moses and Elijah laid their hands upon their heads.[42]

And that is not all.

Luke makes a valuable contribution by noting that Moses and Elijah discussed with Jesus the supreme importance of his suffering and ultimate death. No doubt they wanted to strengthen the Savior for the ordeal which was scheduled in the not too distant future as the climax to his earthly mission.[43] However, the apostles were not allowed to remember the details or true significance of what they had seen and heard until later when the Holy Ghost illuminated their memories so this glorious experience could be recalled in all its glory and power.[44]

None of the three apostles ever mentioned one important segment of the vision which must have been a heavenly secret they were not to disclose. We now know that Peter, James and John were shown a vision of the earth during the Millennium when it would be "transfigured." The Lord mentioned this marvelous manifestation in a modern revelation, but told the prophet Joseph Smith that the fullness of the account of this vision "ye have not yet received."[45]

Apparently Peter thought this flood of panoramic splendor from beyond the veil deserved some kind of memorial or monument, so he said:

---

[41]Matthew 16:19.
[42]*Teachings of the Prophet Joseph Smith*, p. 158.
[43]Luke 9:31.
[44]John 14:26.
[45]Doctrine and Covenants 63:21.

"Lord, it is good for us to be here: if thou wilt, let us make here three tabernacles; one for thee, and one for Moses, and one for Elias [Elijah],"[46]

But Peter had scarcely uttered these words when a glorious illumination enveloped all of them. Matthew writes:

"A bright cloud overshadowed them: and behold a voice out of the cloud, which said, This is my beloved Son, in whom I am well pleased; hear ye him.

"And when the disciples heard it, they fell on their face, and were sore afraid.

"And Jesus came and touched them, and said, Arise, and be not afraid.

"And when they had lifted up their eyes, they saw no man, save Jesus only."[47]

The glorious vision was finally over.

THE IMPACT OF THE TRANSFIGURATION

The scriptures leave no doubt that this night of angelic visitation and panoramic visions left the three humble fishermen of Galilee in a state of completely confused euphoria. They had seen the unbelievable, but what did it all mean? Their state of mind is reflected in the following verses:

"As they came down from the mountain, he charged them that they should tell no man what things they had seen, till the Son of man were risen from the dead.

"And they kept that saying with themselves, questioning one with another what the rising from the dead should mean."[48]

---

[46]Matthew 17:4.
[47]Matthew 17:5-8.
[48]Mark 9:9-10.

414 _Days of the Living Christ_

It is obvious that these humble Galileans still didn't grasp all that they had heard and seen. They were particularly puzzled by the references to the rising of the dead.[49] To change the subject, they said:

"Why then say the scribes that Elias must first come?

"And Jesus answered and said unto them, Elias truly shall first come, and restore all things.

"But I say unto you, That Elias is come already, and they knew him not, but have done unto him whatsoever they listed. Likewise shall also the Son of man suffer of them.

"Then the disciples understood that he spake unto them of John the Baptist."[50]

John the Baptist had tried to make it clear when he first began preaching, that he was the Elias who "came to prepare the way." He said after him there would come another Elias who would "restore all things," and would baptize with fire and the Holy Ghost. This, of course, was the Savior. The word "Elias" means both a "preparer" and a "restorer." John was Elias, the preparer; Jesus was Elias, the restorer.[51]

It would be interesting to know the details of the conversations between Peter, James and John as they carefully made their way down the steep slope of the mountain to join their brethren.

These newly endowed servants of God didn't know it, but—in contrast to their beautiful excursion into the things of the spirit—they were about to walk into a buzz-saw of practical problems that had arisen among the nine apostles who were left behind near Caesarea-Philippi.

*   *   *   *

---

[49]Mark 9:10.
[50]Matthew 17:10-13.
[51]*LDS Bible Dictionary* under "Elias."

TOPICS FOR REFLECTION AND DISCUSSION

1. Can you find Mount Hermon on the map? Can you find Mount Tabor? Can you find Caesarea-Philippi? How did the tribe of Dan happen to select this area as their inheritance after Joshua assigned them a territory down near Jerusalem?

2. How did the rumor get around that Jesus might be the reincarnation of John the Baptist? When Peter was asked who Jesus was, what did he say? What is the "rock" on which Jesus said he would build his church?

3. How would you describe the personality of Peter? When he became president of the church, what did he say the members should be able to do whenever they were asked about a principle of the gospel? Have we received the same command in our own day?

4. Since Jesus told the apostles he would be crucified and resurrected the third day, why couldn't they remember this a short time later? How was the memory of those things Jesus had told them restored to their minds?

5. Jesus knew some of his disciples would be martyrs. What did he say to comfort them and fortify their determination to endure to the end? Which apostles were selected to go up to the Mount of Transfiguration? When had Jesus selected the same three for another special occasion?

6. Is there any indication of jealousy or resentment by the other nine apostles when they were not invited to go with Jesus? Assuming the transfiguration took place on Mount Hermon, why wouldn't Jesus be likely to take his apostles clear to the top? About how far up would they probably go?

7. When they finally arrived, and Jesus went off a short way to pray, what happened to the three apostles? What awakened them? Who were the three people who stood before them? Tell all you can remember about the righteous people who were translated during the Old Testament times. Where do they dwell?

8. What keys did Moses restore? What keys did Elijah restore? When the translators of the New Testament came to the name "Elijah," what name did they use instead? When the Savior, Moses and Elijah laid their hands on the heads of Peter, James and John, what glorious change came over the apostles?

9. Peter was so animated over these events that he suggested to the Savior that they do something to memorialize the occasion. What did he suggest? What suddenly happened before anything could be done? What did the Father say on this occasion? Can you remember any other time when the Father said this same thing?

10. Before they left, what did Moses and Elijah say to strengthen Jesus? After the vision had closed, were the apostles entirely certain about what had happened, and what they had been told? What puzzled them the most? In answer to one of their questions, what did Jesus say about Elias? Had *that* Elias come already? Which Elias would "restore all things"?

*   *   *   *

CHAPTER 23

JESUS ANSWERS
MANY DIFFICULT
GOSPEL QUESTIONS

Following the night of glorious and incredible spiritual experiences on the Mount of Transfiguration, Jesus and his three apostles made their way down the steep slopes of the mountain to Caesarea-Philippi. There they found the other nine apostles in a state of spiritual bankruptcy.

Before the Savior arrived, they had suffered a traumatic and denigrating experience. These men had all gone on missions and on many occasions they had cast out evil spirits from afflicted individuals. But here in Caesarea-Philippi they seemed helpless. They had failed to cast an evil spirit from a terribly afflicted youth whose father had come to them pleading for help.

Luke describes the situation as follows:

"And it came to pass, that on the next day, when they were come down from the hill, much people met him.

"And, behold, a man of the company cried out, saying, Master, I beseech thee, look upon my son: for he is mine only child.

"And, lo, a spirit taketh him, and he suddenly crieth out; and it teareth him that he foameth again, and bruising him hardly departeth from him.

"And I besought thy disciples to cast him out; and they could not."[1]

---

[1]Luke 9:37-40.

WHEN SATAN RESISTS THE
POWER OF THE PRIESTHOOD

When holders of the priesthood have performed great miracles through the power of God, it is totally frustrating and embarrassing to have someone depend upon them only to find they apparently have lost that power. The truth is that the power emanates from God, not the priesthood holder, and this power will only be manifested in the presence of profound faith and the desires of the Lord.

Jesus decided to use this occasion to demonstrate the point. He addressed the large crowd, including his own disciples, and said:

"O faithless and perverse generation, how long shall I be with you? how long shall I suffer you? bring him hither to me.

"And Jesus rebuked the devil; and he departed out of him: and the child was cured from that very hour."[2]

This was the first time these disciples had been unable to use their priesthood power effectively. It shattered their confidence—not in God, but in their feeling of worthiness to represent him. Therefore they said:

"Why could not we cast him out?

"And Jesus said unto them, Because of your unbelief: for verily I say unto you, If ye have faith as a grain of mustard seed, ye shall say unto this mountain, Remove hence to yonder place; and it shall remove; and nothing shall be impossible unto you.

"Howbeit this kind goeth not out but by prayer and fasting."[3]

The lesson here is that when members of the priesthood rebuke an evil spirit and it does not obey, all those connected with the case must fast and pray until they have generated enough faith to compel the evil spirit to leave. They must not give up. As Jesus told them,

[2]Matthew 17:17-18.
[3]Matthew 17:17-21.

there are some evil spirits that will not obey until after much "prayer and fasting."

WHAT IS THE WILL OF THE LORD?

Casting out an evil spirit from an afflicted person is always the will of the Lord. But what about blessing the sick where the will of the Lord is not known? The Lord refers to this in a modern revelation, and says:

"And the elders of the church, two or more, shall be called, and shall pray for and lay their hands upon them in my name; and if they die they shall die unto me, and if they live they shall live unto me....

"And again, it shall come to pass that he that hath faith in me to be healed, and is *not appointed unto death*, shall be healed."[4]

Occasionally the priesthood holder who is blessing a person who is very ill will receive a whispering from the still small voice of the Spirit that the afflicted person can be promised that he or she will get well; and in some cases, where the individual is "appointed unto death," the still small voice will whisper that the individual should be "dedicated" and sent back to the Father.

However, in the absence of very clear instructions from beyond the veil, the priesthood holder should simply pour out a blessing on the individual, and then say to the Father, "Thy will be done," just as Jesus did in the Garden of Gethsemane.

JESUS AND THE APOSTLES
DEPART FOR CAPERNAUM

Later that day, Jesus and his disciples left Caesarea-Philippi and began making their way back down toward the Sea of Galilee.

While the apostles were in a humble mood, Jesus decided to try once more to share with them his troubled feeling concerning his own tribulations. He needed friends with whom he could discuss the

---

[4]Doctrine and Covenants 42:44,48 (emphasis added).

terrible feelings of darkness and anxiety which now appear to have preyed upon him continually. In a rather somber spirit, he said:

"Let these sayings sink down into your ears: for the Son of man shall be delivered into the hands of men."[5]

Matthew says it in more detail:

"Jesus saith unto them, The Son of man shall be betrayed into the hands of men:

"And they shall kill him, and the third day he shall be raised again. And they were exceeding sorry."[6]

The apostles heard what he said, but the awful implications of it failed to penetrate their sense of reality. No doubt Jesus knew that this conversation would later be taken from their minds, but we presume that until then it would have been a comfort to the Savior to just talk about it for awhile. Perhaps he waited expectantly to see if any of these friends would pick up on it, but none of them did. The Savior was therefore left to his own lonely meditations just as before. Luke verifies this by saying:

"But...it was hid from them, that they perceived it not: and they feared to ask him of that saying."[7]

JESUS DEFINES "GREATNESS"

Meanwhile, as they continued their journey toward Capernaum, they began mumbling among themselves about something which gives us the first hint of a possible rift among the twelve.

They were arguing about their respective positions of seniority or greatness and superiority in the kingdom of God. Perhaps the selection of Peter, James and John the night before had left some residual resentment in their hearts after all.

---

[5]Luke 9:44.
[6]Matthew 17:22-23.
[7]Luke 9:45.

Finally they reached Capernaum, and as soon as they were settled, Jesus said:

"What was it that ye disputed among yourselves by the way?

"But they held their peace: for...they had disputed among themselves, who should be the greatest.

"And he sat down, and called the twelve, and saith unto them, If any man desire to be first, the same shall be *last* of all, and *servant* of all."[8]

Now Jesus was back in his role as a teacher. He wanted these apostolic disciples to learn that the first step toward Godhood is acquiring the capacity to find joy in service. Jesus and the Father knew this better than any of their earthly children. The Father and the Son had spent their whole eternal existence— extending over aeons—to bring to pass the immortality and eternal life of man.[9]

So Jesus wanted these men with very special callings to know that "greatness" belongs to that humble servant who is the first to step forward and volunteer to do what others refuse or fear to do. Greatness must not depend on aspiration but on perspiration.

As one pioneer wrote of Brigham Young while they were crossing the western plains: "He sleeps with one eye open and one foot out of bed....when anything is wanted, he is on hand."[10]

GOD'S GREAT LEADERS ARE AS HUMBLE AS LITTLE CHILDREN

Jesus also wanted to emphasize that greatness requires faith, trust, humility and teachability. Therefore, Matthew wrote:

"Jesus called a little child unto him, and set him in the midst of them,

---

[8]Mark 9:33-35.
[9]Moses 1:39.
[10]Susa Y. Gates, *The Life Story of Brigham Young*, p. 63.

"And said, Verily I say unto you, Except ye be converted, and become as little children, ye shall not enter into the kingdom of heaven.

"Whosoever therefore shall humble himself [and be converted and become] as this little child, the same is greatest in the kingdom of heaven."[11]

Of course, the emphasis was on the positive childlike qualities of trust, faith, humility, and a willingness to be taught. He then commented that:

"Whoso shall receive one such [of his disciples who has been converted and become as a] little child in my name receiveth me."[12]

His intent became even clearer in the next verse where he referred to his converted, childlike disciples as "little ones who believe in me." He wanted to emphasize that they are very precious in the sight of heaven. He said:

"But whoso shall offend one of these little ones *which believe in me*, it were better for him that a millstone were hanged about his neck, and that he were drowned in the depth of the sea."[13]

GOD'S DOCTRINE CONCERNING LITTLE CHILDREN

Jesus then returned to the subject of children themselves, giving us a most important doctrine that someone later removed from the King James Translation of Matthew. The original text appears in the Joseph Smith Translation as follows:

"Take heed that ye despise not one of these little ones; for I say unto you, That in heaven their angels do always behold the face of my Father which is in heaven.

---

[11]Matthew 18:2-4.
[12]Matthew 18:5.
[13]Matthew 18:2-6 (emphasis added).

"For the Son of Man is come to save that which was lost, and to call sinners to repentance; *but these little ones have no need of repentance, and I will save them.*"[14]

If this last sentence had not been removed from the original Gospel of Matthew, the fifth century Christian churches would not have accepted Augustine's doctrine of "original sin." That is the concept which became the foundation for the proclamation that infants or little children must be baptized or they will be damned.

Here is what one prophet said about the true doctrine as Jesus originally taught it. He said:

"And their little children need no repentance, neither baptism. Behold, baptism is unto repentance to the fulfilling the commandments unto the remission of sins.

"But little children are alive in Christ, even from the foundation of the world....

"Behold I say unto you, that he that supposeth that little children need baptism is in the gall of bitterness and in the bonds of iniquity....

"For awful is the wickedness to suppose that God saveth one child because of baptism, and the other must perish because he hath no baptism."[15]

It is interesting that when Jesus was instructing his apostles in Capernaum, this is the doctrine he taught them even before this false doctrine of baptizing little children had crept into the church.

WHY IS THERE EVIL IN THE WORLD?

Jesus continually denounced evil wherever it existed, but warned his disciples that it would continue surfacing in every society. In fact, it is the very nature of mortal life. Therefore he said:

---

[14]JST Matthew 18:10-11 (emphasis added).
[15]Moroni 8:11-15, B. of M.

"Woe unto the world because of offences, for it must needs be that offences come; but woe to that man by whom the offence cometh!"[16]

Why would Jesus say that offenses *must* come? Sometimes we forget that our mortal life is a probationary estate, a time of testing and learning. Therefore, the prophet Lehi said:

"It must needs be, that there is an opposition in all things. If not so...righteousness could not be brought to pass."[17]

In other words, if there were no evil, no opposition, and no offenses, there would be no opportunity to demonstrate our determination to choose the good and show forth our desire to live in righteousness. Fortunately, the good and the evil will all be sorted out at the final judgment. The scripture says:

"And he shall separate them one from another, as a shepherd divideth his sheep from the goats:

"And he shall set the sheep on his right hand, but the goats on the left.

"Then shall the King say unto them on his right hand, Come, ye blessed of my Father, inherit the kingdom prepared for you from the foundation of the world."[18]

HOW SHOULD WE DEAL WITH EVIL
WHEN IT APPEARS IN OUR MIDST?

Now Jesus repeated something he had mentioned in the Sermon on the Mount but it bears repeating here. He wanted to stress the need to resist those who commit offenses among his saints—or even in one's own family—but without abandoning the offender. He started out by repeating something similar to what he had said in the Sermon on the Mount:[19]

---

[16]Matthew 18:7.
[17]2 Nephi 2:11.
[18]Matthew 25:32-34.
[19]See Matthew 5:30.

"Wherefore if thy hand or thy foot offend thee, cut them off, and cast them from thee: it is better for thee to enter into life halt or maimed, rather than having two hands or two feet to be cast into everlasting fire.

"And if thine eye offend thee, pluck it out, and cast it from thee: it is better for thee to enter into life with one eye, rather than having two eyes to be cast into hell fire."[20]

Of course we are left wondering what Jesus meant by an offending hand, an offending foot, or an offending eye. The explanation is found in the Inspired Version, which says:

"And a man's hand is his friend, and his foot also; and a man's eye, are they of his own household."[21]

As we pointed out earlier, the inspired version of Mark makes the same point. Mark quotes Jesus as saying:

"Therefore, if thy hand offend thee, cut it off; or if thy brother offend thee and confess not and forsake not [his sins], he shall be cut off. It is better for thee to enter into life maimed, than having two hands, to go into hell.

"For it is better for thee to enter life without thy brother, than for thee and thy brother to be cast into hell; into the fire that never shall be quenched, where their worm dieth not, and the fire is not quenched.

"And again, if thy foot offend thee, cut it off; for he that is thy standard [teacher], by whom thou walkest, if he become a transgressor, he shall be cut off....

"Therefore, let every man stand or fall, by himself, and not for another; or not trusting another."[22]

---

[20]Matthew 18:8-9.
[21]JST Matthew 18:7-8.
[22]JST Mark 9:40-44.

BUT WHAT ABOUT THE OFFENDER?

Now Jesus turned to the needs of the offender. Even the offender is very precious to the Lord. If at all possible, he or she must be induced to be brought back into a harmonious relationship with God and his servants. As Jesus emphasized:

"For the Son of man is come to save that which was lost.

"How think ye? if a man have an hundred sheep, and one of them be gone astray, doth he not leave the ninety and nine, and goeth into the mountains, and seeketh that which is gone astray?

"And if so be that he find it, verily I say unto you, he rejoiceth more of that sheep, than of the ninety and nine which went not astray.

"Even so it is not the will of your Father which is in heaven, that one of these little ones should perish."[23]

Notice how Jesus seems to refer to all mankind as "little ones." In reality, they are all the children of God.

HOW DID JESUS PERCEIVE "GOOD" IN PEOPLE WHO ARE NOT HIS DISCIPLES?

God has always had compassion for those who are seeking to do good even though they may not be within the ranks of his immediate disciples.

Just as Cornelius, the Roman commander, was counted a "just man" and received certain administrations of the Holy Ghost even before he was baptized, so the Lord judges men according to the desires of their hearts and blesses them accordingly.

Peter, who was brought up as a Pharisee, marveled when he discovered what the Lord was doing for Cornelius, a righteous Gentile. He therefore said:

---

[23]Matthew 18:11-14.

"Of a truth I perceive that God is no respecter of persons:

"But in every nation he that feareth him, and worketh righteousness, is accepted with him."[24]

This same generous spirit was taught by Jesus when his disciples saw a man casting out evil spirits in the name of Jesus, but the man declined to join the disciples.

This is the way Mark describes this incident:

"John answered him, saying, Master, we saw one casting out devils in thy name, and he followeth not us: and we forbad him, because he followeth not us.

"But Jesus said, Forbid him not: for there is no man which shall do a miracle in my name, that can lightly speak evil of me.

"For he that is not against us is on our part."[25]

Luke gives the final verse as:

"Forbid him not; for he that is not against us is for us."[26]

This writer has sometimes wondered if there might not be a bit of humor hidden in this story. Note the elements of the account. The Savior learns that devils are fleeing when his name is used, even though the exorcist was not one of his disciples. But if the devils flee at the sound of the Savior's name, can it be such a loss even though the exorcist is not a disciple?

Note this subtle suggestion in the Savior's interesting comment:

---

[24]Acts 10:34-35.
[25]Mark 9:38-40.
[26]Luke 9:50.

"Forbid him not; for there is no man which shall do a miracle in my name, that can lightly speak evil of me."[27]

In other words, Since the *devils* believed him and fled, isn't it a gain for good on our side?

HOW MANY TIMES SHOULD AN OFFENDER BE FORGIVEN?

It was about this time that the apostle Peter raised a question which brought an unexpected reply. Matthew says:

"Then came Peter to him, and said, Lord, how oft shall my brother sin against me, and I forgive him? till seven times?"[28]

The Savior's most complete answer is recorded by Luke:

"Take heed to yourselves: If thy brother trespass against thee, rebuke him; and if he *repent*, forgive him.

"And if he trespass against thee seven times in a day, and seven times in a day turn again to thee, saying, I *repent*, thou shalt forgive him."[29]

Note that an important ingredient in this process, is a sincere desire on the part of the offender to mend his ways. However, in the case of alcoholics, addicts, kleptomaniacs, and other repetitive offenders, the process of offending and repenting can be like a revolving door at the mall. And it can try the patience of Job.

In a modern revelation the Lord extended some practical advice for those who find themselves burdened with chronic offenders. He said the goal is to help the offender through:

"...persuasion, by long-suffering, by gentleness and meekness, and by love unfeigned...

---

[27]Ibid.
[28]Matthew 18:21.
[29]Luke 17:3-4.

"*Reproving* betimes with *sharpness*, when moved upon by the *Holy Ghost*; and then showing forth afterwards an increase of love toward him whom thou hast reproved, lest he esteem thee to be his enemy;

"That he may know that thy faithfulness is stronger than the cords of death."[30]

BUT WHAT IF THE OFFENDER DOES NOT REPENT?

It is interesting that all through the Savior's teaching there is a strong element of pacification, or tolerance for the rudeness or crudeness of some people in the ordinary course of life. His admonition to "turn the other cheek" is an example. We also have just seen how far the Savior expects us to go along with the offender who repeatedly professes to repent, yet later returns to his old ways.

But what if there is no remorse for the offense and no evidence of any desire to repent? In response to this question, the Savior said:

"If thy brother shall trespass against thee, go and tell him his fault between thee and him alone: if he shall hear thee, thou hast gained thy brother.

"But if he will not hear thee, then take with thee one or two more, that in the mouth of two or three witnesses every word may be established.

"And if he shall neglect to hear them, tell it unto the church: but if he neglect to hear the church, let him be unto thee as an heathen man and a publican."[31]

Jesus wanted the apostles to know that the church has a special interest in all these problems, and if the parties cannot be reconciled, then outside parties should be brought in to arbitrate the matter. Finally, if the offender is so stubborn and obnoxious that no

---

[30]Doctrine and Covenants 121:41-44.
[31]Matthew 18:15-17.

settlement can be reached, then he should be advised that his membership in the church is at risk.

To make sure the apostles understood both their responsibility and their authority, he said:

"Verily I say unto you, Whatsoever ye shall bind on earth shall be bound in heaven: and whatsoever ye shall loose on earth shall be loosed in heaven."[32]

In other words, the same priesthood power that sealed the offender's membership in the church can unseal it and relegate the offender to the status of "a heathen and a publican."

A HEAVENLY PRINCIPLE: GOD FORGIVES OUR TRESPASSES AS WE FORGIVE OTHERS

Sometimes we forget that from God's point of view, we are all chronic offenders in one way or another. Of course, he is a loving God, and we expect to be forgiven. However, Jesus set forth one of the eternal principles that will be in operation on judgment day. As Jesus had mentioned earlier, men and women will be forgiven according to a divine scale of justice which measures the way each individual has forgiven others.

Jesus dramatized this principle by relating the parable of the unforgiving debtor.

A man owed the king ten thousand talents (which is a fabulous amount of several million dollars). This debtor was about to lose everything and go to the debtors' prison because he could not pay the king. So the man fell on his knees before the king and pleaded for mercy. The king's sense of compassion was aroused and he forgave the entire debt.

However, this same man had a servant who owed him a hundred pence. When the servant could not pay, he pleaded for mercy, but the man was heartless and threw the servant in prison.

---

[32]Matthew 18:18.

But news of this action reached the king. He was furious. The king thereupon reimposed the original debt of ten thousand talents on the man and told him he would be beaten and tormented until he paid every farthing of it.

Jesus concluded by saying:

"So likewise shall my heavenly Father do also unto you if ye from your hearts forgive not every one his brother their trespasses."[33]

THE ANXIETY OF THE FATHER TO FILL
THE NEEDS OF ALL HIS CHILDREN

The Father is mindful of the needs of all his children, but he is particularly sensitive to the requirements of those who are in the front line trenches of the kingdom of God.

Jesus therefore addressed his apostles and said:

"I say unto you, that if two of you shall agree on earth as touching any thing that they shall ask, it shall be done for them of my Father which is in heaven.

"For where two or three are gathered together in my name, there am I in the midst of them."[34]

There are numerous instances in church history where General Authorities have been desperately in need of advice or assistance, and the Lord has responded in a glorious and marvelous way. Many of these responses have been recorded in the Doctrine and Covenants or the archives of the church.

Of course, there are some instances where the responses have been so sacred and personal that they have remained cloistered in the hearts and minds of those who received them.

---

[33]Matthew 18:35.
[34]Matthew 18:19-20.

YE ARE THE SALT OF THE EARTH

It will be recalled that this question and answer session arose because of a dispute over who would be the greatest in the kingdom of heaven. Jesus therefore closed this marvelous dialogue with his disciples by reminding them of a doctrine he had taught them in the Sermon on the Mount. He said they were the salt of the earth and that he is depending upon them to season the church with spirituality and create a climate of love and unity among the members. Therefore he said:

"Salt is good: but if the salt have lost his saltiness, wherewith will ye season it? Have salt in yourselves, and have peace one with another."[35]

We should mention that pure salt never loses its savor, but as Dummelow's *Commentary* states:

"Salt in Palestine, being gathered in an impure state, often undergoes chemical changes by which its flavor is destroyed while its appearance remains....[Furthermore] salt mixed with insolvable impurities may be dissolved out by moisture, leaving the insoluble residue slightly salty. The lesson of the Lord's illustration is that spoiled salt is of no use."[36]

Thus we come to the end of one of those special times in the lives of the apostles when they enjoyed the marvelous opportunity to hear the Master Teacher share his innermost thoughts and repeat several doctrines he had explained to them before. In the coming years, as they moved out across the earth, these servants of the Lord must have reflected a hundred times on these pearls of wisdom which Jesus left for their guidance.

*   *   *   *

---

[35]Mark 9:50.
[36]Quoted by Talmage, *Jesus the Christ*, p. 248.

TOPICS FOR REFLECTION AND DISCUSSION

1. When the apostles were unable to cast out an evil spirit, what did Jesus say they should do to gain the necessary spiritual strength to achieve it? When administering to the sick, what should the priesthood say at the end of a blessing unless the Spirit indicates otherwise?

2. Why do you think Jesus kept bringing up the subject of his crucifixion, death, and resurrection? Did any of the apostles comprehend what he was saying? Why do you think they were afraid to ask him about it?

3. In what way does the apostles' discussion of who would be the greatest in heaven reflect their spiritual immaturity at this stage of their ministry? What did Jesus say will determine who is the greatest? What is the first and most important step in preparing oneself for Godhood? Did Jesus and the Father set the pattern? Did Brigham Young have this attribute?

4. What qualities in a little child should be emulated by those who wish to gain favor with God? Why do you think Jesus said this is the kind of person who joyfully receives the Savior and his gospel message? What did Jesus say would happen to those who persecute and abuse his humble, childlike disciples as they go forth to share the gospel?

5. What doctrine relating to children was taught by Jesus but later lost? In what way did Augustine's theory of "original sin" lead to the baptizing of little children? What covers the mistakes of little children up to the age of accountability?

6. While discussing evil which may arise in the midst of the saints, what did Jesus mean by an offending hand, an offending foot, or an offending eye? If a person repents, what does Heavenly Father expect of those he offended? But what about the offender who keeps backsliding and has to repent over and over? As long as the person keeps trying, does the Lord expect us to keep forgiving?

7. What did Jesus say the procedure should be if the offender has not repented? What does the offender risk losing if he stubbornly refuses to respond to this procedure?

8. What is God's attitude toward people who go around doing a lot of good, but don't join the kingdom? What should our attitude be toward them? In the beginning, why did Peter have a difficult time sharing the gospel with the Gentiles? What did the Lord do to help Peter get a more generous feeling toward "outsiders"?

9. Heavenly Father is a loving God, and he wants to forgive us of our trespasses, but what determines the extent to which he will forgive us? Is this just?

10. What did Jesus tell the apostles to do if they were in difficulty and needed divine help? What was there about salt in the days of the Savior that allowed it to lose its savor? Did he warn his disciples that this could happen to them?

*   *   *   *

Chapter 24

JESUS SENDS FORTH THE SEVENTY

*Pronounces Judgment on Three Cities
And Departs for Jerusalem*

Altogether, Jesus and his disciples spent at least two years in Galilee. However, a short time after the glorious events on the Mount of Transfiguration, Jesus prepared to close his Galilean ministry.

SHOULD JESUS HAVE PAID TRIBUTE?

But before Jesus and his disciples departed from Capernaum, the officials who collected tribute money for the temple visited this community. They came to Peter and asked:

"Doth not your master pay tribute?

"He saith, Yes. And when he was come into the house, Jesus prevented [*rebuked*—JST] him, saying, What thinkest thou, Simon? of whom do the kings of the earth take custom or tribute? of their own children, or of strangers?

"Peter saith unto him, Of strangers. Jesus saith unto him, Then are the children free."[1]

Jesus was pointing out that religious leaders and those associated with the temple are exempt from this annual tribute. This was not a regular tax levied by the government. It was an ecclesiastical tax for the specific purpose of maintaining the temple, and therefore rabbis, religious leaders, and those connected with the temple were exempt from this tax.

---

[1]Matthew 17:24-26.

436 *Days of the Living Christ*

For the moment, Peter forgot about his apostolic calling, and thought of himself as merely a professional fisherman. But certainly he should have remembered that under Jewish law, his Master, being a great religious leader, was not obligated to pay the tax.

However, since Peter had already said they would pay the tax, Jesus did not want to make an issue out of it. Therefore, he said:

"Notwithstanding [our being exempt], lest we should offend them, go thou to the sea, and cast an hook, and take up the fish that first cometh up; and when thou hast opened his mouth, thou shalt find a piece of money: that take, and give unto them for me and thee."[2]

We are led to assume that when Peter cast out a line, the first fish to take the hook was indeed found to have the coin in its gullet and the tribute money was duly paid.

The very fact that Jesus was aware that there was a fish in the nearby Galilee that had seen a shiny coin and swallowed it, tells us something about the Savior's well-nigh omniscient mental processes, even in mortality. This is further evidenced by his ability to read the minds of men even before they spoke.

JESUS SENDS FORTH THE SEVENTY

Jesus now prepared to do two things before concluding his ministry in Galilee.

The first task was to appoint and send forth "other" seventy. The Lord gave seventy men to Moses to assist him in the administration of his labors,[3] and the Sanhedrin illegitimately claimed to be the heirs of that body. Perhaps this is why Luke refers to this body as the "other" seventy, meaning they were the Lord's true and legitimate seventy who would now assist the apostles in the spreading of the gospel.[4]

---

[2]Matthew 17:27.
[3]Numbers 11:24-25.
[4]Luke 10:1.

It is said that the word "*other*" means "in addition to" but there is no record of any previous quorum of seventy in the New Testament; hence our conclusion that he was referring to his own seventy "other" than the Sanhedrin.

If one compares the Savior's instructions to the seventies in Luke, chapter 10, with his instructions to the twelve in Matthew, chapter 10, it will be noted that the two are very similar even though his directions to the twelve were more detailed.

JESUS PRONOUNCES JUDGMENT ON THREE CITIES

As for the second task, Jesus felt compelled to pronounce judgment on the three major cities where he had lived and preached during much of the time in Galilee.

These three cities were all closely associated together on the northern shore of the Galilee. One was Chorazin, the second was Capernaum, and the third was Bethsaida. Chorazin is not mentioned in any other place, but St. Jerome states that it was within two miles of Capernaum.[5]

Bethsaida is believed to have been about the same distance south of Capernaum.

The Savior's judgment on these cities carried the pungent odor of hell, fire and brimstone. After all, these were the people who had seen him heal hundreds of people—the blind, deaf and crippled. They had seen or heard many witnesses testifying that he had cast out evil spirits, raised the dead, miraculously fed thousands and repeatedly explained the gospel in greater detail than any other people would ever hear it. From among them he had selected all of his apostles, save one (Judas Iscariot of Judea), and from these cities he probably selected most of the seventies as well.

To all these who had received such monumental blessings and then rejected him, Jesus said:

---

[5]Peloubet's *Bible Dictionary*, under "Chorazin."

"Woe unto thee, Chorazin! woe unto thee, Bethsaida! for if the mighty works, which were done in you, had been done in Tyre and Sidon, they would have repented long ago in sackcloth and ashes.

"But I say unto you, It shall be more tolerable for Tyre and Sidon at the day of judgment, than for you.

"And thou, Capernaum, which art exalted unto heaven, shalt be brought down to hell: for if the mighty works, which have been done in thee, had been done in Sodom, it would have remained until this day.

"But I say unto you, That it shall be more tolerable for the land of Sodom in the day of judgment, than for thee."[6]

THE LORD'S SORTING OUT PROCESS
DURING THE SECOND ESTATE

Jesus knew these people better than they knew themselves. He knew they had stiff necks and doubting minds in spite of what they had seen and heard. Nevertheless, he also knew that if they had been converted and then apostatized, their fate would have been far worse than if they remained blind to the truth pending the time when they would hear it in the spirit world. Therefore, Jesus spoke to his Father and said:

"I thank thee, O Father, Lord of heaven and earth, because thou hast hid these things from the wise and prudent, and hast revealed them unto babes."[7]

In Galilee it had been the "little ones," the babes, who generally responded to his call. They were the humble fishermen, the poor, the despised publicans, or an occasional Roman or Phoenician who felt the power of God's Spirit. Jesus knew that long range, it was better for the "wise and the prudent" to remain blinded by their rabbinical indoctrination than have the Spirit illuminate them so that their rejection of the gospel in mortality would deprive them of a celestial

---

[6]Matthew 11:21-24.
[7]Matthew 11:25.

endowment even if they later accepted it in the spirit world. For these it is better that the scintillating elements of godly knowledge remain hidden until a more propitious time.

This helps us appreciate how carefully the Father has structured our mortal existence so that it will work for the ultimate good of as many as possible. He knows that some are not ready to embrace the gospel in this life, and those heavenly principles therefore remain hidden from them for the present, even when they hear them. Many who, by worldly standards, are considered "wise and prudent" belong to this category. But not all, of course.

In the final analysis the key ingredient for service in God's kingdom is the depth of a person's conversion. And the key to conversion is humility, childlike submissiveness and commitment. Historically, God has taken the unlearned like the youthful Jeremiah, or the well educated scholar like Isaiah, and molded them both to serve faithfully and brilliantly.

As Jesus looked at his faithful disciples, he knew they were special gifts from the Father to help him in his ministry. He therefore said:

"All things are delivered unto me of my Father: and no man knoweth the Son, but the Father; neither knoweth any man the Father, save the Son, and he to whomsoever the Son will reveal him."[8]

This was like saying, "Everything I accomplished in gathering up converts was given to me by my Father. He is the only one who really knows and understands each individual. And no one understands the Father like the Son, and those to whom the Son is allowed to reveal the Father."

Now Jesus was ready to close his ministry in Galilee.

---

[8]Matthew 11:27.

THE ANXIETY OF THE JEWS TO HAVE JESUS
ATTEND THE FEAST OF THE TABERNACLES

At this stage of his ministry, Jesus was now barely six months away from the day he was dreading. It was late fall, and nearly time for the Feast of the Tabernacles which would last eight days.

As the people in Jerusalem were making elaborate preparations for this feast, we learn from John that the big question among thousands of the Jews was whether or not Jesus would dare to come to this celebration. He had now become so famous, everybody wanted to see him.[9] Perhaps he would perform some of his miracles. There were others who wanted him to come in hopes they could find an excuse or an opportunity to kill him.[10]

Meanwhile, up in Capernaum, the Savior's brothers were urging Jesus to go down to Judea and preach where more people could witness a demonstration of his miraculous healing powers. They said:

"Depart hence, and go into Judaea, that thy disciples also may see the works that thou doest.

"For there is no man that doeth any thing in secret, and he himself seeketh to be known openly. If thou do these things, shew thyself to the world."[11]

This is rather ironic since John says:

"Neither did his brethren believe in him."[12]

Of course, these brothers knew he could perform miracles; practically everybody in Galilee had seen or heard of him doing that. But they were quite certain he was not the Messiah. After all, they knew him. He was their older brother.

---

[9]John 7:11.
[10]John 7:1; Luke 22:2.
[11]John 7:3-4.
[12]John 7:5.

But they had to admit he had made the family famous, and they couldn't help basking in the notoriety and the limelight of this older brother's fame. To their minds, that is why he should go to the feast. Let more people see him and watch him demonstrate his miraculous healing powers.

It will be recalled that Matthew had indicated that Jesus had four brothers, and at least two sisters. The names of the brothers are given as James, Joses (Joseph), Simon and Judas.[13]

We do not have the names of his sisters.

It is interesting that John would record that these brothers did not believe in Jesus at this stage of the Savior's ministry. Little did they know what the future held in store for them.

As we have previously mentioned, the oldest half-brother, named James, would be one of those who would get to see the resurrected Christ.[14] He would not only become a devout believer, but he would be ordained an apostle.[15] However, like Paul, who became an apostle,[16] he does not appear to have been one of the original twelve. He is believed to be the author of the book of James.

The other half-brothers also must have become Christians shortly after the resurrection. In Acts 1:14 it says they were numbered among the members of the church. Most authorities believe it was the Savior's youngest half-brother, Judas, who wrote the book of Jude, since he describes himself as "the brother of James," who by then was an apostle and prominent among the saints. The original James, brother of John, had long since been martyred.[17]

---

[13]Matthew 13:55.
[14]1 Corinthians 15:7.
[15]Galatians 1:19.
[16]Romans 1:1.
[17]Acts 12:2.

JESUS SENDS HIS BROTHERS AHEAD WHILE
HE FOLLOWS A DIFFERENT PLAN

But at the time of which we are speaking—when Jesus was in Capernaum—John says the brothers were not believers, and in spite of their urging, Jesus refused to go to Jerusalem to satisfy the curiosity of the people. He had a different plan. Therefore, Jesus said to his brethren:

"Go ye up unto this feast: I go not up yet unto this feast; for my time is not yet full come."[18]

Notice that Jesus did not say he would *not* go up to the feast, but merely that he would not go up "yet." It is easy to understand how the brothers might have assumed he was not coming at all.

So Jesus tarried in Galilee, and his apostles tarried with him. In Jerusalem, however, his absence from the feast was a major subject of conversation. John writes:

"Then the Jews sought him at the feast, and said, Where is he?

"And there was much murmuring among the people concerning him: for some said, He is a good man: others said, Nay; but he deceiveth the people.

"Howbeit no man spake openly of him for fear of the Jews."[19]

LUKE'S TRAVEL NARRATIVE THAT CHALLENGES
THE STUDENT OF THE GOSPELS

At this point, Luke takes over the narration of the travels of the Savior and his apostles for about seven chapters.

Much of what he tells us is not mentioned by the other Gospel writers, and since he leaves out both the Feast of the Tabernacles and the Feast of Dedication—the two events for which the dates are

---

[18]John 7:8.
[19]John 7:11-13.

known—there is no time frame by which we can be certain when most of the events actually occurred.

Keeping this in mind, the student of the New Testament should not be surprised to find different writers arranging these events in a variety of patterns. But perhaps that is not so important. The most vital part is knowing that the events transpired and understanding their significance in the Savior's life story.

We should also remind ourselves that Jesus taught the same lessons in Samaria and Judea that he taught in Galilee. Therefore, we undoubtedly have a certain amount of duplication of the Savior's teachings and stories.

In this present study, where two or more of the Gospel writers have covered the same subject, we have tried to concentrate on the one who told it best or explained it in the greatest detail.

Having said this, let us continue.

THE JOURNEY TOWARDS JERUSALEM BEGINS

After Jesus had sent out the seventies and passed judgment on Chorazin, Bethsaida and Capernaum, Luke says Jesus was ready to attend the Feast of the Tabernacles.

"And it came to pass, when the time was come...he steadfastly set his face to go to Jerusalem,

"And sent messengers before his face: and they went, and entered into a village of the Samaritans, to make ready for him.

"And they did not receive him, because his face was as though he would go to Jerusalem."[20]

It will be recalled that when Jesus was coming *from* Jerusalem, the Samaritans received him gladly, but now that he is going *to* Jerusalem to worship, they rejected him. We also need to remember

[20]Luke 9:51-53.

that it was in the Samaritan city of Shechem that Jesus and the apostles had converted so many. On this particular journey it does not identify the Samaritan community which refused to receive Jesus. Unlike Shechem, it may have been a village that had never heard of Jesus.

Be that as it may, James and John were furious that the Master had been rejected. Luke says:

"And when his disciples James and John saw this, they said, Lord, wilt thou that we command fire to come down from heaven, and consume them, even as Elias [Elijah] did?"[21]

Jesus knew that even good men can sometimes listen to spirits from below rather than above, and Elijah did not call down fire from heaven until God commanded it. Therefore Jesus said to the two apostles:

"Ye know not what manner of spirit ye are of.

"For the Son of man is not come to destroy men's lives, but to save them. And they went to another village."[22]

Nevertheless, this incident clearly illustrates the feelings of the apostles concerning the Savior's role as a King-Messiah. They thought the destruction of the Romans and the setting up of the kingdom under the Savior's direction would come just as Daniel had predicted. The evil powers would be overthrown, and if there were to be fire and brimstone from heaven, to get things under way why not start with these obnoxious Samaritans?

JESUS ATTEMPTS TO VISIT JERUSALEM SECRETLY

John said that the Savior and his apostles tried to go up to Jerusalem secretly, but Jesus was far too well known to pass along unnoticed.[23] Therefore Luke says:

---

[21]Luke 9:54.
[22]Luke 9:55-56.
[23]John 7:10.

"As they went in the way, a certain man said unto him, Lord, I will follow thee whithersoever thou goest."[24]

Apparently Jesus read his heart and saw that he was not prepared to undertake the hardships that lay ahead for his disciples. Therefore he did not encourage him, but said:

"Foxes have holes, and birds of the air have nests; but the Son of man hath not where to lay his head."[25]

A little later Jesus saw a man who could have been a good disciple. He therefore extended an invitation to him, saying:

"Follow me. But he said, Lord, suffer me first to go and bury my father.

"Jesus said unto him, Let the dead bury their dead: but go thou and preach the kingdom of God."[26]

This may seem like a harsh response, but Jesus was already beginning to sense the avalanche of oncoming events which would require the complete devotion of men like his apostles who had forsaken all to serve him. Whether or not the man responded to the call, we are not told.

"And another also said, Lord, I will follow thee; but let me first go bid them farewell, which are at home at my house.

"And Jesus said unto him, No man, having put his hand to the plough, and looking back, is fit for the kingdom of God."[27]

Once again, we see Jesus discouraging any fair-weather disciple who was not prepared to maintain the strictest priorities in helping

---

[24]Luke 9:57.
[25]Luke 9:58.
[26]Luke 9:59-60.
[27]Luke 9:61-62.

the Savior accomplish his ministry within the extremely short limit of time that was left.

A LAWYER ATTEMPTS TO SNARE THE SAVIOR

While Jesus and his disciples were in the vicinity of Jerusalem, the Savior was approached by a lawyer. This particular Pharisee wanted to tempt Jesus and used a very subtle and deceptive method of doing it. He said:

"Master, what shall I do to inherit eternal life?

"He said unto him, What is written in the law? how readest thou?

"And he answering said, Thou shalt love the Lord thy God with all thy heart, and with all thy soul, and with all thy strength, and with all thy mind; and thy neighbour as thyself.

"And he said unto him, Thou hast answered right: this do, and thou shalt live."[28]

Obviously, Jesus had completely outwitted the shrewd lawyer, and made him answer his own question, which was intended to snare Jesus. The lawyer therefore floundered around in his mind trying to keep this encounter from being totally fruitless, and finally tossed out an ancillary question, saying:

"Who is my neighbour?"[29]

One can almost hear Jesus thinking to himself, "I thought you would never ask!"

PARABLE OF THE GOOD SAMARITAN

Jesus had a beautiful story to answer this very question. He just needed someone to bring it up. He said:

---

[28]Luke 10:25-28.
[29]Luke 10:29.

"A certain man went down from Jerusalem to Jericho, and fell among thieves, which stripped him of his raiment, and wounded him, and departed, leaving him half dead."[30]

The road to Jericho was notorious for the number of highway robbers who infested it. One section was known as the Red Path, or the Bloody Way, because of the frequent atrocities which occurred there. Jesus continued:

"And by chance there came down a certain priest that way: and when he saw him, he passed by on the other side.

"And likewise a Levite, when he was at the place, came and looked on him, and passed by on the other side.

"But a certain Samaritan, as he journeyed, came where he was: and when he saw him, he had compassion on him,

"And went to him, and bound up his wounds, pouring in oil and wine, and set him on his own beast, and brought him to an inn, and took care of him.

"And on the morrow when he departed, he took out two pence, and gave them to the host, and said unto him, Take care of him; and whatsoever thou spendest more, when I come again, I will repay thee."[31]

Now Jesus was ready to make his point. Obviously, the hero of the story was a Samaritan, and he could not have selected a more odious essence in the nostrils of a Pharisee lawyer than a Samaritan who turns out to be a hero. Therefore, with the satisfaction of a tale well told, Jesus asked:

"Which now of these three, thinkest thou, was neighbour unto him that fell among the thieves?

---

[30]Luke 10:30.
[31]Luke 10:31-35.

"And he said, He that shewed mercy on him."[32]

It would have been interesting to see the face of the lawyer as he painfully said these words. Notice how carefully he avoided saying "the Samaritan."

Jesus then ended the whole matter by saying simply:

"Go, and do thou likewise."[33]

James and John must have listened to this parable with fascinated amazement. Just a short time before, the Samaritans had been so obnoxious that the two apostles thought Jesus should begin using fire and brimstone to clear them out of the way, yet here he was making a Samaritan the hero of his story. They must have realized there were many things about Jesus they still didn't understand.

JESUS VISITS ONE OF HIS
FAVORITE FAMILIES

It would appear that shortly after the encounter with the lawyer, Jesus and his apostles drew near to Jerusalem. Jesus seems to have separated from his companions temporarily so he could visit one of his favorite families. These friends consisted of Lazarus and his two sisters, Mary and Martha, who lived in the village of Bethany.

Bethany is on the eastern slope of the Mount of Olives, and is therefore only about two miles from Jerusalem. The ancient Roman road makes a loop around the southern end of the mountain and is therefore considerably further than going straight up over the Mount of Olives and down the other side. Even today, the natives nearly always take the more direct route over the Mount when they are walking to Bethany.

Certain passages suggest that Jesus took the pathway that went over the Mount of Olives when he went to visit the home of Mary, Martha and Lazarus. It is believed this is what the Gospel writers

[32]Luke 10:36-37.
[33]Luke 10:37.

mean when they say Jesus "abode in the mount that is called the mount of Olives."[34] Bethany is part of this mount, but on the eastern side.

On a number of occasions I have taken groups of friends over the Mount of Olives and then down the path that leads to Bethany. Along this path, especially at evening, there is a certain feeling or mood that hovers over the trees and shrubs. As one walks along this quiet lane there seems to be a spirit that whispers, "He walked this way."

JESUS WITH MARY AND MARTHA

When Jesus reached the home of his friends, he found that Lazarus was away, undoubtedly at the Feast of the Tabernacles which was now at its height. But Mary and Martha were there, and they joyfully welcomed him.

It is very likely that this is where Jesus stayed each night while the Feast of the Tabernacles was in progress. The same thing would happen during the last eventful week of his life. So far as we can tell, when Jesus was in Jerusalem and its environs, this was the Savior's home.

Martha immediately busied herself getting something to eat. Mary, on the other hand, sat at the Savior's feet, anxiously extracting from him all the latest news, his latest encounters, and his latest teachings.

It is doubtful anyone was writing books about "Fascinating Womanhood" at that early date, but perhaps Mary's anxious questions about the debate in the temple, the lawyer who had tried to trick Jesus, the calling of the Seventies, or many other recent events, drew an enthusiastic response from this beloved guest whom Mary and Martha both believed to be the Messiah.

No doubt Martha came in to catch snatches of the conversation from time to time, perhaps even smiling cordially before she hurried

---

[34]Luke 21:37; John 8:1.

back again to check the lamb stew or whatever she was cooking. We learn that Martha even wished that Mary would come and help her so there would be no delay in the meal.[35]

It is not difficult to portray this scene because it often happens to church leaders while visiting among the saints. Somebody scurries about the kitchen, hurriedly preparing the dinner, while others stimulate the visiting authority with tantalizing questions that he thoroughly enjoys answering.

Finally, Martha's bustling about as she prepared the dinner became disturbing to the Savior. He knew Martha was sharing her love for him by preparing this special meal. But he had something to share with her, and she was missing it. Surely she should be hearing these things as much as Mary.

All of this finally came to a head when Martha suddenly came into the room and said:

"Lord, dost thou not care that my sister hath left me to serve alone? bid her therefore that she help me.

"And Jesus answered and said unto her, Martha, Martha, thou art careful and troubled about many things:

"But one thing is needful: and Mary hath chosen that good part, which shall not be taken away from her."[36]

About six months later, there would be another dinner prepared for Jesus in Bethany, and Martha would once more be doing what she did so well, cooking and serving. Mary, on the other hand, would be kneeling before the Savior, and while she listened, anointing his feet with a precious ointment and wiping off the excess perfume with her long hair.

---

[35]Luke 10:40.
[36]Luke 10:40-42.

But that was something for the future. After visiting in Bethany, Jesus probably rejoined his disciples the next morning to attend the final rites at the Feast of the Tabernacles.

* * * *

TOPICS FOR REFLECTION AND DISCUSSION

1. Why did Jesus and Peter pay tribute for the upkeep of the temple even though they were exempt from this tax? Where did Peter get the money?

2. What is the office and calling of a seventy? (See Doctrine and Covenants 107:34, 37.) The Jews also claimed to have a Council of Seventy. What was it called? What were the names of the three cities upon which Jesus pronounced a "woe"? Why did he say they deserved this harsh judgment?

3. Why do you think so many of the Jews were anxious to have Jesus appear at the Feast of the Tabernacles? Why did his brothers want him to go? Were they believers at this time? What happened to them after Christ's resurrection?

4. What happened when the apostles tried to get accommodations from the Samaritans? Why was their attitude different when Jesus had passed that way returning *from* Jerusalem?

5. How did James and John recommend that the Samaritans be punished? What was the Savior's response? Do holders of the priesthood have power to call down fire from heaven or do they have to wait until God commands it?

6. What was the lawyer trying to do when he asked Jesus how he should inherit eternal life? Who ended up answering his question? Was it the right answer?

7. Who was the hero in the story about the man who was robbed on the way to Jericho? Why was it difficult for the lawyer to admit who the hero was? What did Jesus tell the lawyer to do after he had told this story?

8. How far is Bethany from Jerusalem? Apparently where was Lazarus when Jesus arrived at the home of his favorite friends in this village?

9. When church leaders visit the saints in their various localities, do you think they like to be asked gospel questions, or is it an imposition? Do they seem anxious to report on the progress of the work?

10. Was Jesus enthusiastic about visiting with Mary and Martha? How do you think Martha felt when she was trying to fix a nice dinner and Jesus said it would have been better for her to sit down and listen? What were the priorities of each of the women? Why is it so difficult to decide which is right? Is it important to choose the appropriate time for each?

* * * *

CHAPTER 25

THE SAVIOR'S LAST FEAST OF THE TABERNACLES

The Feast of the Tabernacles was celebrated the last of September and extended over into early October. In a way, this was a thanksgiving feast which Moses called the Feast of the Ingathering.[1]

Its primary purpose was to commemorate the time when the Israelites escaped from the captivity of the Pharaoh and began their long trek across the desert.

During their flight from Egypt, the Israelites had to live in tents or improvised huts made of palm fronds or branches of trees. Therefore, during the Feast of the Tabernacles, the more faithful Jews lived out of doors all week in "booths" or tiny "tabernacles." This is what gave the Feast of the Tabernacles its name.

The eighth day, at the end of the feast, was the grand finale, with a massive convocation of all the people participating in certain holy rites.

JESUS AND HIS APOSTLES ARRIVE IN JERUSALEM

This was the feast to which Jesus and his apostles now came. The people were no longer expecting him, and therefore Jesus was able to enter the compound of the temple unnoticed.

Nevertheless, it did not take long for a crowd to gather around him once the word spread that he was there. For Jesus, this was the opportunity he wanted, and he immediately began teaching them his gospel message.

---

[1]Exodus 23:16.

After listening to the Savior for awhile, the people began murmuring among themselves, and said:

"How knoweth this man letters, having never learned?"[2]

Apparently he perceived what they were saying, and he answered:

"My doctrine is not mine, but his that sent me.

"If any man will do his will, he shall know of the doctrine, whether it be of God or whether I speak of myself."[3]

The proof of the gospel has always been in its practice. Every disciple of Jesus could speak of his doctrine with the greatest of confidence and say, "Try it, you'll like it."

The Savior also wanted to make it completely clear that his entire mission was to glorify his Father, not himself. Jesus therefore went on to say:

"He that speaketh of himself seeketh his own glory: but he that seeketh his glory that sent him, the same is true, and no unrighteousness is in him."[4]

The Savior never talked very long before he managed to get around to the subject of repentance; therefore Jesus began to lay the foundation for a real scorcher. He said:

"Did not Moses give you the law, and yet none of you keepeth the law?"[5]

---

[2]John 7:15.
[3]John 7:16-17.
[4]John 7:18.
[5]John 7:19.

This theme could have been developed into a sermon of at least an hour's duration, but suddenly the Savior stopped. He turned on the people like an avenging angel and said:

"Why go ye about to kill me?"[6]

In this crowd Jesus must have begun to see some of his deadly enemies. Ever since the last feast, they had been trying to find him and slay him. But at this moment the spies and others who had been part of the plot were caught by surprise. Like wounded birds, they immediately began to flutter. They said:

"Thou hast a devil: who goeth about to kill thee?"[7]

THE BASIS FOR THE PLOT TO KILL JESUS

To appreciate the tenseness of this situation it is necessary to recall that at the last feast Jesus had come upon a crippled man at the pool of Bethesda near the temple. The man was thirty-eight years old and had been paralyzed and helpless all the days of his life. Jesus had said to him:

"Rise, take up thy bed, and walk."[8]

This was on a sabbath day, and the man had not gone far before some horrified Pharisees had stopped him and said, "It is not lawful for thee to carry thy bed."[9]

He told them he had just been healed by a man who told him to rise up and walk and carry his bed away.

They were even more outraged when they learned it was Jesus of Nazareth who had healed him. The scripture says they "sought to slay him, because he had done these things on the sabbath day."[10]

---

[6]John 7:19.
[7]John 7:20.
[8]John 5:8.
[9]John 5:10.
[10]John 5:16.

Now Jesus was back for the Feast of the Tabernacles, and challenging those who wanted to slay him. He knew the basis for their murderous plot was merely that he had healed a man on the sabbath. Therefore he decided to put them on the defensive.

He reminded them that under the law of Moses, a male child should be circumcised on his eighth day. Then he pointed out that in order to obey this law, the Jews had never hesitated to perform circumcision even if the eighth day happened to be a sabbath. He let that sink in for a moment, and then asked them why were they angry with him because he had "made a man every whit whole on the sabbath day?"[11]

The people who were listening began to realize that this conversation could become a matter of life and death for Jesus. Therefore they asked one another:

"Is not this he, whom they seek to kill?

"But, lo, he speaketh boldly, and they say nothing unto him. Do the rulers know indeed that this is the very Christ?"[12]

As their discussion continued they finally decided Jesus could not be the Christ because they knew he was from Nazareth, and "when Christ cometh, no man knoweth whence he is."[13]

Jesus perceived what they were saying among themselves, so he spoke directly to them and said:

"Ye both know me, and ye know whence I am: and I am not come of myself, but he that sent me is true, whom ye know not.

"But I know him: for I am from him, and he hath sent me."[14]

---

[11]John 7:23.
[12]John 7:25-26.
[13]John 7:27.
[14]John 7:28-29.

No man could come with greater credentials than one who was sent by the Father, so John says:

"Many of the people believed on him, and said, When Christ cometh, will he do more miracles than these which this man hath done?"[15]

However, the Savior's enemies who were in the audience had heard him talk this way before. They knew the high priest and leading Pharisees considered these claims to be rank blasphemy. Imagine this uneducated Galilean claiming that his Father was the very God of heaven!

THE ORDER TO ARREST JESUS

Apparently the spies hurried to the nearby quarters where the leaders of the Sanhedrin were meeting and reported what Jesus was saying. That distinguished body of dignitaries decided to take decisive action. Their officers were called in and ordered to arrest Jesus without delay.

But when the officers arrived and joined the crowd surrounding Jesus, they made the mistake of listening for awhile instead of taking Jesus immediately into custody. What they heard fascinated them, so they continued to listen.

However, at one point Jesus caused them to wonder what he meant. He said:

"Yet a little while am I with you, and then I go unto him that sent me.

"Ye shall seek me, and shall not find me: and where I am, thither ye cannot come.

"Then said the Jews among themselves, Whither will he go, that we shall not find him? will he go unto the dispersed among the Gentiles, and teach the Gentiles?

---

[15]John 7:31.

"What manner of saying is this that he said, Ye shall seek me, and shall not find me: and where I am, thither ye cannot come?"[16]

It is amazing that the officers did not conclude from this statement that Jesus was about to flee and go into hiding somewhere. However, the record is clear that they did not arrest him. We conclude that they were fascinated with his teachings and undecided as to just what action they should take.

This incident occurred at the close of the day and so the officers apparently decided to come back and hear him further on the morrow, which would be the last day of the Feast. John says:

"In the last day, that great day of the feast, Jesus stood and cried, saying, If any man thirst, let him come unto me, and drink.

"He that believeth on me, as the scripture hath said, out of his belly shall flow rivers of living water."[17]

This was the Savior's reference to the "living water" or the outpouring of the Spirit—the burning of the bosom—which would animate their souls if they would open their hearts to receive the gospel. Some began to feel the Spirit working on them and almost immediately the people began to engage in a warm discussion concerning Jesus. The scripture says:

"Many of the people therefore, when they heard this saying, said, Of a truth this is the Prophet.

"Others said, This is the Christ. But some said, Shall Christ come out of Galilee?

"Hath not the scripture said, That Christ cometh of the seed of David, and out of the town of Bethlehem, where David was?"[18]

[16]John 7:33-36.
[17]John 7:37-38.
[18]John 7:40-42.

This statement is highly significant. The day before, some of the people said that no one knew "from whence" the Christ would come,[19] but here we have people who knew their scriptures and said the Christ or Messiah would be of the seed of David and come from the town of Bethlehem.

It is very apparent that the Savior's birth in Bethlehem and all the dramatic events connected with it were not generally known among the Jews, even among those who knew their scriptures. They thought Jesus was born in Nazareth and therefore they decided he could not be the Christ. John concludes by saying:

"So there was a division among the people because of him.

"And some of them would have taken him; but no man laid hands on him."[20]

THE OFFICERS REPORT BACK
TO THEIR LEADERS

By this time the officers decided they had better go back to the leaders of the Sanhedrin and report. To the amazement of these high officials, the soldiers came back without Jesus. They were outraged. This was insubordination. The soldiers were asked why they didn't arrest Jesus. They replied:

"Never man spake like this man.

"Then answered them the Pharisees, Are ye also deceived?"[21]

At this point one of the more notable Pharisees intervened and said:

"Doth our law judge any man, before it hear him, and know what he doeth?"[22]

---

[19]John 7:27.
[20]John 7:43-44.
[21]John 7:45-47.
[22]John 7:51.

The others deeply resented this interference and shot back:

"Art thou also of Galilee? Search, and look: for out of Galilee ariseth no prophet.

"And every man went unto his own house."[23]

If Jesus had witnessed this brief dialogue, he might have been very surprised. The man who broke up the plot to have Jesus arrested was none other than Nicodemus,[24] the learned Pharisee who had come to Jesus at night two and a half years before.

John says that as evening came on, Jesus went up on to the Mount of Olives, but it is very likely that after praying to his Father, he proceeded on to the other side of the mountain to nearby Bethany where Lazarus and his two sisters, Mary and Martha, resided.

THE PHARISEES ATTEMPT TO TRAP JESUS

The next morning, when the Feast was over, Jesus returned to the temple where he found a crowd of scribes and Pharisees, hoping he would put in an appearance. The scripture says:

"And the scribes and Pharisees brought unto him a woman taken in adultery; and when they had set her in the midst,

"They say unto him, Master, this woman was taken in adultery, in the very act.

"Now Moses in the law commanded us, that such should be stoned: but what sayest thou?

"This they said, tempting him, that they might have to accuse him."[25]

---

[23]John 7:52-53.
[24]John 3:1.
[25]John 8:3-6.

Stoning was a form of capital punishment, but the Jews were not allowed to take human life without the consent of the Roman governor. It is quite certain that no approval would have been granted since the Roman law did not consider adultery a capital crime. In this complicated situation, the Pharisees demanded that Jesus make a judgment. Would he come down on the side of Moses or on the side of Rome? Either way, they thought they would have an excuse to bring an accusation against him.

Notice that they did not bring the man. The Law of Moses required that both of the parties had to be brought in for judgment, not just the woman.[26]

But Jesus was not going to waste time debating the technicalities of the Law. He had something more fundamental in mind. What he then did must have been uncomfortably frustrating for those who thought they had trapped him. He virtually ignored them. Furthermore, he said nothing. All he did was to kneel on the pavement of the temple courtyard and start making nondescript marks in the dust that had accumulated on the stones.

They immediately began to heckle and harass him, demanding that he give his judgment in this case. Finally, John says:

"He lifted up himself, and said unto them, He that is without sin among you, let him first cast a stone at her.

"And again he stooped down, and wrote on the ground."[27]

For a moment nothing happened, and then gradually the crowd began to thin out. At last none of the accusers was left, but only the people who stood around wondering what was going to happen next. After a period of time, the scripture says:

"And they which heard it, being convicted by their own conscience, went out one by one, beginning at the eldest, even unto

---

[26]Leviticus 20:10.
[27]John 8:7-8.

the last: and Jesus was left alone, and the woman standing in the midst [of the crowd of curious onlookers].

"When Jesus had lifted up himself, and saw none but the woman, he said unto her, Woman, where are those thine accusers? hath no man condemned thee?

"She said, No man, Lord. And Jesus said unto her, Neither do I condemn thee: go, and sin no more."[28]

At this point, the Joseph Smith Translation includes a gratifying sentence which is missing from the modern Bible. It says:

"And the woman glorified God from that hour, and believed on his name."[29]

We observe that Jesus had refused to act as judge to condemn this woman, but he had not consented to her offense or said she was forgiven. Nevertheless, once she believed on the Savior, she could be baptized and gain complete forgiveness. That is the happy ending to this story.

JESUS BEARS WITNESS THAT HE IS INDEED THE CHRIST

Meanwhile, Jesus turned to the crowd that had gathered and began giving these listeners a moving testimony concerning his own divinity and the eternal relationship he had with his Father.

This is interesting, because he had admonished his apostles just a few days earlier that *they* should *not* tell people that he was the Christ.[30]

---

[28]John 8:9-11.
[29]JST John 8:11.
[30]Matthew 16:20.

Perhaps he desired, from this time forward, to be the one voice testifying of his divinity. Certainly, he did not want his own people to complain at the final judgment that they had never heard Jesus personally reveal his true identity.

In any event, there was no doubt in the minds of the apostles as they listened to the Savior that he intended to put the brand of his personal testimony on the heart of every Jew within the sound of his voice.

"Then spake Jesus again unto them, saying, I am the light of the world: he that followeth me shall not walk in darkness, but shall have the light of life."[31]

It is interesting that by these very words, the Savior's critics thought they had evidence of his duplicity. They cried out:

"Thou bearest record of thyself; thy record is not true."[32]

Then there began a very instructive dialogue between Jesus and the agitators:

"Jesus answered and said unto them, Though I bear record of myself, yet my record is true: for I know whence I came, and whither I go; but ye cannot tell whence I come, and whither I go...

"It is also written in your law, that the testimony of two men is true.

"I am one that bear witness of myself, and the Father that sent me beareth witness of me."[33]

---

[31]John 8:12.
[32]John 8:13.
[33]John 8:14-18.

CONCERNING THE FATHER

The scribes and Pharisees decided this attack was not going anywhere, so they used a diversionary tactic. They said: "Where is thy Father?"

If Jesus had said, "God dwells on a celestial planet near Kolob,"[34] Abraham would have understood, but this would have meant nothing to these learned men blinded by their own sophistry. They didn't really want to know where the Savior's Father was. The question was purely polemic and part of their tactical strategy. In response Jesus said:

"Ye neither know me, nor my Father: if ye had known me, ye should have known my Father also."[35]

John says this dialogue took place in the treasury of the temple. When those who had hoped to trap Jesus realized they had failed, "no man laid hands on him."[36]

WHAT IT MEANS *"NOT* TO BE WITH CHRIST"

This gave Jesus an opportunity to plant a few more shafts of light in his adversaries for the benefit of those who were standing around listening. Jesus repeated something he had said before, but with a new touch. He said:

"I go my way, and ye shall seek me, and shall die in your sins: whither I go, ye cannot come.

"Then said the Jews, Will he kill himself? because he saith, Whither I go, ye cannot come."[37]

This had reference to the fact that the Jews believed all suicides went to Gehenna or hell, a place where no other Jew would be

---

[34]Abraham 3:9
[35]John 8:19.
[36]John 8:20.
[37]John 8:21-22.

allowed to go since they were presumed to be scheduled for a place in heaven.[38]

Jesus was really talking about the fact that all those who knowingly reject the gospel, and then die in their sins, are cast into outer darkness and must partake of their share of the second death until they have paid for their own sins to the uttermost farthing. As John would later explain in his Apocalypse:

"He that overcometh shall inherit all things; and I will be his God, and he shall be my son.

"But the...unbelieving, and the abominable, and murderers, and whoremongers, and sorcerers, and idolaters, and all liars, shall have their part in the lake which burneth with fire and brimstone: which is the second death."[39]

And as Jesus explained in modern times:

"For behold, I, God, have suffered these things for all, that they might not suffer if they would repent;

"But if they would not repent they must suffer even as I.

"Which suffering caused myself, even God, the greatest of all, to tremble because of pain, and to bleed at every pore, and to suffer both body and spirit—and would that I might not drink the bitter cup, and shrink."[40]

Those who pay for their own sins must do so in a place which is outside the glorious enlightenment of God's realm. The Lord has it all take place:

---

[38]Talmage, *Jesus the Christ*, p. 408.
[39]Revelation 21:7-8.
[40]Doctrine and Covenants 19:17-18.

"Even in outer darkness, where there is weeping, and wailing, and gnashing of teeth."[41]

And the Lord says those who have to pay for their own sins remain there until they are:

"Redeemed in the due time of the Lord, after the sufferings of his wrath."[42]

To all of these who were seeking to entrap and slay him, Jesus could truly say: "Where I am, thither ye cannot come."[43]

THEY SAID TO JESUS, "WHO ART THOU?"

The baffled band of accusers decided they would try to get Jesus to speak straight out and commit blasphemy by saying he was the Messiah. So they said: "Who art thou?"[44] Jesus replied:

"Even the same that I said unto you from the beginning...

"When ye have lifted up the Son of man, then shall ye know that I am he, and that I do nothing of myself; but as my Father hath taught me, I speak these things."[45]

Now a remarkable thing happened. The Spirit was beginning to touch some of those who were listening, so John says:

"As he spake these words, many believed on him."[46]

Jesus therefore turned toward those who were beginning to believe in him, and said:

"If ye continue in my word, then are ye my disciples indeed;

---

[41]Doctrine & Covenants 101:91.
[42]Doctrine & Covenants 76:38.
[43]John 7:34.
[44]John 8:25.
[45]John 8:25-28.
[46]John 8:30.

"And ye shall know the truth, and the truth shall make you free."[47]

His accusers thought they saw a chance to embarrass Jesus, so they tried to get their oar back in the water again by saying:

"We be Abraham's seed, and were never in bondage to any man: how sayest thou, Ye shall be made free?

"Jesus answered them, Verily, verily, I say unto you, Whosoever committeth sin is the servant of sin."[48]

Now Jesus was ready to close in on these sycophants of sin and level a few charges at them. He said:

"I know that ye are Abraham's seed; but ye seek to kill me, because my word hath no place in you.

"I speak that which I have seen with my Father: and ye do that which ye have seen with your father."[49]

YE ARE OF YOUR FATHER THE DEVIL

"They answered and said unto him, Abraham is our father.

"Jesus saith unto them...Ye seek to kill me...Ye are of your father the devil, and the lusts of your father ye will do. He was a murderer from the beginning, and abode not in the truth, because there is no truth in him. When he speaketh a lie, he speaketh of his own: for he is a liar, and the father of it.

"Then answered the Jews, and said unto him, Say we not well that thou art a Samaritan, and hast a devil?" [50]

---

[47]John 8:31-32.
[48]John 8:33-34.
[49]John 8:37-38.
[50]John 8:39-44.

In the past, when the Pharisees spoke contemptuously of Jesus, they usually called him a Galilean, but now they felt the need for stronger epithets so they spat out that he was "a Samaritan" with a devil.

"Jesus answered, I have not a devil; but I honour my Father, and ye do dishonour me...

"Verily, verily, I say unto you, If a man keep my saying, he shall never see death."[51]

The accusers immediately thought Jesus was speaking of the physical death, whereas he was merely reiterating the glorious gospel promise we have already mentioned. He wanted them to know that all those who follow the sayings of Jesus would never taste of that second death in outer darkness where there will be "weeping and wailing and gnashing of teeth."

The debate continued for a few more minutes, and then his accusers could not endure it any longer. The last straw was when Jesus made a statement that he even existed before Abraham.[52] That did it. They all rushed to pick up stones and kill him on the spot.

But a miracle happened.

Jesus suddenly veiled himself so he could not be seen. The scripture says:

"But Jesus hid himself, and went out of the temple, *going through the midst of them,* and so passed by."[53]

For Jesus and his apostles, the Feast of the Tabernacles was over.

*   *   *   *

---

[51]John 8:49-51.
[52]John 8:58.
[53]John 8:59.

Now we are ready for volume II of this study which is the most illuminating portion of the Savior's entire ministry. There are many scriptural surprises in the closing weeks of the Savior's life.

* * * *

TOPICS FOR REFLECTION AND DISCUSSION

1. When did the Feast of the Tabernacles take place? What did it represent? As Jesus began talking at the temple, what caused the people to admire him? According to Jesus, what did he advise them to do in order to determine the validity of his teachings?

2. What did Jesus start to talk about, but suddenly stopped and never went back to it? What did he say to some of his enemies whom he saw in the crowd?

3. What had he done at the previous feast that was the principal reason why they felt he should be slain? Why did the people who started to believe in him finally convince themselves that he couldn't be the Christ?

4. When Jesus said his Father had sent him, what did the spies do? Whom did it alarm the most? What did they decide to do?

5. Why didn't the soldiers arrest Jesus? What did Jesus say that would have ordinarily made the soldiers think Jesus was going to flee out of their jurisdiction? Instead of being alarmed, what did they decide to do?

6. When the soldiers reported back to the officials, who was it that intervened to break up the plot to have Jesus arrested? Did some of the people know that the Messiah should come from Bethlehem? Did any of them seem to know about the marvelous events that happened at the Savior's birth?

7. Was Jesus willing to judge the woman taken in adultery? Did he forgive her or just tell her to sin no more? What circumstances occurred which allowed her to be forgiven?

8. Who did Jesus say bore witness of him besides himself? Hadn't he told his apostles NOT to bear witness of him? Then why did HE do it?

9. What happens to people who knowingly reject the gospel and die in their sins? How long do they stay there? Is this tasting of the "second death"? What is the place called where this occurs?

10. Who did Jesus say was the father of his accusers? Did his accusers try to kill Jesus in the temple? What saved him? Was this the first time he had done this or had it happened before?

*   *   *   *